HEIDE CHRISTIANSEN

Charming PORTUGAL

teNeues

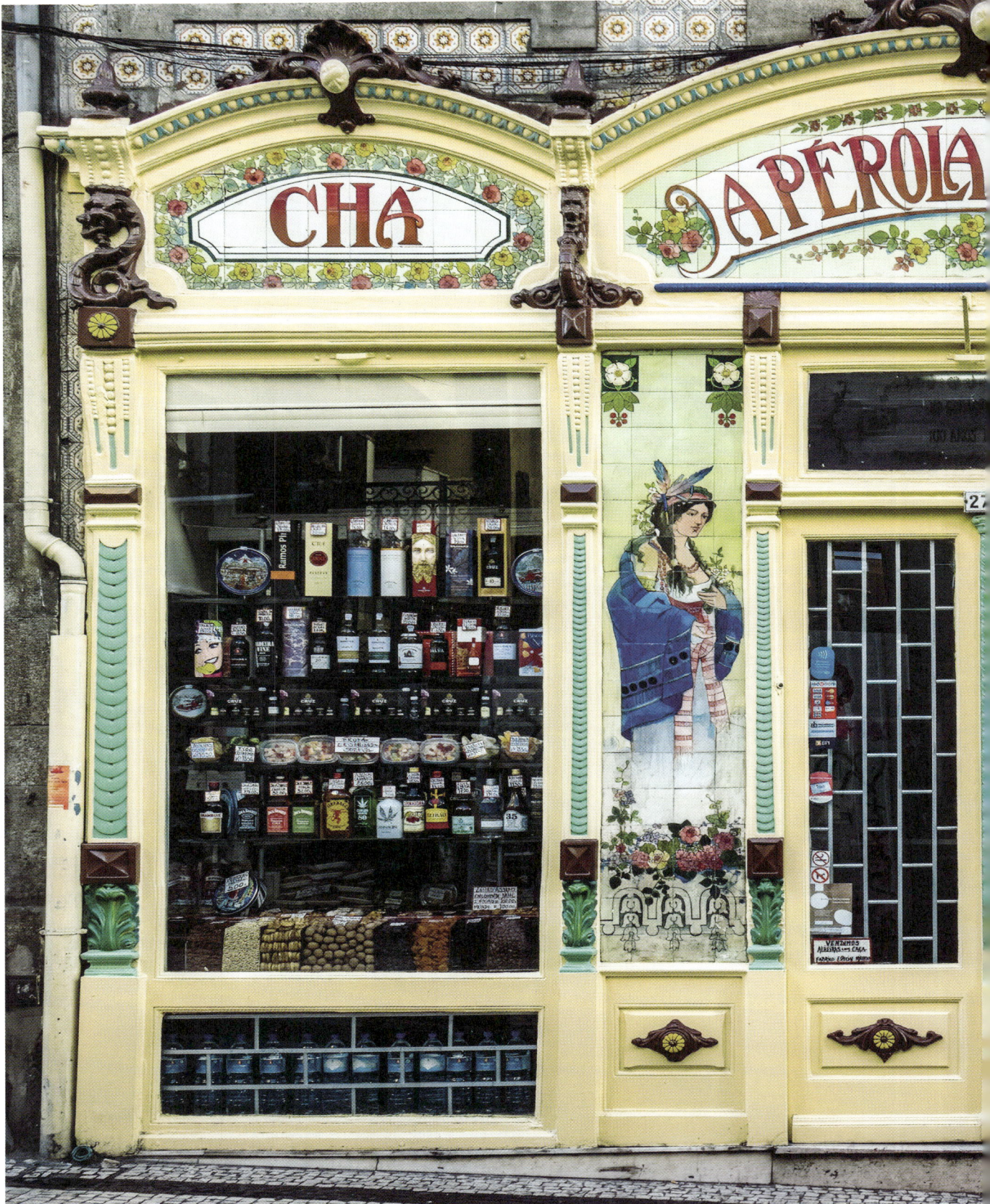

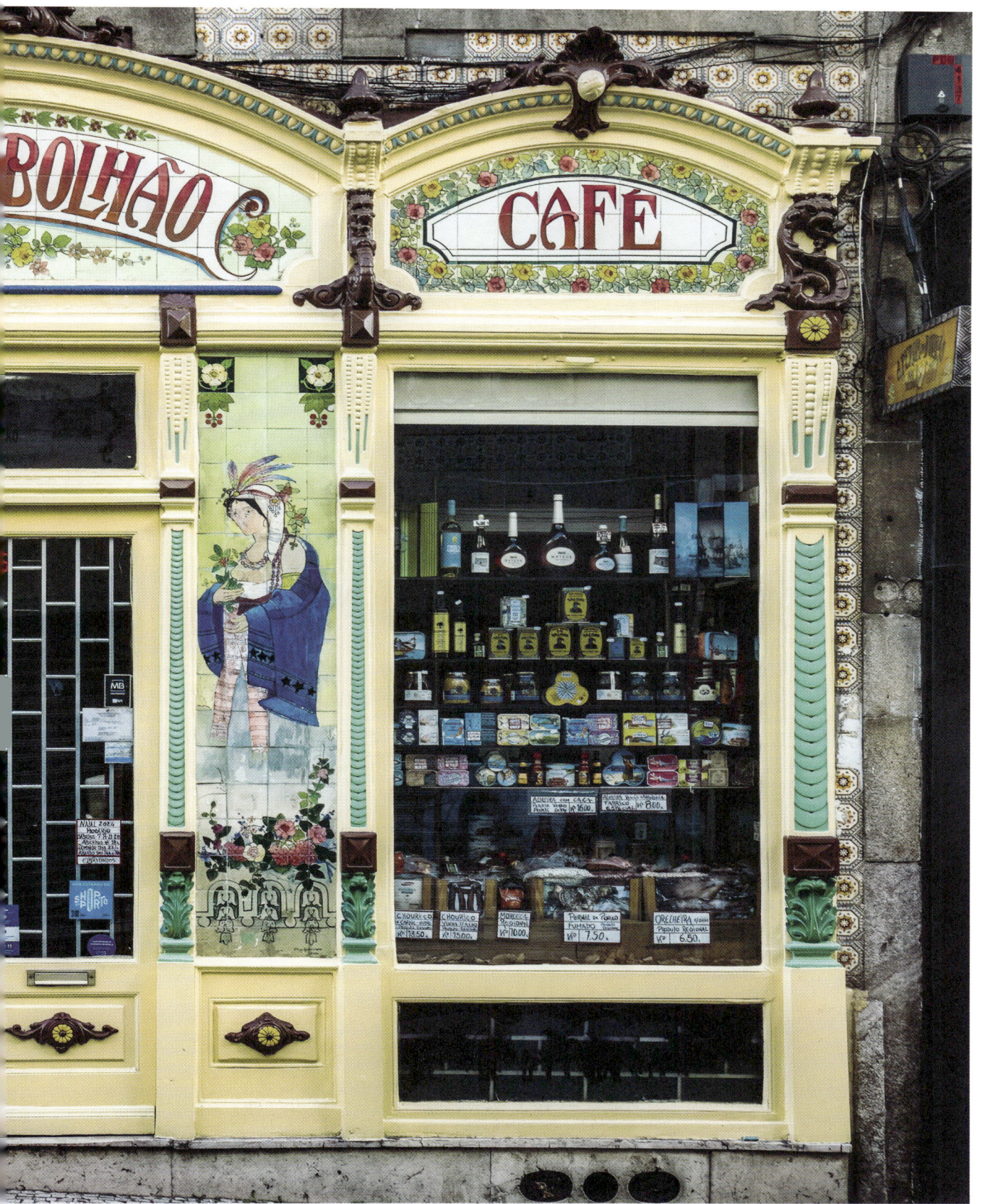

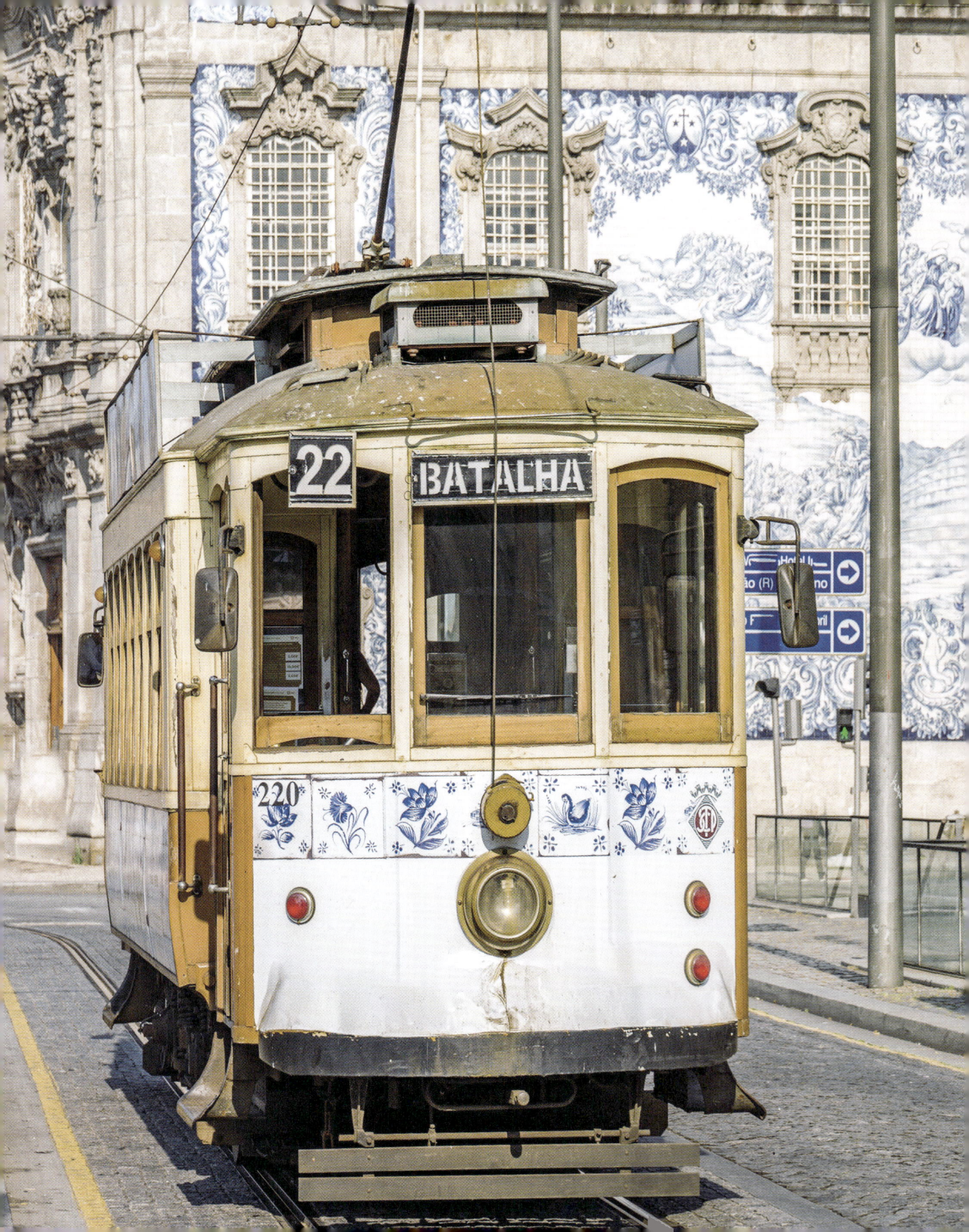

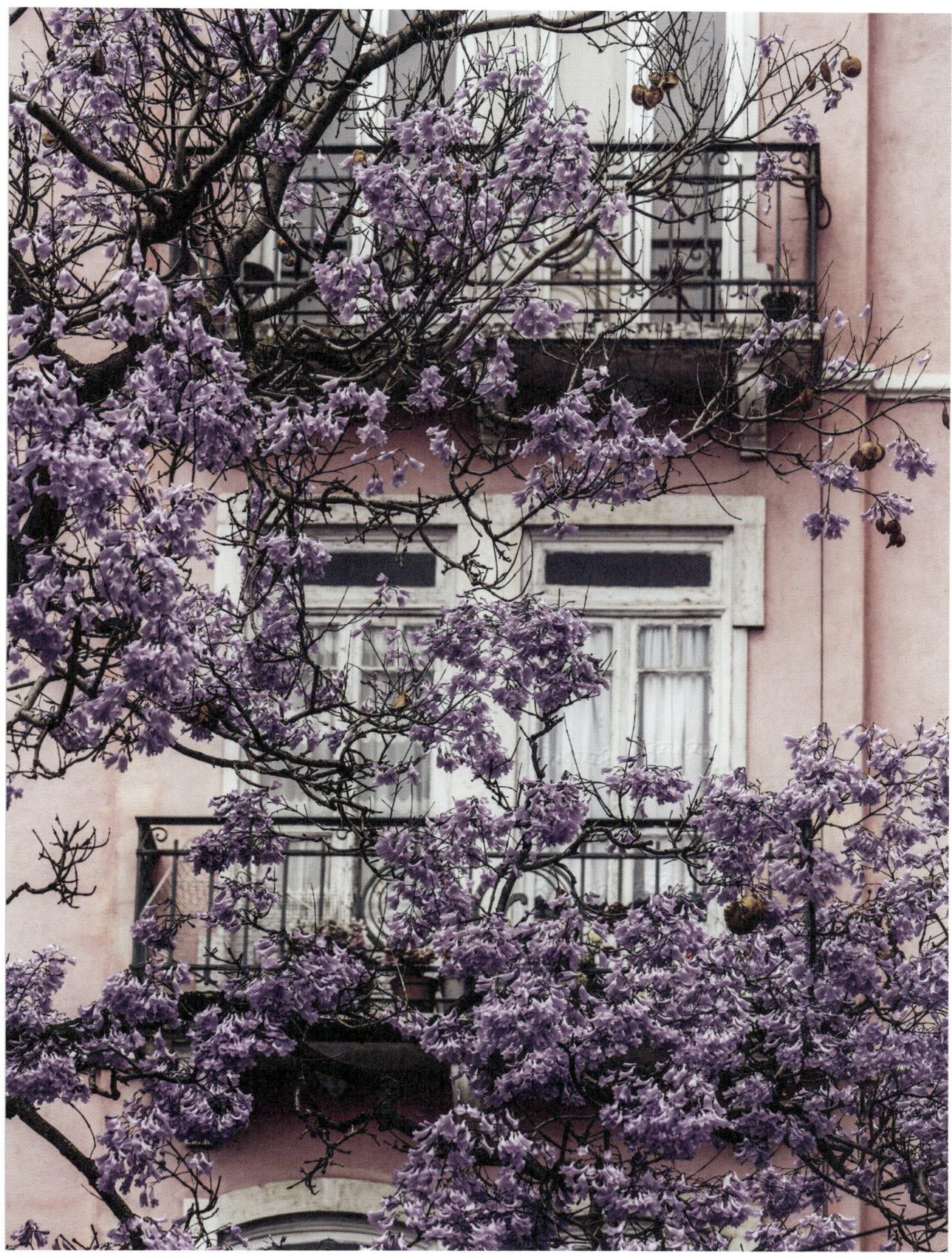

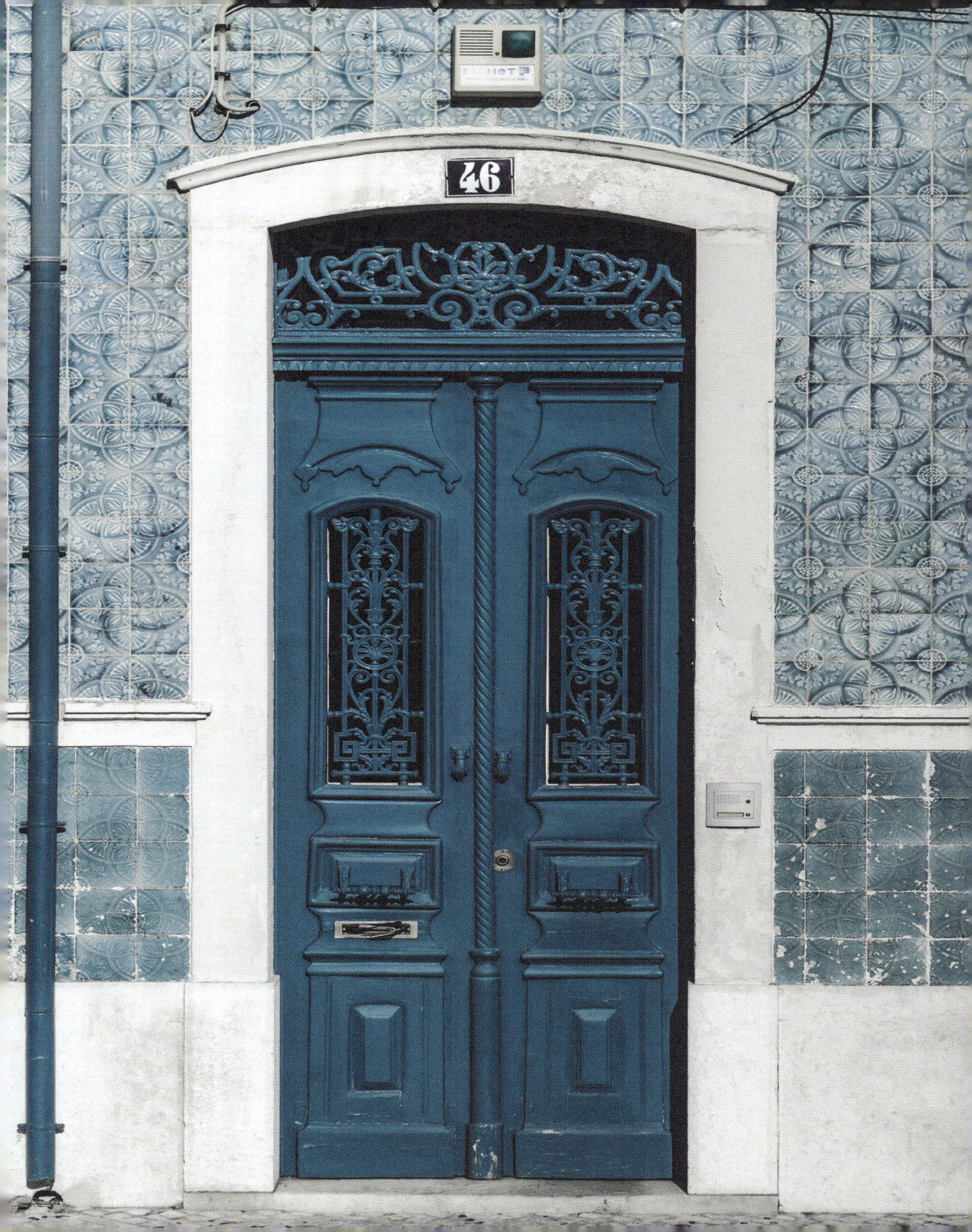

FOREWORD

BETWEEN AZULEJOS AND THE BLUE OF THE ATLANTIC, BETWEEN CORK-OAK GROVES AND MONASTERIES WITH MEDIEVAL SPLENDOR, PORTUGAL UNFOLDS AS A COUNTRY OF LIGHT, TEXTURE, AND CONTRAST

My vision is shaped by photography: light, color, and the search for new angles. That is one reason Portugal, often called the "land of light," keeps drawing me back. During the day the sun makes the whitewashed houses glow; in the evening, everything takes on a warm, golden tone as it sinks into the Atlantic.

Portugal offers a wide range of landscapes and settings. Along the coast, bright rock formations and long beaches meet an ocean that shifts from soft aquamarine to steel-blue surf. Inland, monasteries and churches stand near mountain villages tucked behind old stone walls, where traces of the Middle Ages remain visible, and broad plains stretch out under olive trees and cork oaks. Between Atlantic and uplands, between rural quiet and city life, the country moves through many registers: the melancholy of *fado,* the lightness of painted fishing boats and tiled façades, the gravity of sacred buildings, and the slow fade of sunset along the shore.

This variety makes Portugal a place that suits many moods and moments. The photographs that follow trace that range, moving through some of the places that define the country's character.

Heide Christiansen explores places through her camera, using light and composition to tell visual stories. Anja Klaffenbach, who shares her interest in travel and observation, puts those experiences into words.

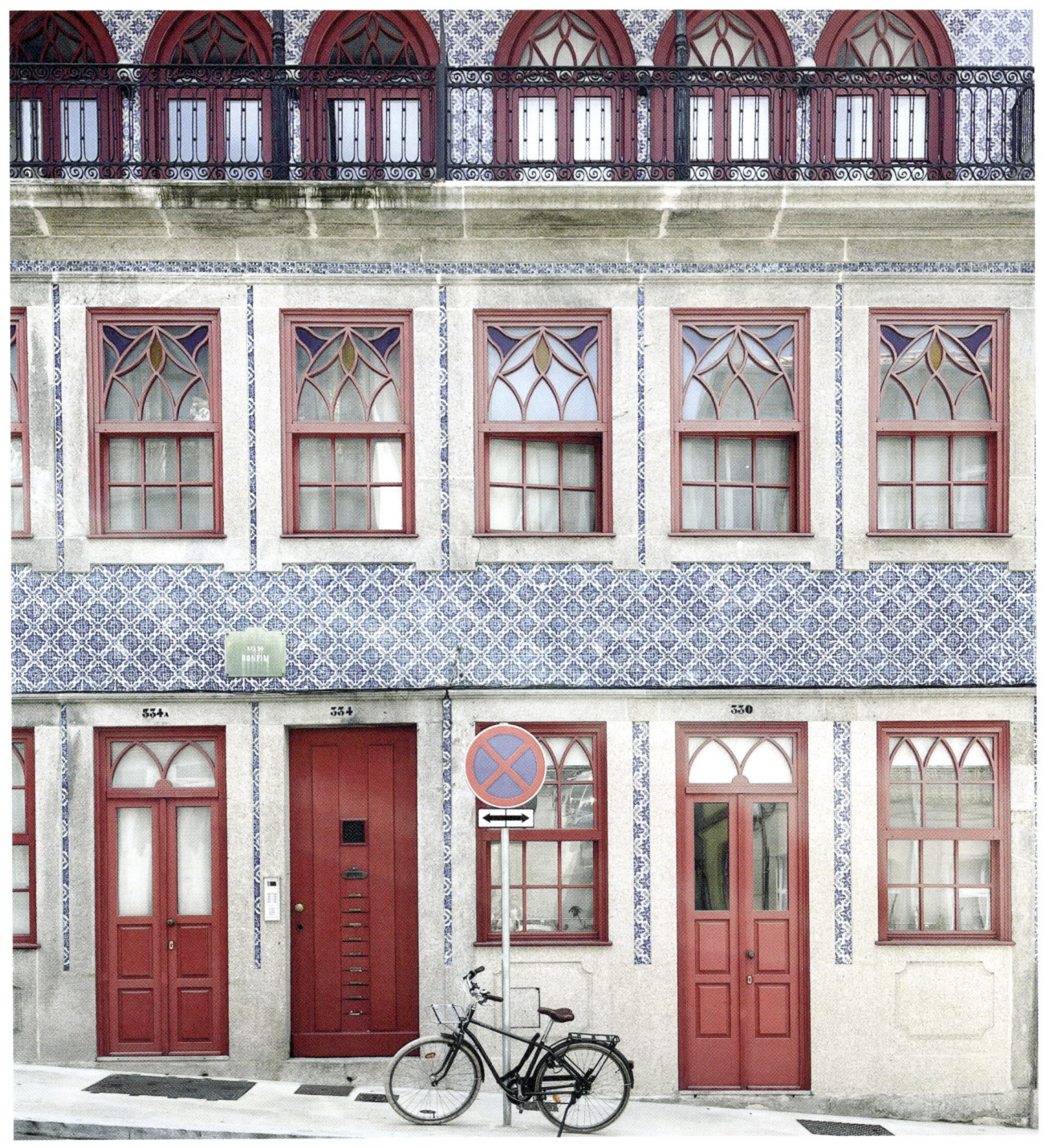

PREVIOUS: *From Lisbon to Porto and across the country, colorful azulejos and the playful charm of old Art Nouveau houses give Portugal its characteristic appearance.*

ABOVE: Bem-vindo a Bonfim. *A walk through Porto's burgeoning creative district with old façades. Precisely because Bonfim saw so little development for so long, details and everyday architectural features have been preserved.*

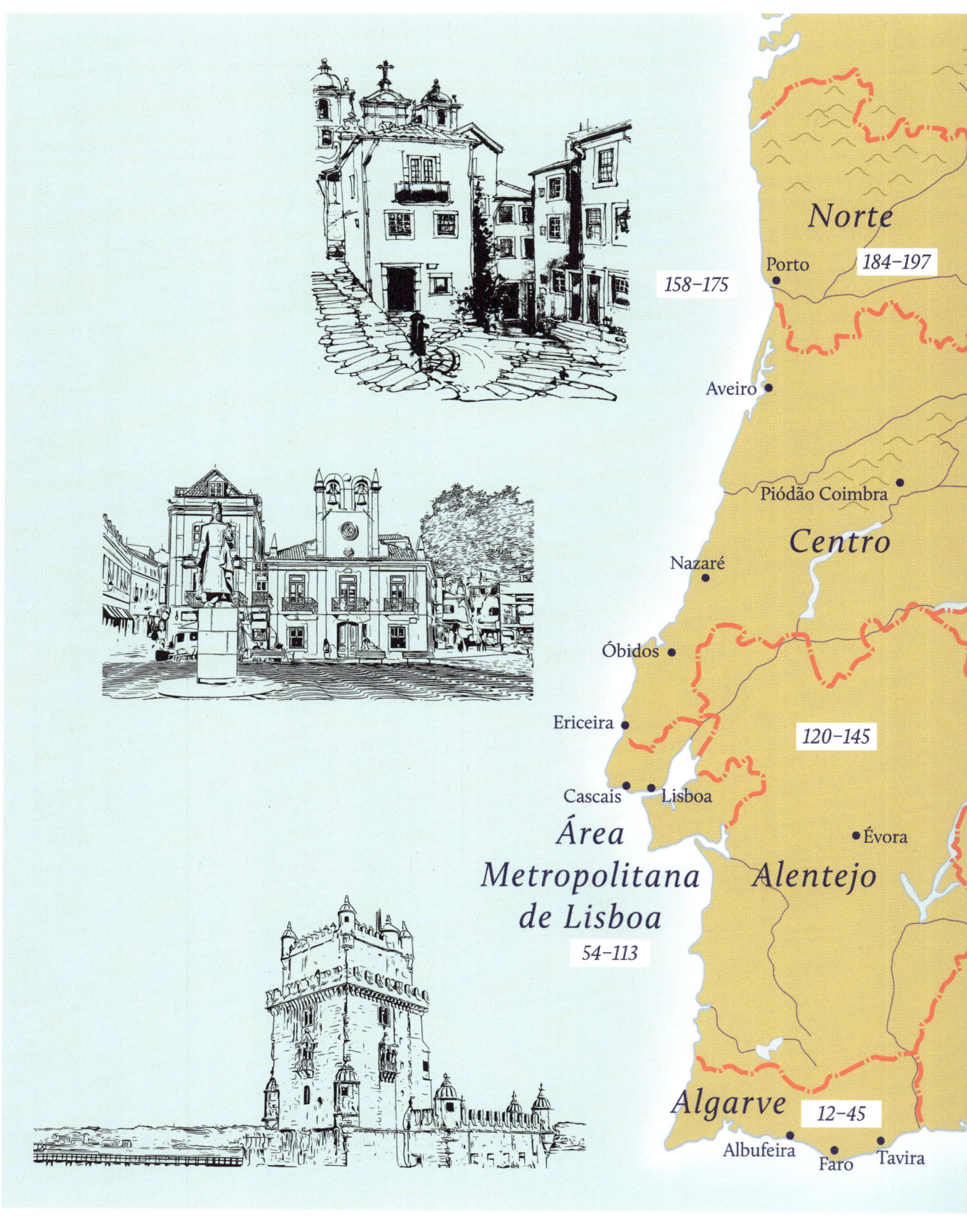

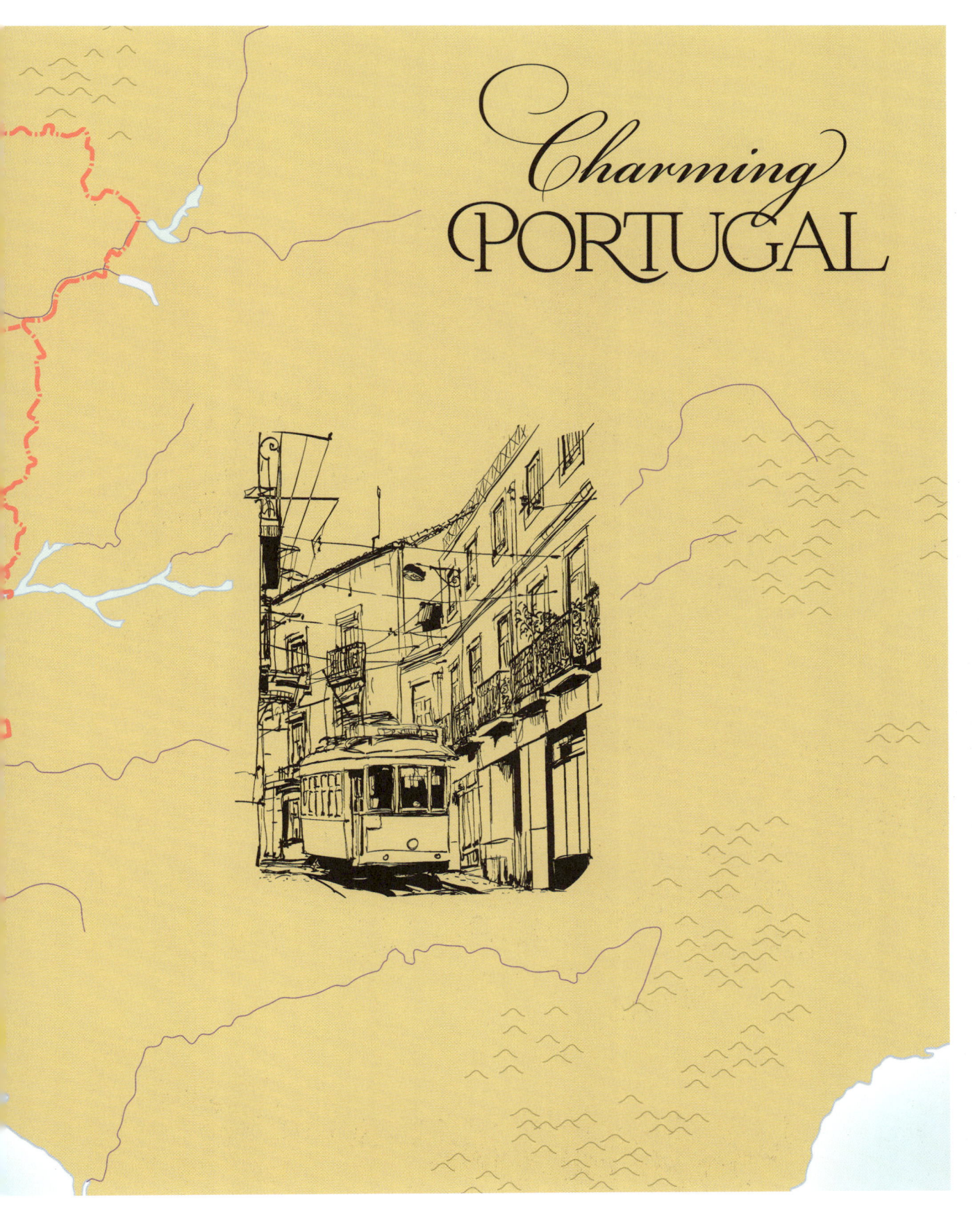

Charming
PORTUGAL

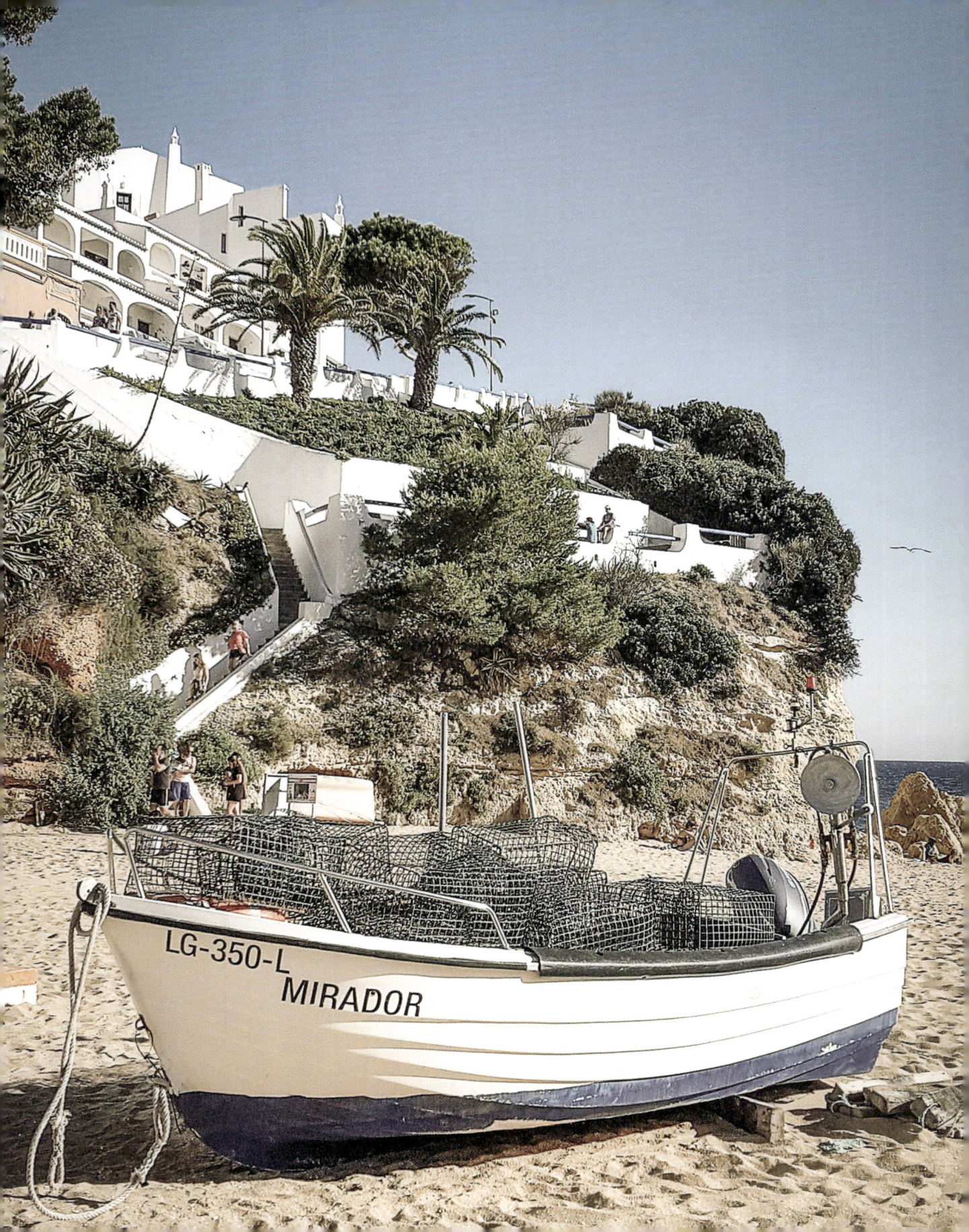

THE ALGARVE

PORTUGAL'S SOUTHERN COAST DRAWS BEACHGOERS WITH MORE THAN 300 SUNNY DAYS A YEAR, THE CHARM OF OLD FISHING VILLAGES, AND A LONG CULTURAL HISTORY

The name Algarve comes from the Arabic *al-gharb*, meaning "the west." The invocation of a cardinal direction is reason enough to go and see where it leads. Near the Spanish border lies Tavira. Sheltered by long sandbanks along the lagoon, the town sits on the Gilão and carries both Roman and Moorish traces. In the old quarter, pastel façades alternate with patterned azulejos. Farther west, Olhão shows a clear North African note. Its cubic, flat-roofed houses recall towns across the water in Morocco. In Faro, urban life takes on a Mediterranean cast. Behind heavy city walls, the area around the thirteenth-century cathedral feels quiet and contained. From the old bell tower, the view sweeps across the city and the winding channels of the Ria Formosa. Inland, Estoi is shaped by Rococo detail. The *palácio* now operates as a hotel, but its formal gardens and azulejos remain open to visitors. Albufeira on the rocky Algarve is defined by contrast: golden beaches, blue-green water, ochre and red sandstone cliffs, and whitewashed houses above the shore. The former fishing village reveals itself best in the quiet moments along its narrow streets. Ferragudo shares that slower rhythm. Bougainvillea and whitewashed houses line its cobbled lanes, while along the quay small taverns offer shade and brightly painted fishing boats bob just offshore. Lagos is known for its historic old town, but the surrounding cliffs and hidden coves often leave a stronger mark.

LEFT: *As in Carvoeiro, many small fishing villages along the Algarve have grown into lively seaside resorts. Some have retained the unhurried feel of earlier days.*

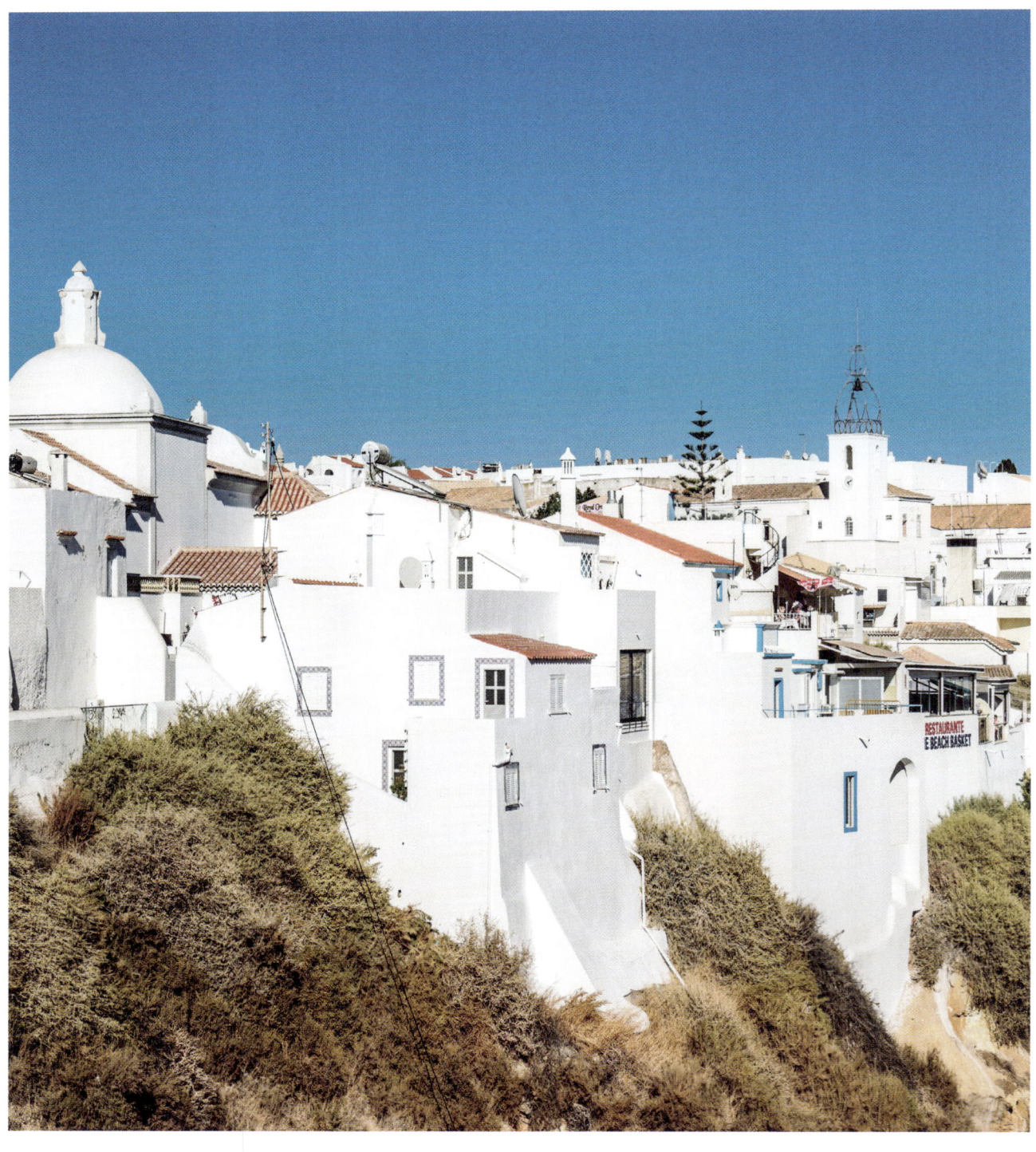

ABOVE AND RIGHT: *A trace of North Africa on the Algarve. The angular, brightly whitewashed fishermen's houses of Albufeira reflect Moorish influence, remnants from the period when the town was known as Al-Buhera, the "castle by the sea." From above the golden cliffs, the broad curve of the bay comes into view, with a wide sandy beach.*

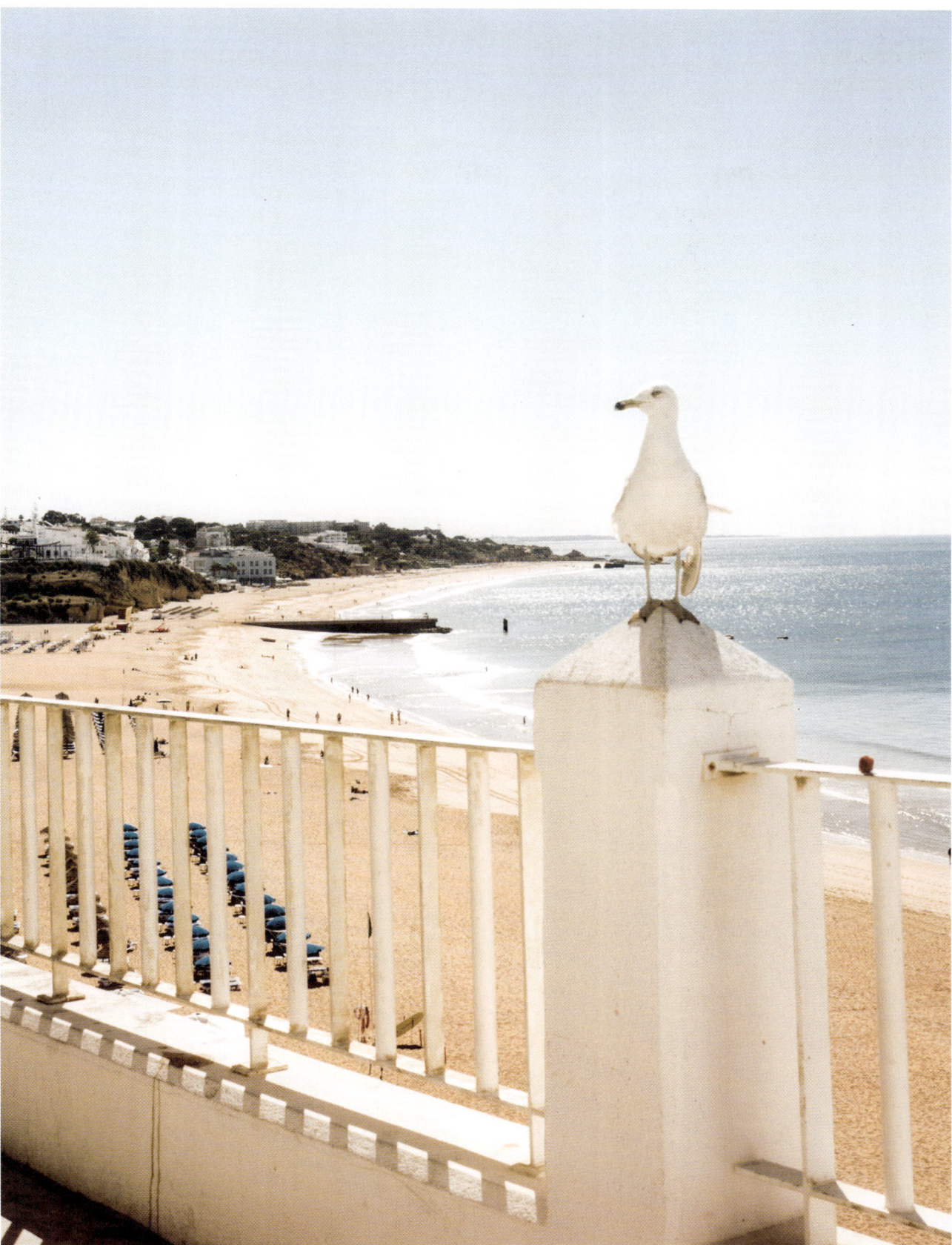

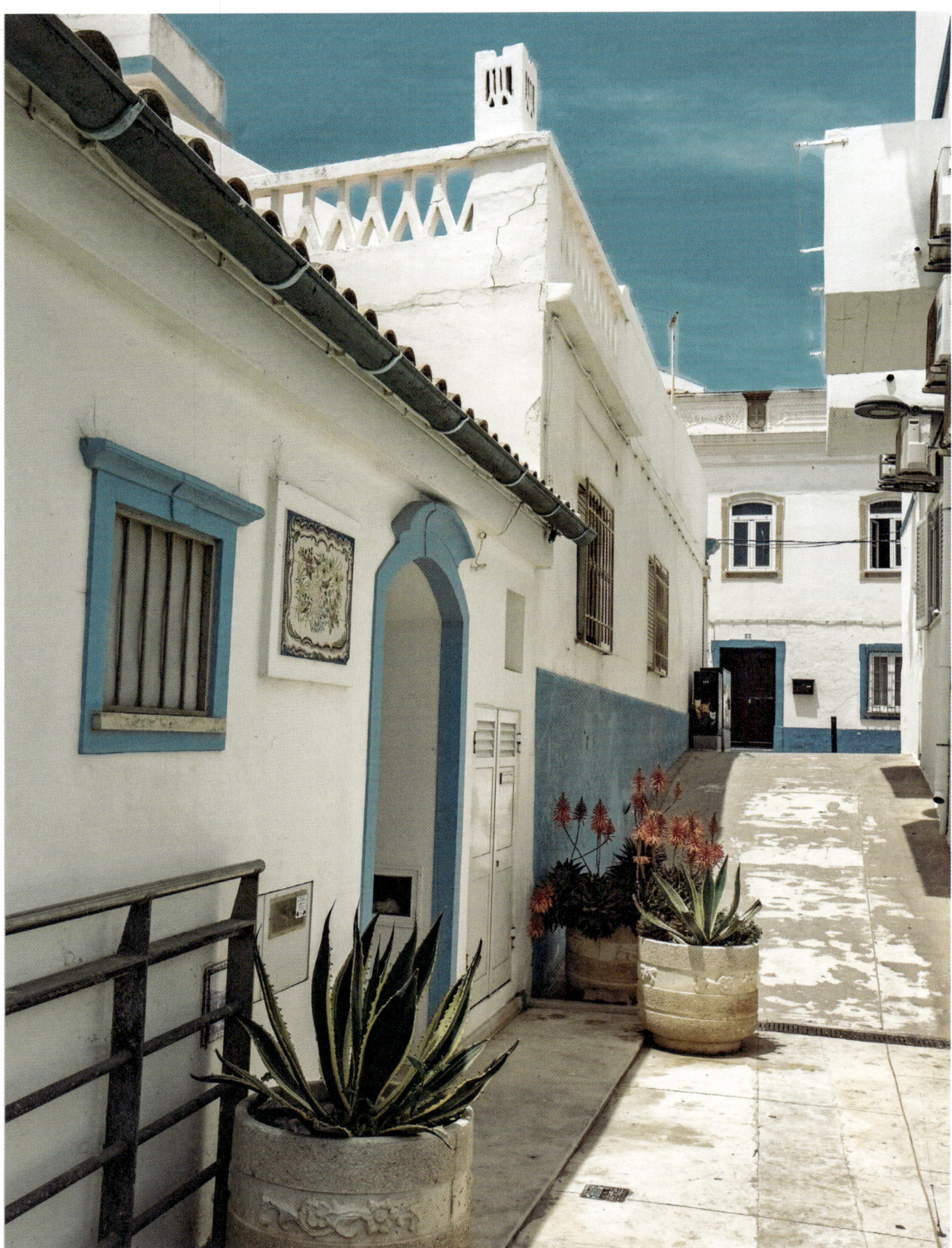

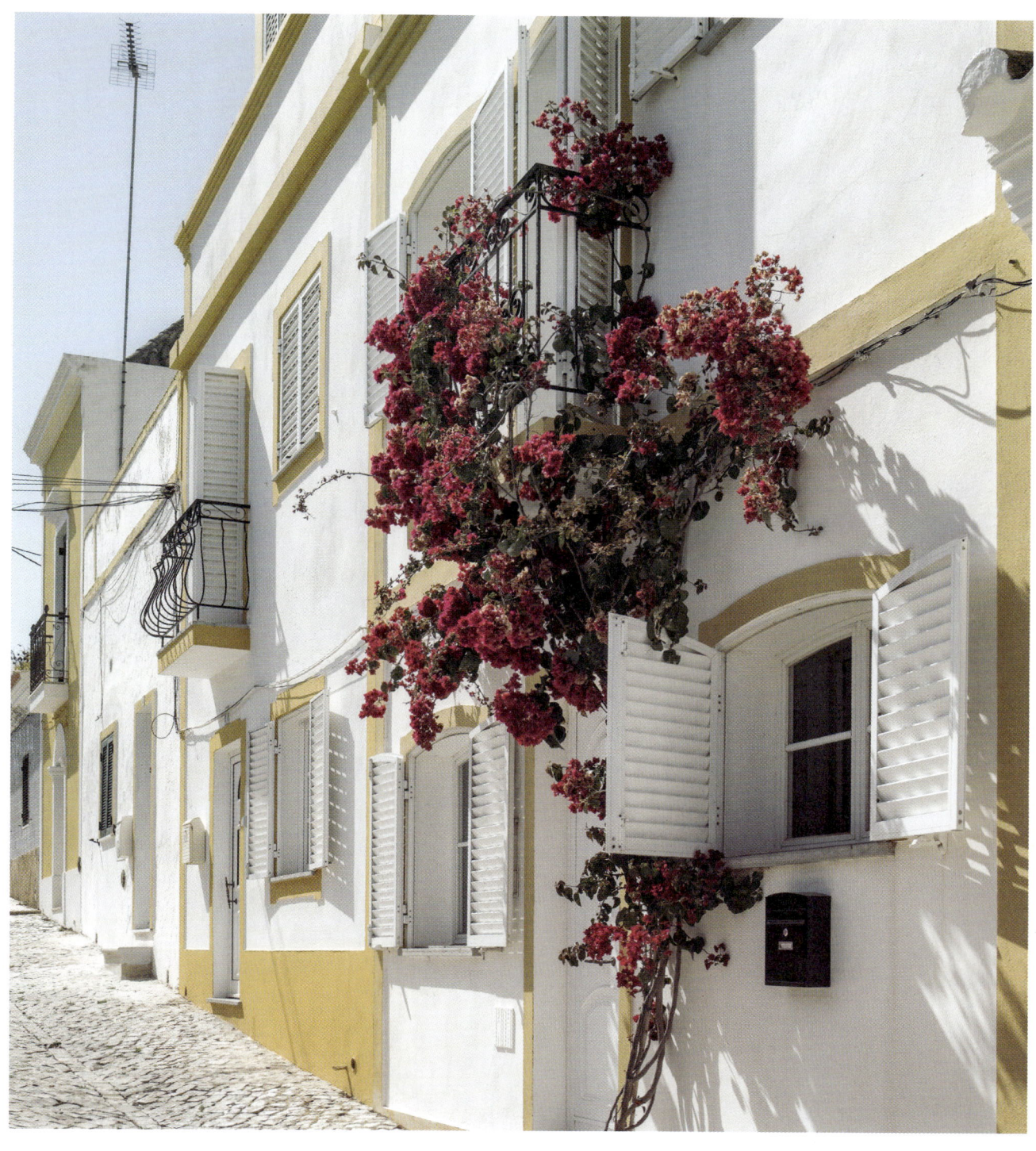

ABOVE AND LEFT: *In Albufeira (left) and Tavira (above), colorful accents brighten the white houses of the old town. Elements of Moorish architecture recall a period of active trade between Portuguese ports and cities in North Africa.*

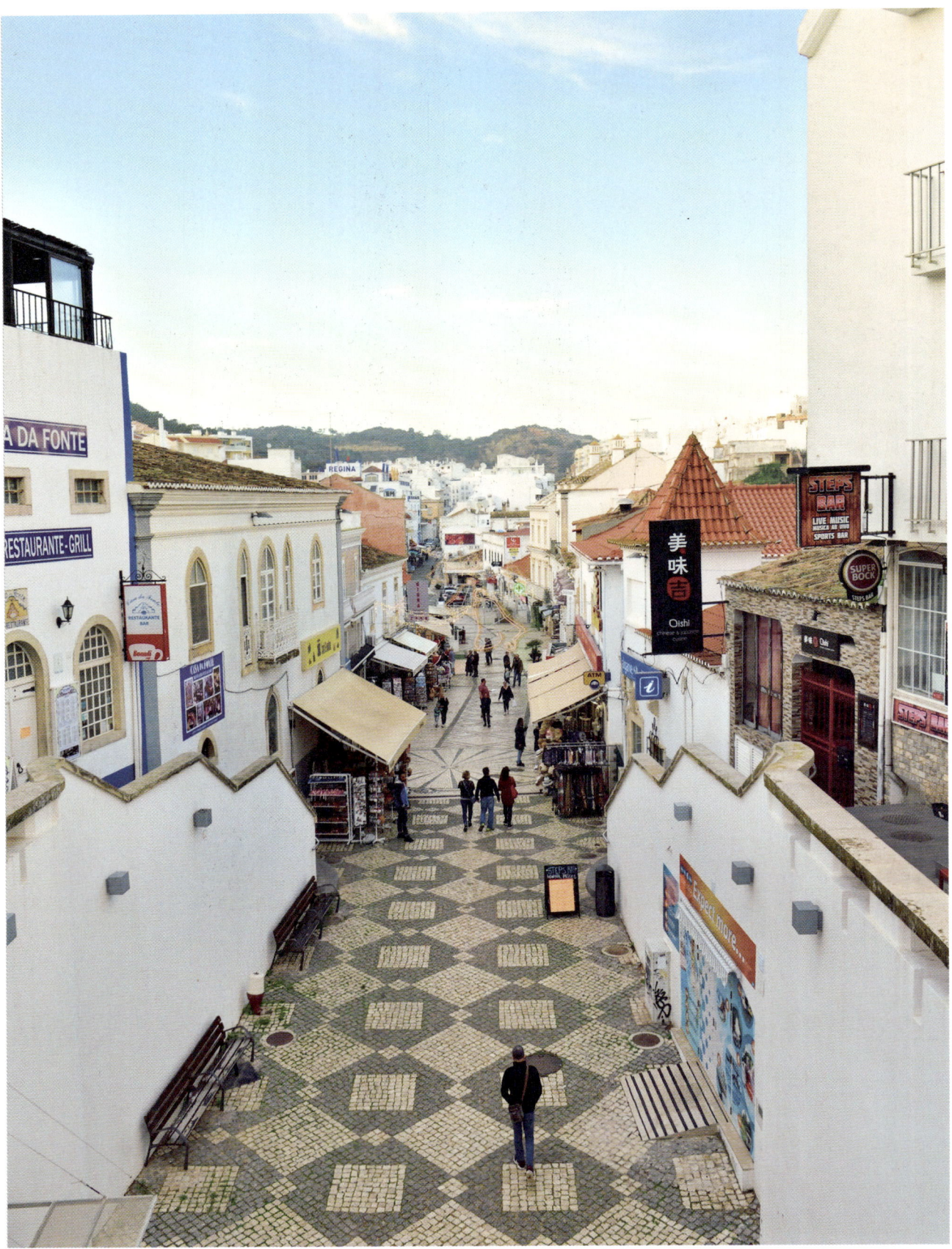

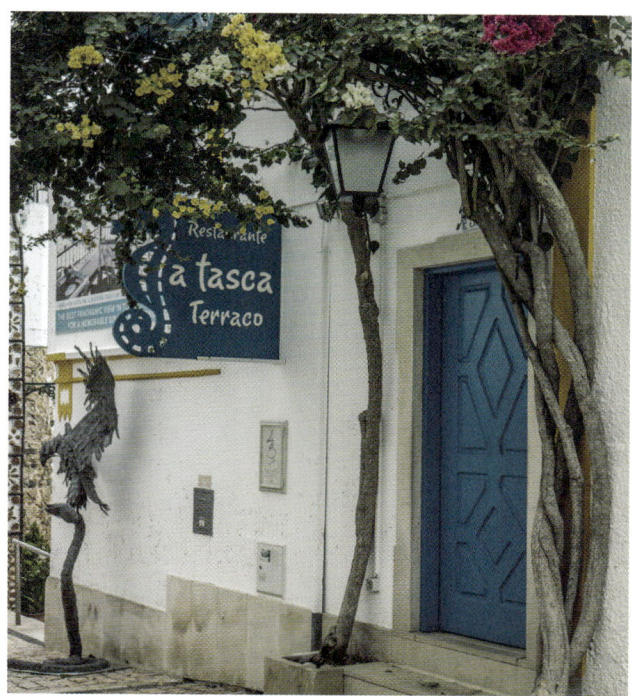

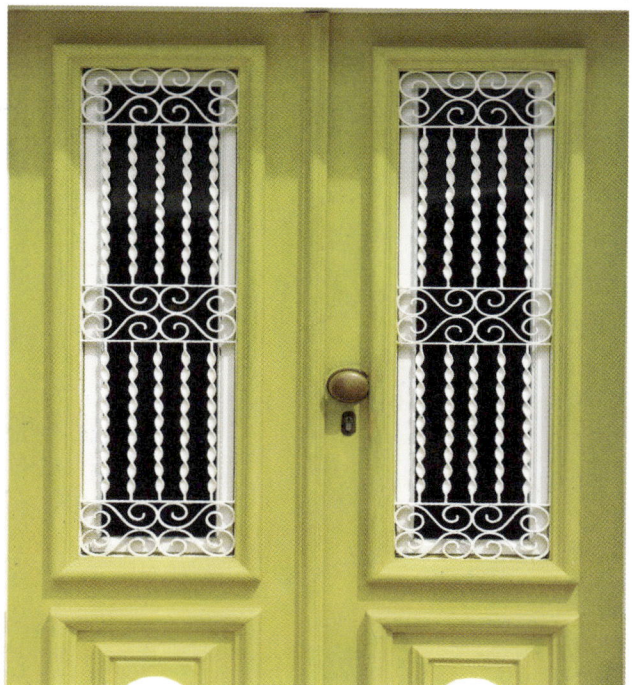

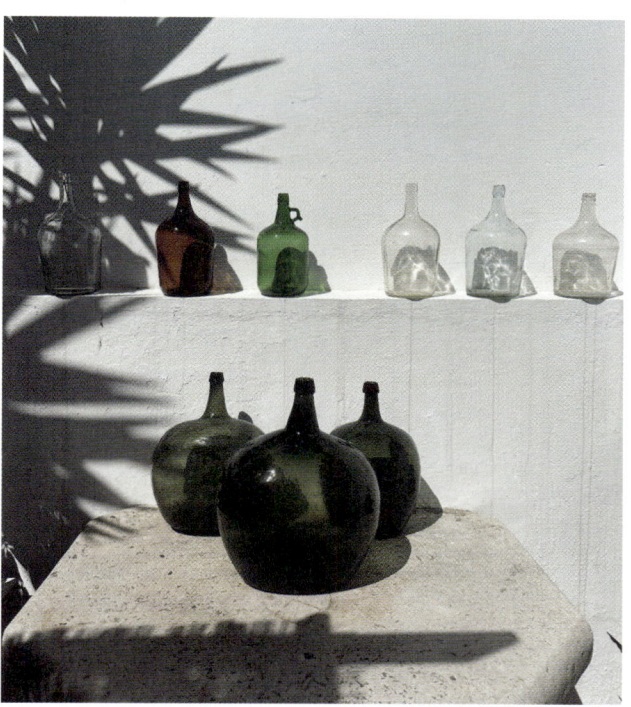

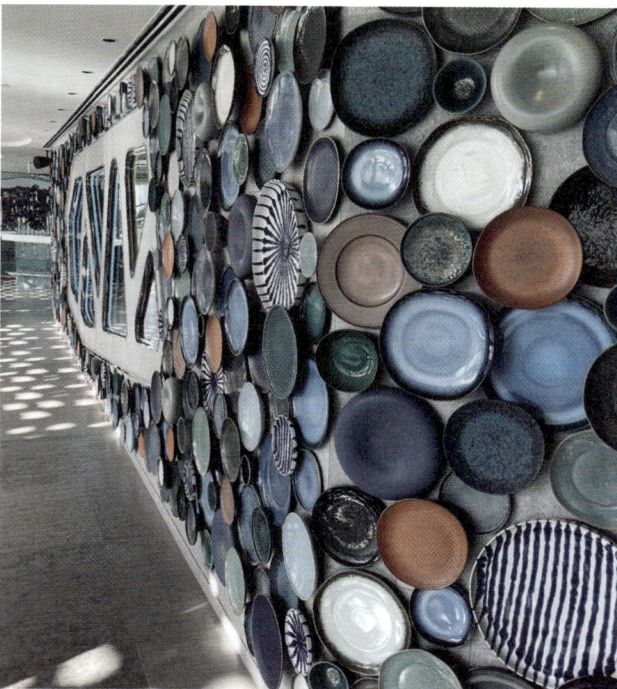

ABOVE AND LEFT: *Once a quiet fishing village, Albufeira has become a busy resort, with cafés and bars for night owls and many small shops in the old town. Those who look closely are rewarded with surprising details at every turn.*

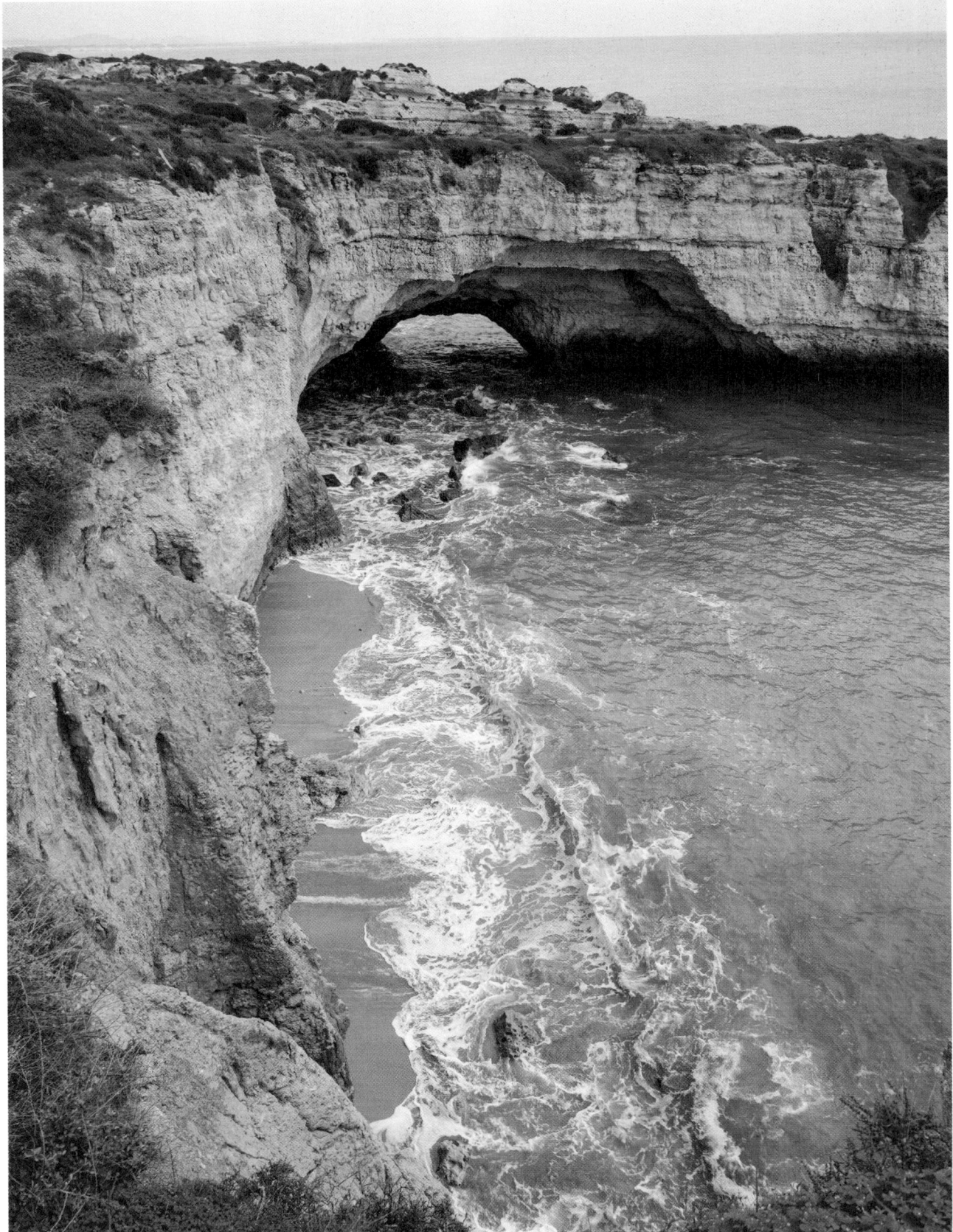

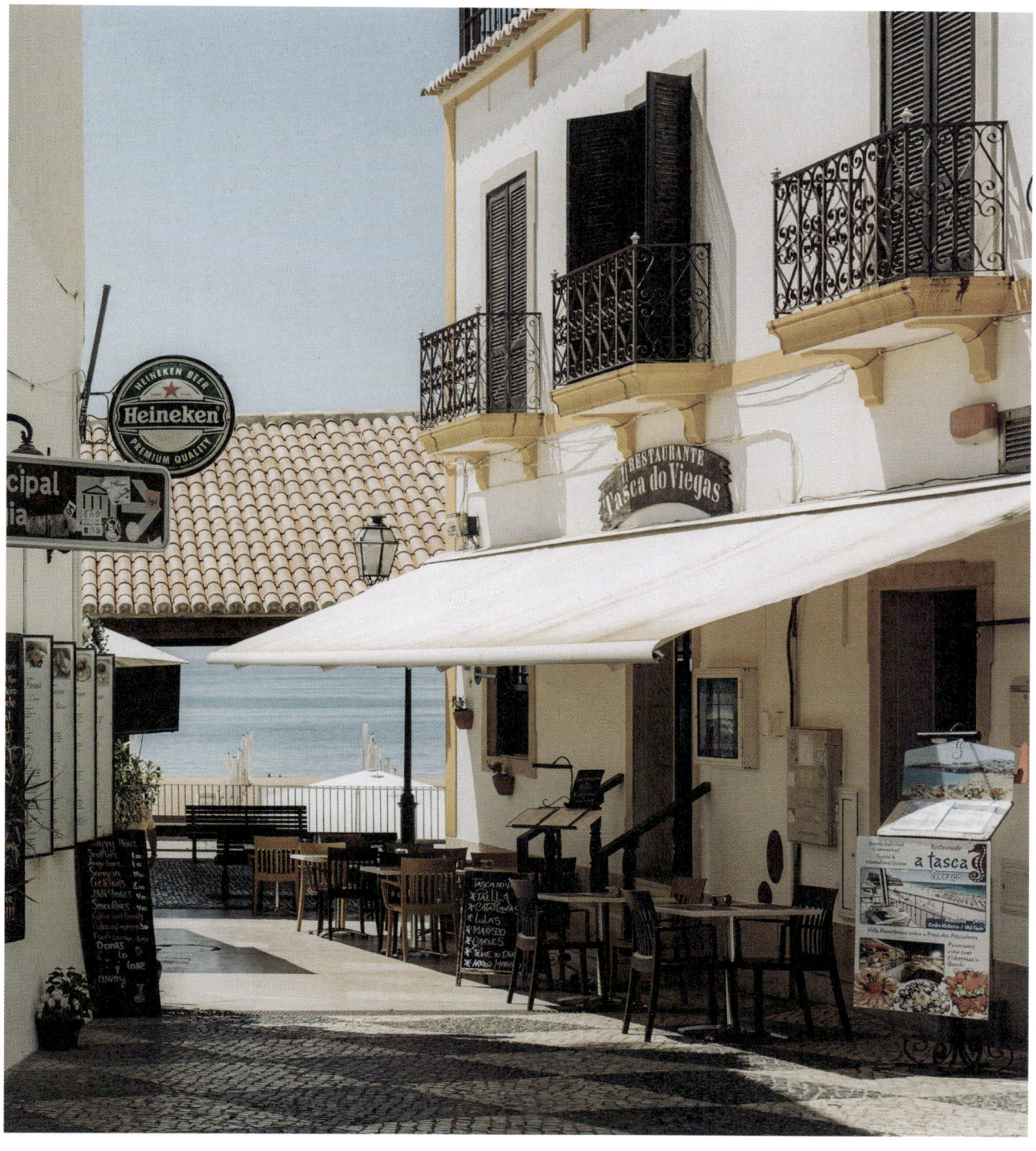

ABOVE: *Even in lively Albufeira, small, off-the-beaten-path* tascas *along narrow lanes serve plainly prepared but very fresh fish.*

LEFT: *West of Albufeira, dramatic cliffs frame small sandy coves. Tidal action at Praia da Ponte Pequena has carved a striking natural sandstone arch.*

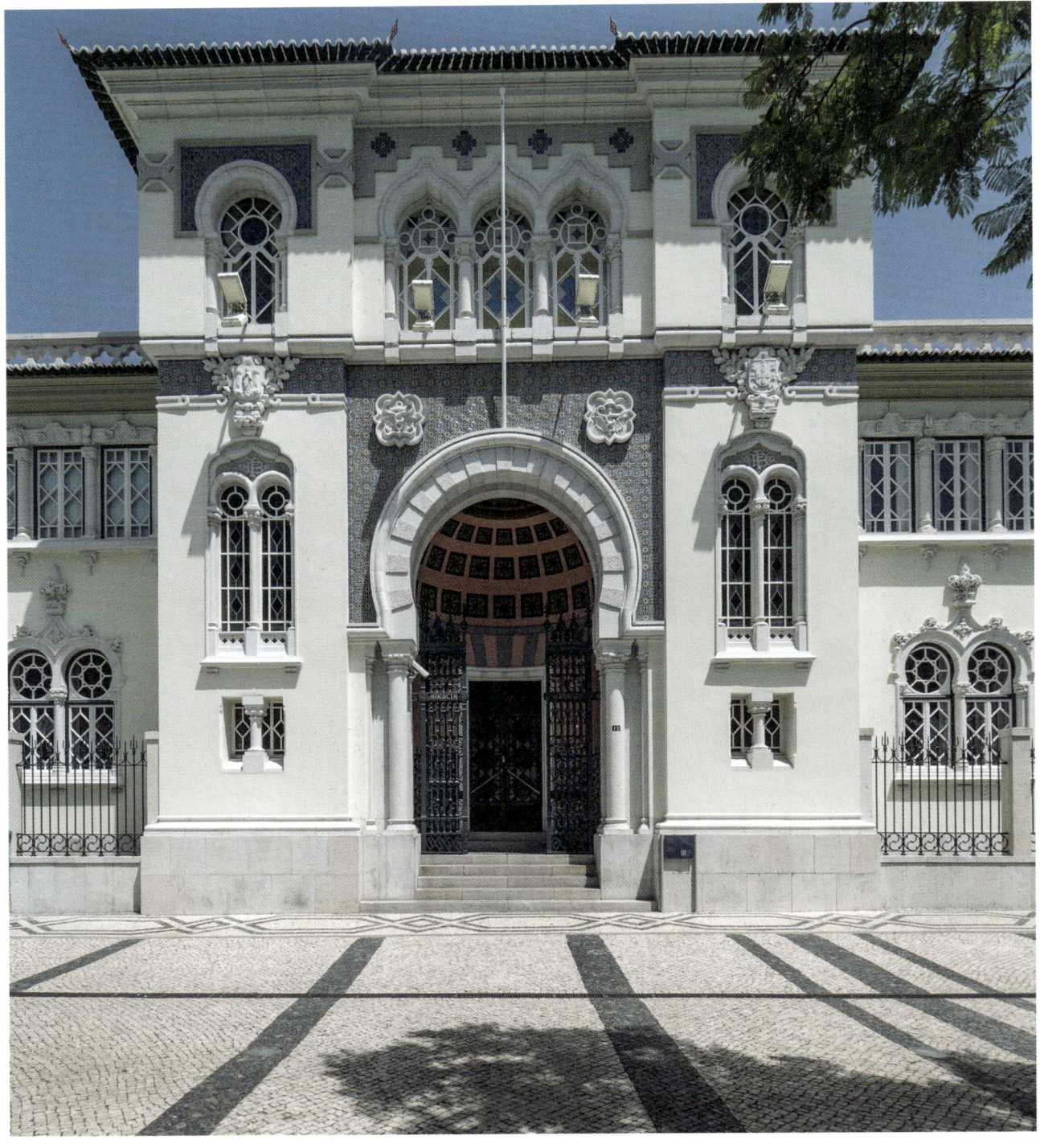

ABOVE AND RIGHT: *Faro features ornate Art Nouveau buildings with Moorish references. The opulent Banco de Portugal building could pass for a church.*

RIGHT: *Beyond the gardens of the palácio, quiet corners all around the village of Estoi. Bougainvillea adds shots of color along the narrow cobblestone streets.*

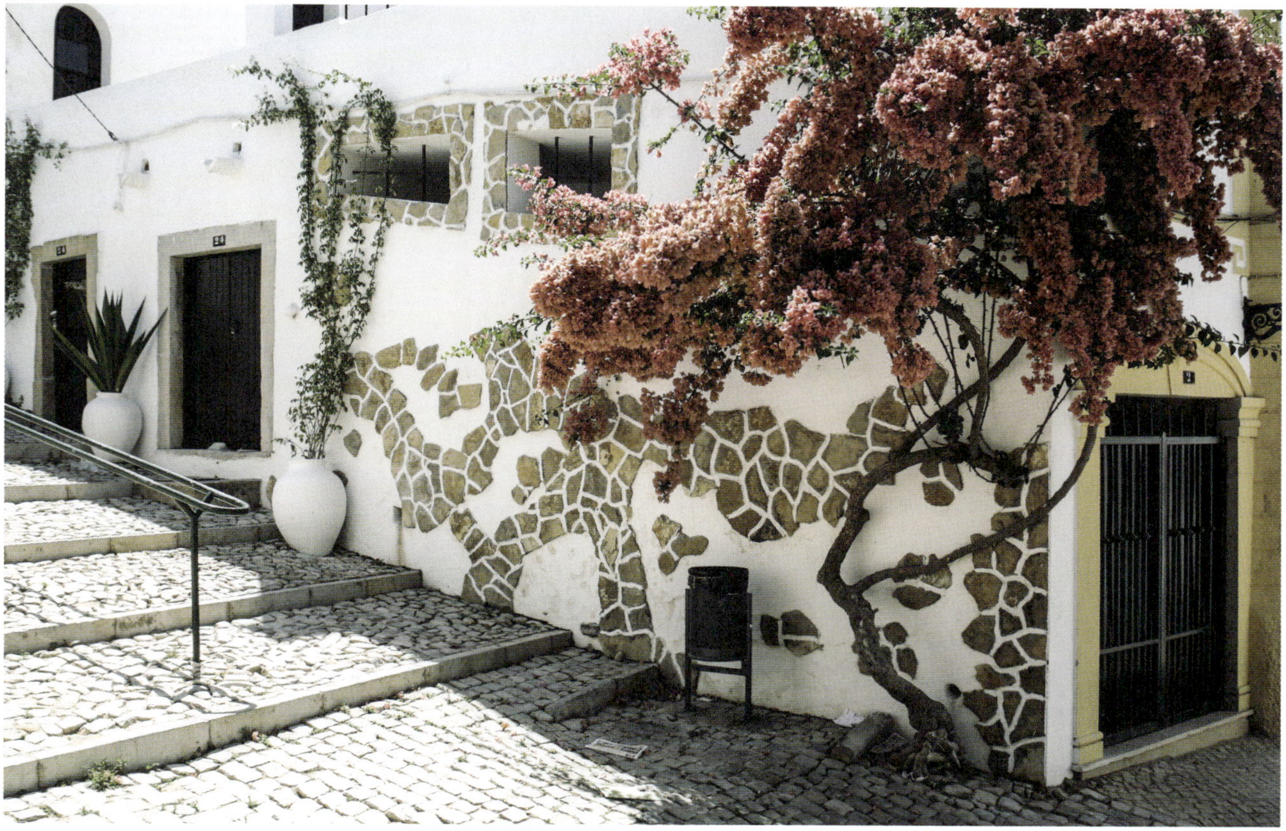

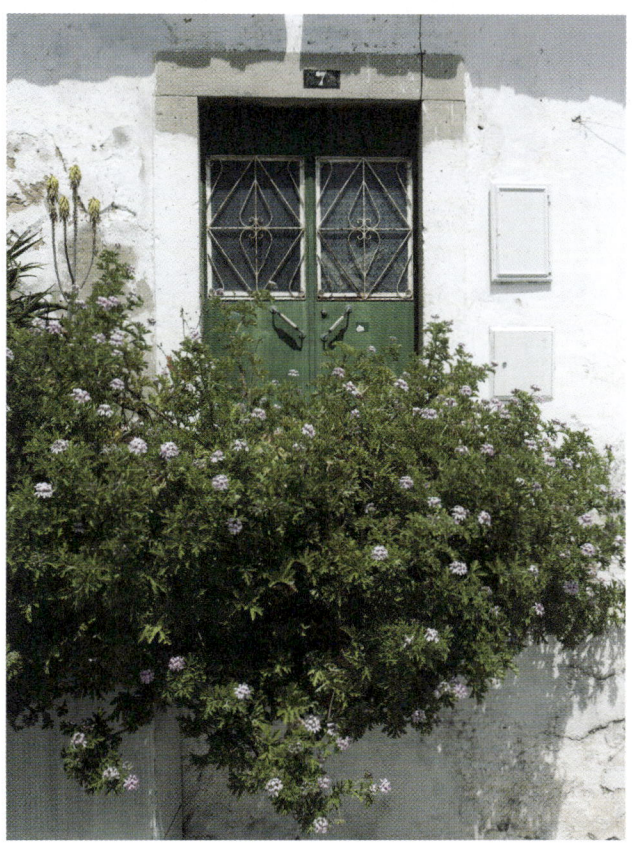
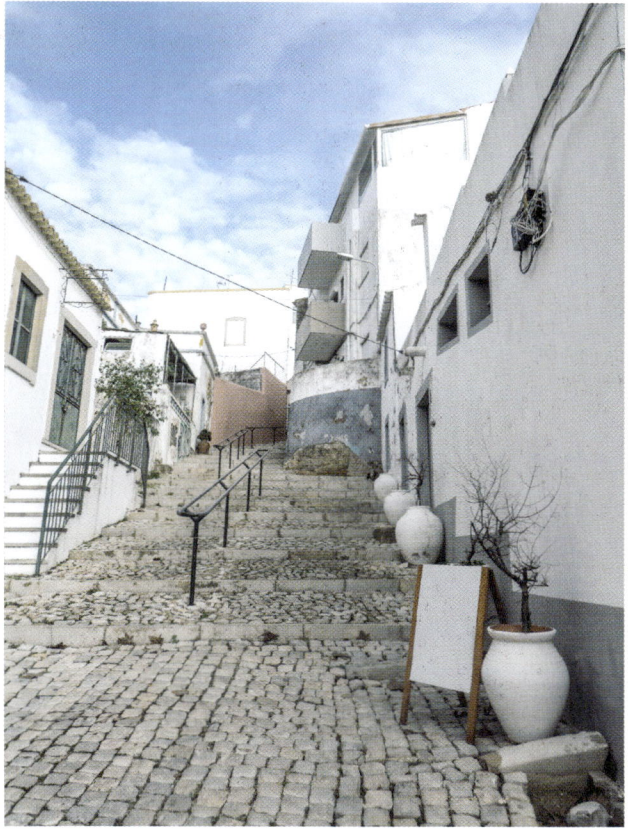

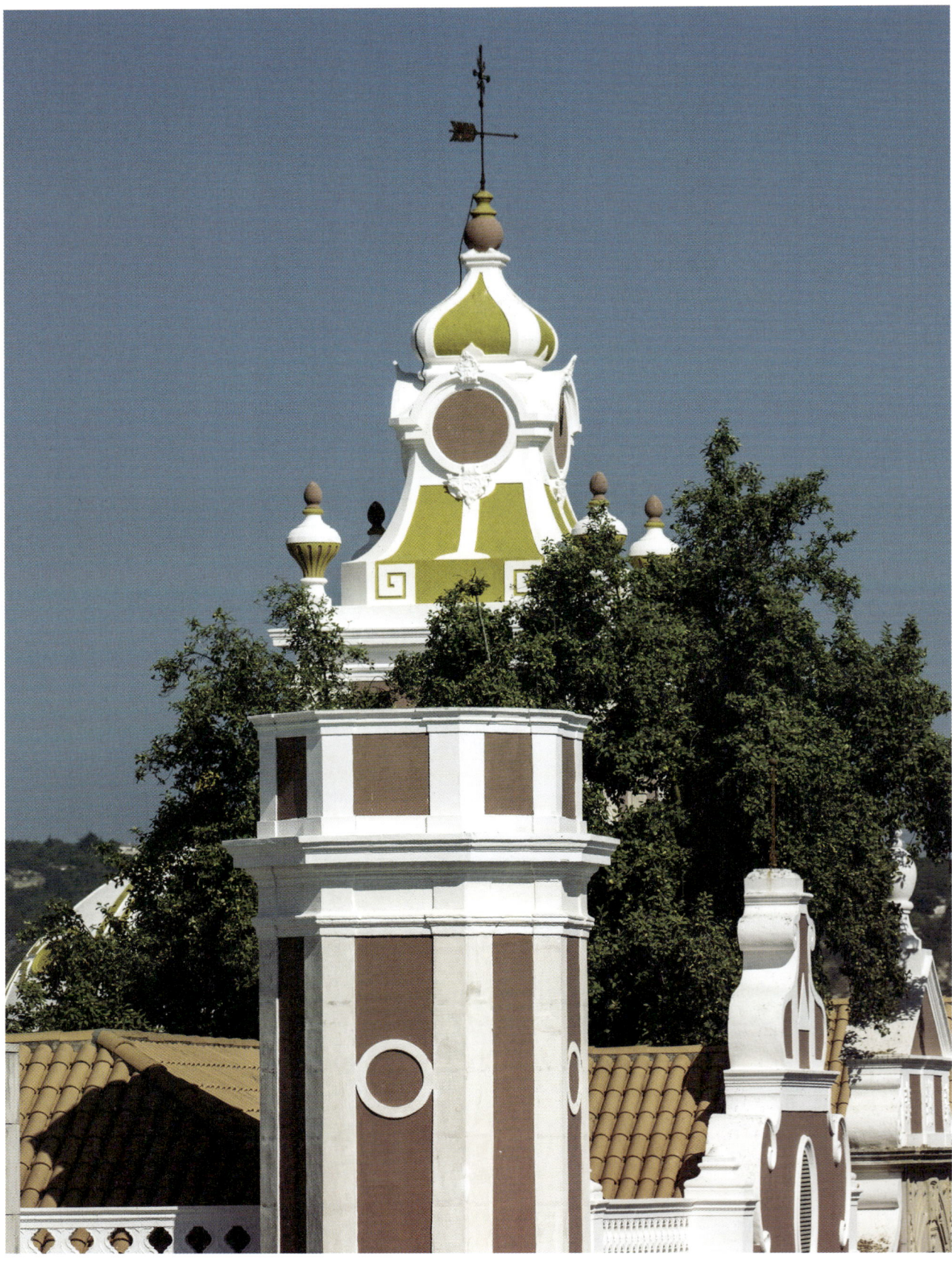

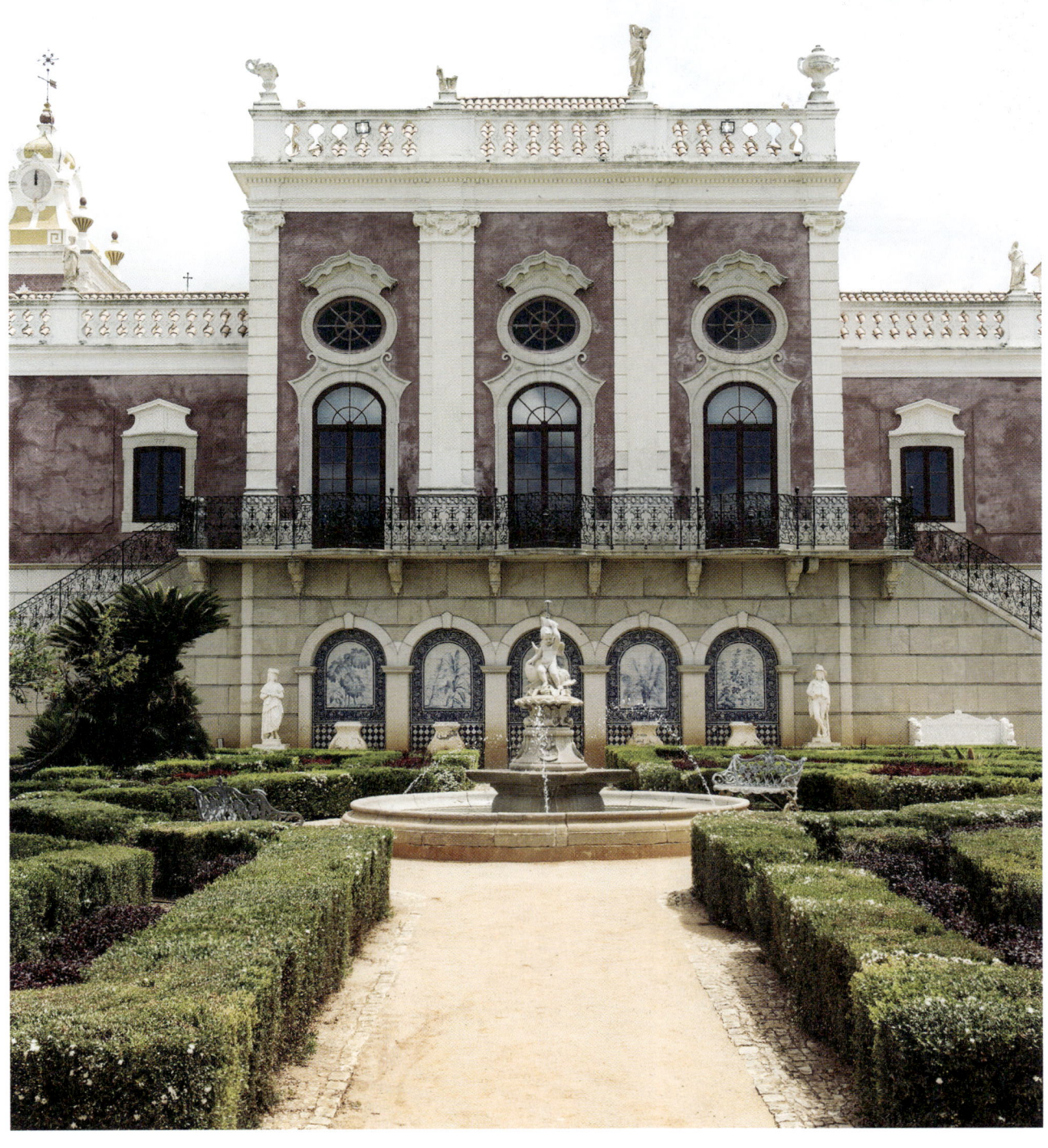

ABOVE AND LEFT: *The distinctive colors of the Rococo façade of the Palácio de Estoi. Once neglected, the building now houses a luxury hotel whose rates only the most generous travel budgets can absorb. But the gardens and elaborate staircases are open to the public.*

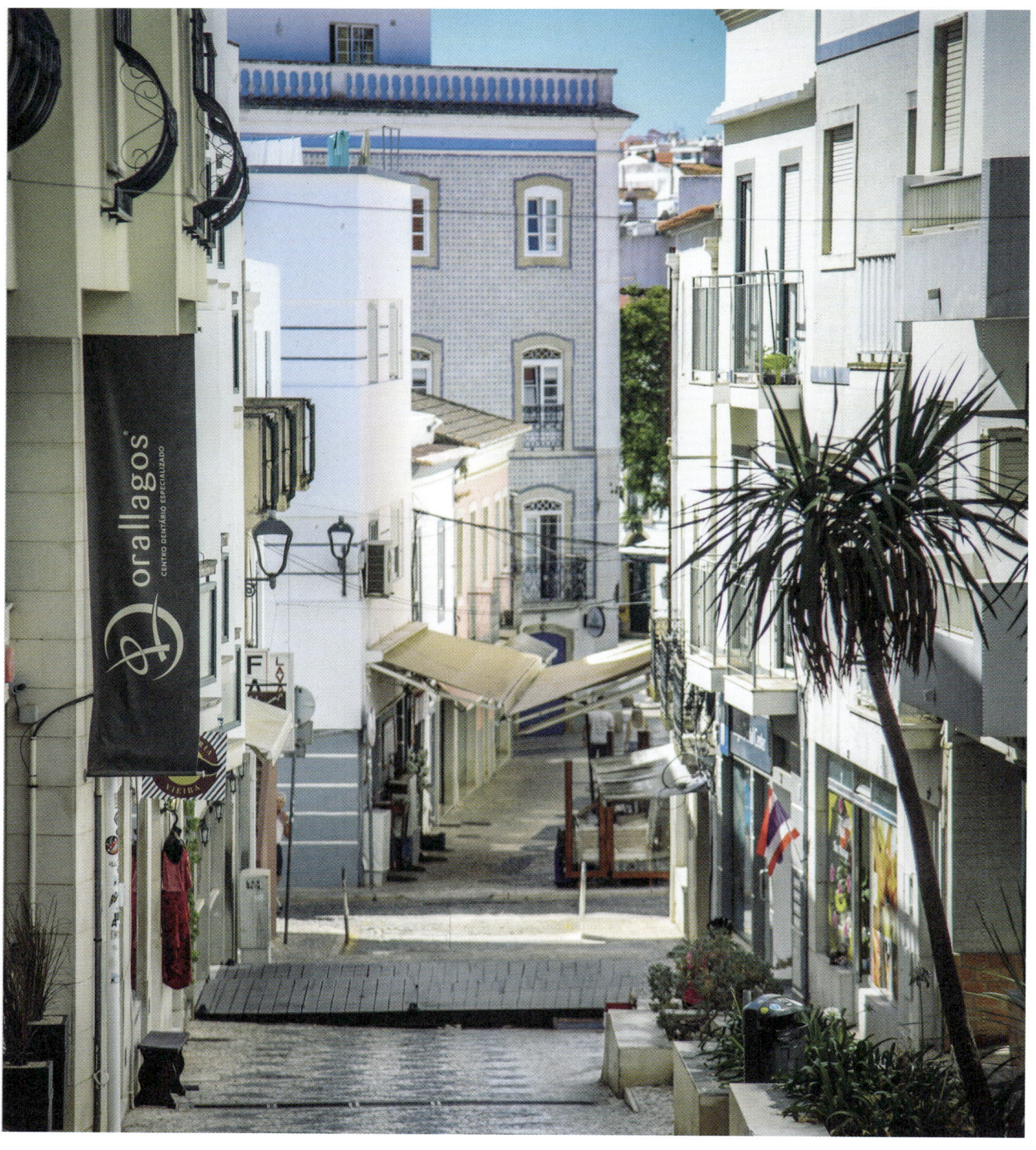

ABOVE AND RIGHT: *Lagos, one of the most attractive towns in the Algarve. In the old town, elegant façades along shaded streets attest to the former wealth of this important port. It was from here that Henry the Navigator set out to explore the coast of West Africa in the fifteenth century.*

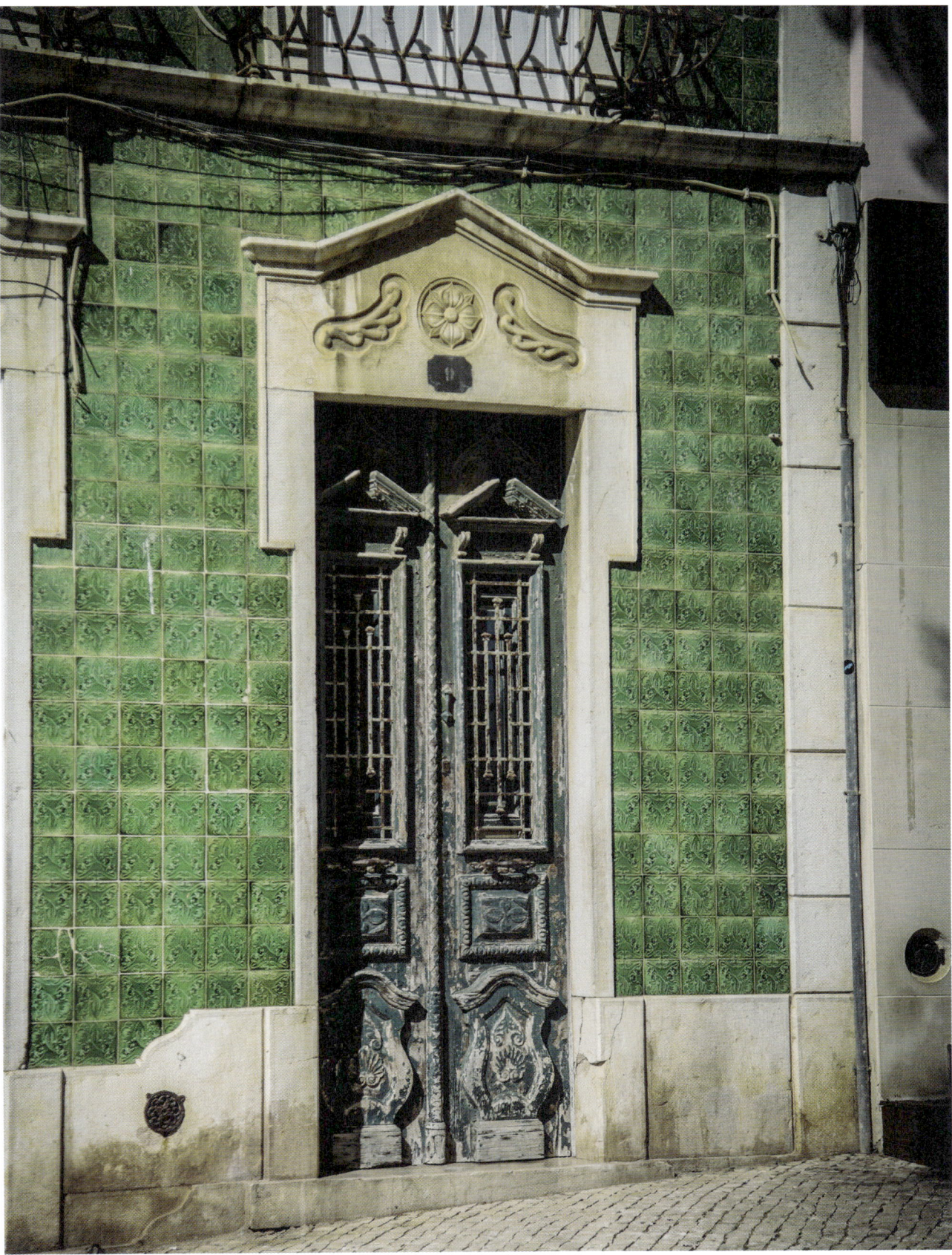

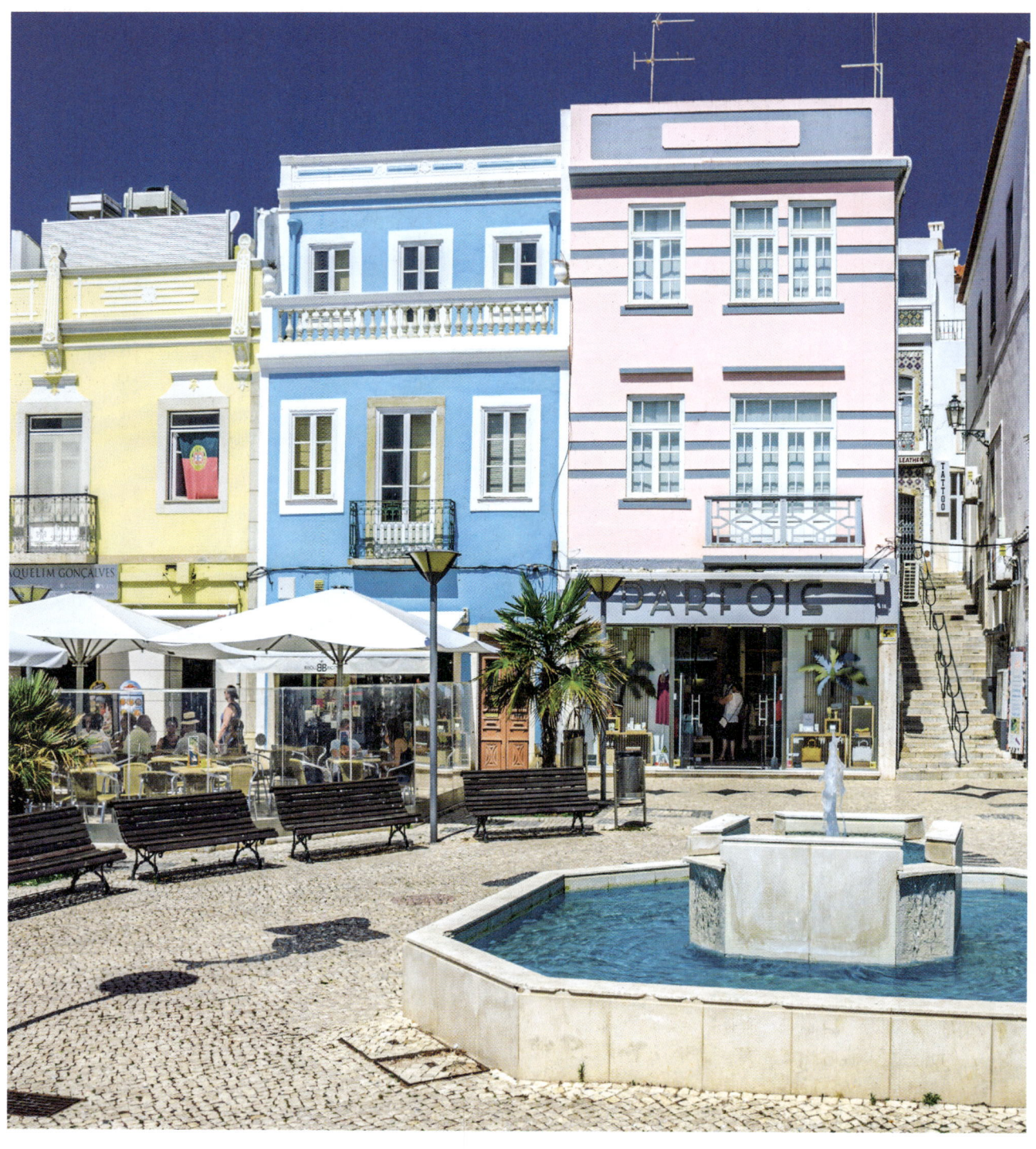

ABOVE AND RIGHT: *Layers of color in the old town and along the port of Lagos, with soft pastels and vivid tile façades. The "Green House" on Praça Luís de Camões. On the town's squares, people gather to chat at cafés beneath the trees.*

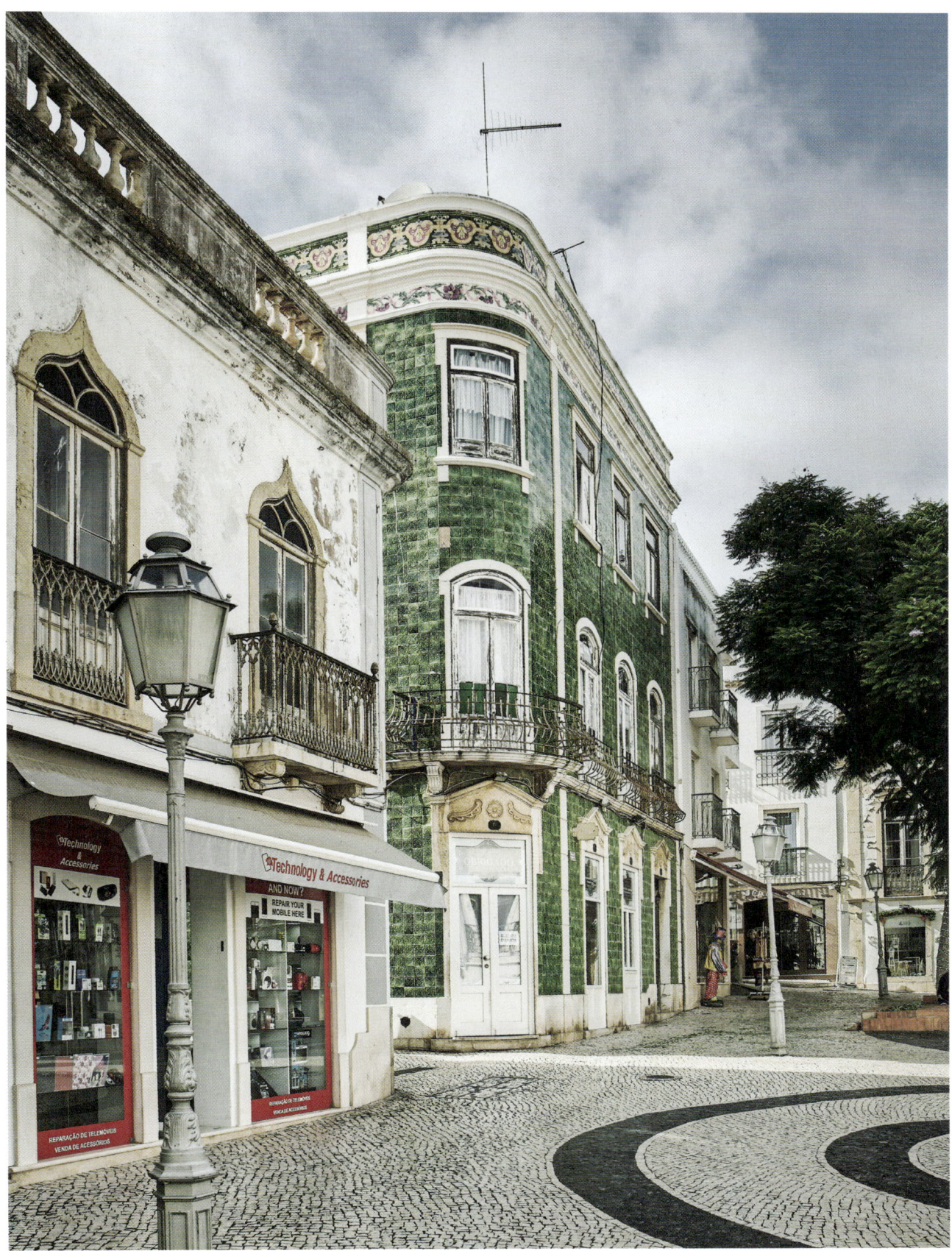

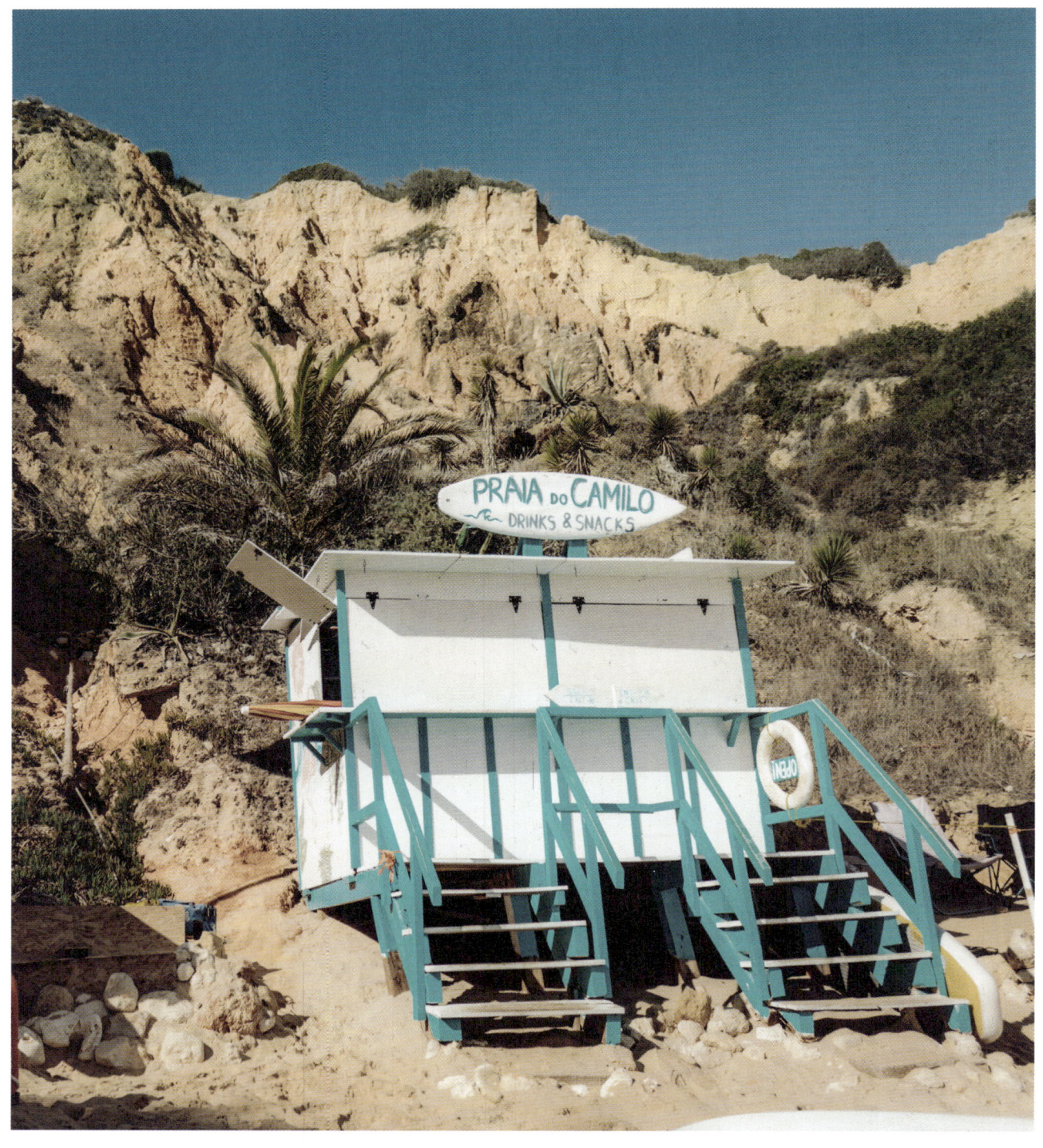

ABOVE AND RIGHT: *Around Lagos, small coves delineated by jagged rocks open onto turquoise water, like at Praia do Camilo (above). Farther south, steep steps descend to the bay of Ponte da Piedade (right). Pink rock arches and grottos draw kayakers and paddlers.*

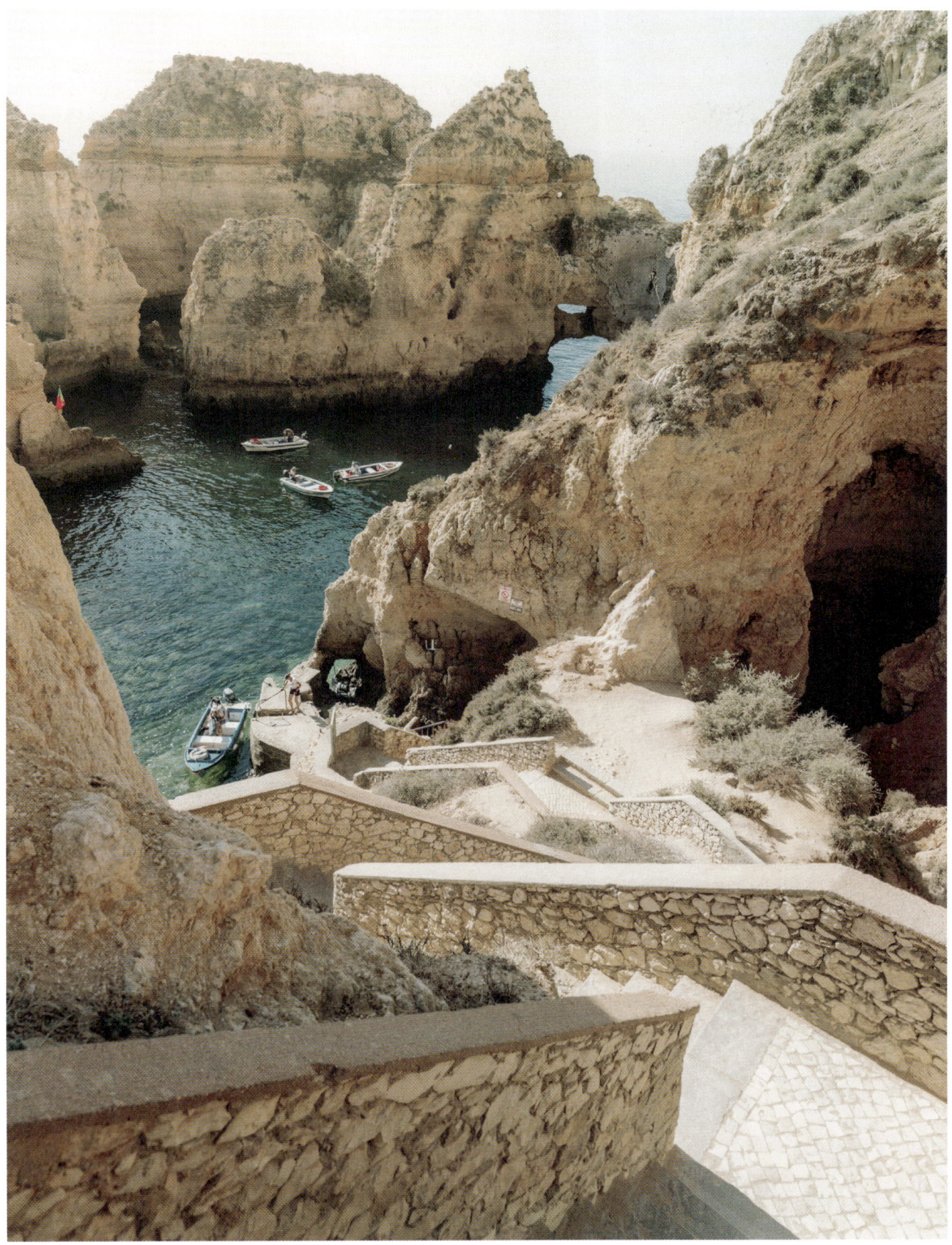

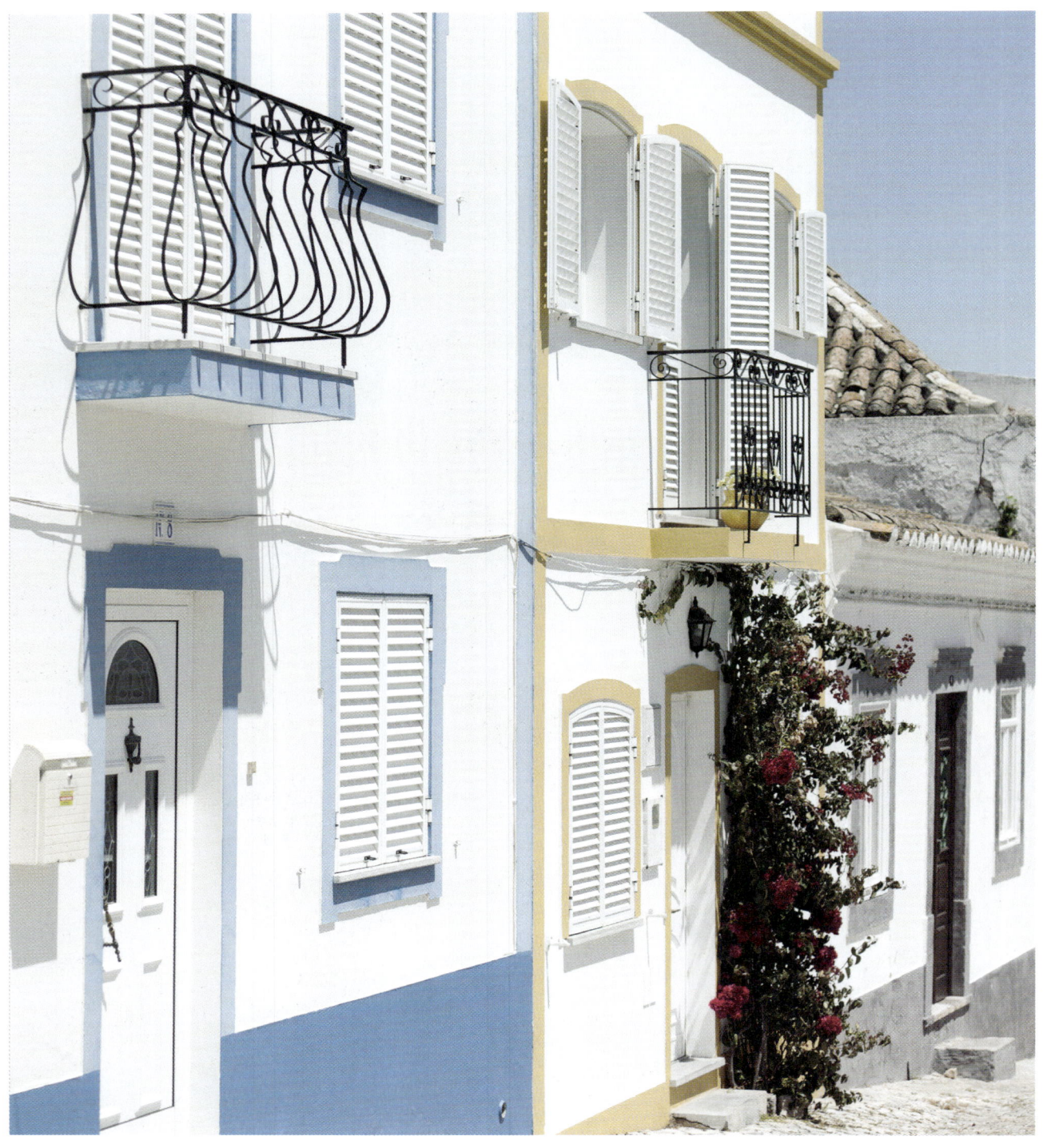

ABOVE AND RIGHT: *The lagoon setting of the maze-like old town of Tavira in the eastern Algarve. Colorful window frames punctuate white houses along narrow streets.*

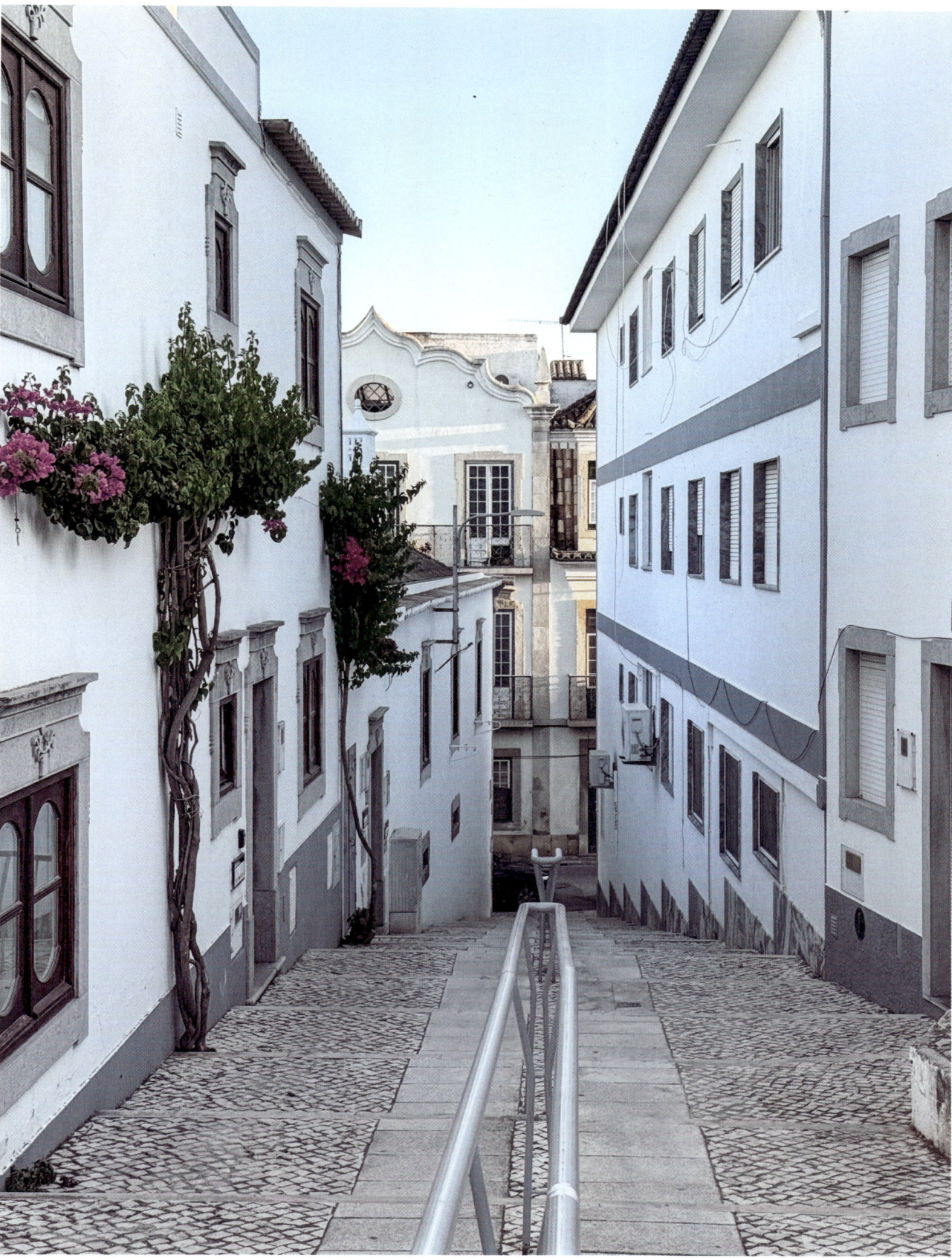

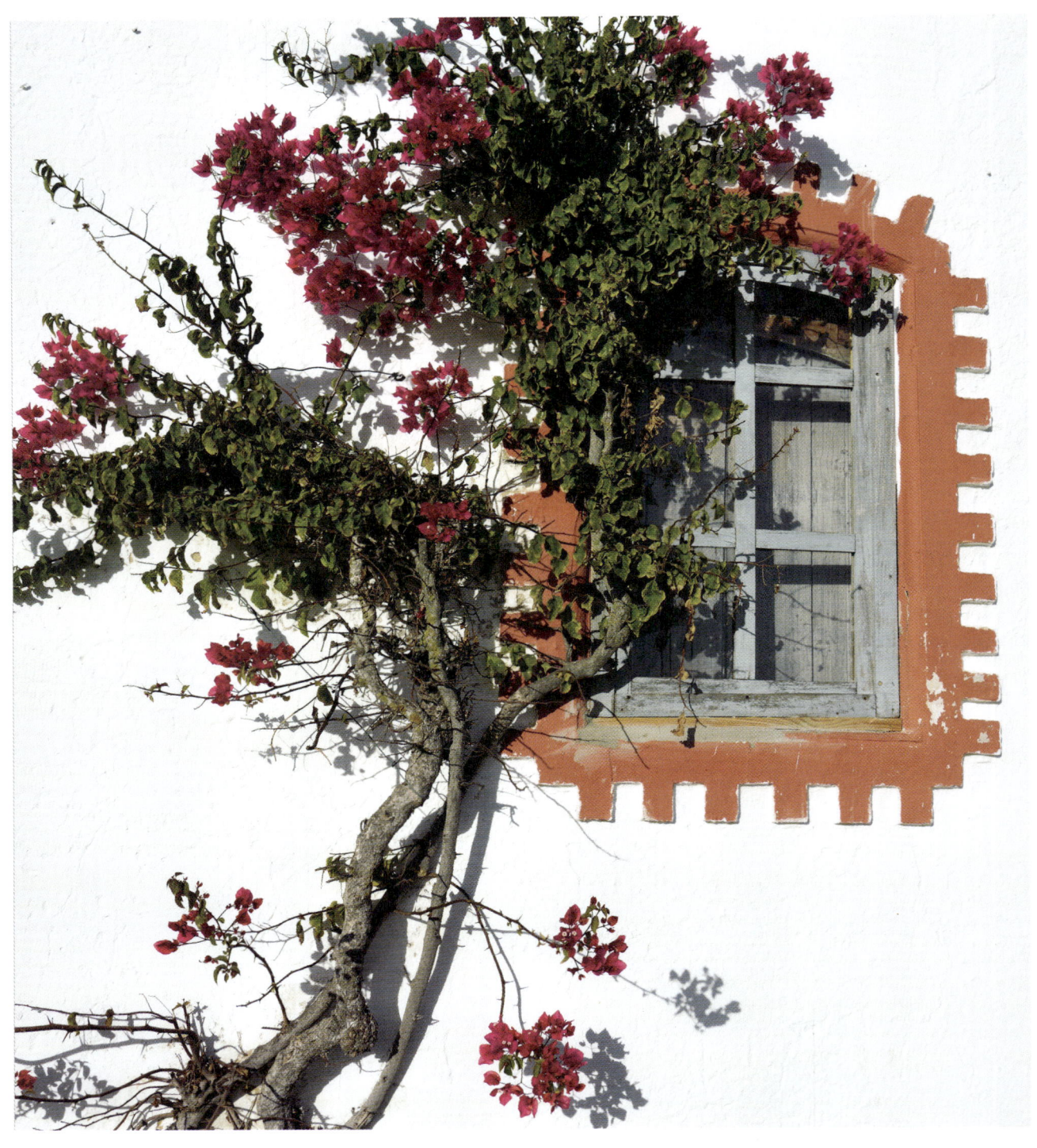

ABOVE AND RIGHT: *Tavira is understated compared with larger Algarve resorts. Shade can be found here in narrow alleyways even on hot summer days between oleander and bougainvillea. A short respite from the bustle.*

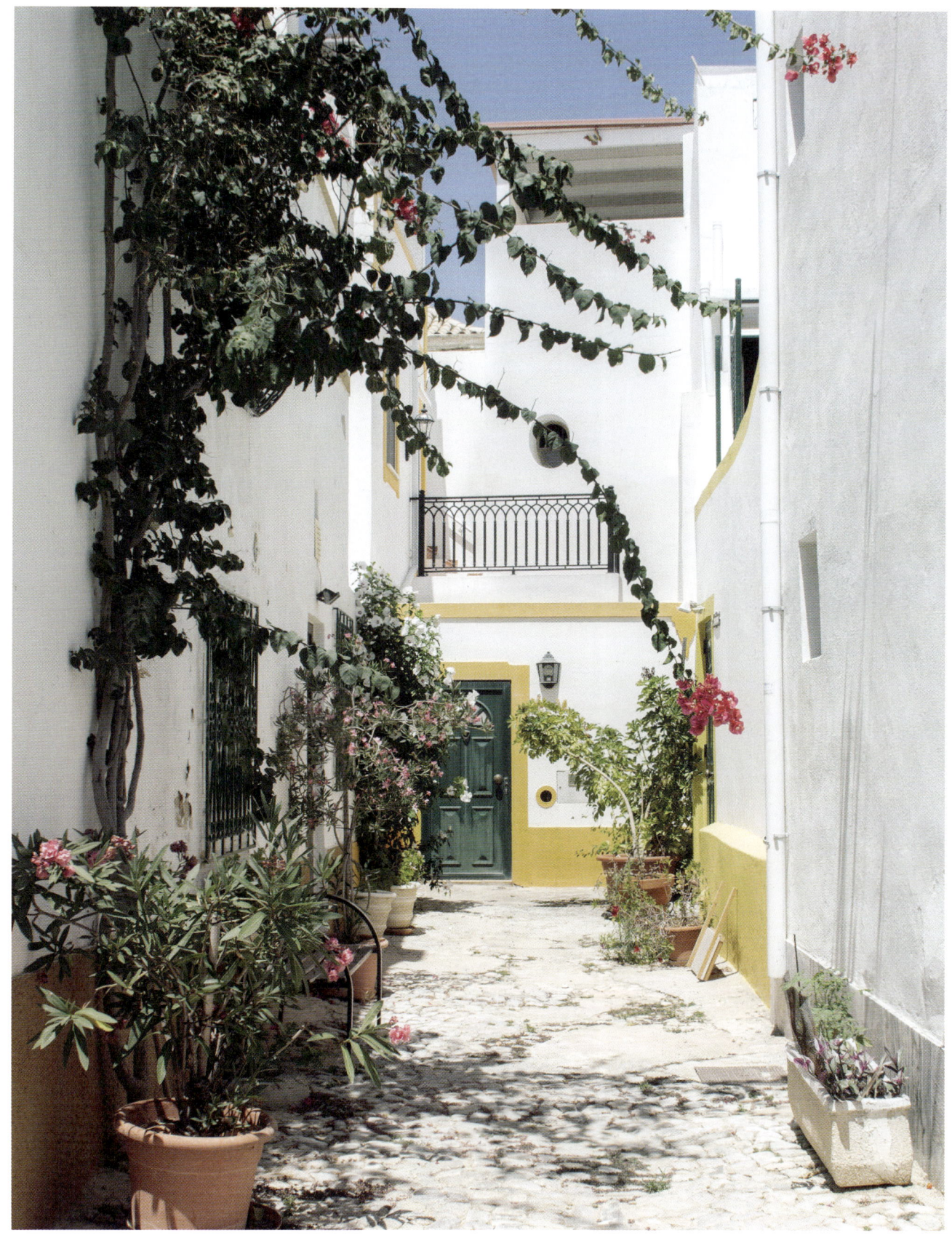

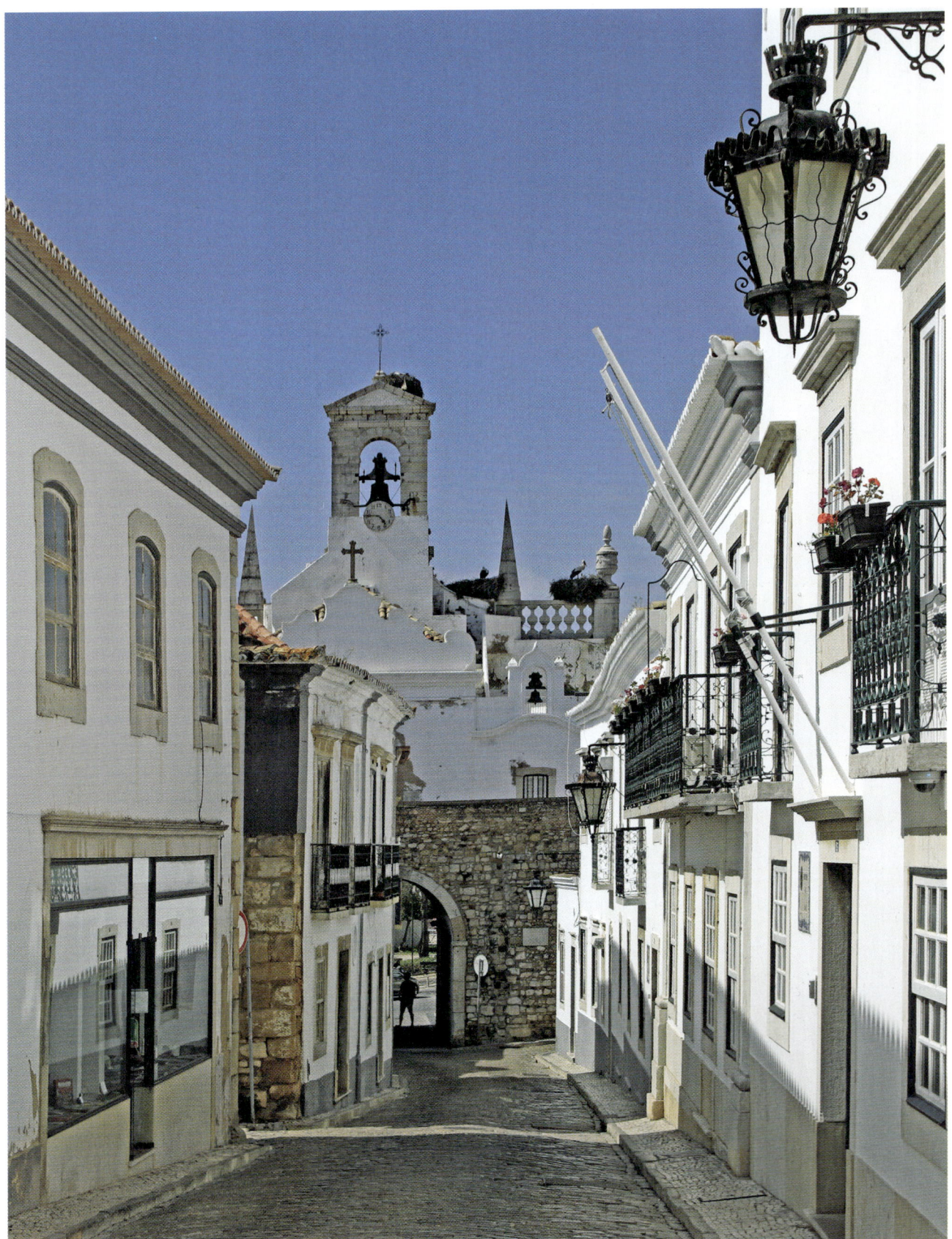

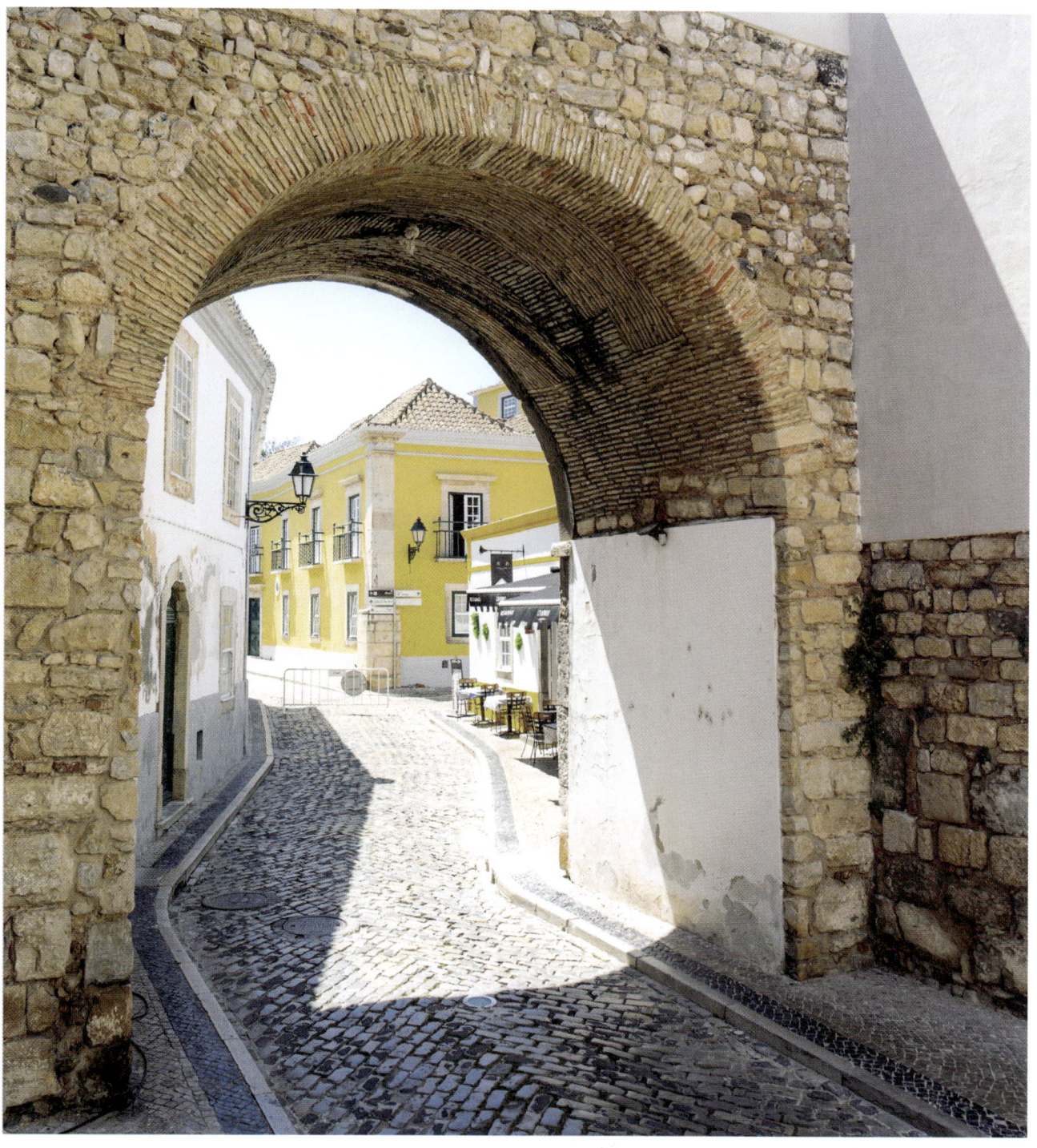

ABOVE AND LEFT: *Faro's old town is compact and easy to navigate. A leisurely pace leaves time to spot the details on many a historic building. Passing through the classical Arco da Vila (left) or the massive Arco do Repouso leads directly to Faro's thirteenth-century cathedral, whose bell tower rises above the city.*

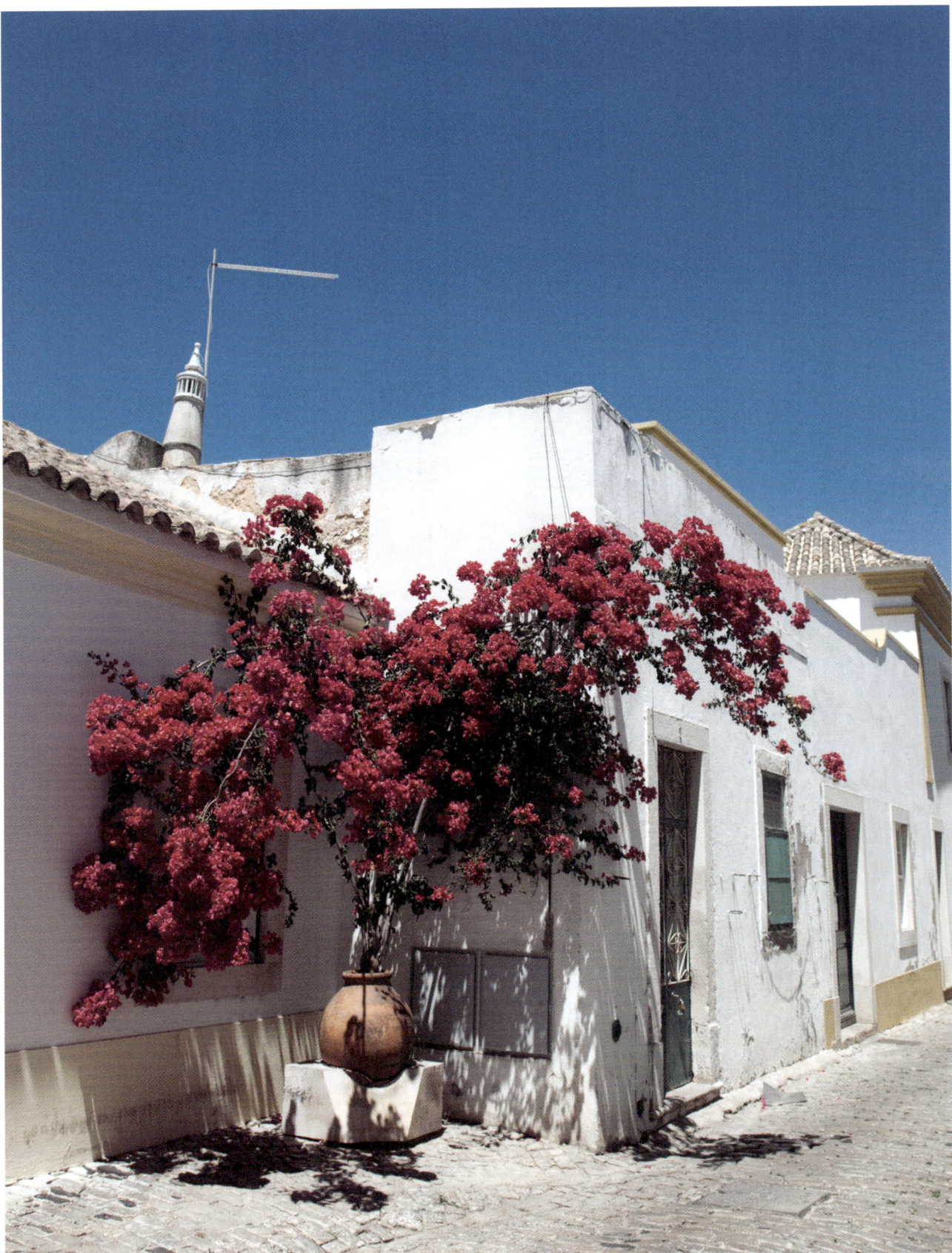

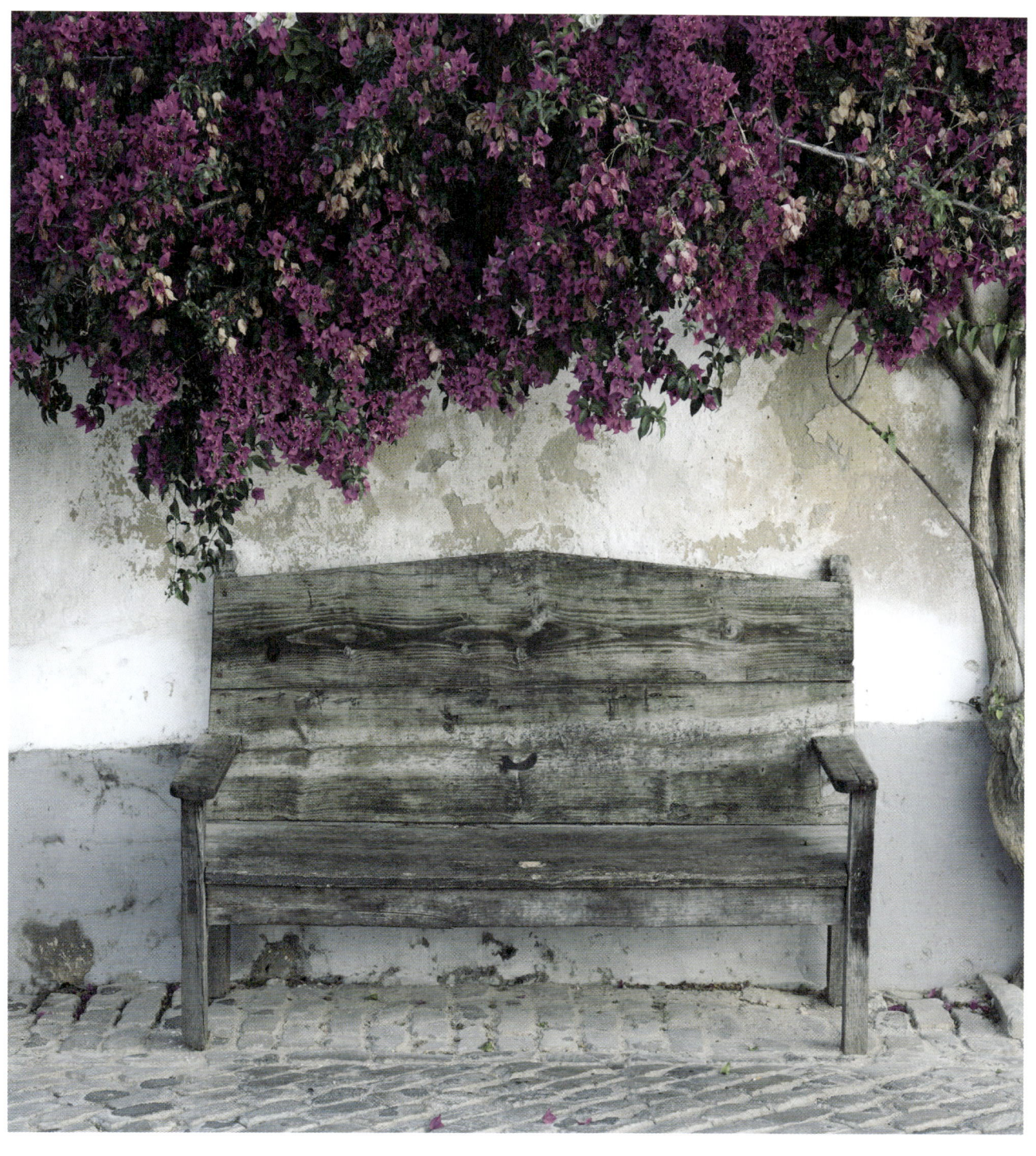

ABOVE AND LEFT: *However narrow the streets and alleys of the Algarve's former fishing villages may be, bougainvillea always gains a foothold. Purple blossoms stand out sharply against whitewashed walls in Faro.*

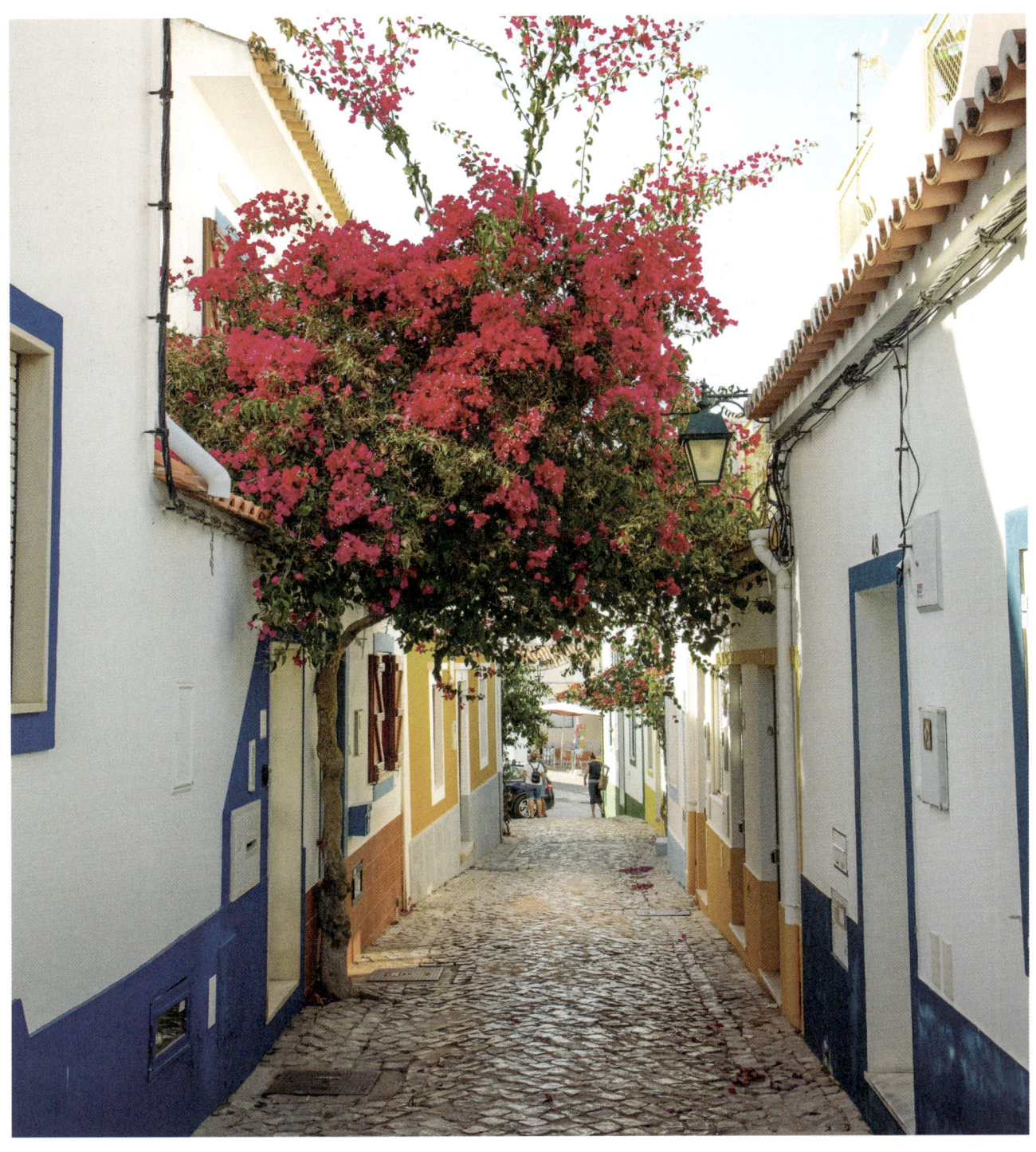

ABOVE AND RIGHT: *The houses of Ferragudo cluster around a gentle hill near where the Arade pours into the Atlantic. Charming tableaux of bougainvillea and painted façades abound.*

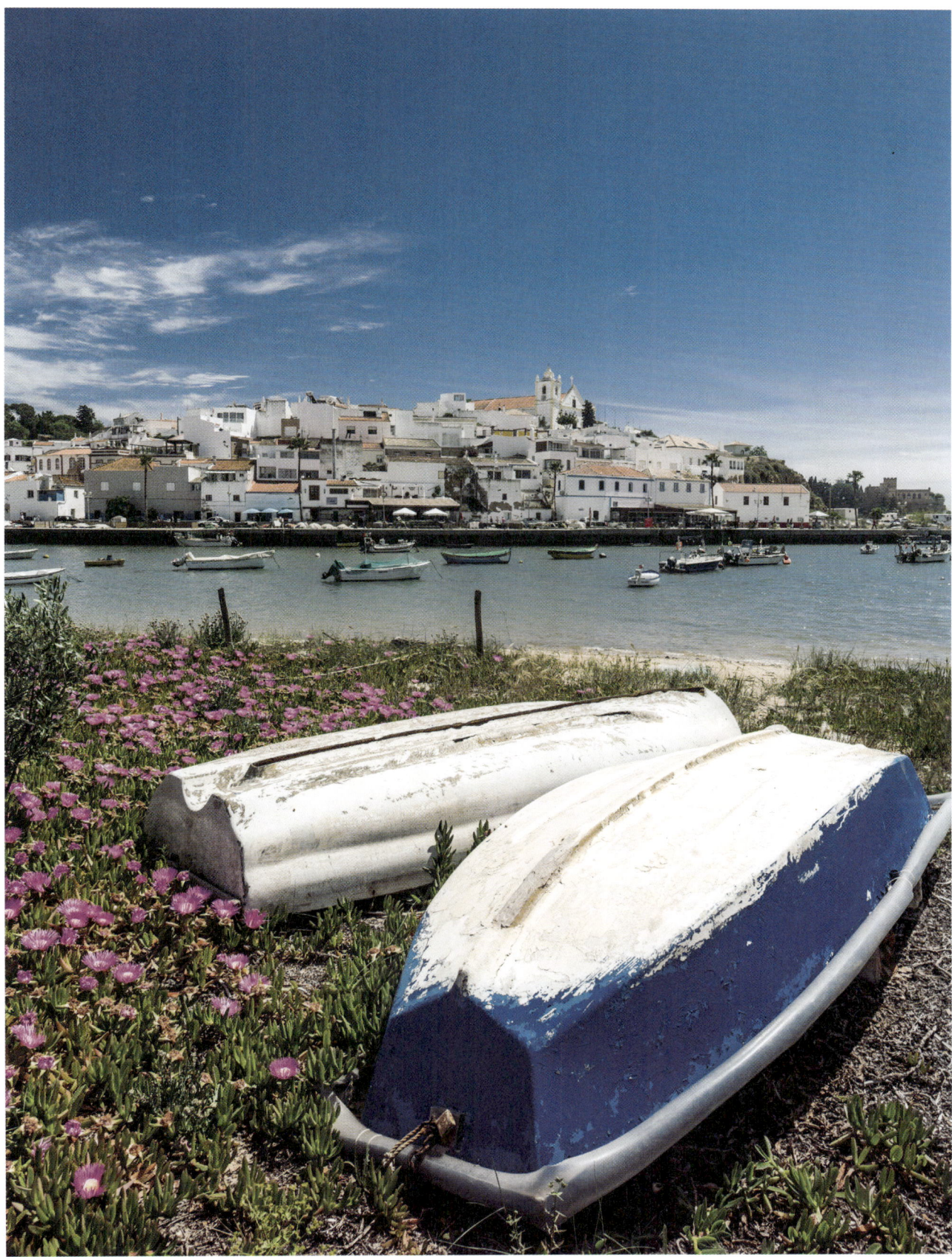

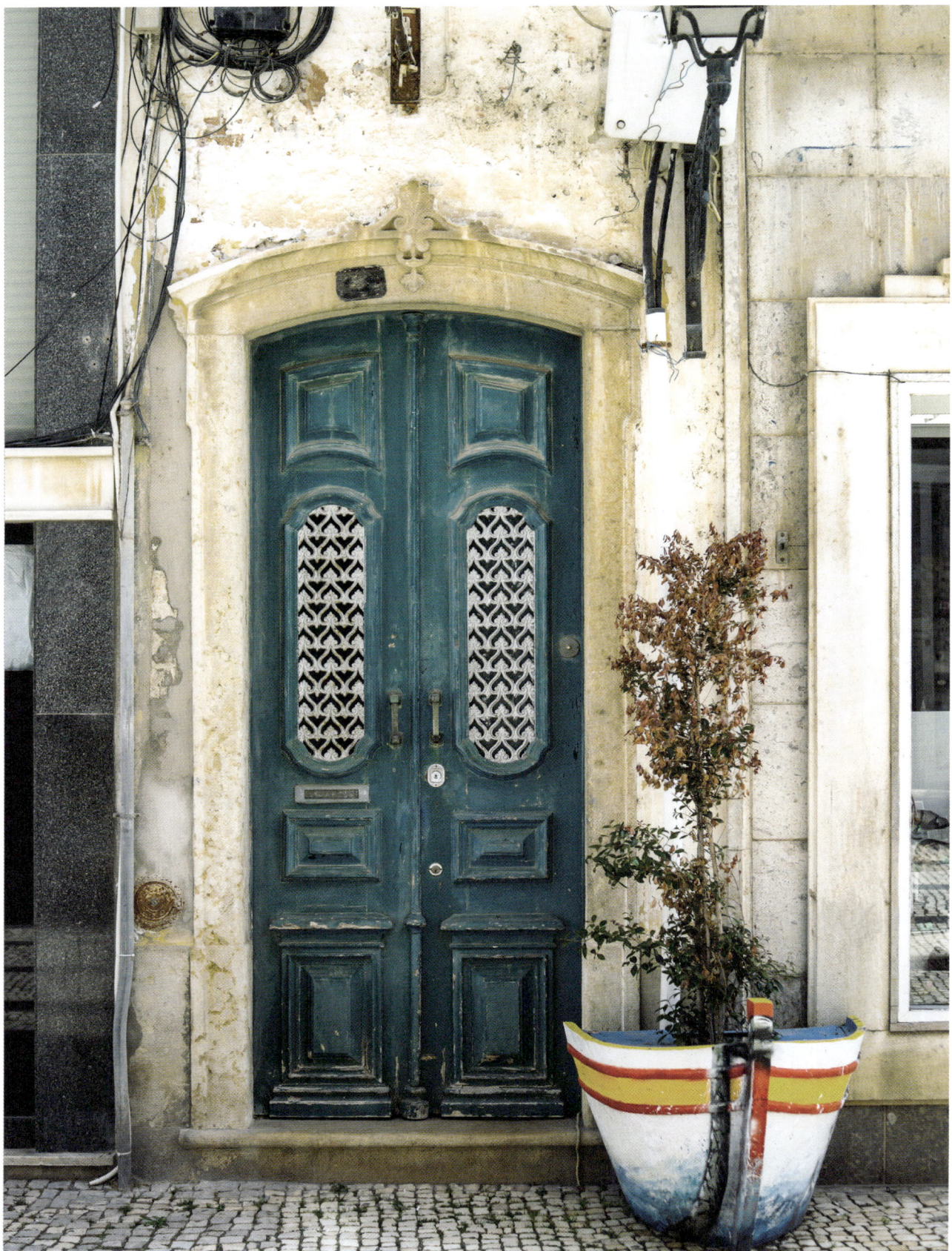

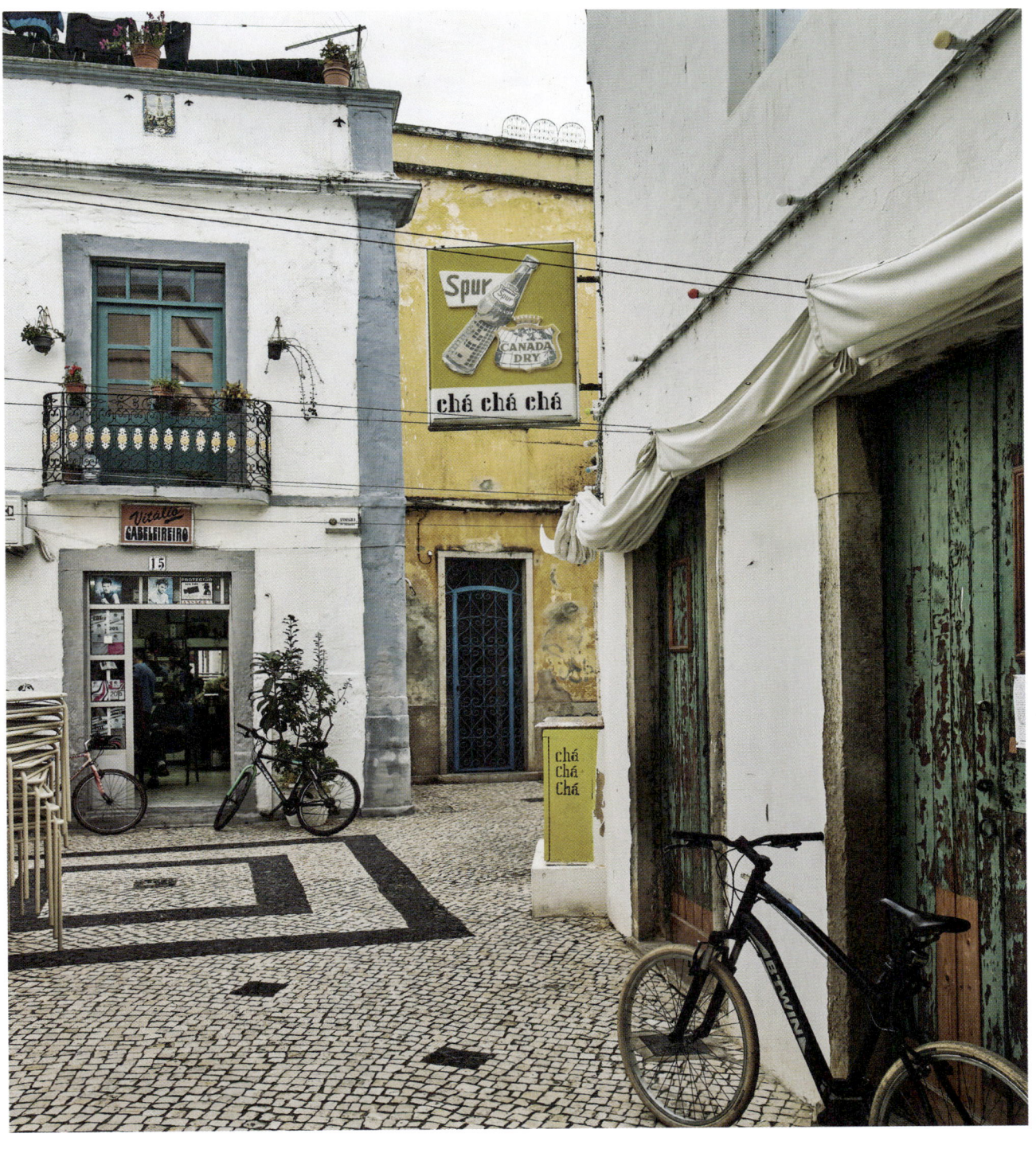

ABOVE AND LEFT: *Nostalgic doorways recall the past in Olhão's old town. Cubic houses with roof terraces seem a nod to northern Africa.*

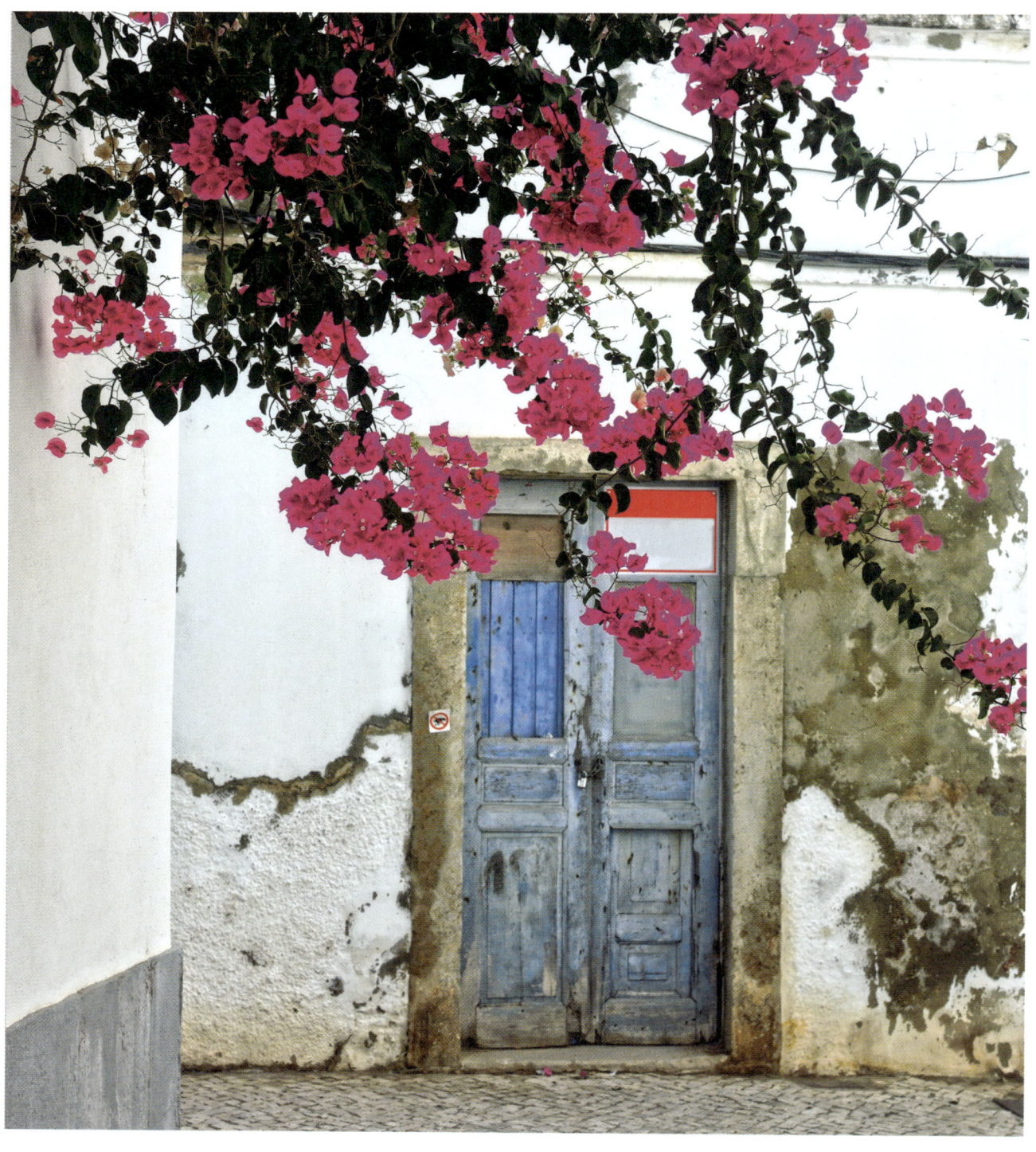

ABOVE AND RIGHT: *In Olhão, weathered façades, explosions of color, and a slightly run-down patina look both lively and muted at the same time.*

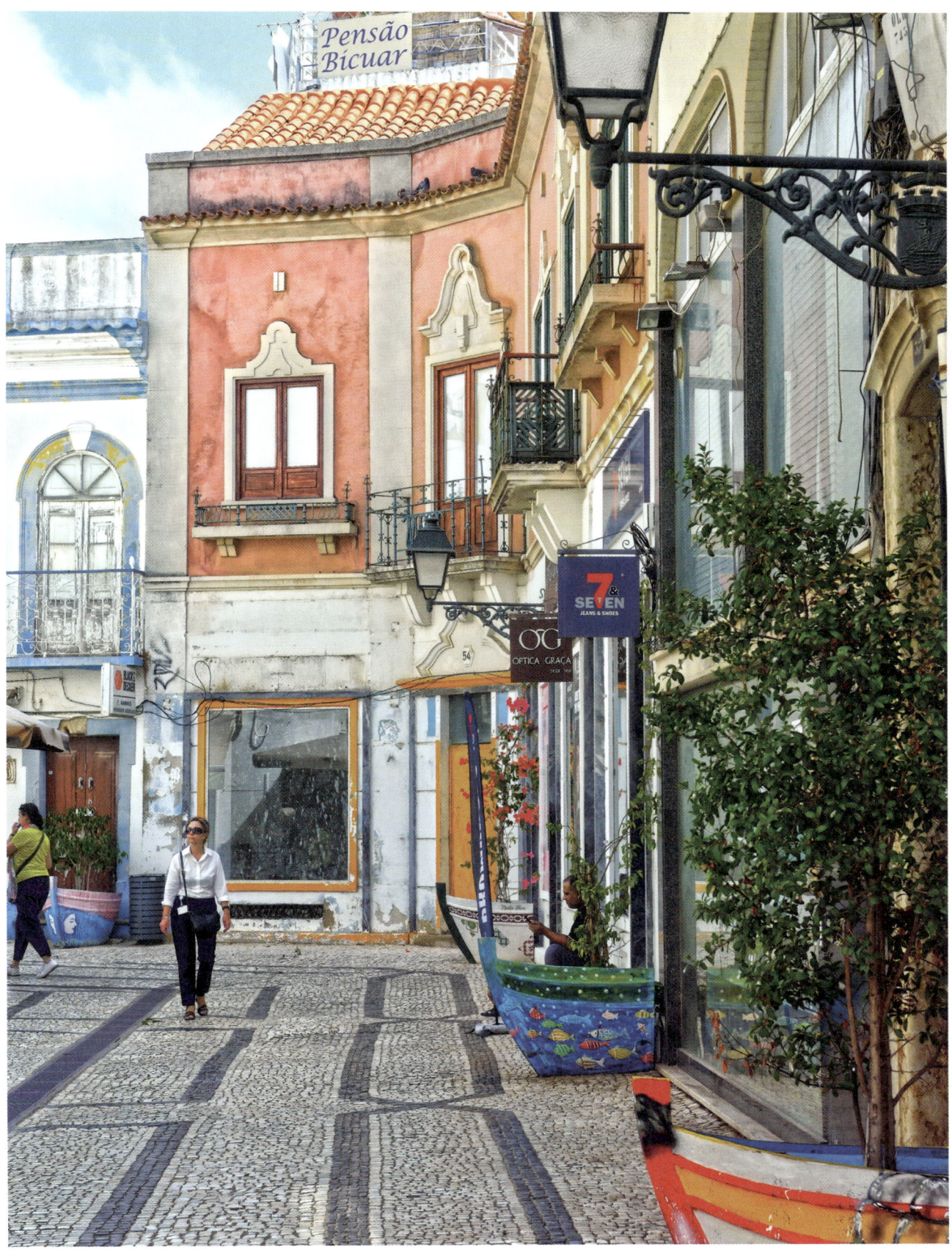

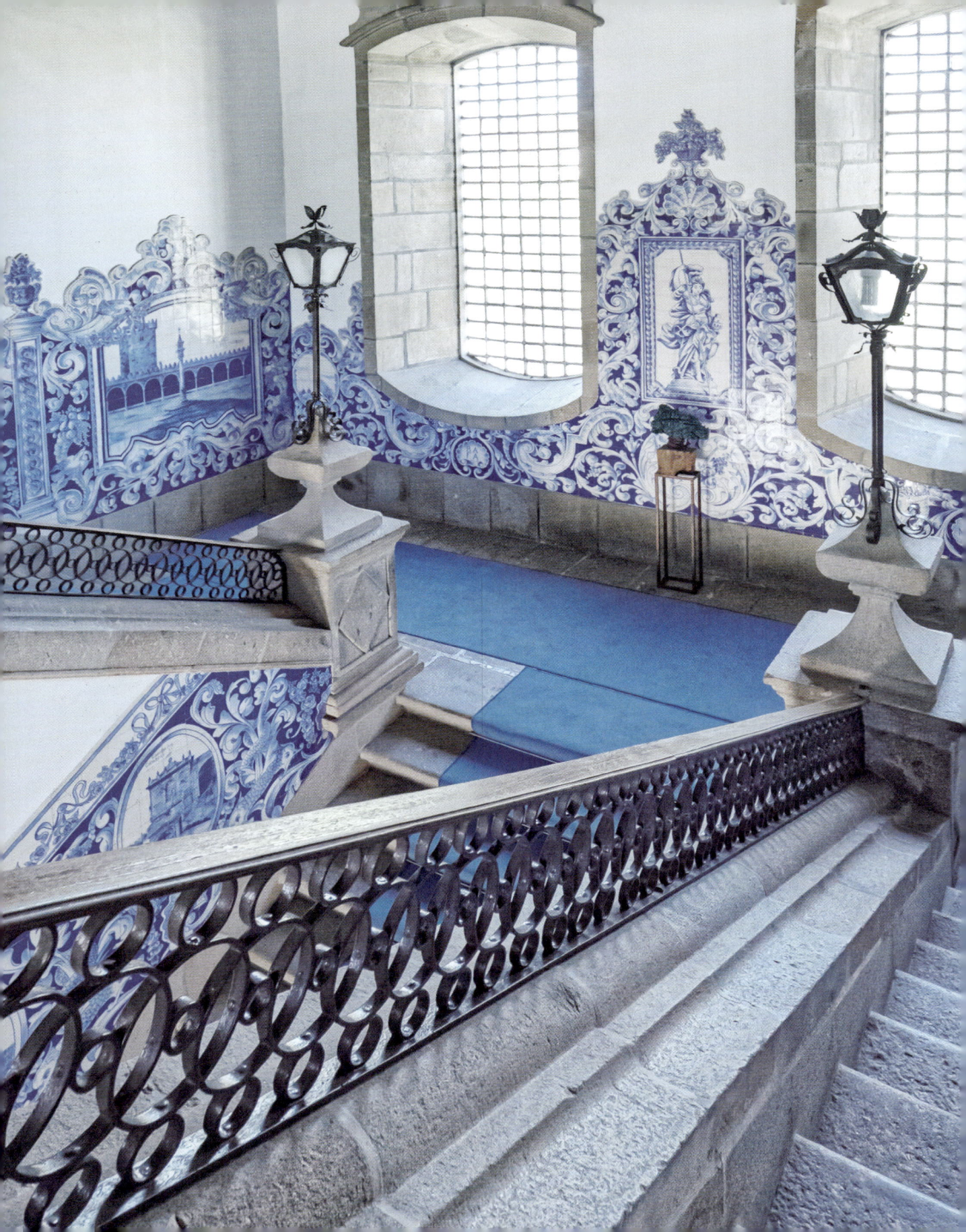

AZULEJOS

AS PORTUGUESE AS VINHO VERDE AND FADO, AZULEJOS APPEAR ON FAÇADES AND DOORWAYS ACROSS THE COUNTRY

These intricately designed, vividly colored ceramic tiles form an artistic signature within Portugal's cultural history. While the word may suggest the blue of the sea, it actually comes from the Arabic *al-zuléija*, meaning "polished stone." King Manuel I of Portugal (1469–1521) encountered Moorish ceramic craftsmanship in Spain and brought the technique back to Portugal. Soon royal palaces were decorated with tiles, from traditional mosaics to precise geometric patterns. Before long, azulejos also took the form of large painted panels. The *Grande Panorama de Lisboa*, attributed to Gabriel del Barco, which is more than twenty-three meters long and dates from around 1700, is now displayed at the Museu Nacional do Azulejo. It presents the city in a sweeping, bird's-eye view along the Tagus. The detail and clarity of this image made it an invaluable record of Lisbon before the earthquake of 1755 and a reference for rebuilding. Via churches and monasteries, tilework entered everyday architecture, especially once nineteenth-century industrial production made it more affordable. What had once marked status now also served a practical purpose, protecting walls from the weather. In the older quarters of Lisbon and Porto, geometric patterns and floral motifs still frame windows and doors or cover entire façades. Ceramic lovers should also look underground: Since the 1950s, Lisbon's metro stations have featured large azulejo murals by leading artists.

LEFT: *The ornate staircase of the Câmara Municipal in Braga, one of Portugal's most striking examples of Baroque architecture.*

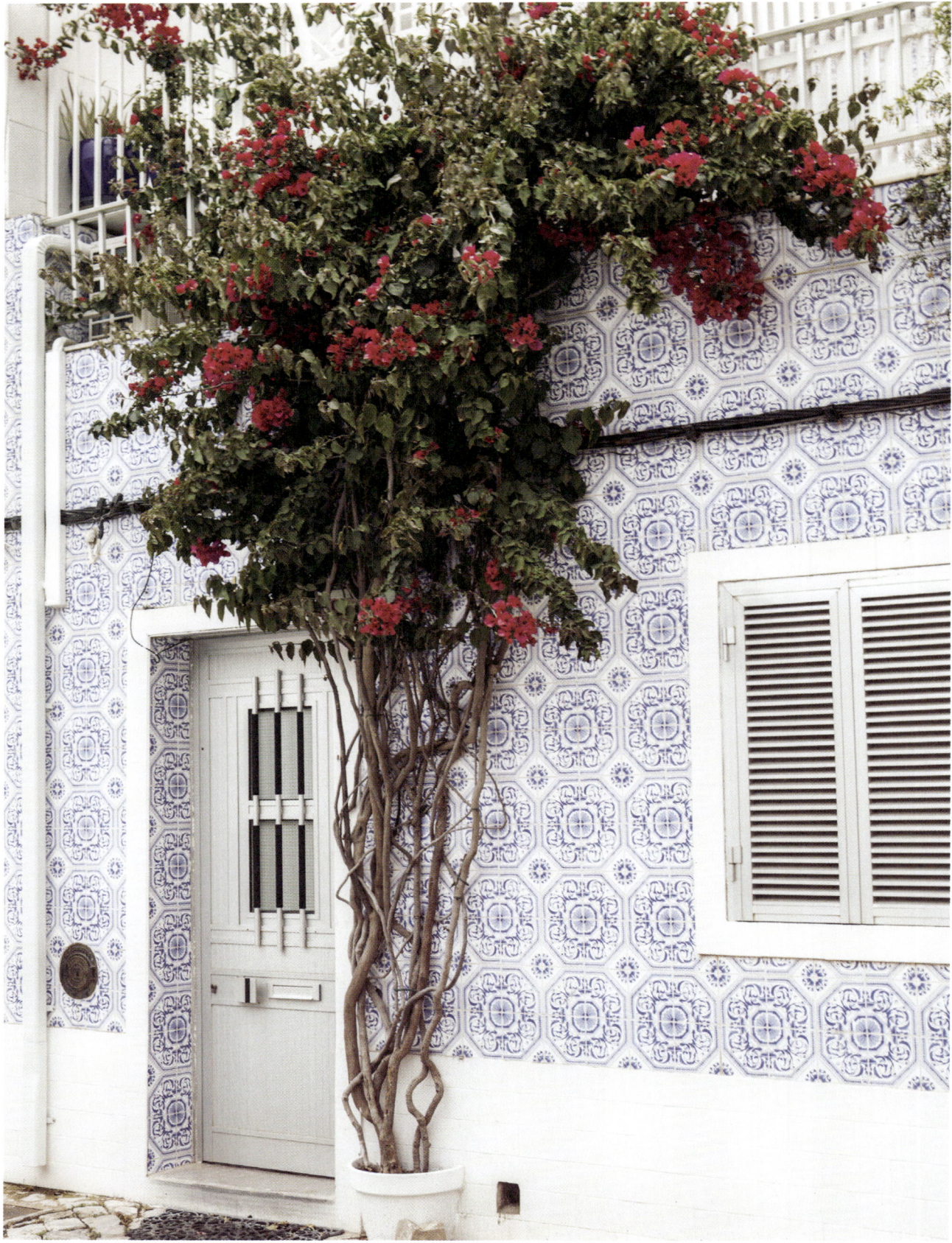

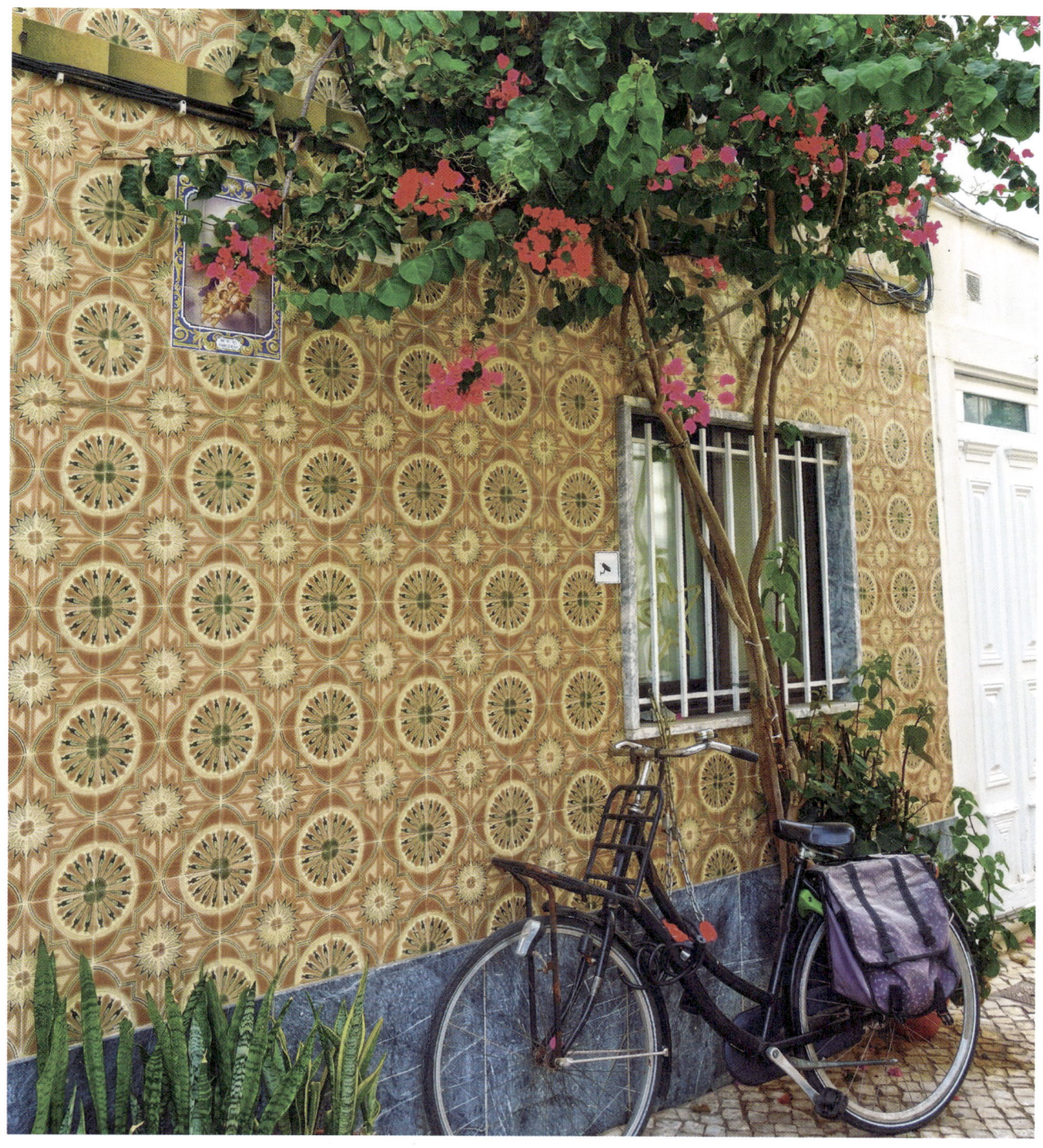

ABOVE: *Bold floral and geometric patterns became widespread in the nineteenth century as industrial production of tiles put azulejos on the façades of ordinary townhouses.*

LEFT: *Many azulejos are dominated by blue and white, an influence of Delft blue in the Dutch ceramic tradition.*

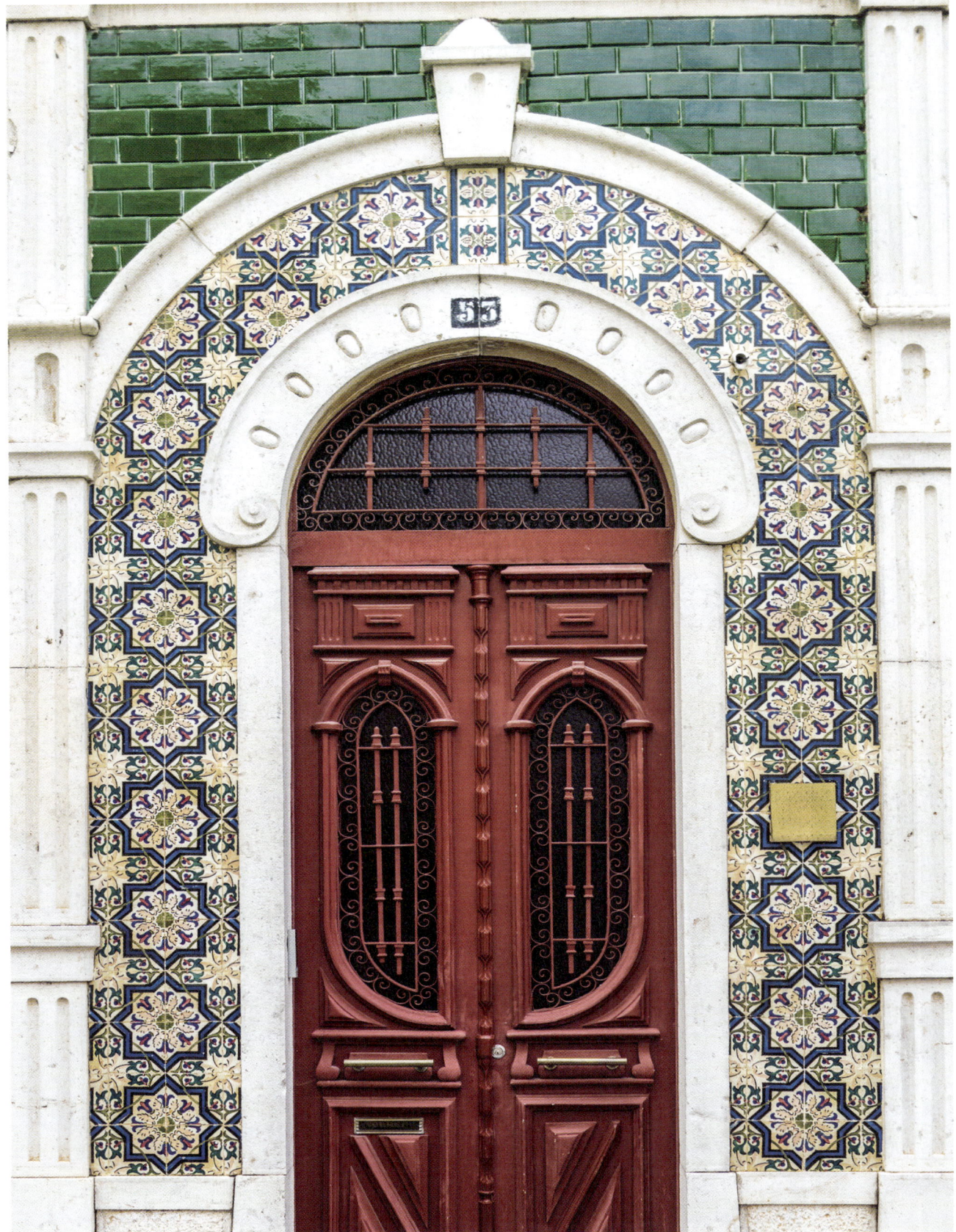

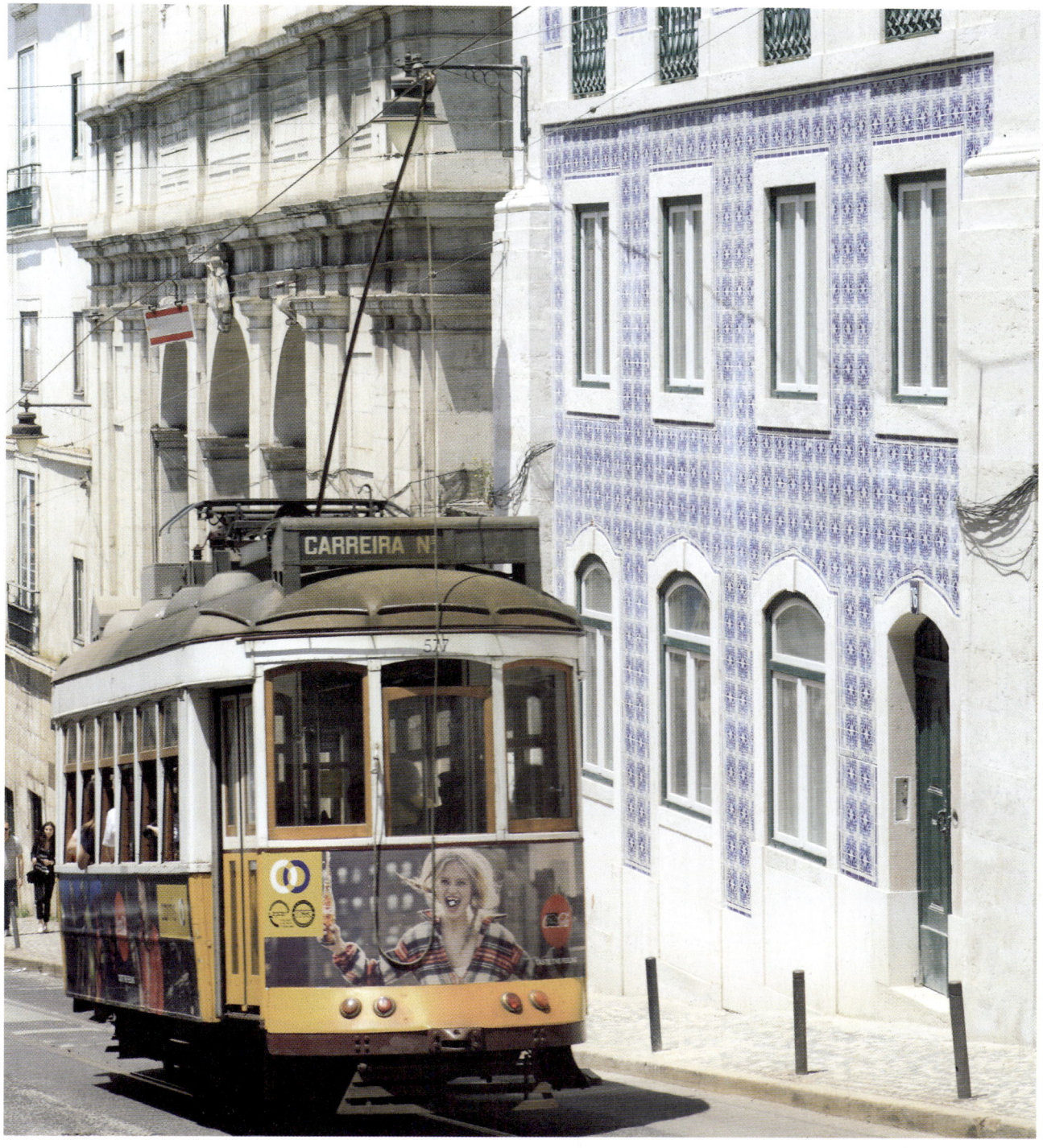

ABOVE: *Façades rich with azulejos along the Elétrico line through Lisbon's older neighborhoods.*

LEFT: *Geometric ornament and octagonal patterns point to the Moorish origins of azulejos.*

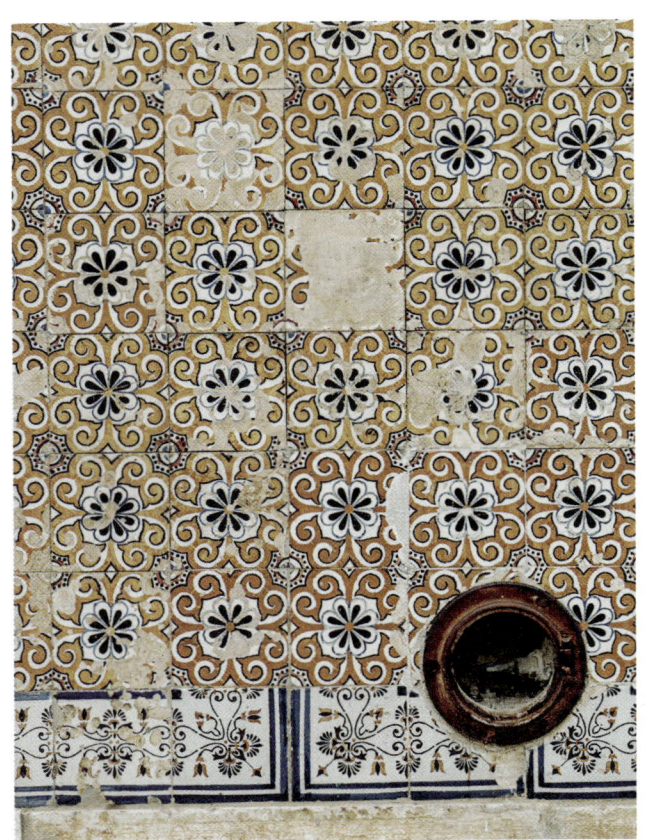
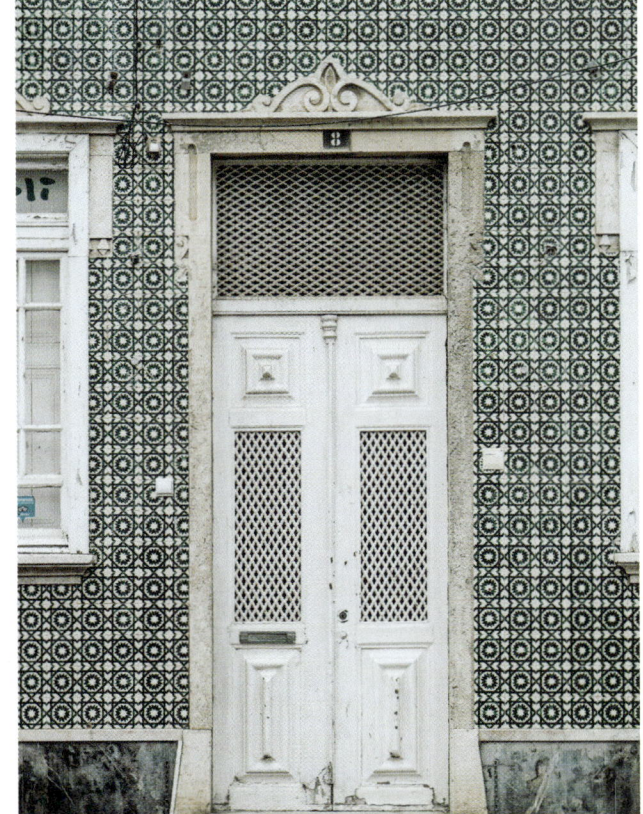
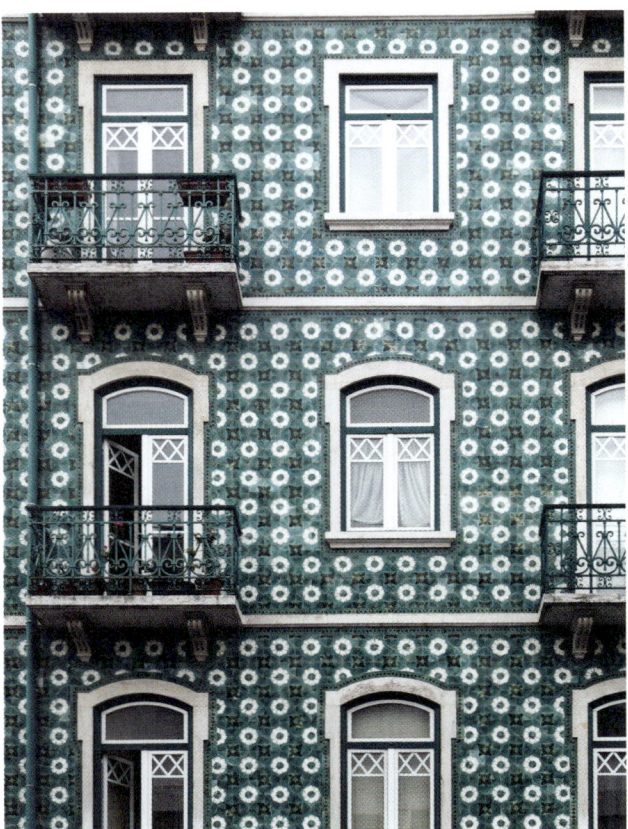
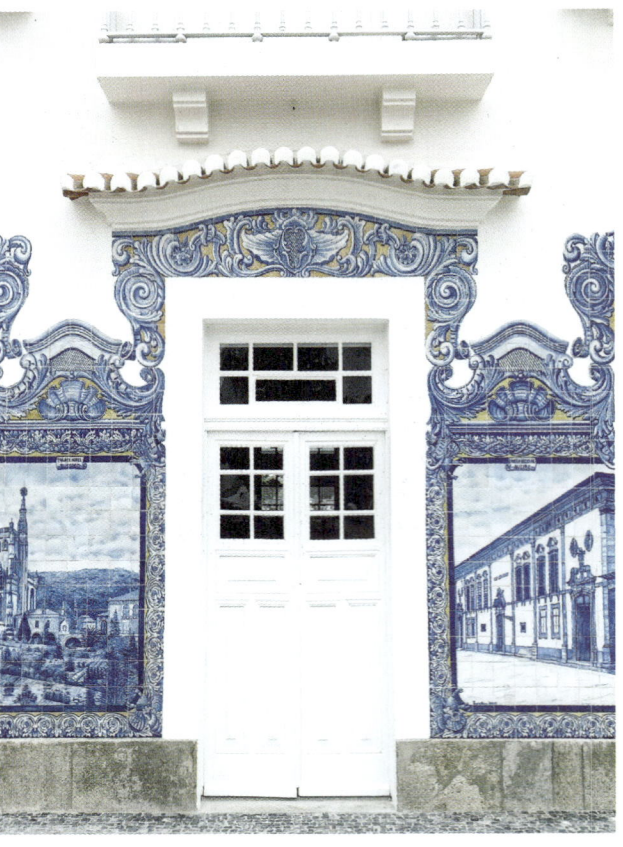

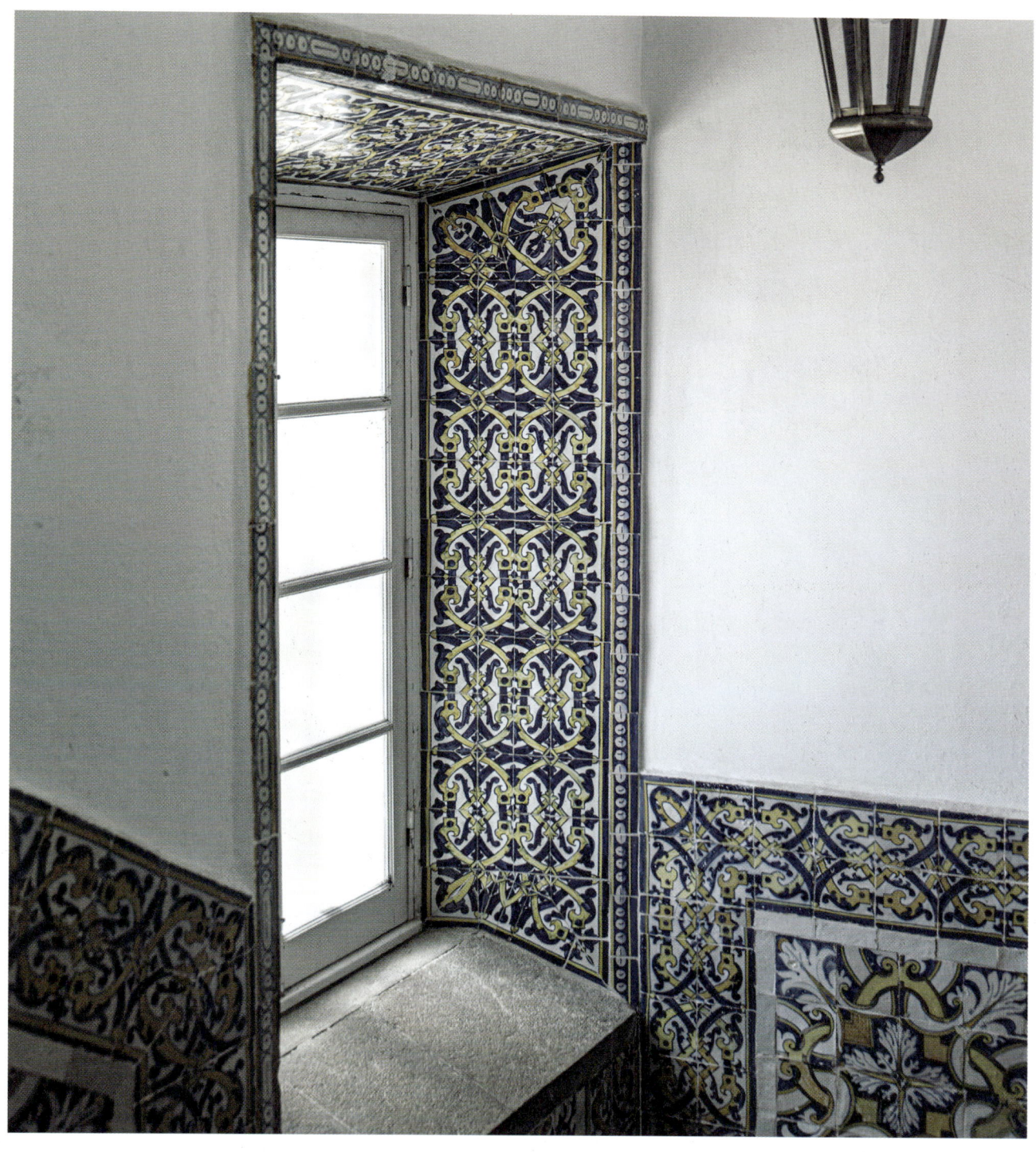

ABOVE AND LEFT: *The range of azulejo ornamentation, often framing windows and doorways, as seen on a walk through Faro (above and top left). Classic blue-and-white tiles depict local history around Aveiro's former train station (left, bottom right), which now hosts art exhibits.*

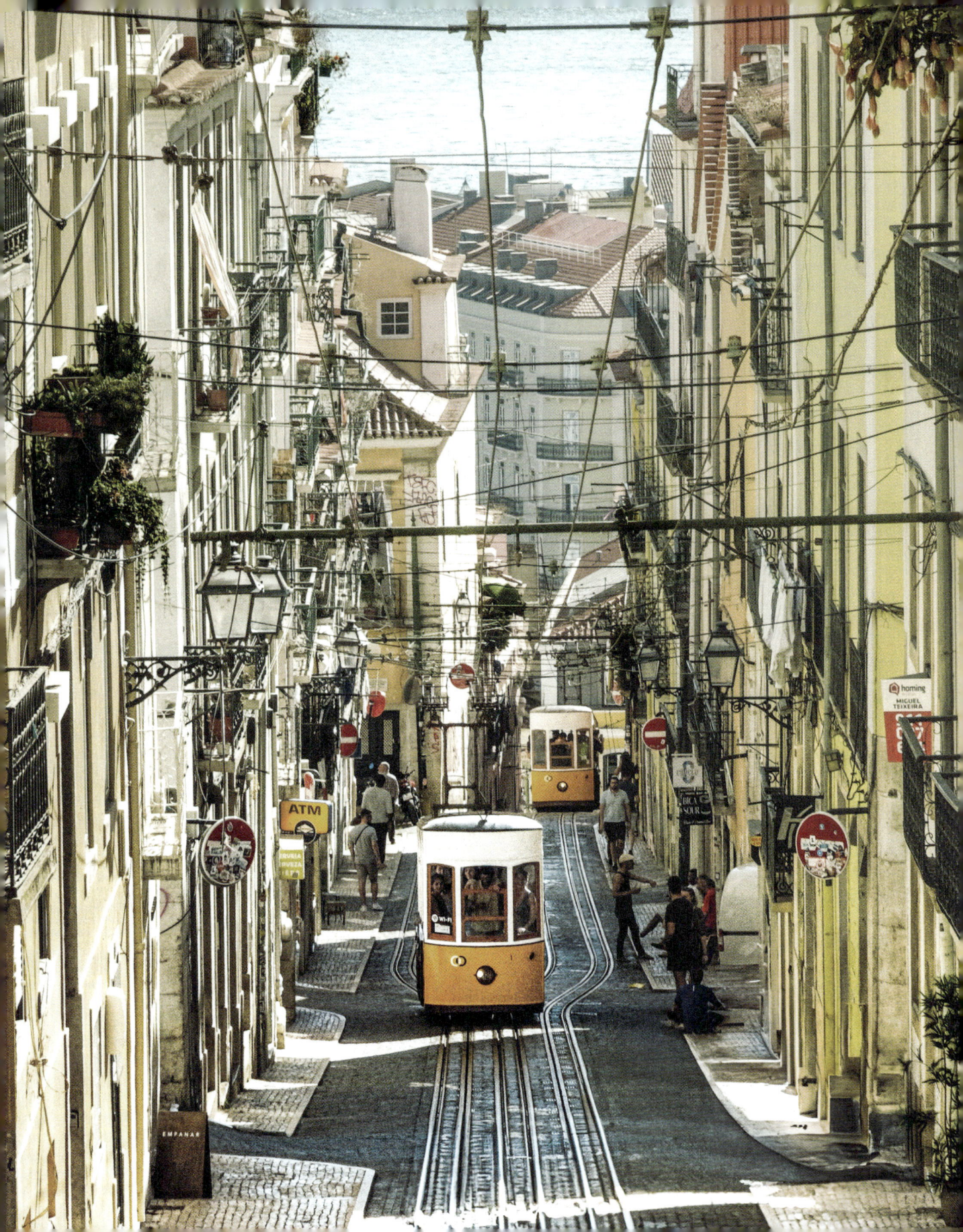

LISBON

THE METROPOLIS ON THE TAGUS IS BUILT ON CONTRASTS. NARROW HILL STREETS LEAD TO MIRADOUROS WITH WIDE VIEWS, WHILE ART NOUVEAU FAÇADES AND AZULEJOS STAND BESIDE STREET ART

Many visits begin in Alfama, the city's oldest quarter. The former fishing district still shows traces of an earlier time. Narrow lanes climb the hillside, and in the evening fado melodies drift out of small restaurants. Alfama is the cradle of fado, and the music is still performed here. The old Elétrico tram runs up the steep slopes to the Miradouro da Graça. From there, the view stretches across the roofs of the old town to the arched bridge over the Tagus. Below lies Baixa, set apart from the tangled streets and former fishermen's houses above. After the earthquake of 1755, the Marquês de Pombal rebuilt Baixa with earthquake-resistant construction and broad, straight avenues. The use of prefabricated elements allowed the work to proceed quickly. The uniform, symmetrical façades from that period still define the district. In 1902, the Elevador de Santa Justa was built to connect Baixa with Chiado and Bairro Alto. The 45-meter cast-iron lift tower in neo-Gothic style remains one of Lisbon's best-known landmarks. In Chiado, Art Nouveau buildings, old bookshops, and cafés preserve the atmosphere of the city's literary and bohemian past. Farther west lies Belém, where the Tagus opens toward the Atlantic. Along the river, the stonework of the Jerónimos Monastery and the Torre de Belém stands in contrast to the modern lines of the MAAT museum. A visit to Lisbon often includes a trip to Óbidos. A heavy ring of walls surrounds the medieval town, which Portuguese kings once gave to their queens as a wedding gift.

LEFT: *The Elevador da Bica runs along the steep Rua da Bica de Duarte Belcio. It is one of three historic funiculars that define Lisbon.*

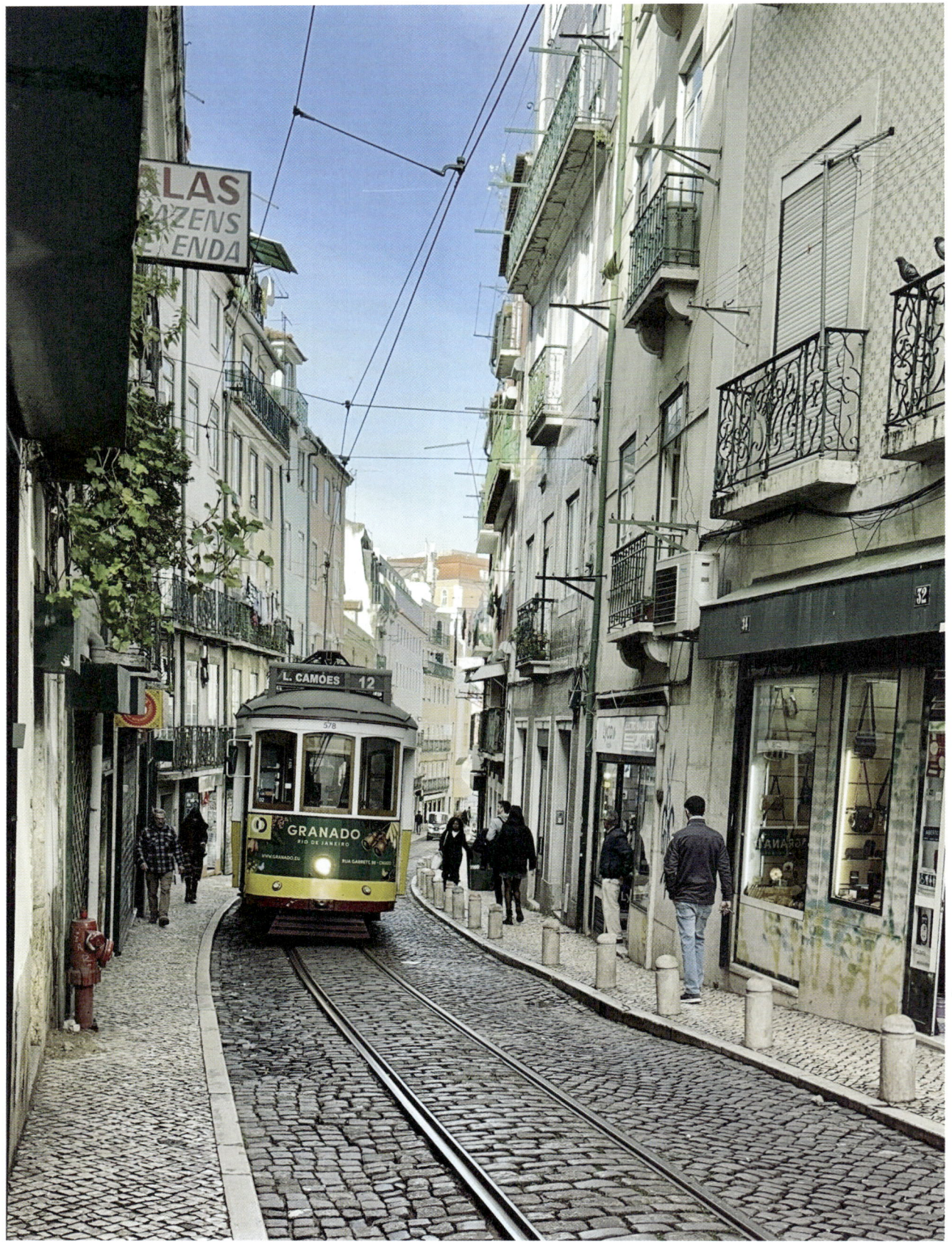

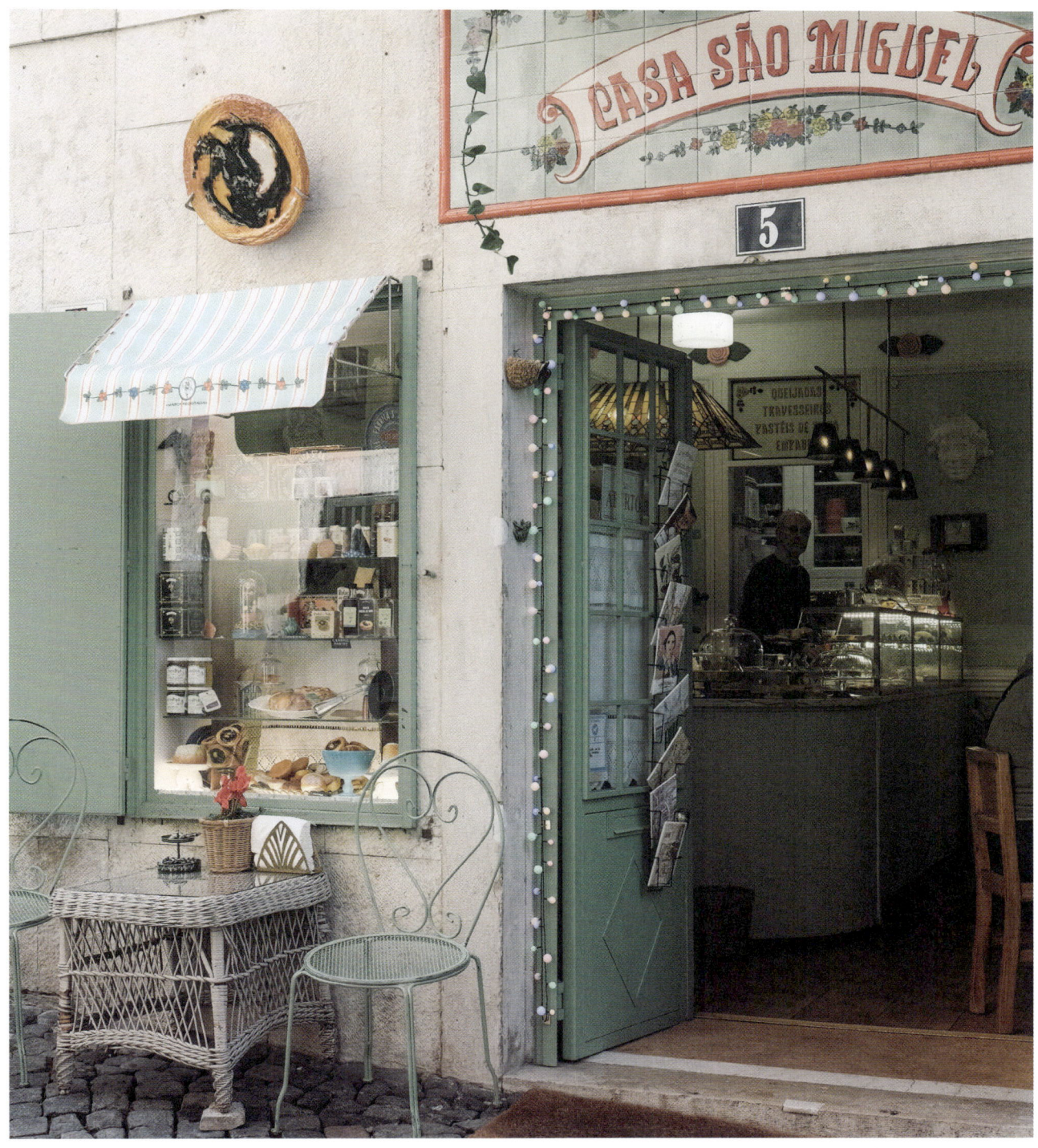

ABOVE: *A tiny café in Alfama like the set of a Wes Anderson film. A good place for* pastéis de nata, *Portugal's signature pastry.*

LEFT: *The historic trams of line 12E still run the steep gradients and tight curves of the Alfama district in Lisbon.*

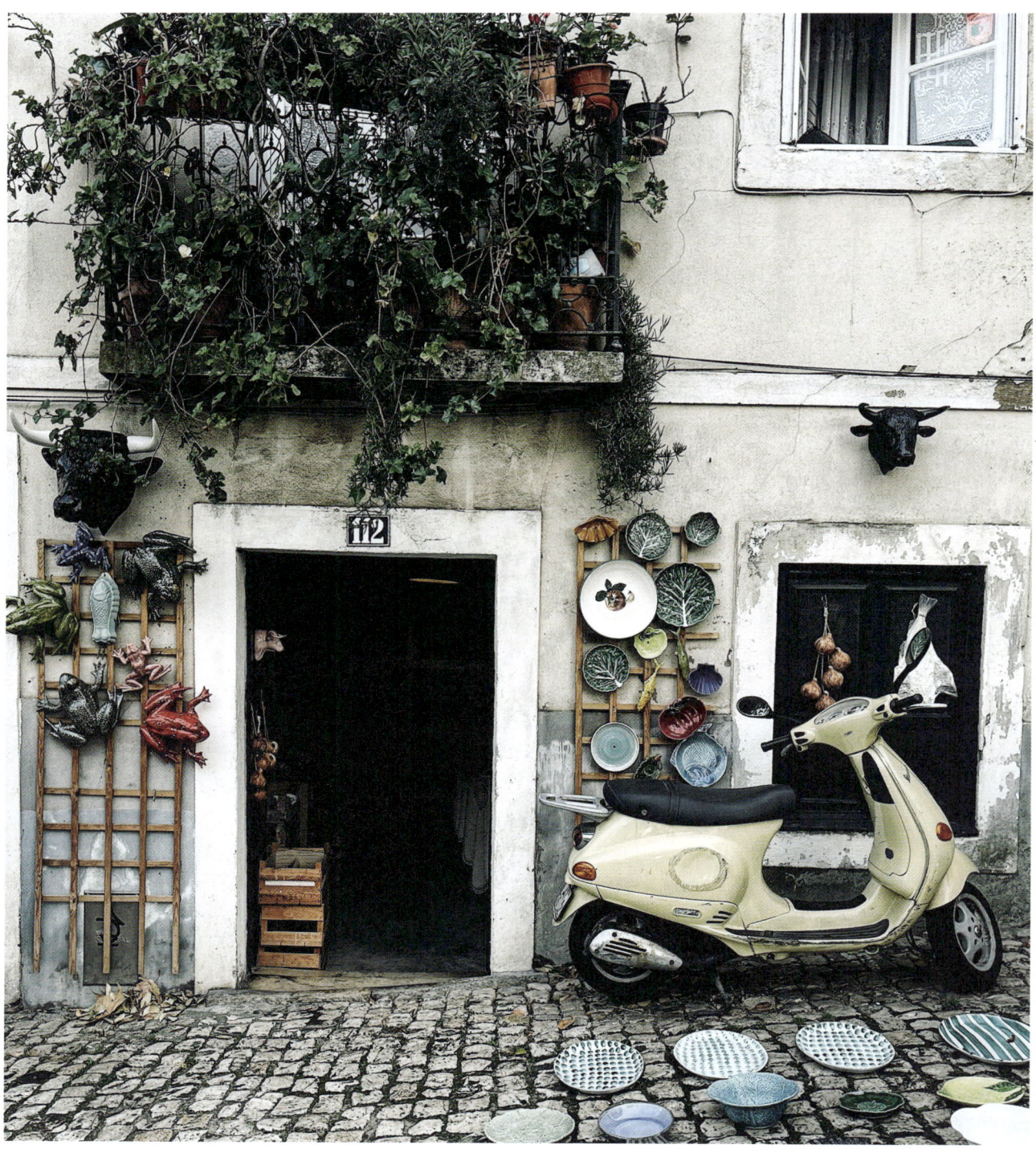

ABOVE AND RIGHT: *In Alfama, fado melodies drift from small, hidden bars. Façades sport traditional azulejos next to contemporary street art along narrow passages. Quintessential Portugal.*

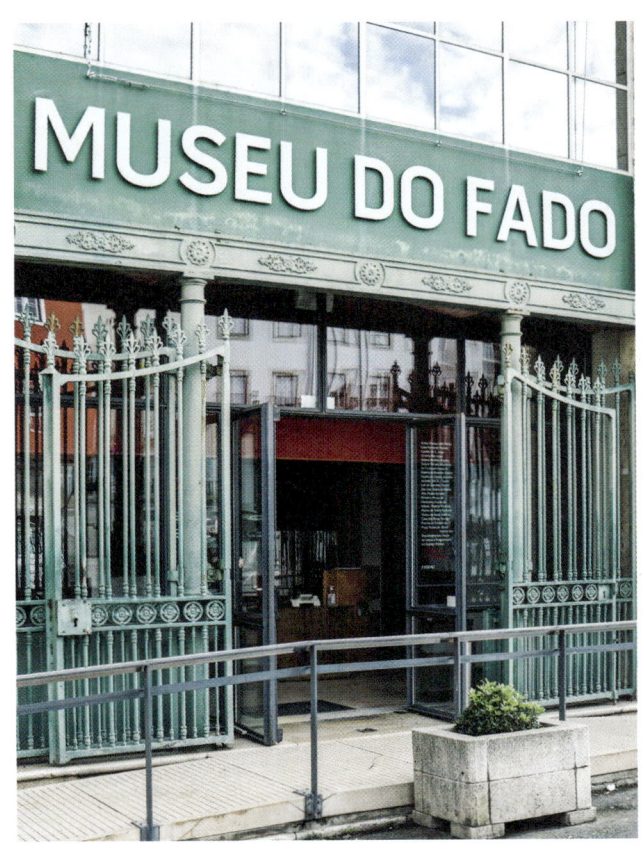

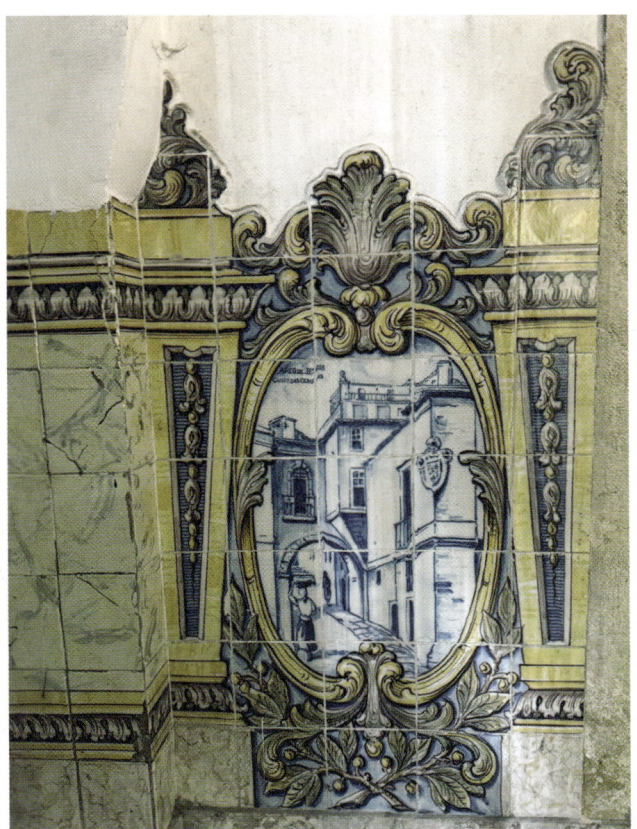

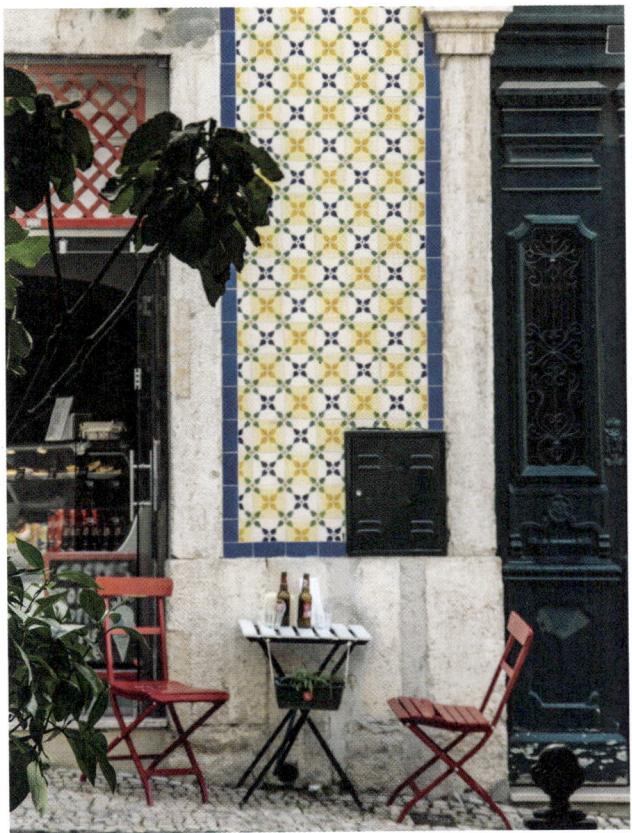

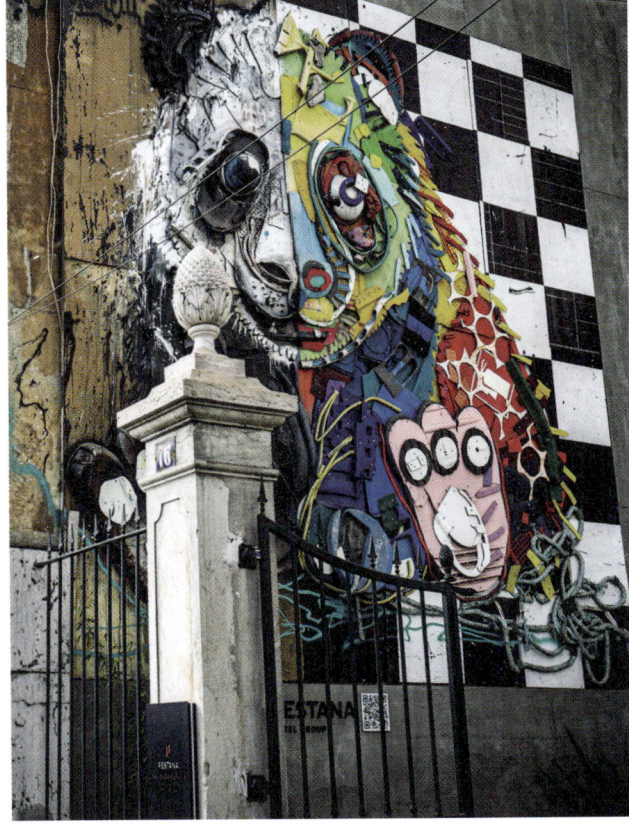

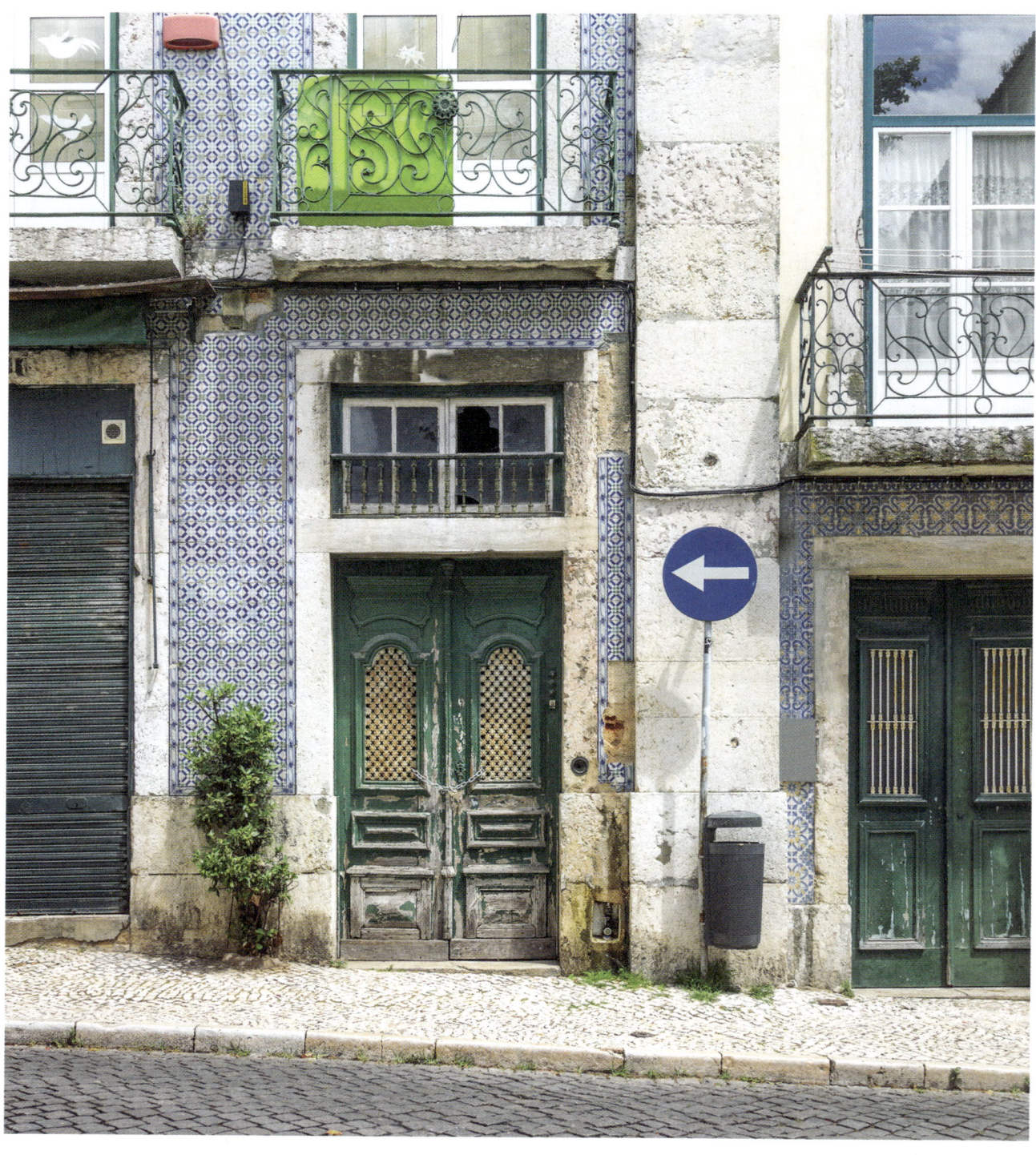

ABOVE AND RIGHT: *Paint peels from old doors and azulejos once carefully crafted are now marked by time. Such is the charm of Alfama's steep streets and stairways.*

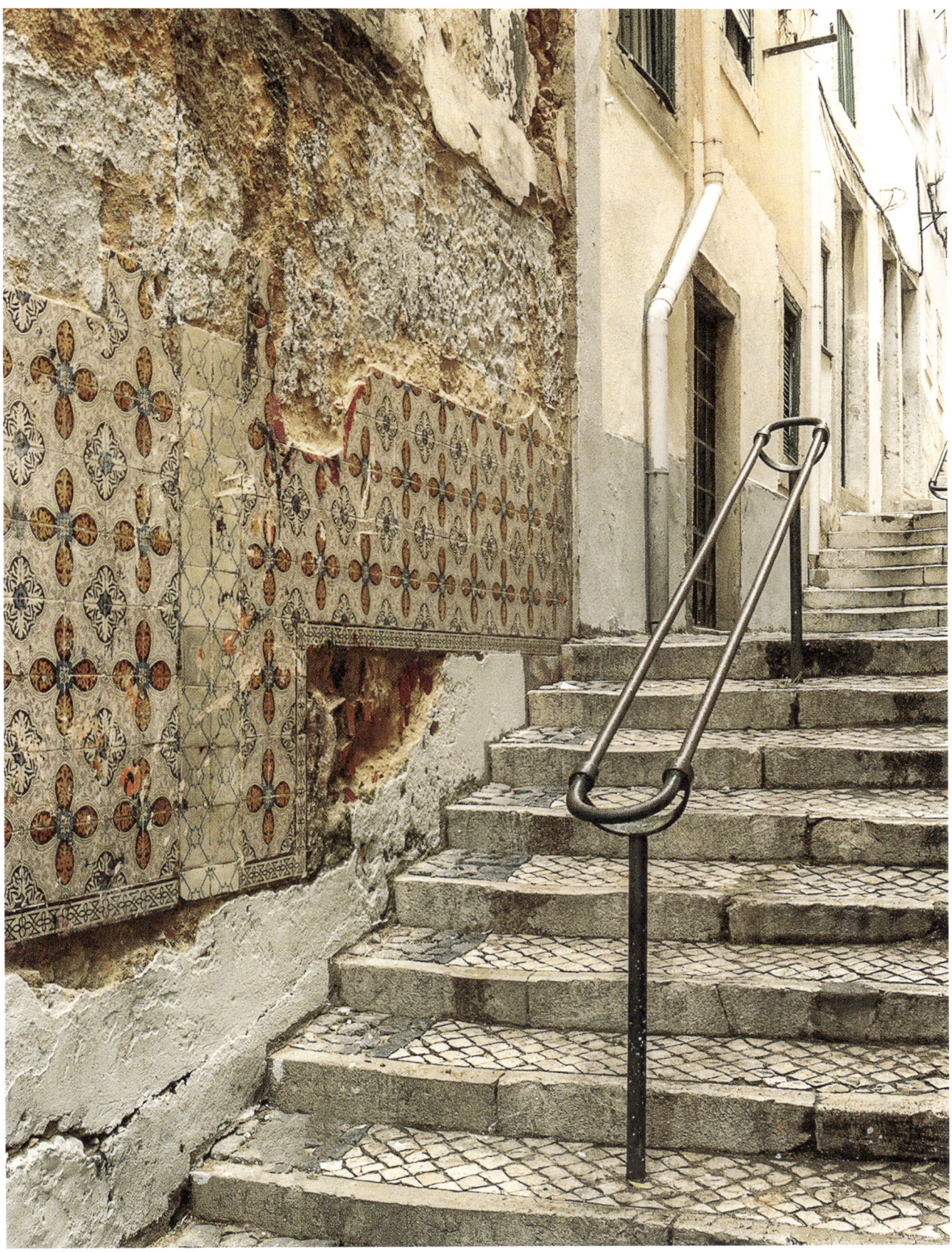

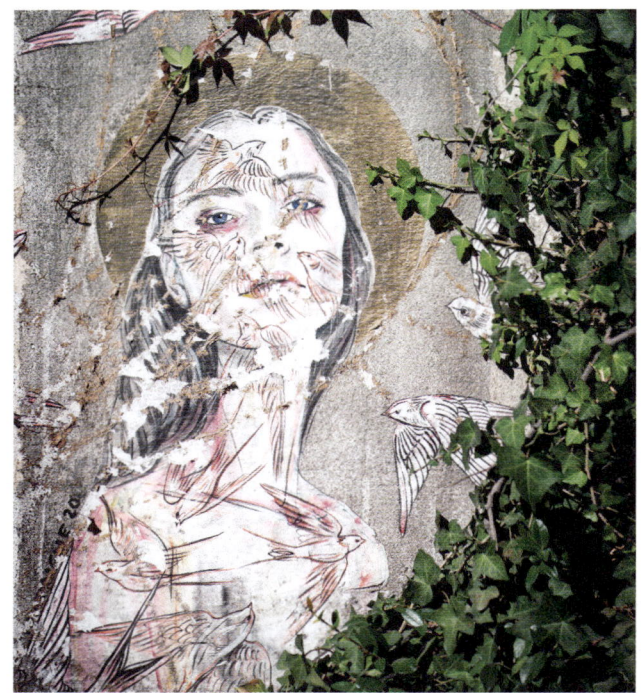
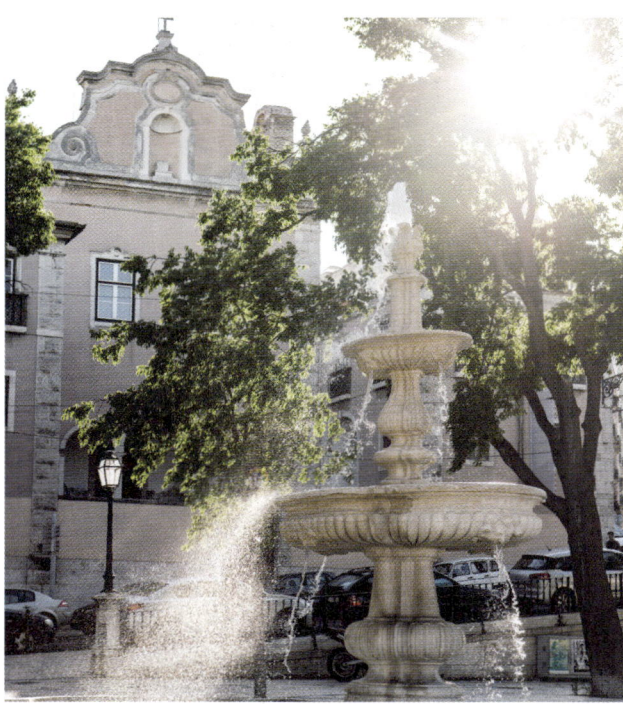
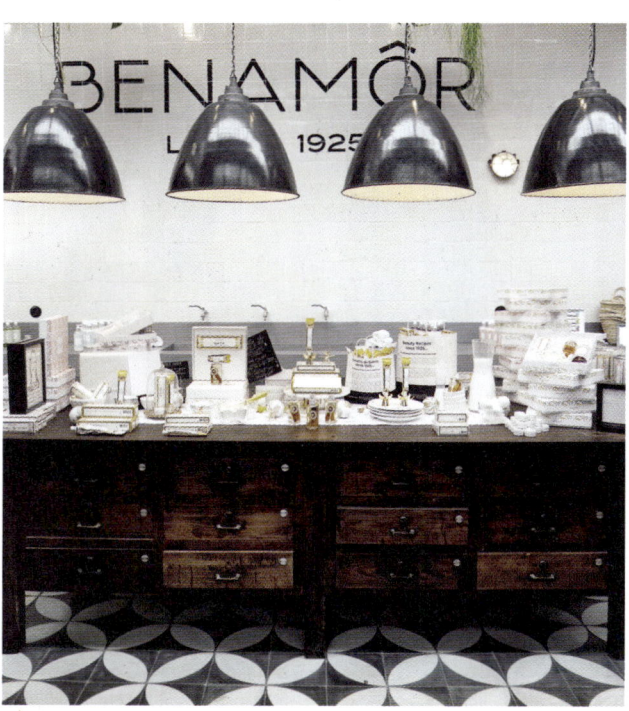
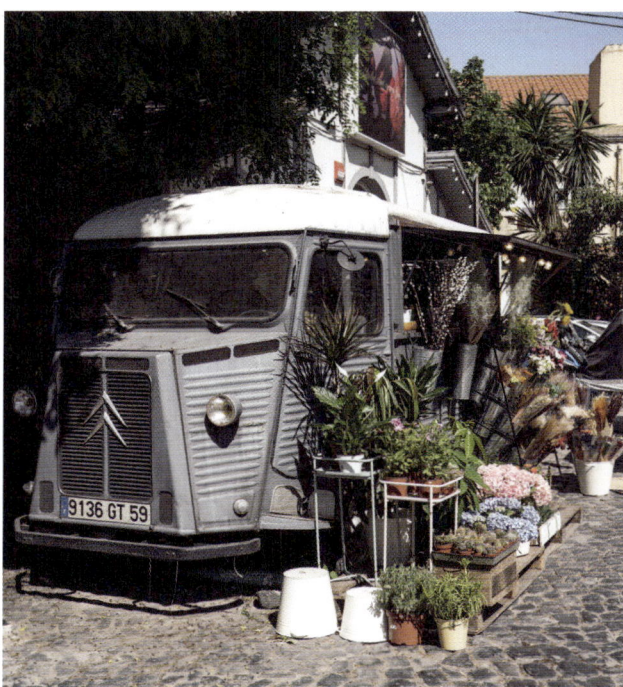

ABOVE AND RIGHT: *Old factory buildings in the former industrial zone of Alcântara, now home to a youthful subculture. Street art all around the streets near the LX Factory.*

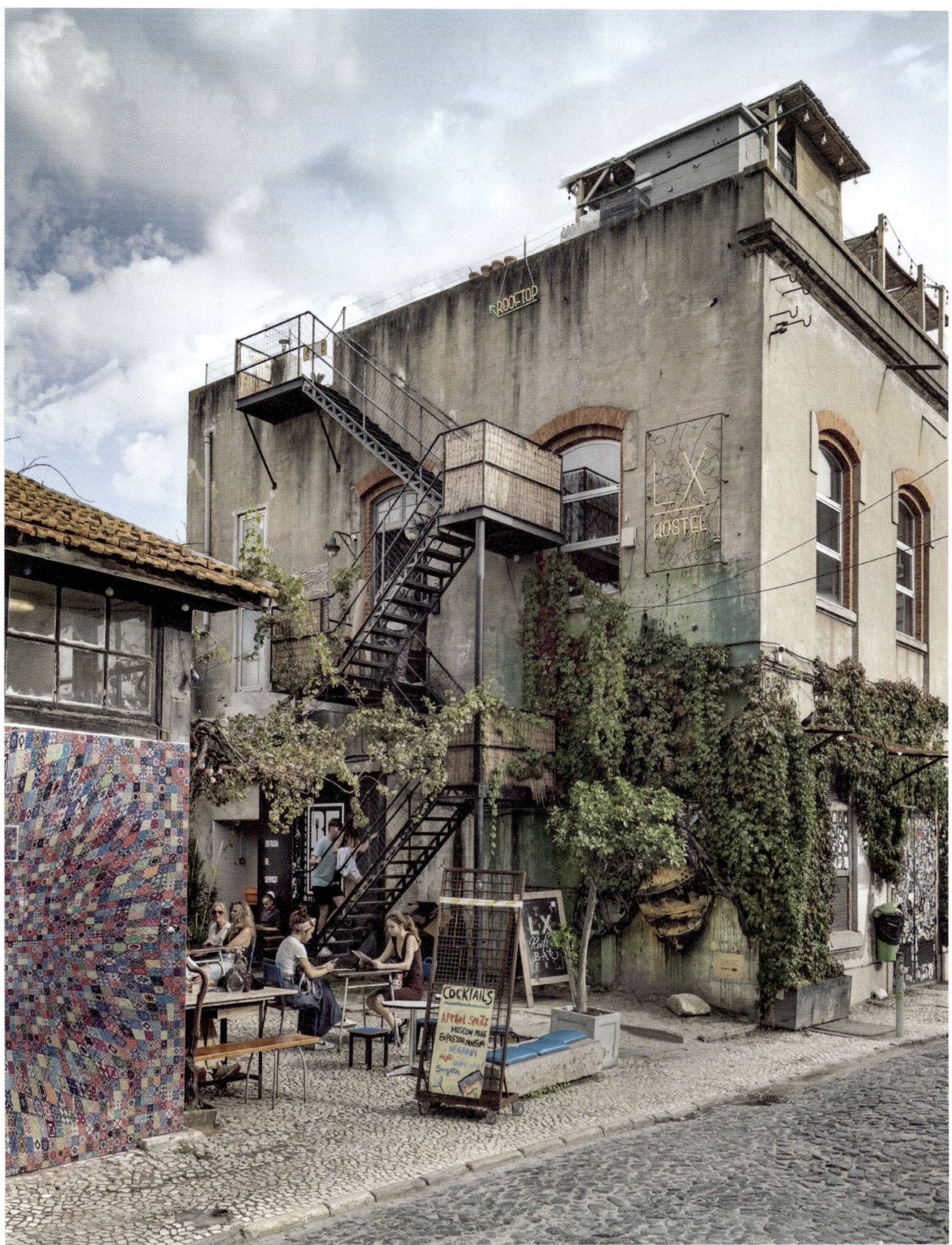

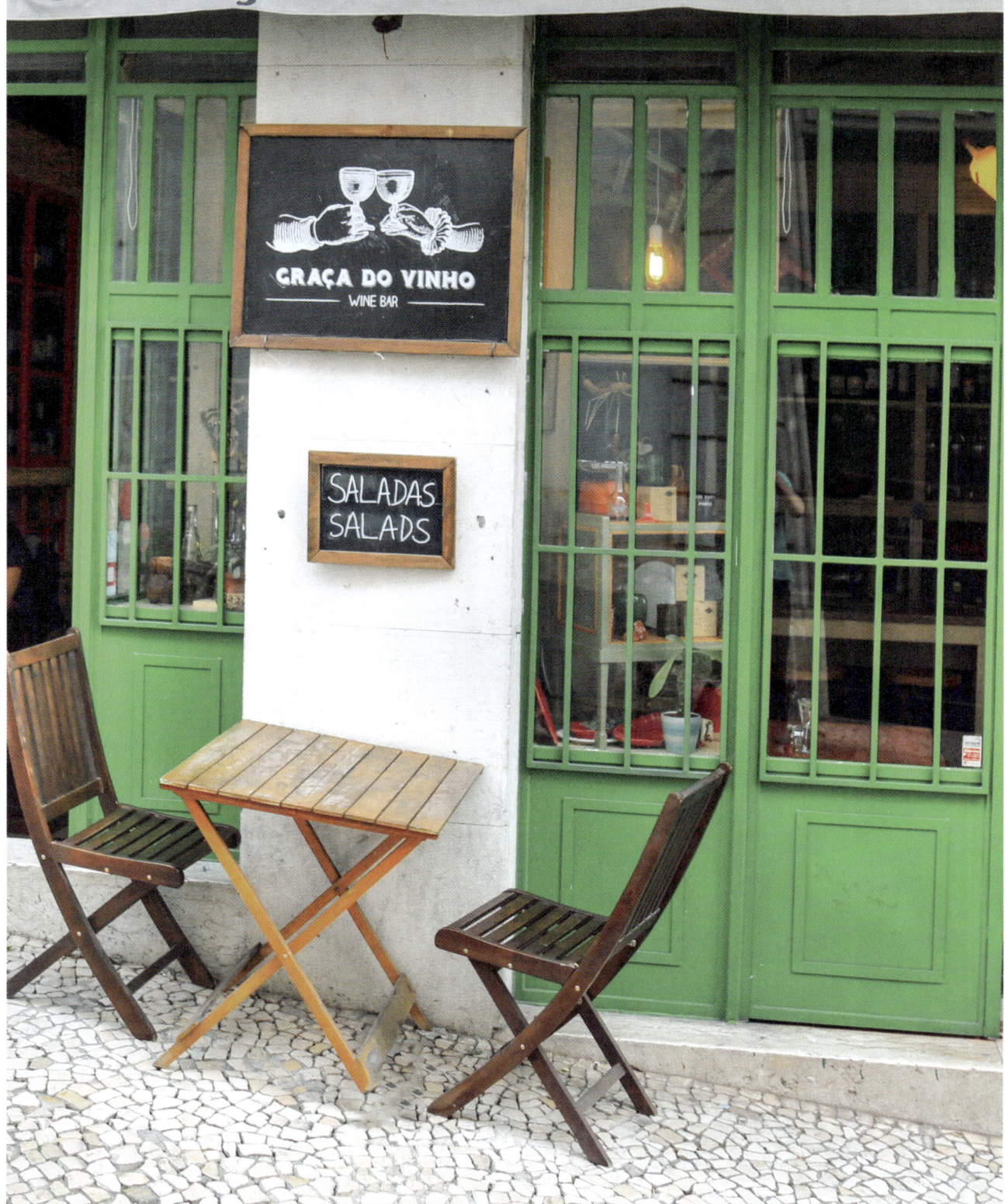

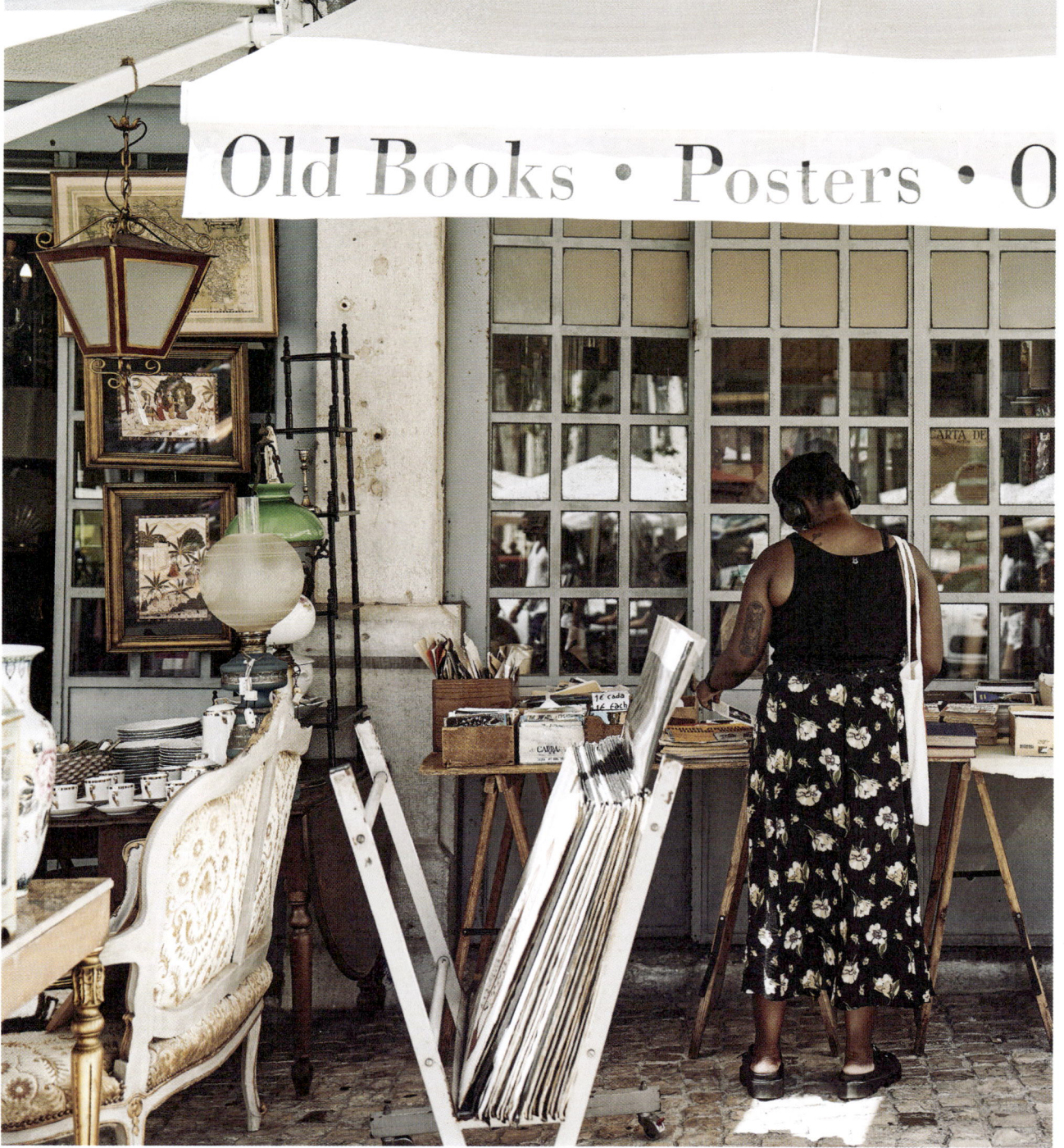

ABOVE: *At Campo de Santa Clara in the Graça district, near the Feira da Ladra—the "market of the thief lady." Great finds at a flea market; plenty of color.*

LEFT: *At the foot of the Miradouro da Graça, narrow streets lead through one of Lisbon's long-established working-class neighborhoods. No shortage of wine bars here.*

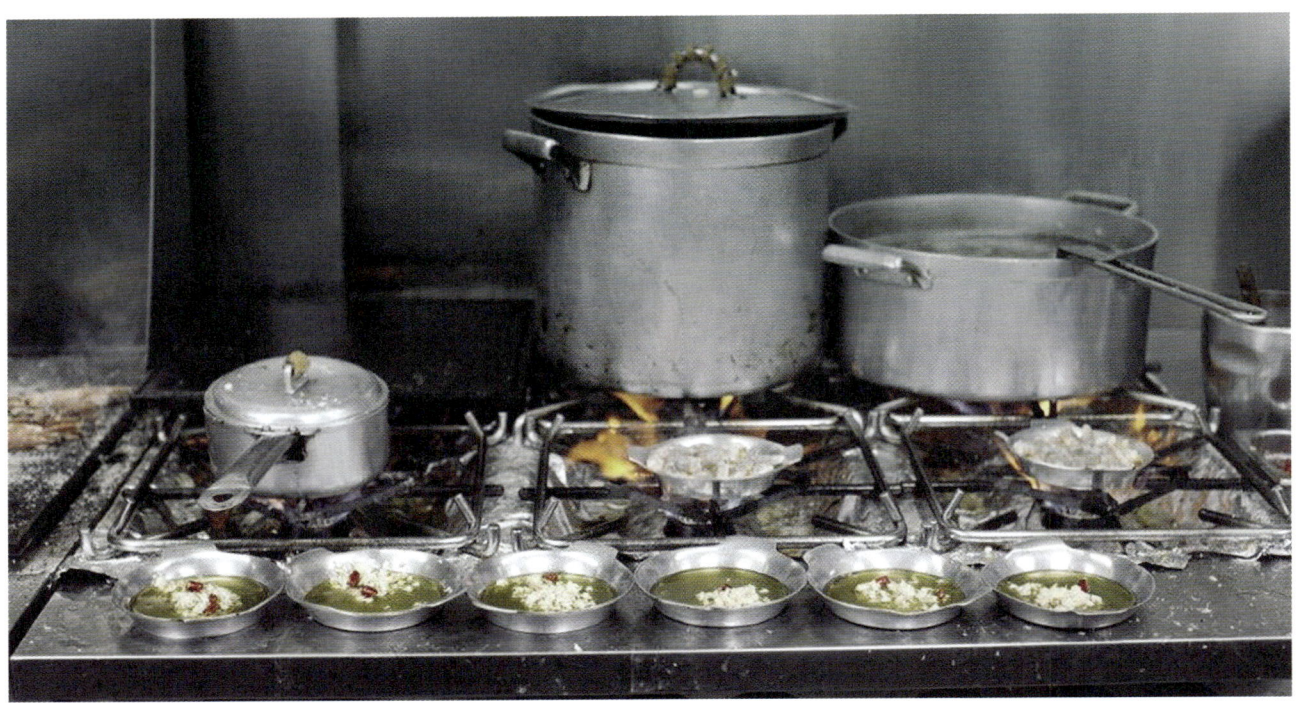

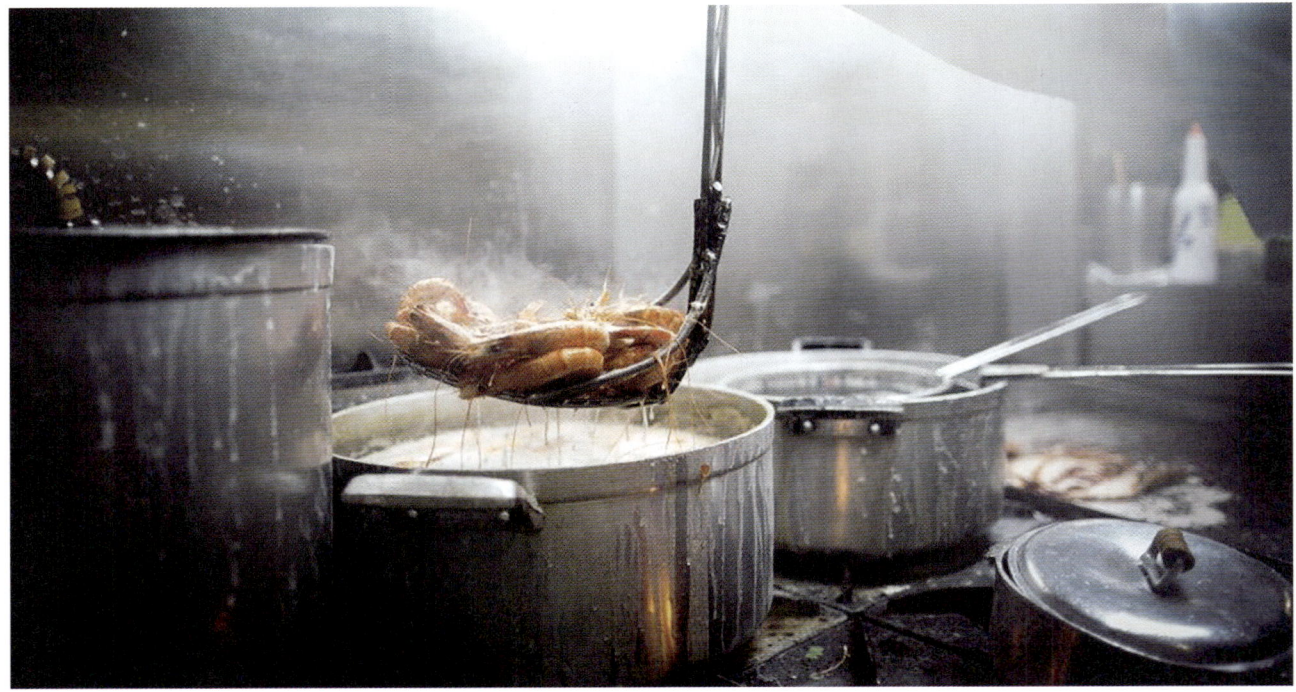

ABOVE AND RIGHT: *Fresh seafood and beer in a retro setting at the venerable establishment of Cervejaria Ramiro.*
Many residents insist it's the best; no surprise that foodies have taken notice of the outwardly drab restaurant.

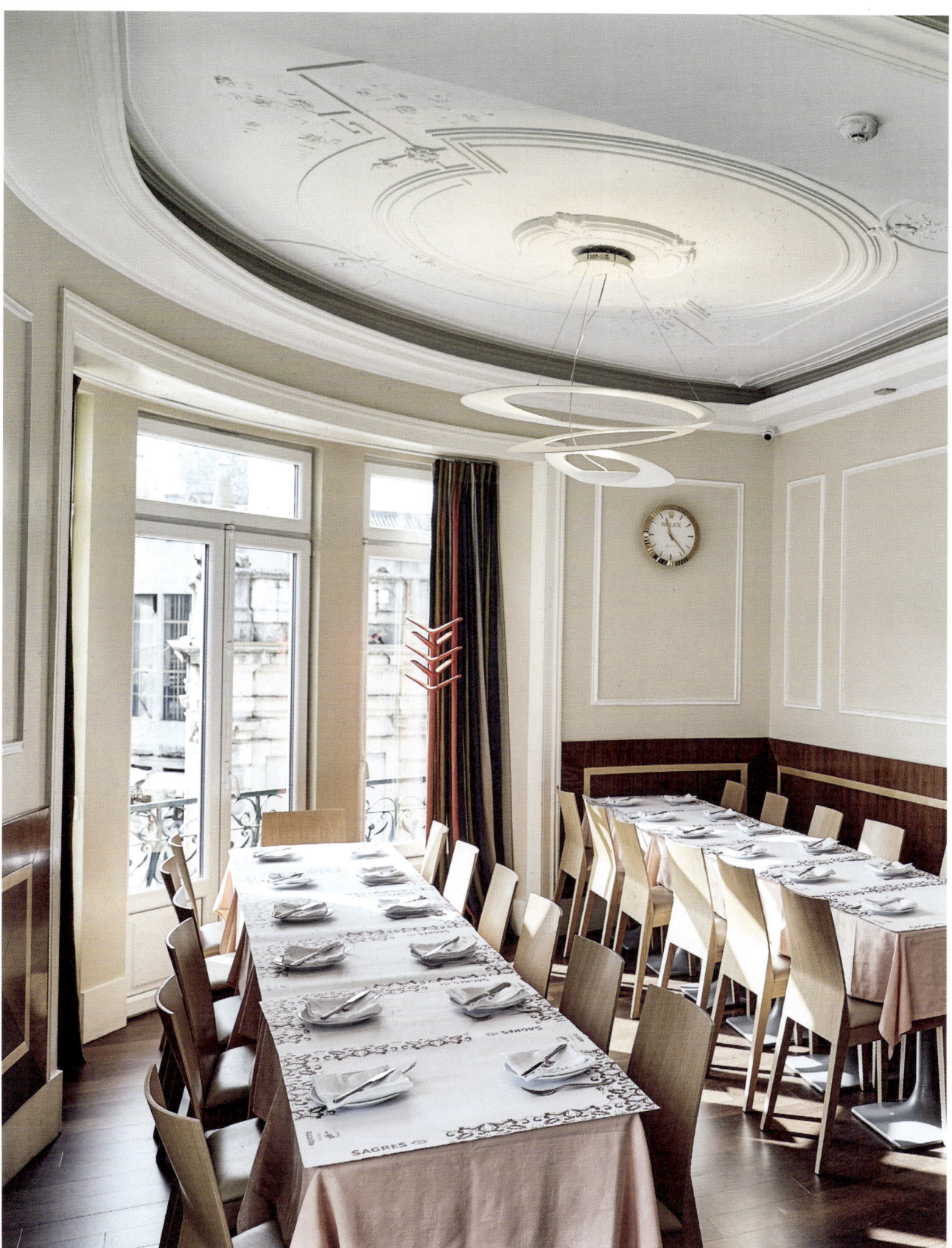

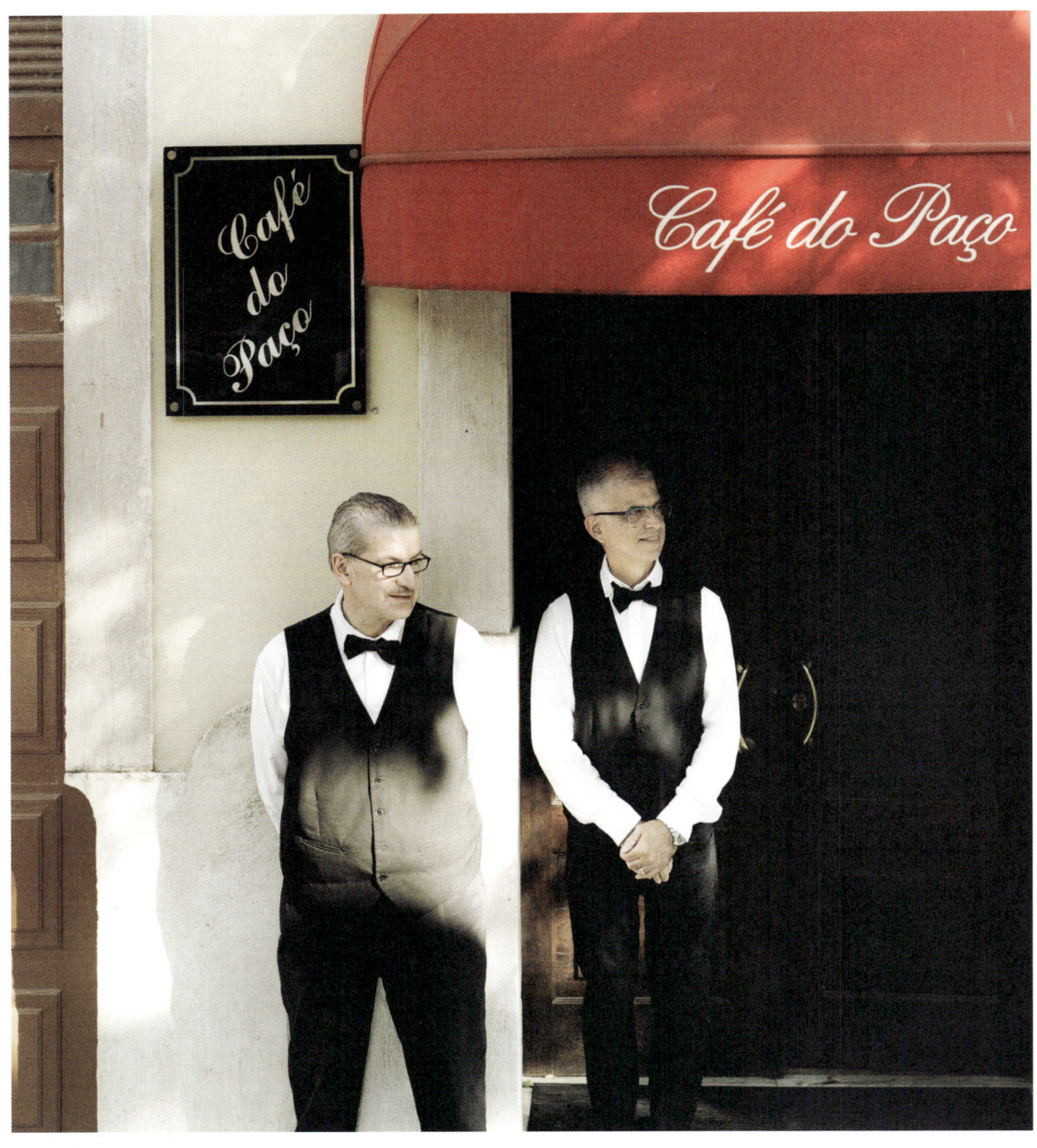

ABOVE AND RIGHT: *In Lisbon's theater district of Chiado, small establishments such as Café do Paço serve simple, carefully prepared classic Portuguese cuisine. Interiors recall the old days. Regulars of the cultural scene go for a traditional* bife: *steak with fries and a fried egg.*

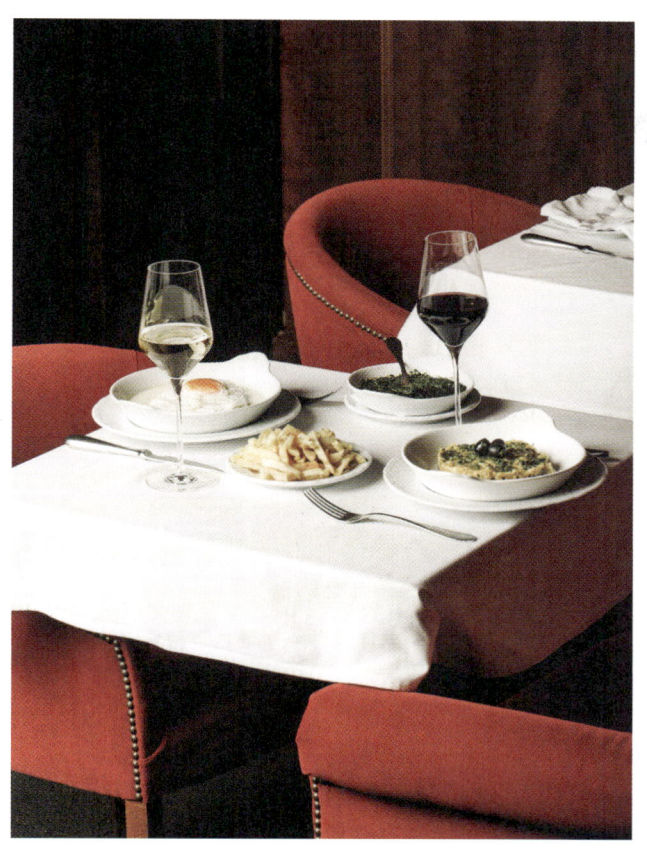

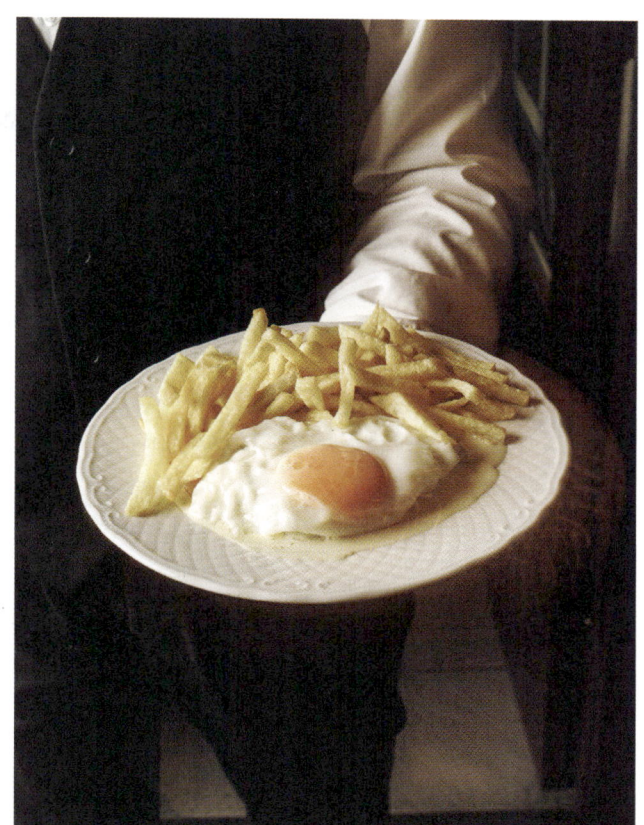

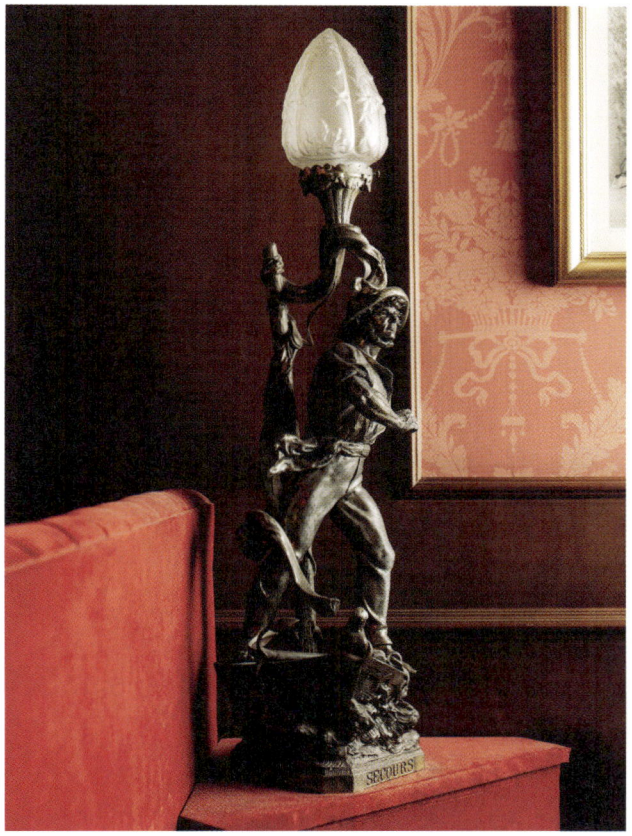

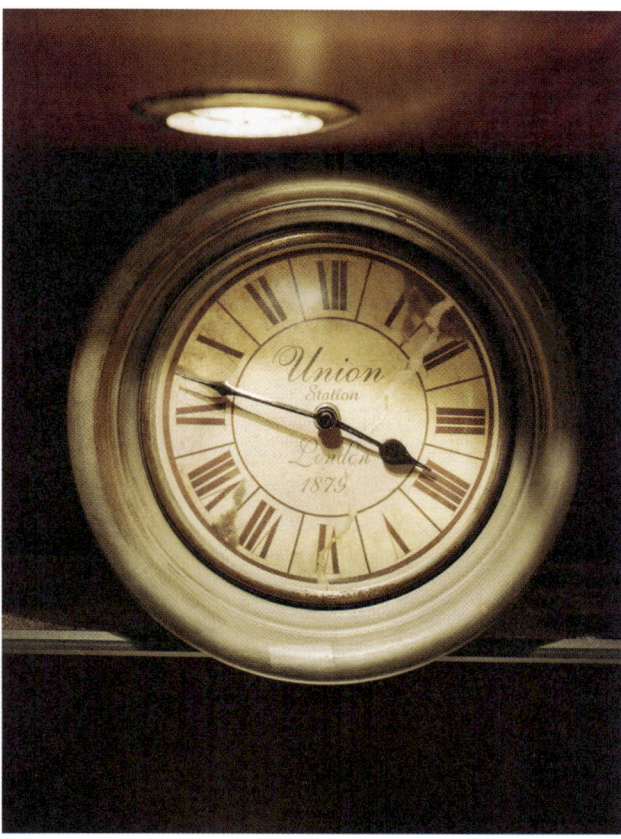

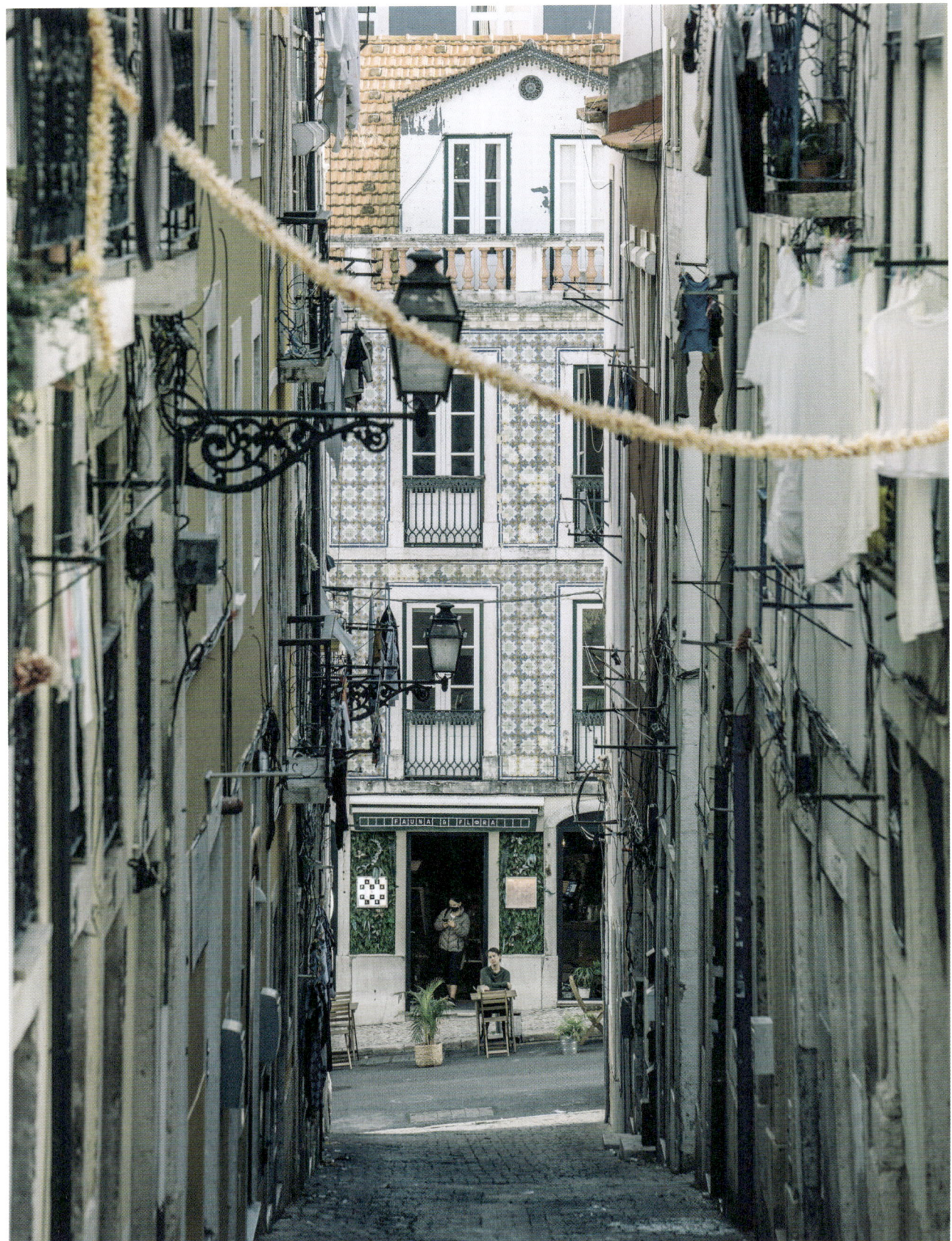

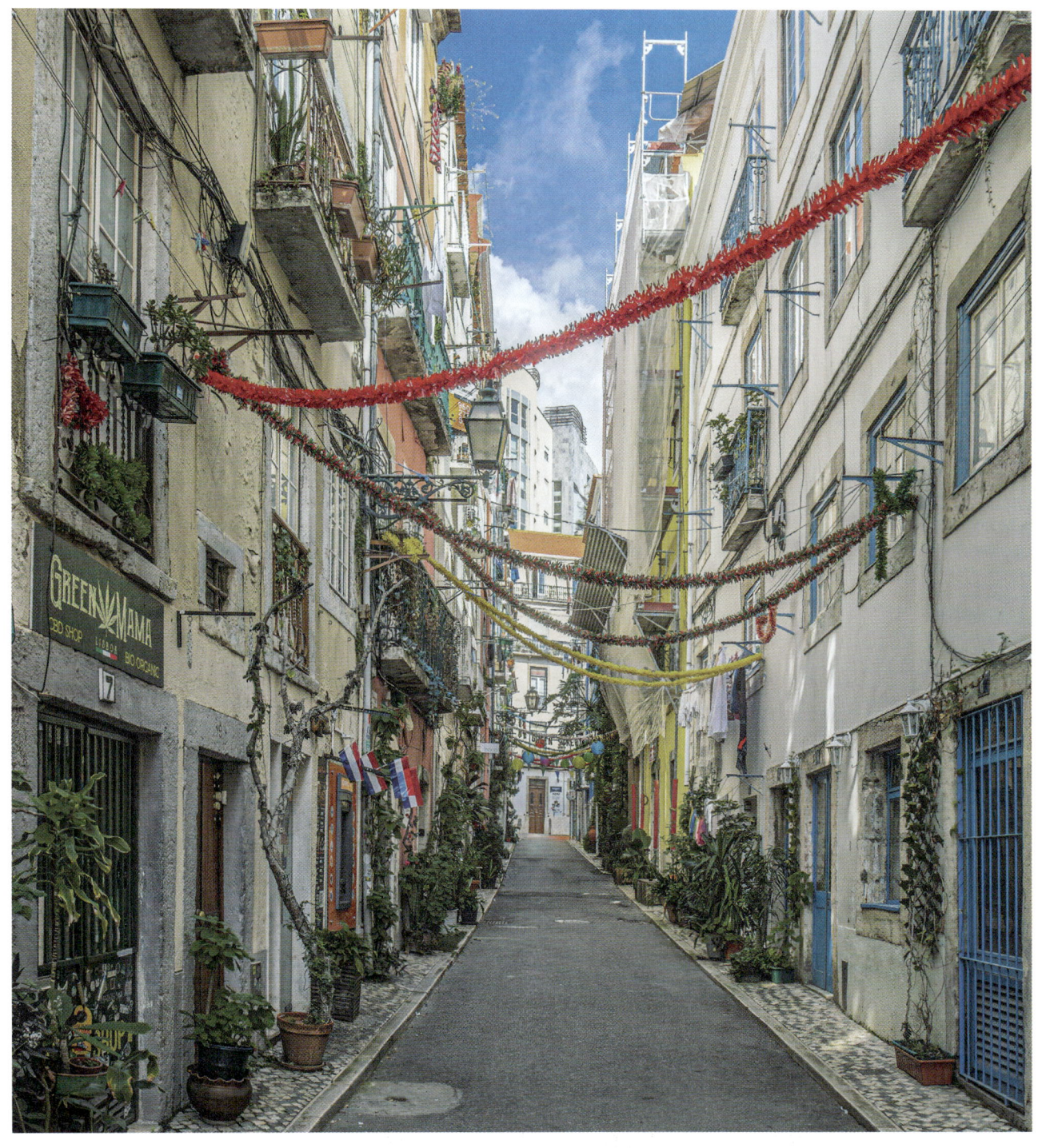

ABOVE AND LEFT: *During the summer street-festival season, narrow streets in Alfama and Madragoa are decorated with garlands and flowers. Rua da Silva (above) is now known as Lisbon's "green street" and draws photography enthusiasts from around the world.*

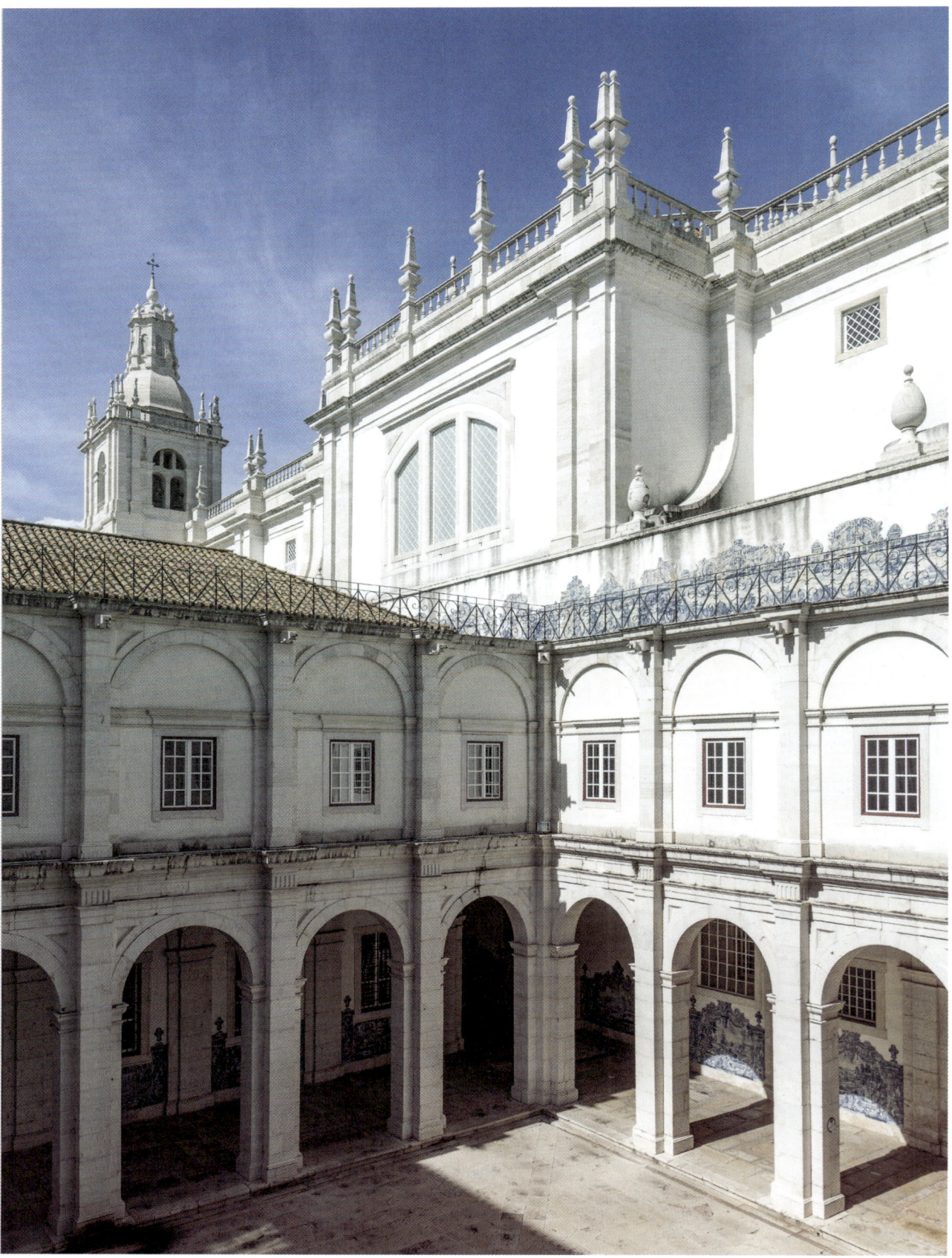

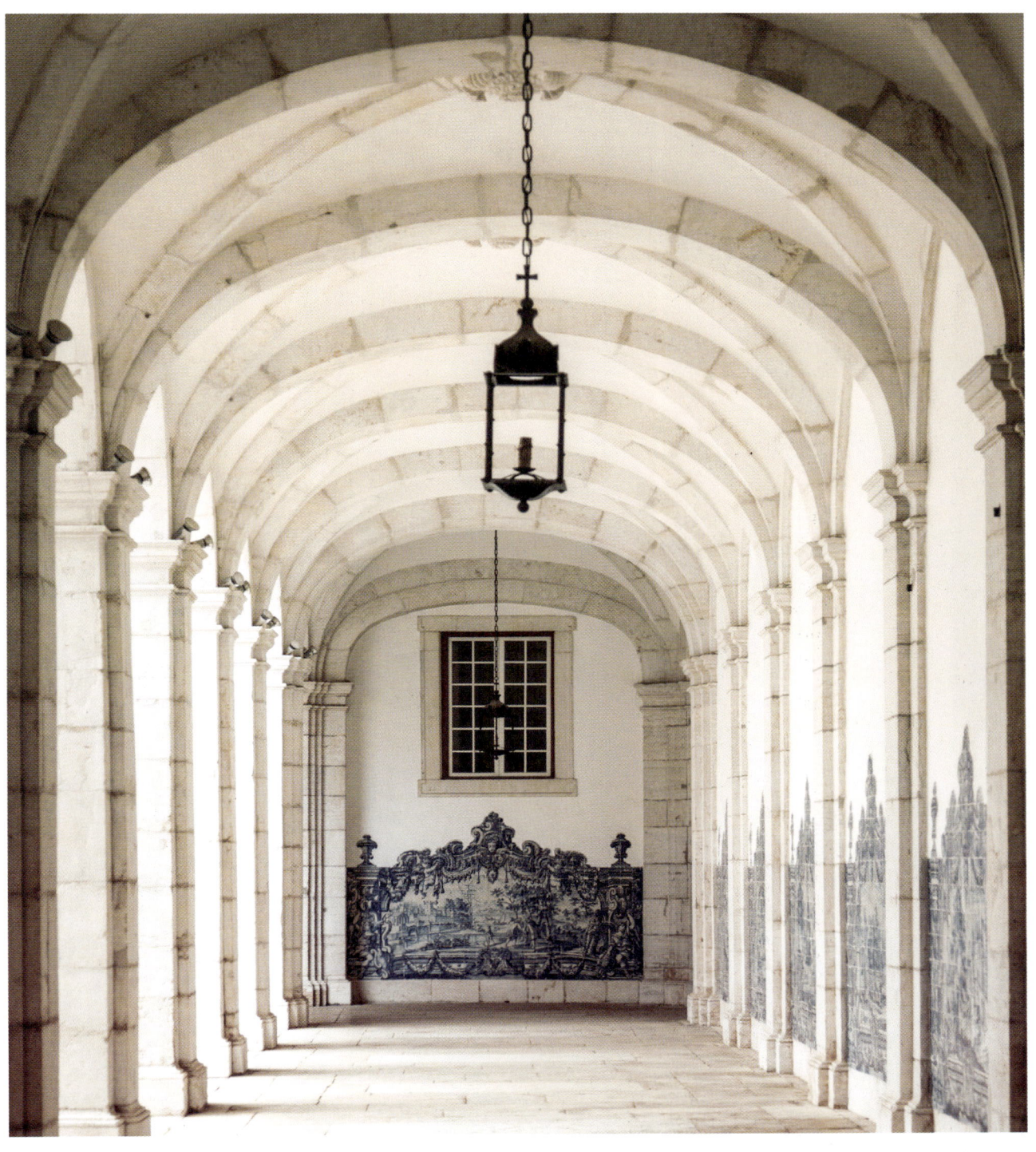

ABOVE AND LEFT: *At the Monastery of São Vicente de Fora (left), one of the most extensive collections of preserved seventeenth-century azulejos. More than 100,000 tiles form an elaborate tableau in the cloister courtyard.*

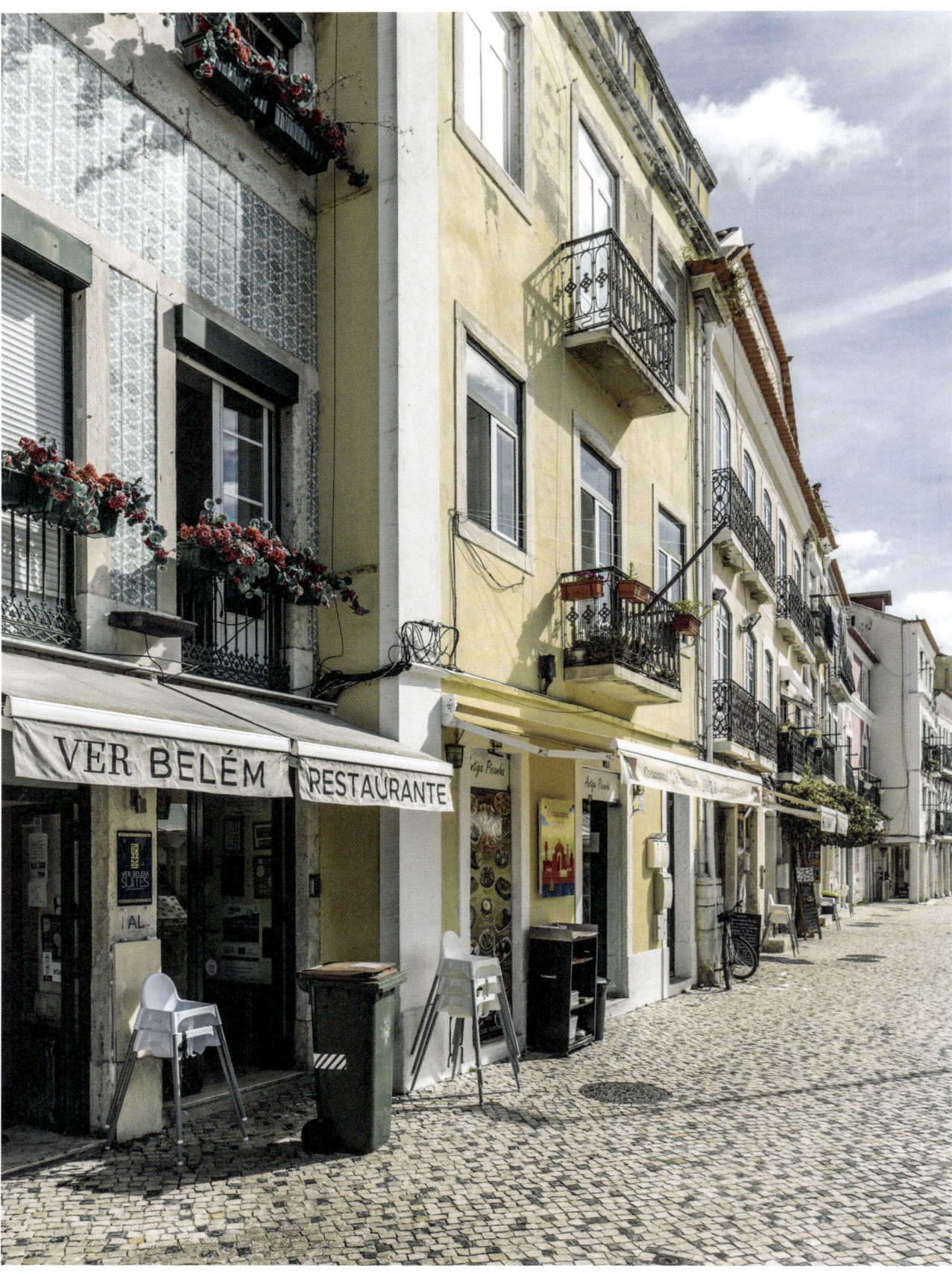

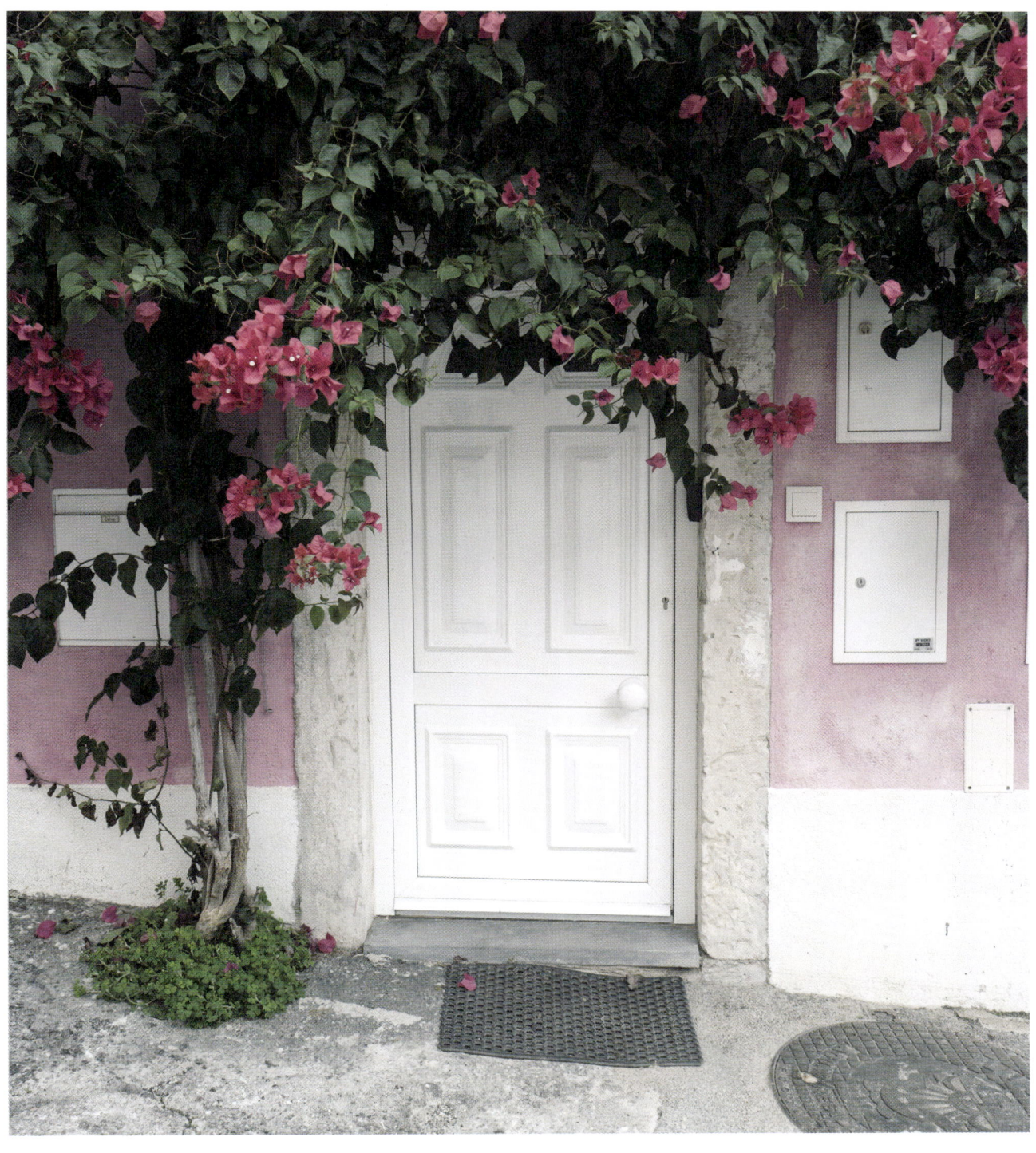

ABOVE AND LEFT: *Many small restaurants in the streets along the Tagus in Belém. Colorful façades and bright bougainvillea everywhere.*

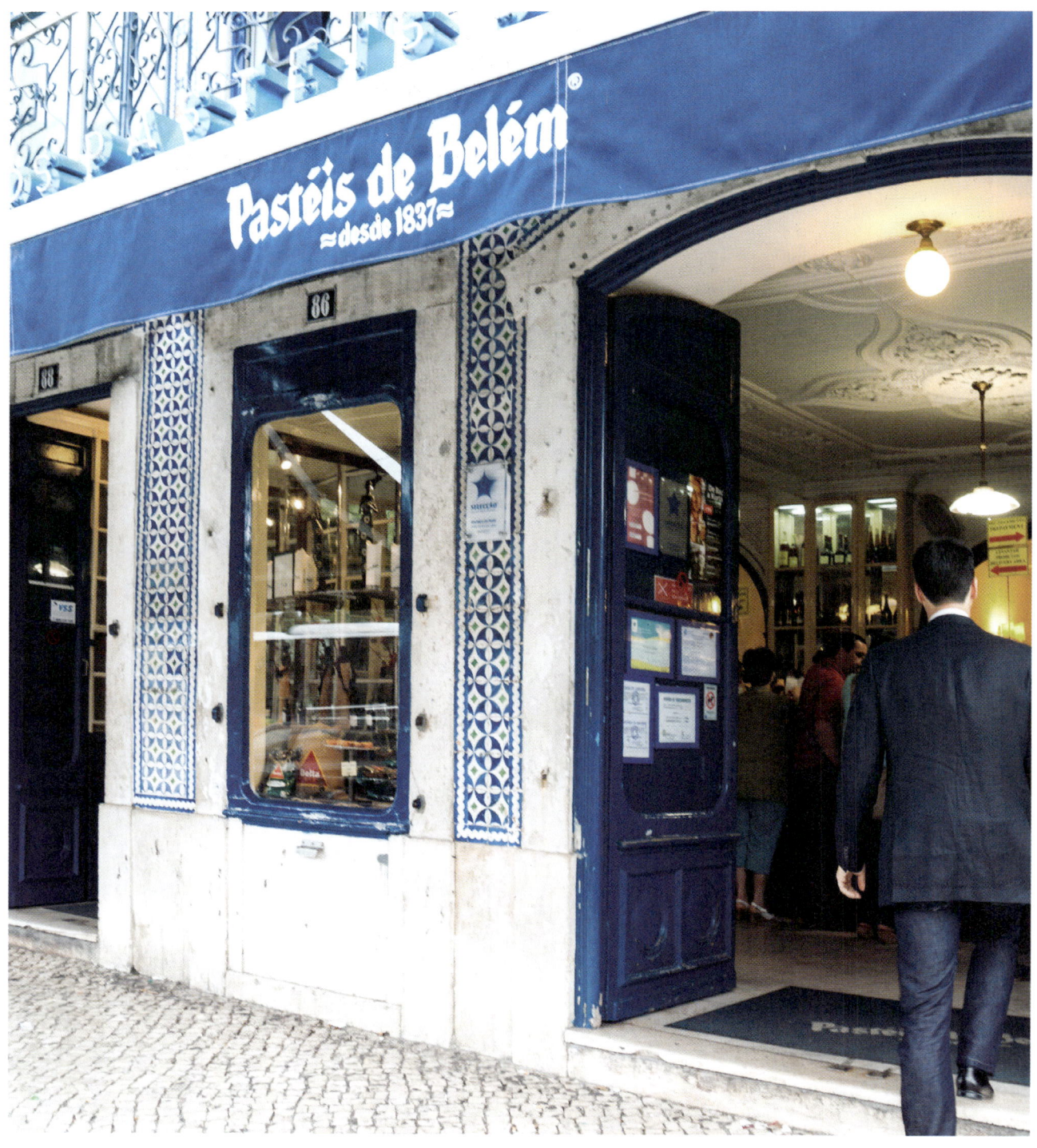

ABOVE AND RIGHT: *Belém is regarded as the birthplace of Portugal's best-known goodie: no pastéis de nata here; only pastéis de Belém. The Antiga Confeitaria de Belém has kept customers coming in for their custard tarts since 1837, baked according to a closely guarded original recipe purchased from the monks at the neighboring monastery.*

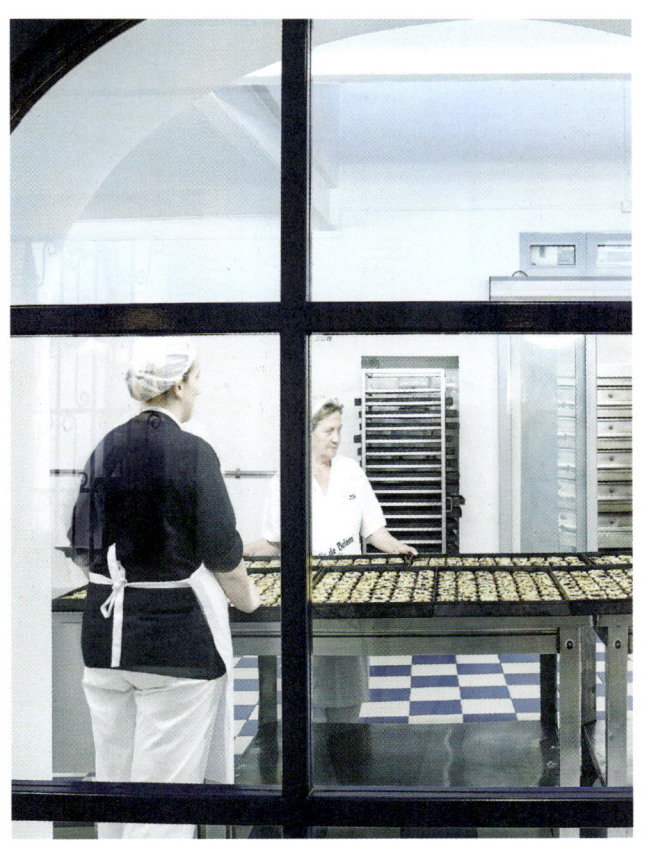
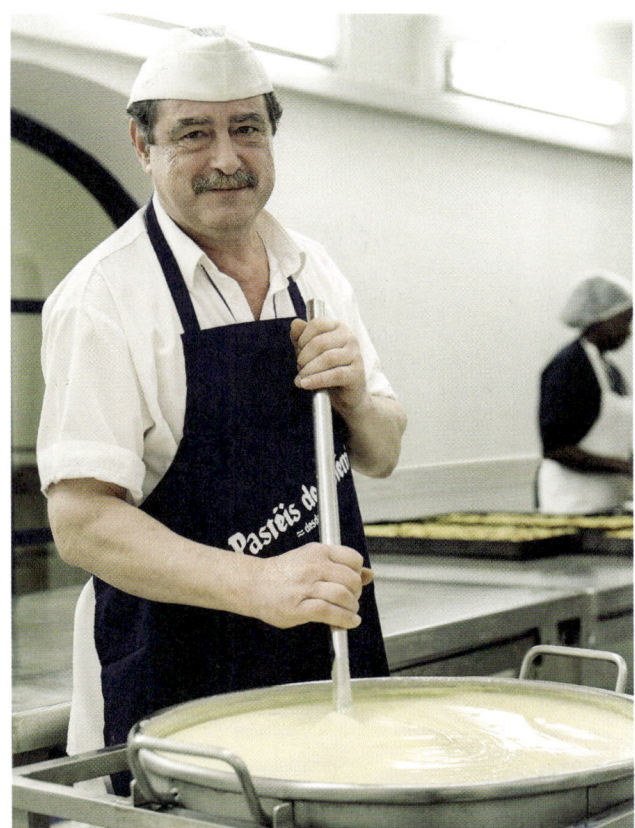
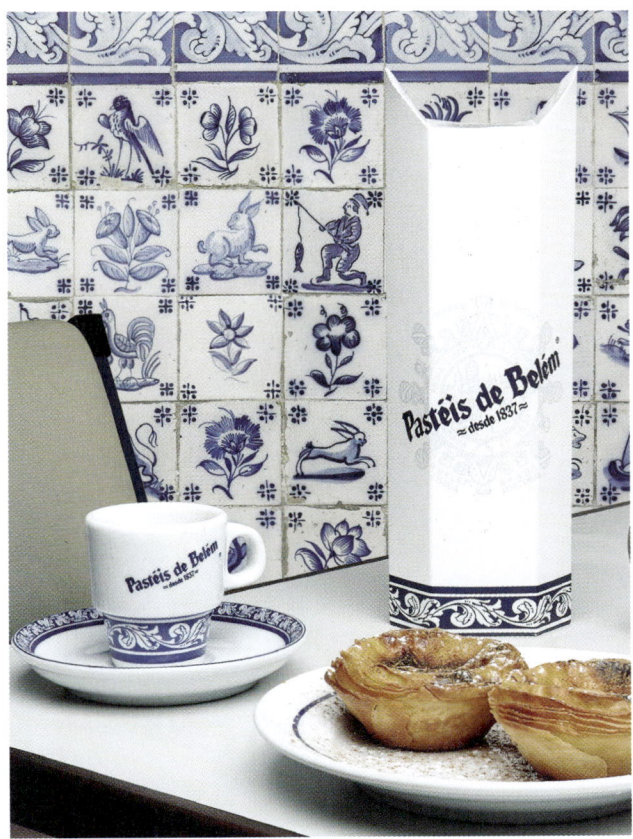
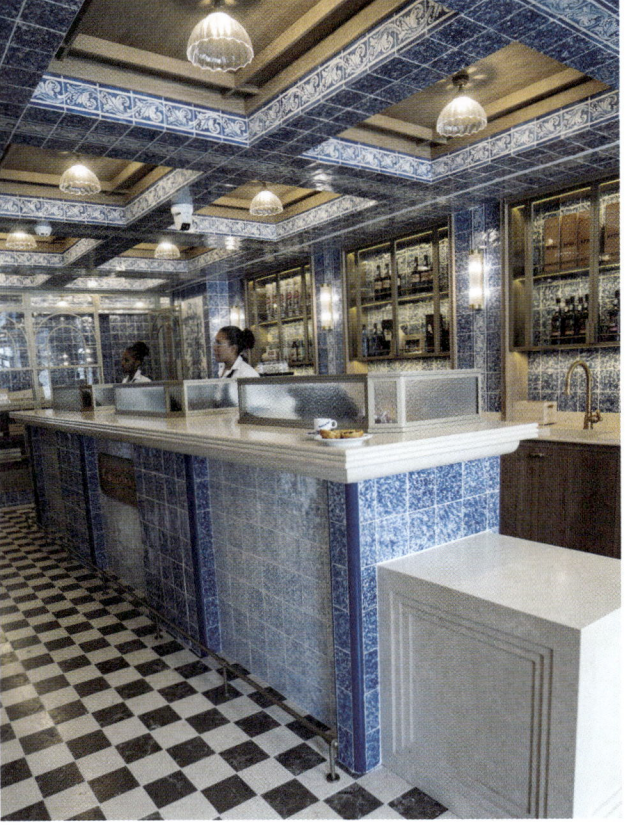

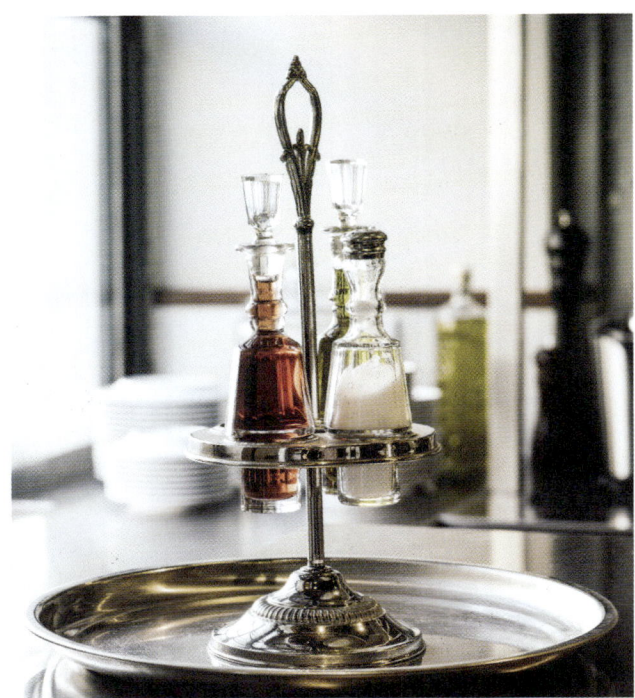
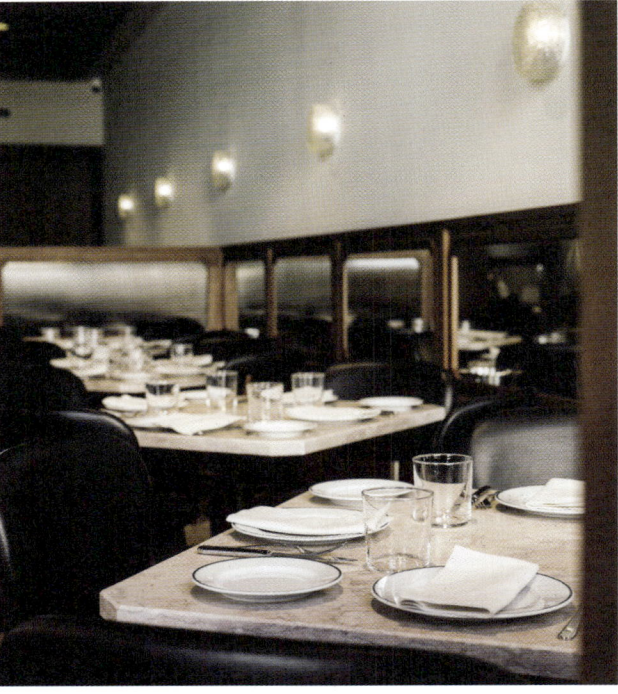
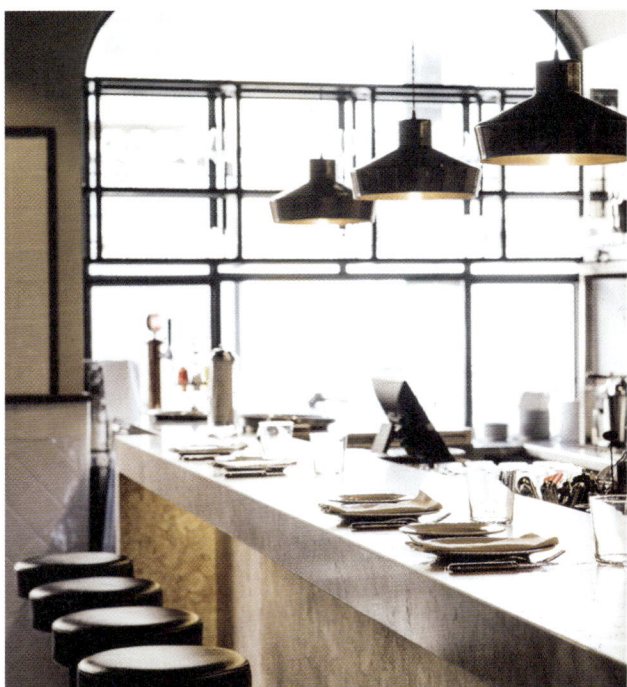
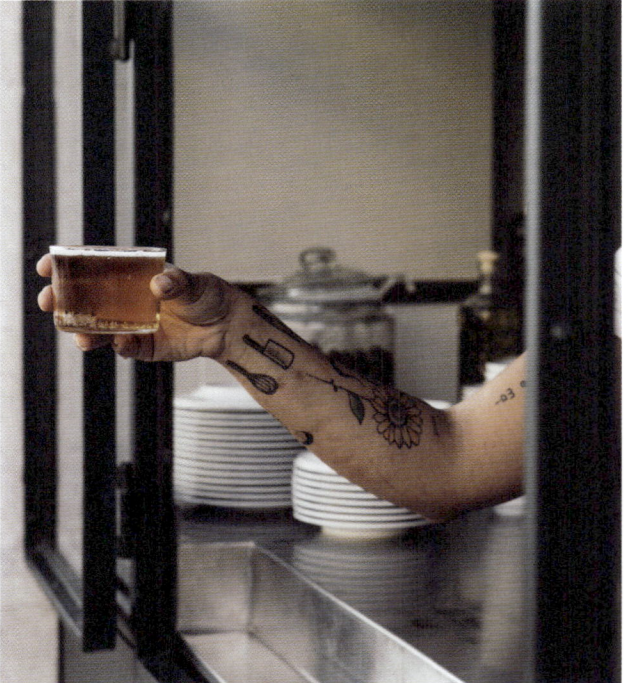

ABOVE AND RIGHT: *The restaurant Canalha in Belém serves fine traditional Portuguese fare. That and a modern tavern interior have made this small brasserie a destination for epicures.*

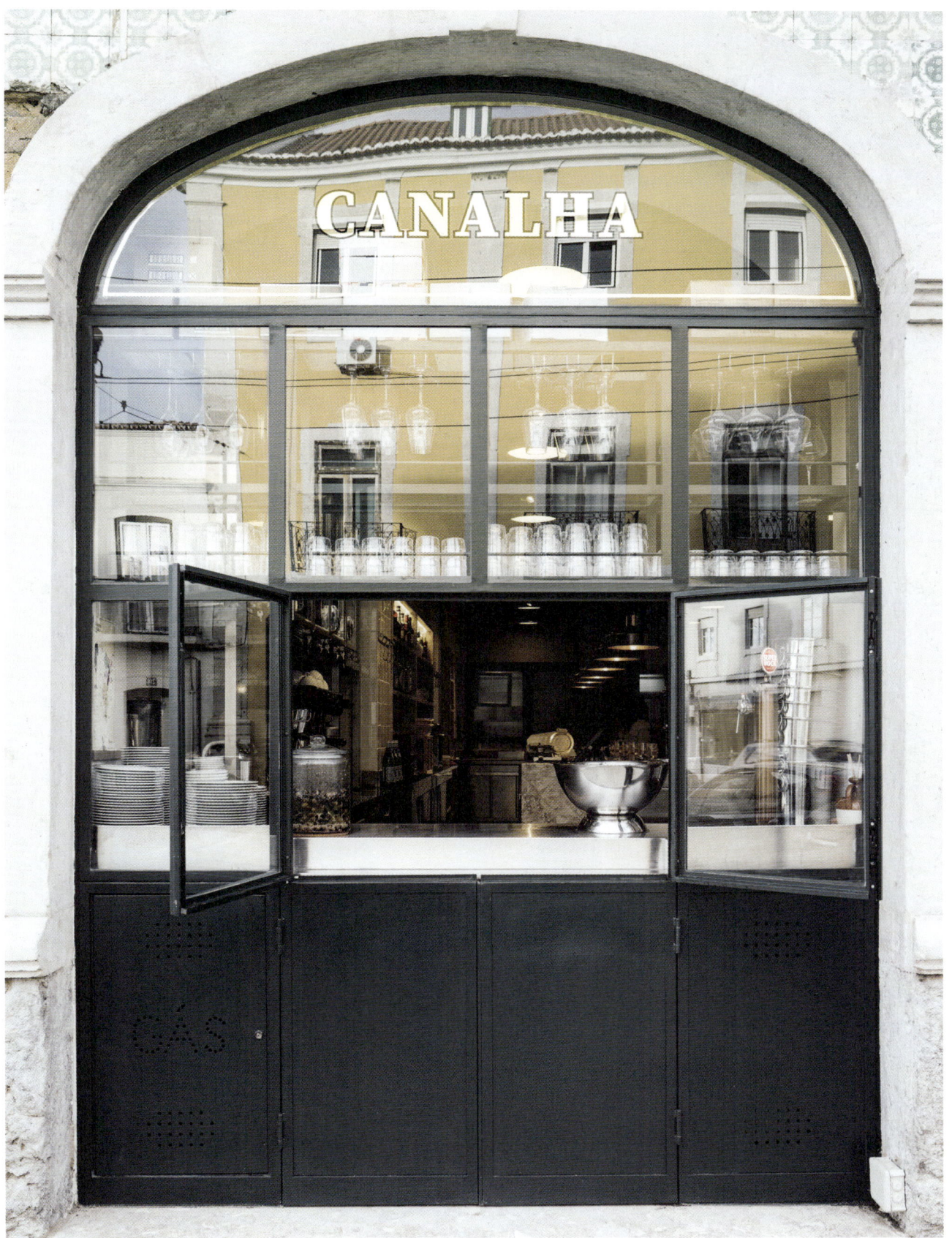

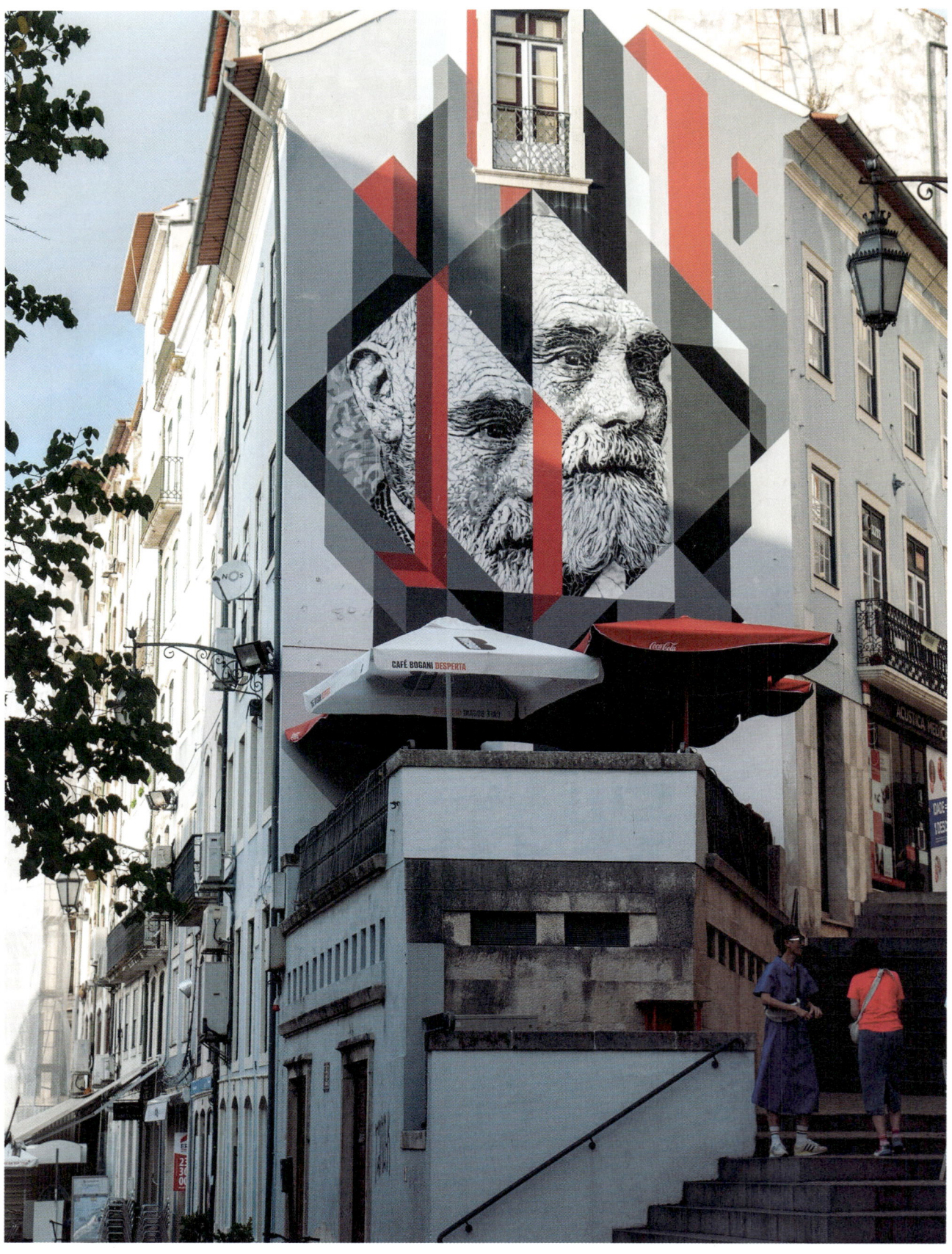

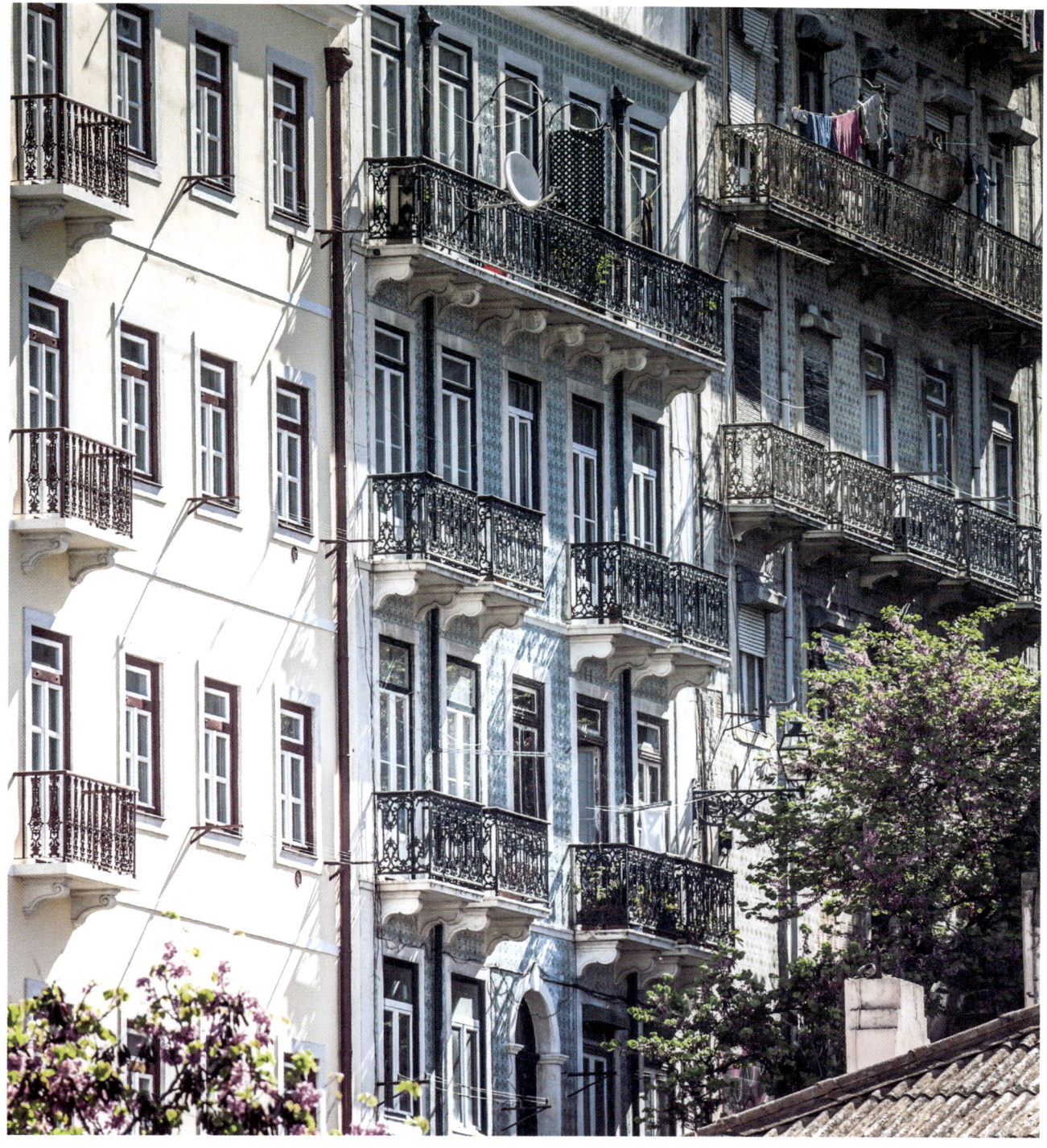

ABOVE: *A light-blue tiled building with wrought-iron balconies in the Alfama neighborhood of Lisbon.*

LEFT: *The historic blue-and-white façades are readily associated with Portugal. Lesser known is the thriving street art scene for which many modern buildings stand out.*

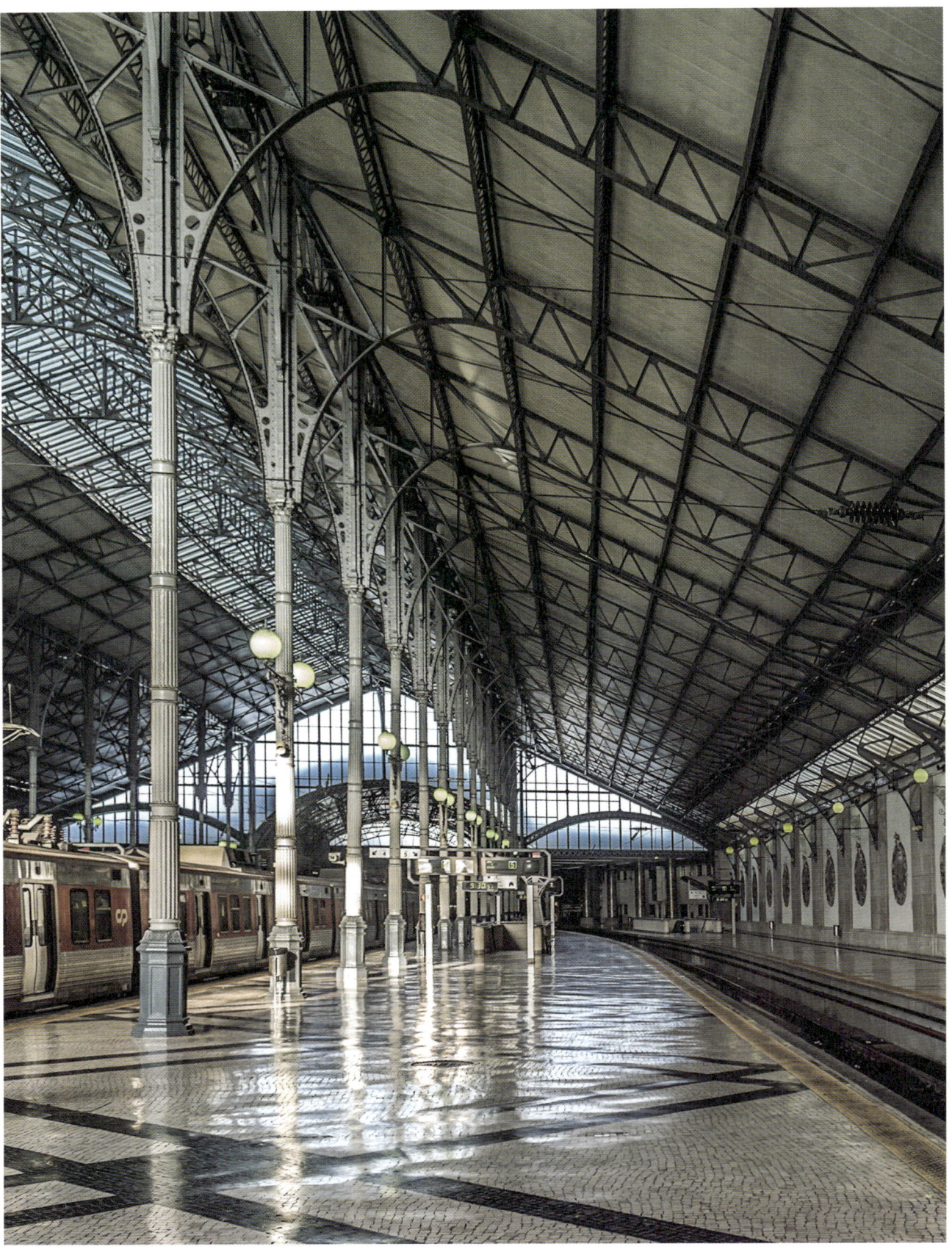

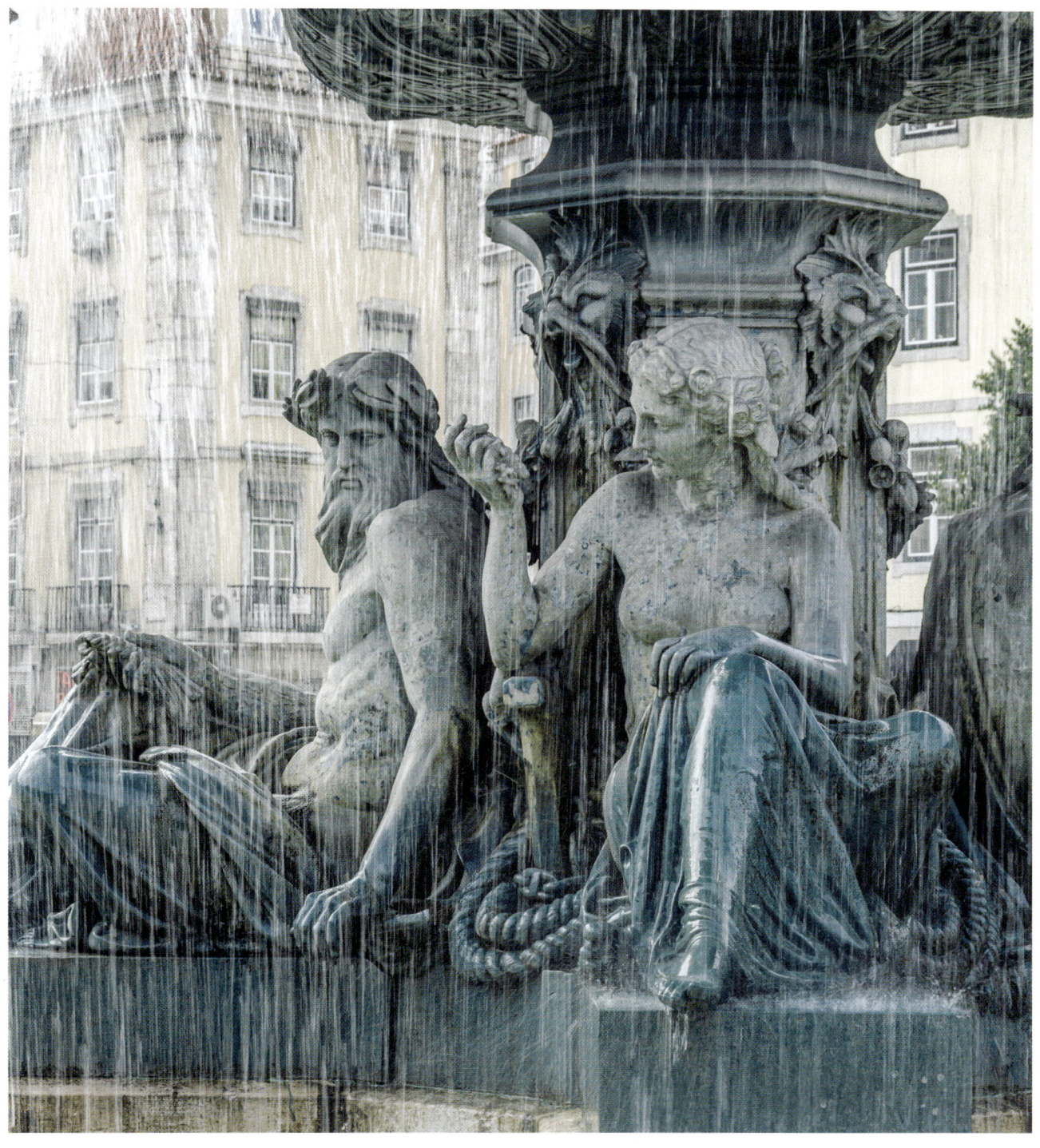

ABOVE: *Praça do Rossio north of the Baixa Pombalina is a busy meeting place. Street performers draw in passersby among jacaranda trees and two monumental fountains.*

LEFT: *Railway nostalgia at Lisboa Rossio station, with elegant cast-iron structures still in use.*

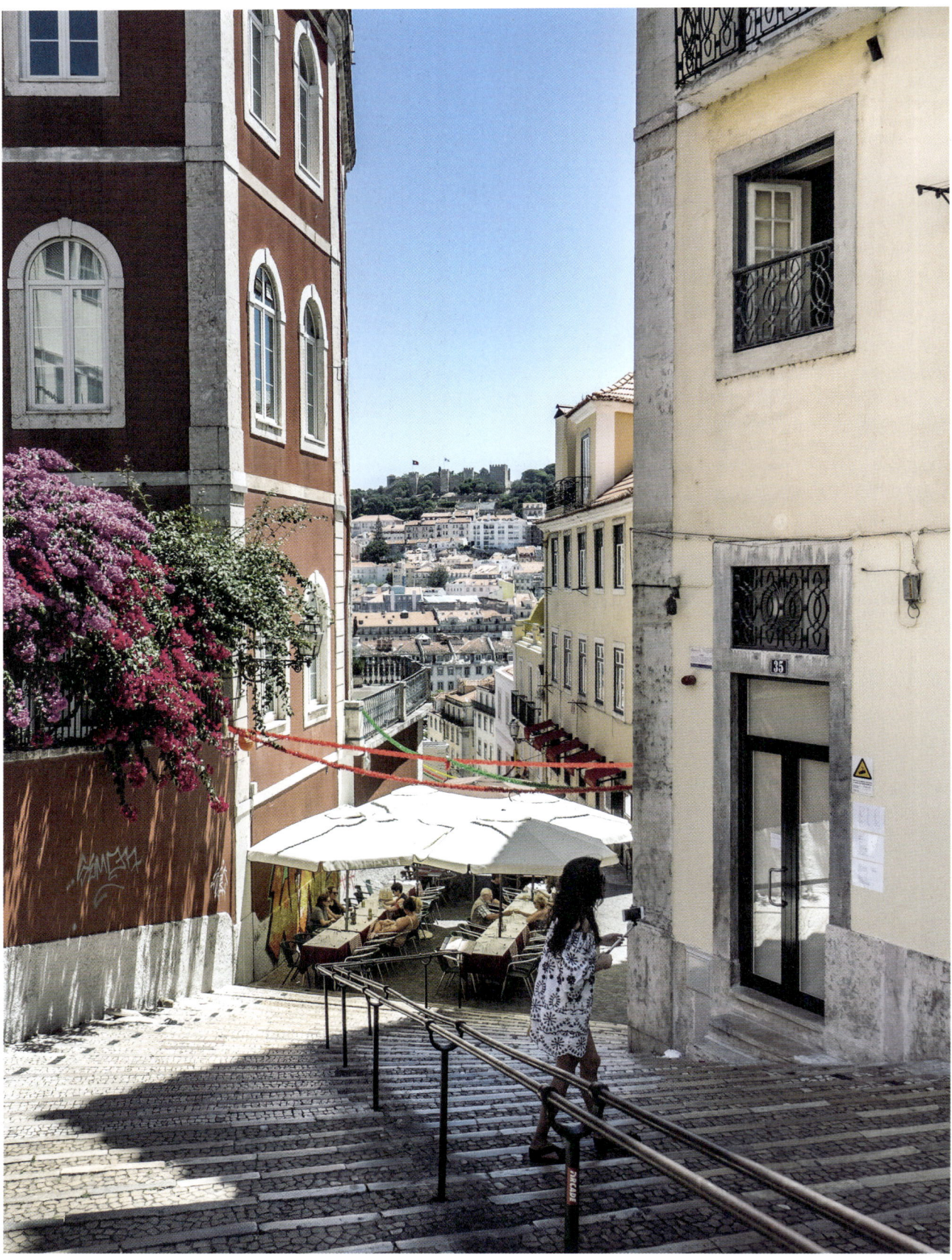

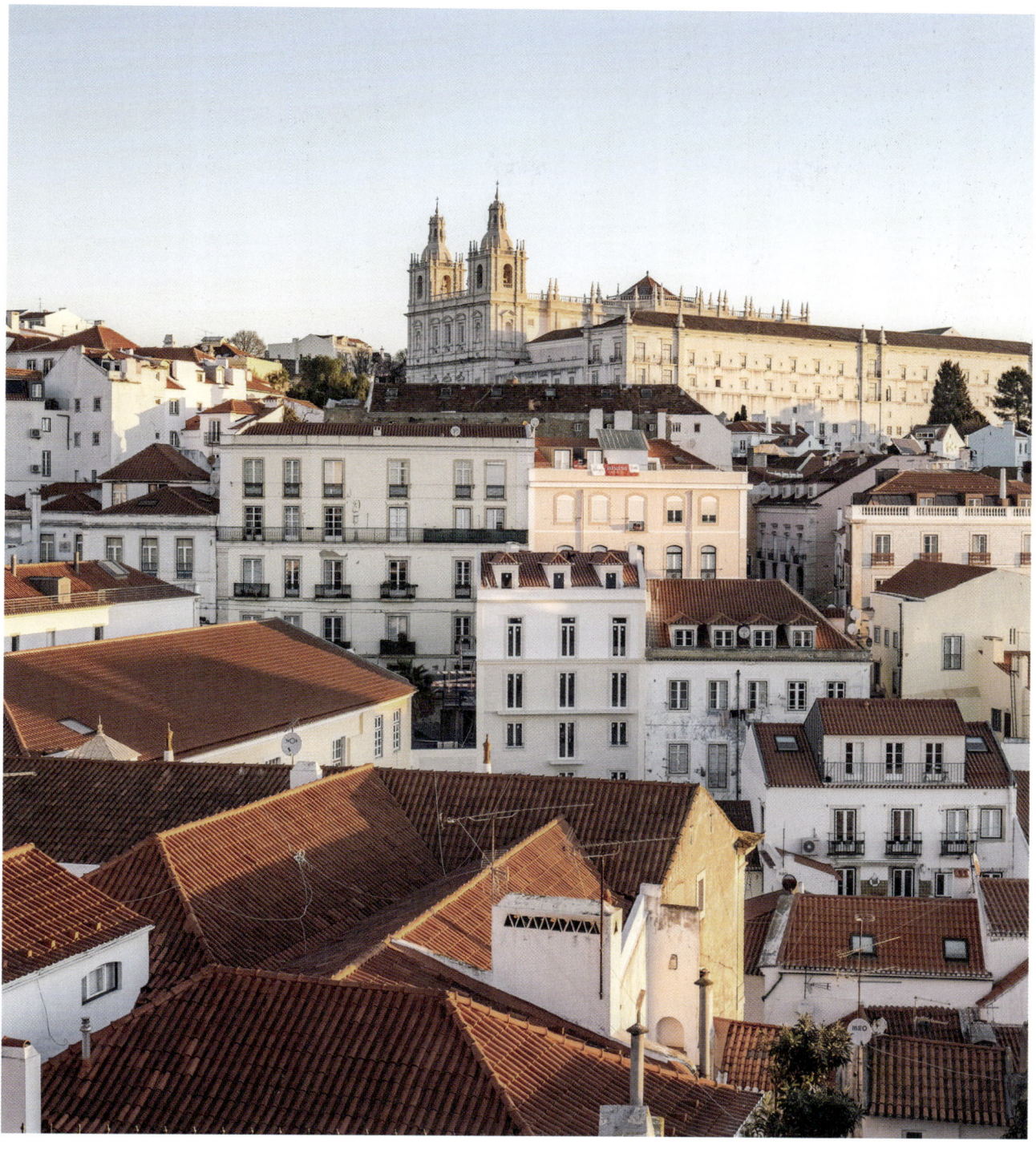

ABOVE: *The façade of the Monastery of São Vicente de Fora glows above the rooftops of Alfama in the evening light.*

LEFT: *Along the stepped Calçada do Dunque, street cafés line the way down from Bairro Alto. The route leads from shaded, irregular streets into the straight lines of the Baixa Pombalina.*

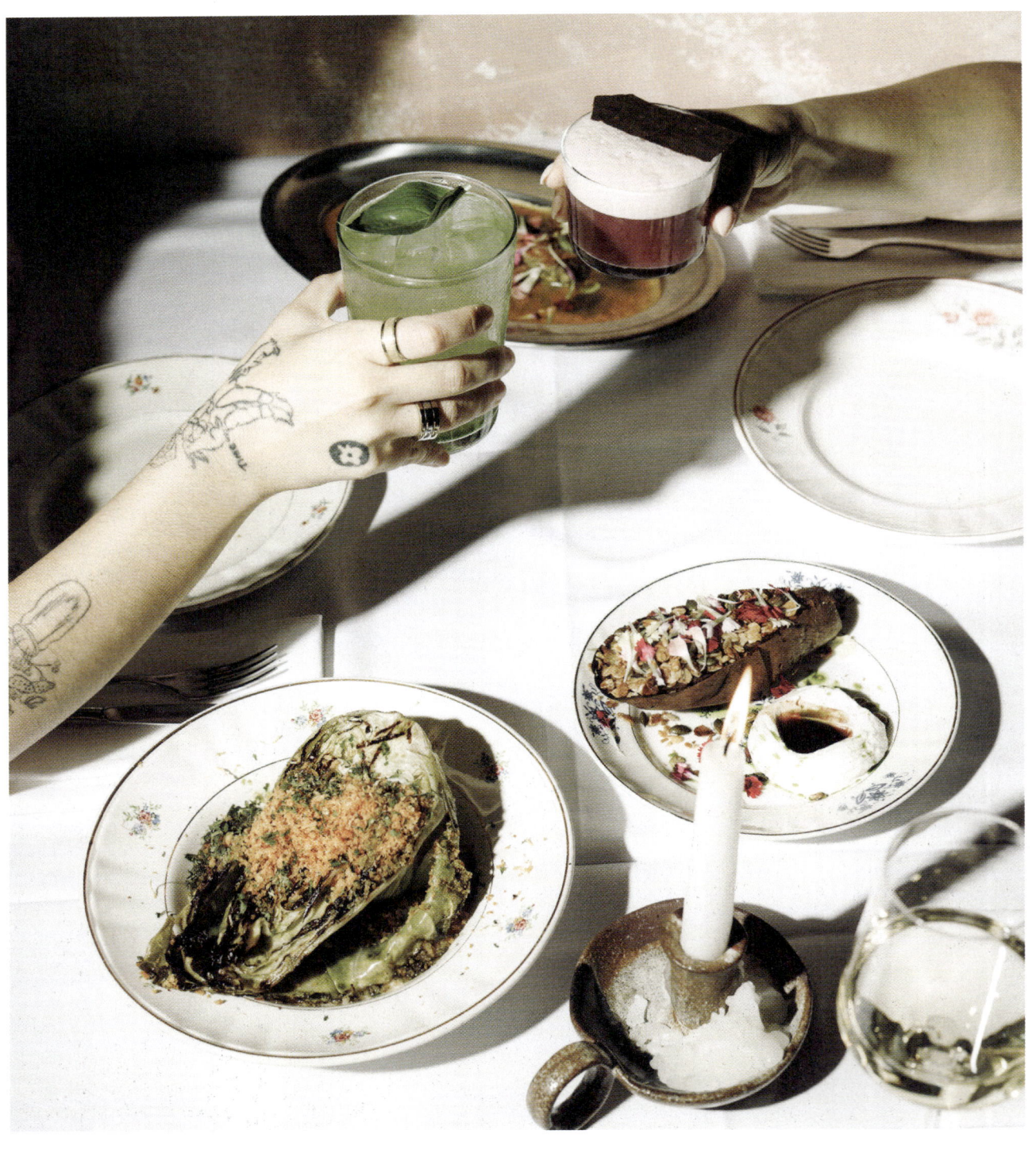

ABOVE AND RIGHT: *At the Gandaia, a club in the upscale Príncipe Real district, The Decadent Restaurant serves contemporary fusion cuisine with carefully mixed cocktails in an intimate setting.*

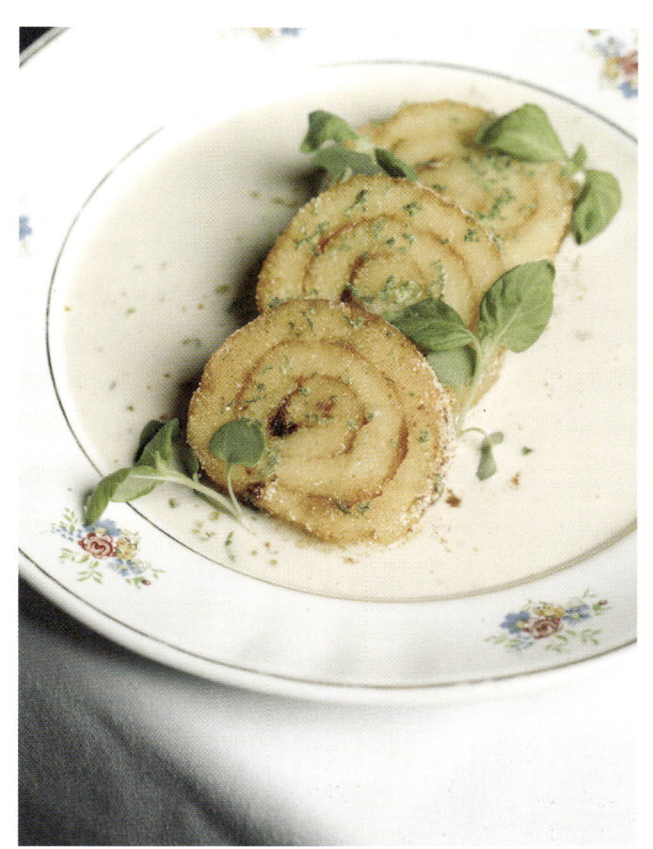
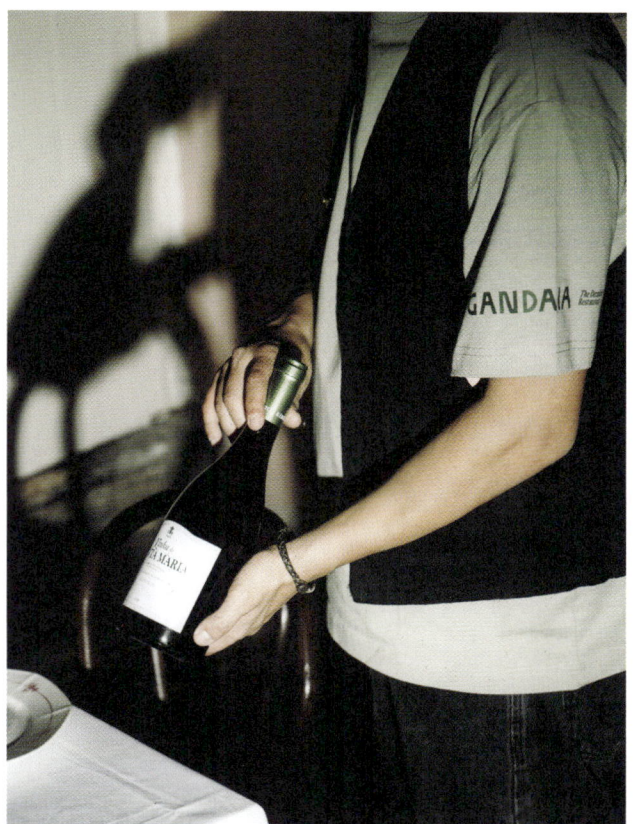
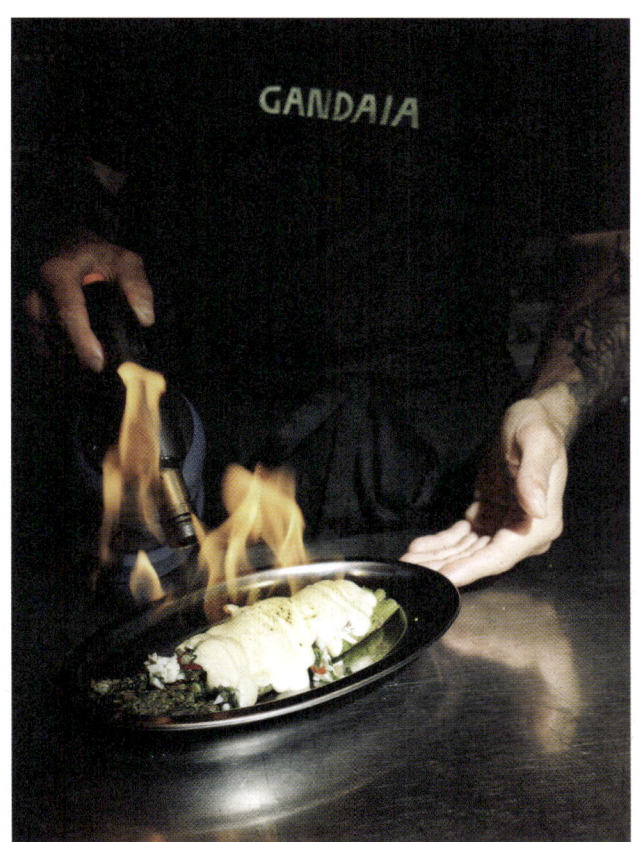
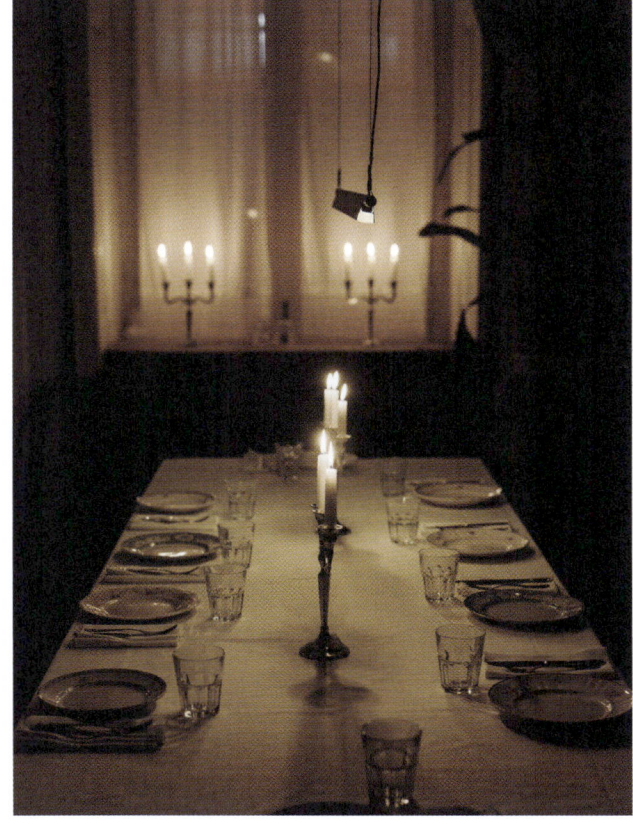

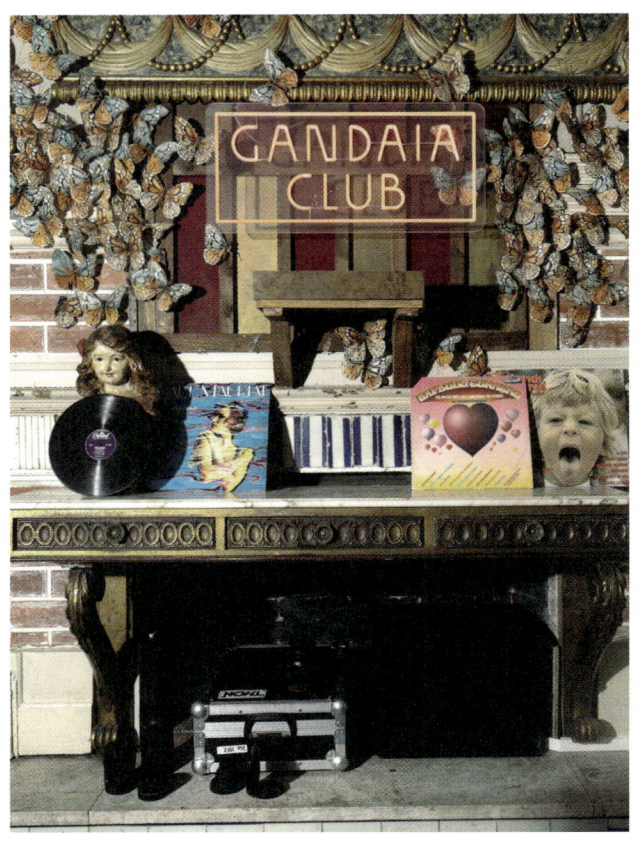
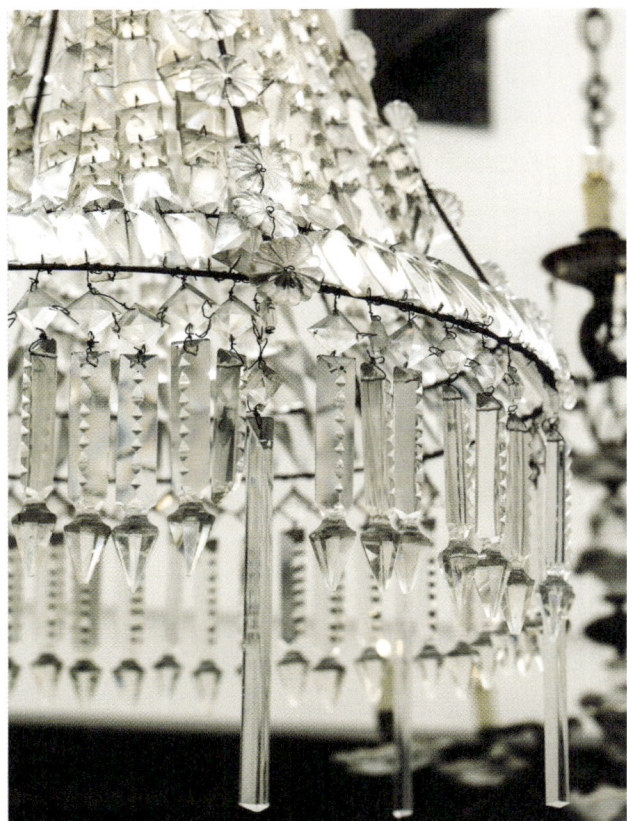
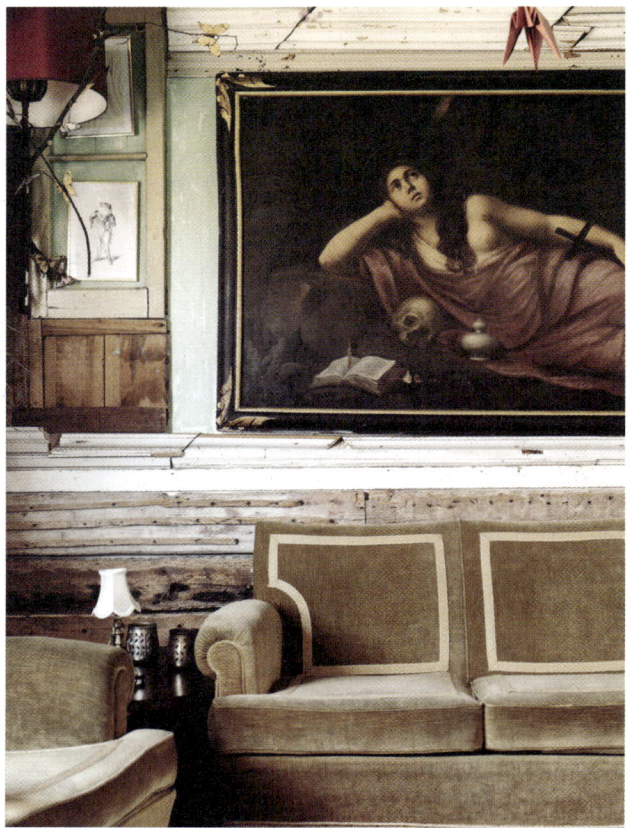
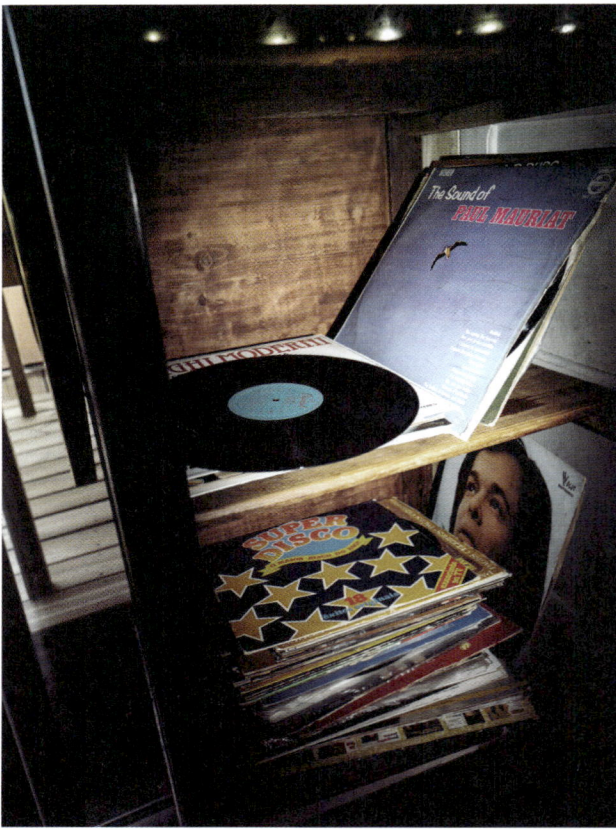

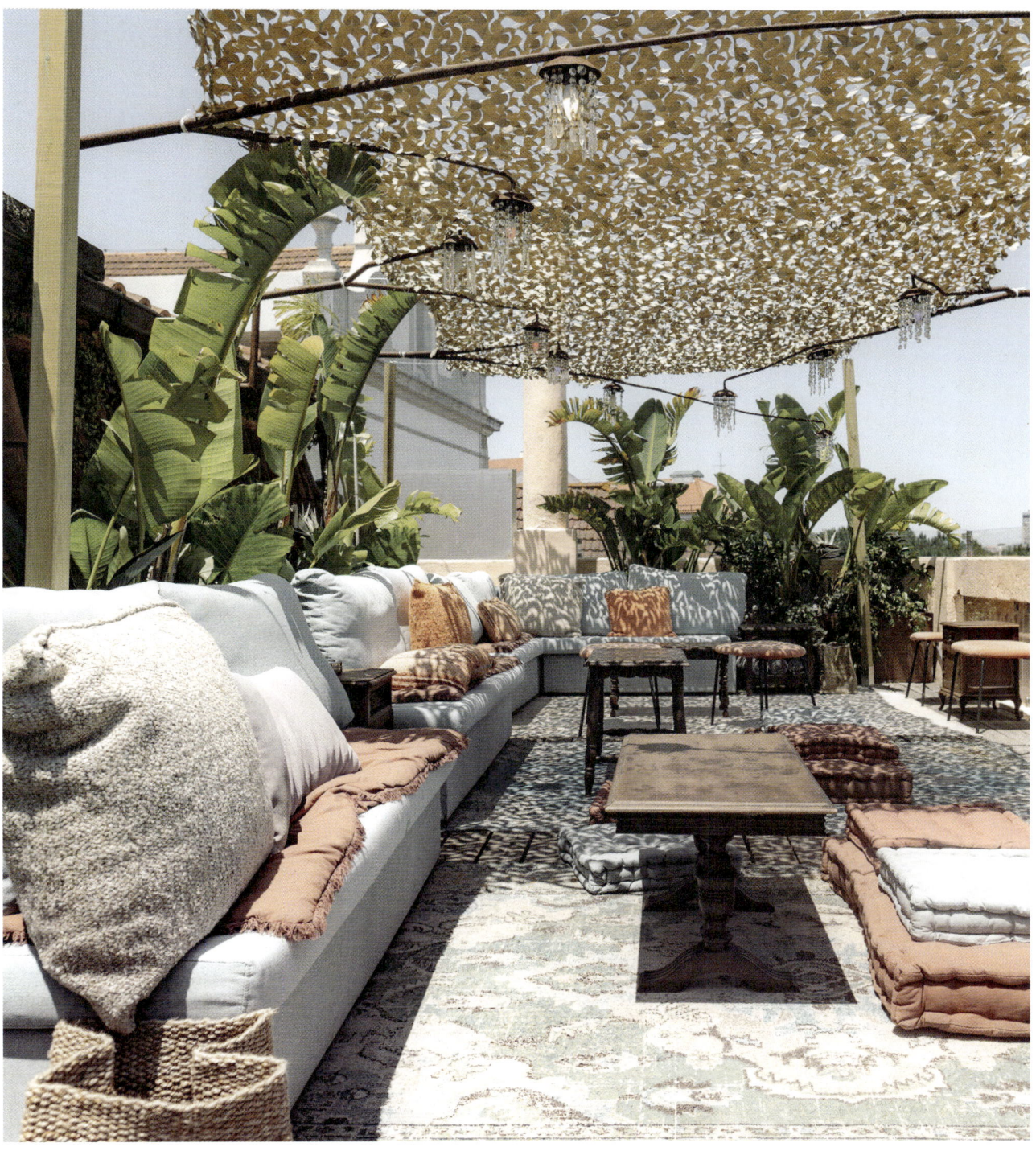

ABOVE AND LEFT: *Rooftop terrace at the Gandaia: Coffee during the day, cocktails and views across Lisbon's rooftops at night.*

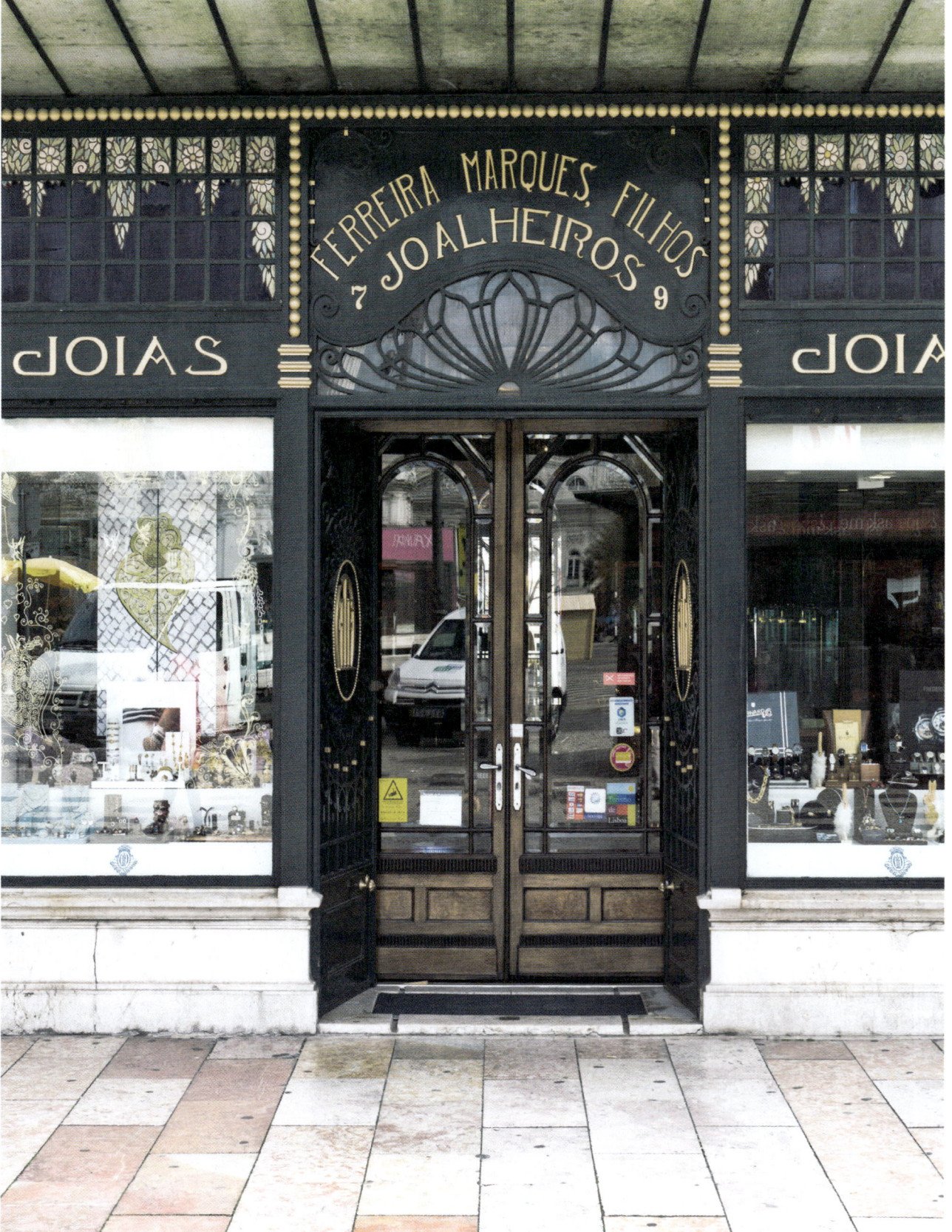

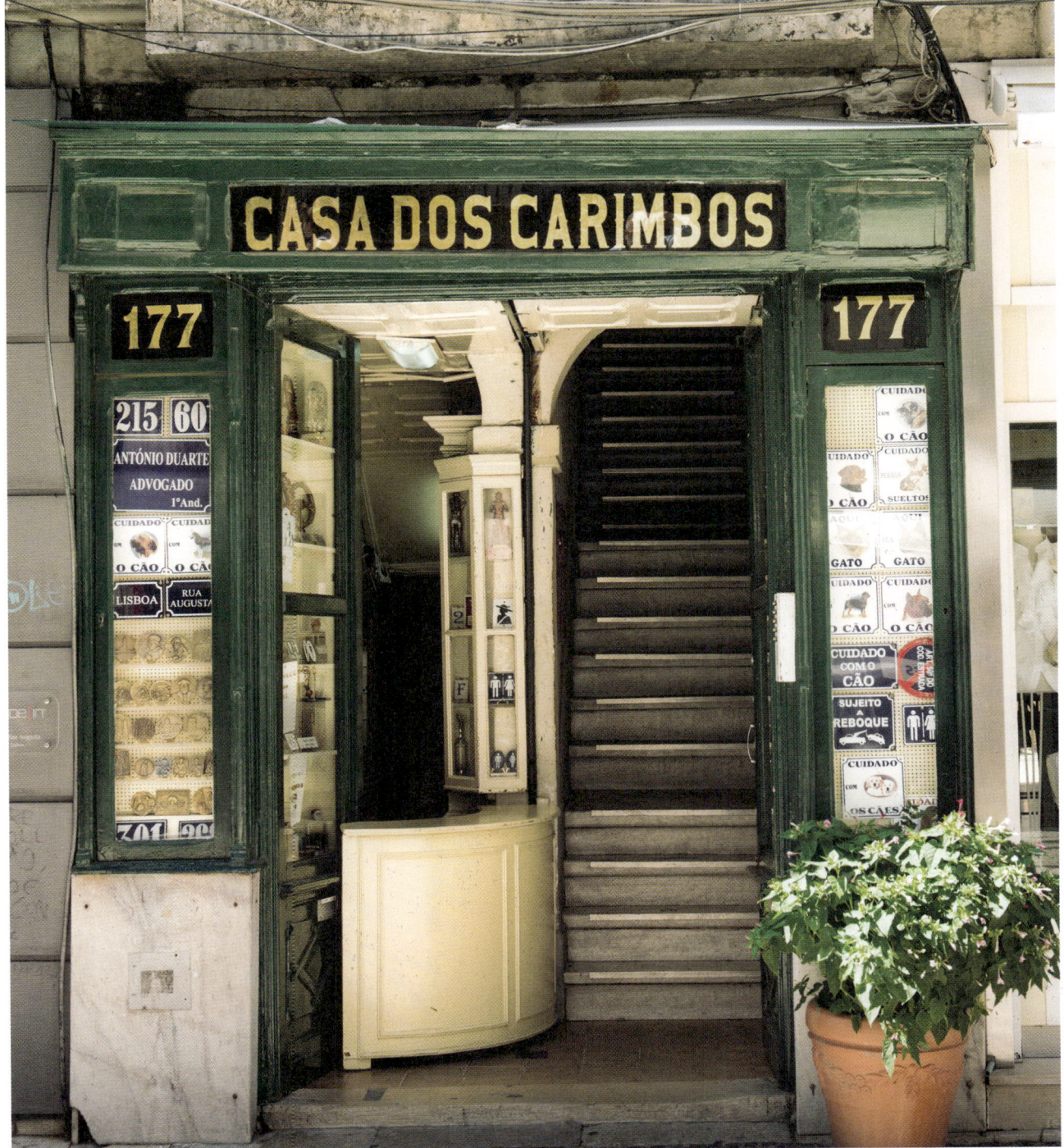

ABOVE: *Small discoveries throughout Lisbon: the nostalgic shopfronts of storied workshops.*

LEFT: *The exterior of the traditional Ferreira Marques jewelry store stands out on its own. A James Bond production filmed on location here.*

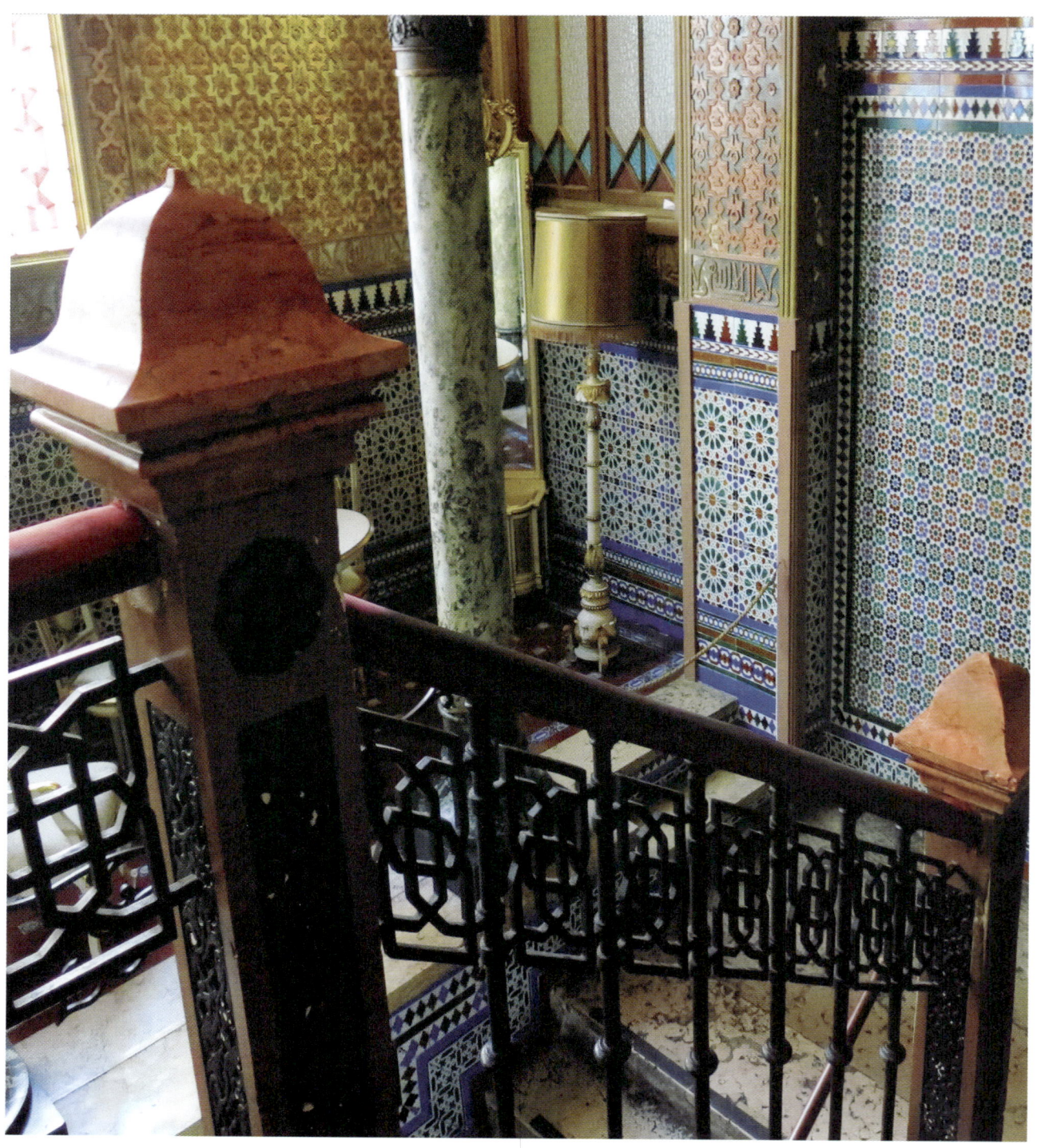

ABOVE AND RIGHT: *A few steps from Rossio Square, Casa do Alentejo opens onto a richly decorated staircase, and a Moorish courtyard conjures up a bygone world of fantasy. Large azulejo panels line the walls.*

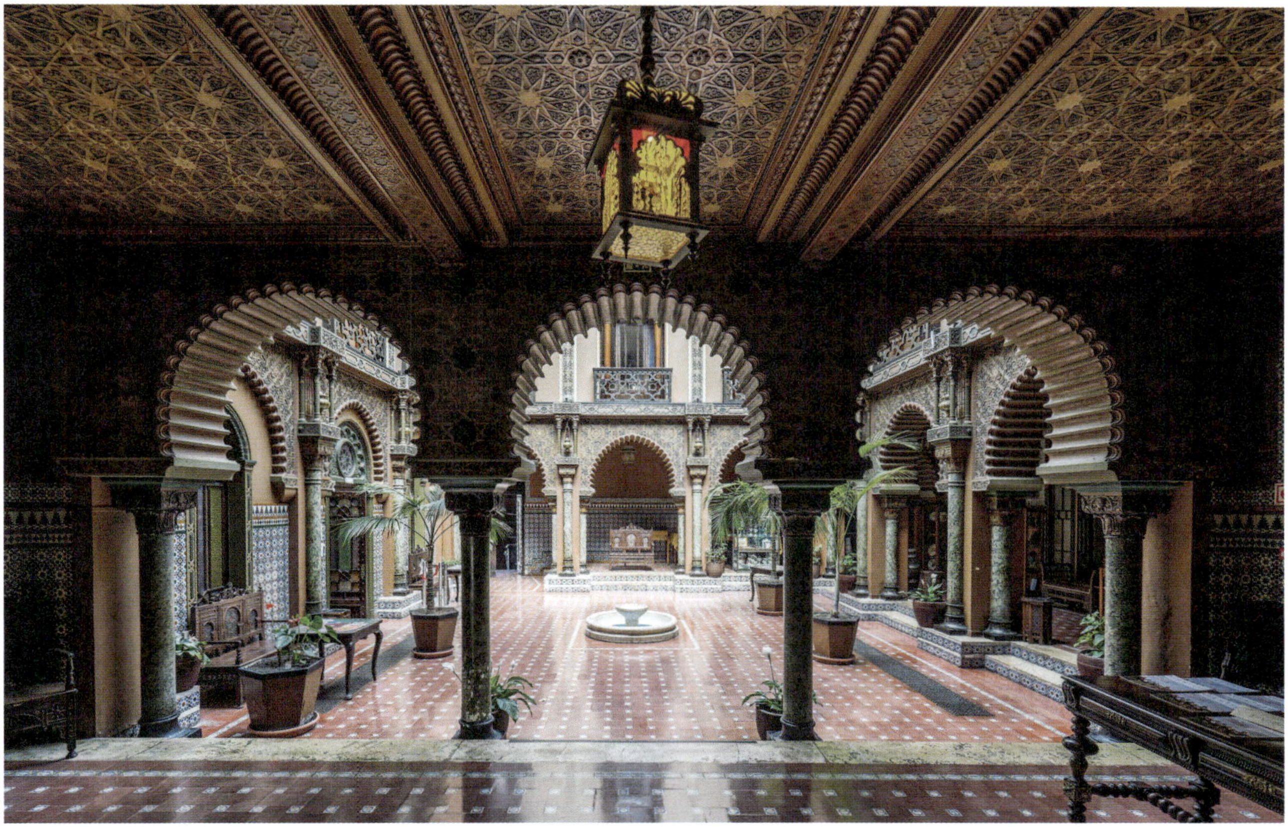

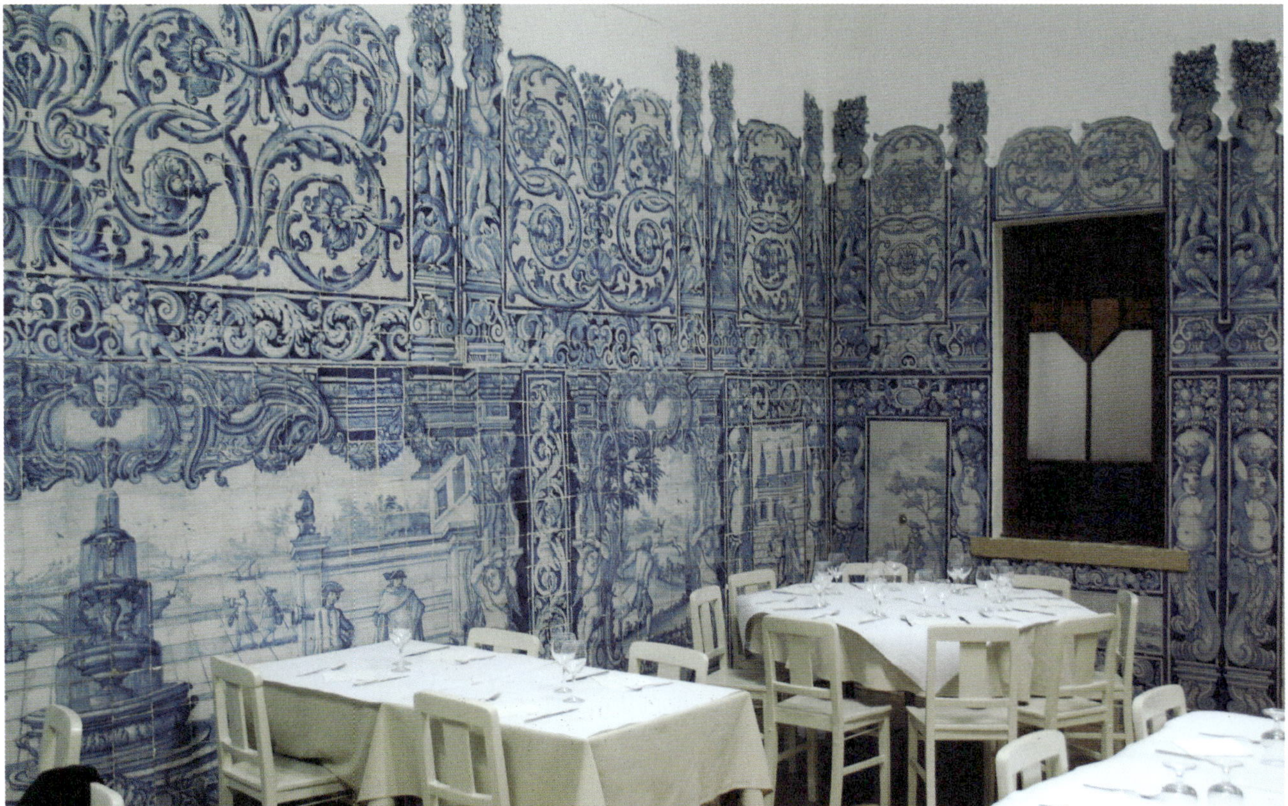

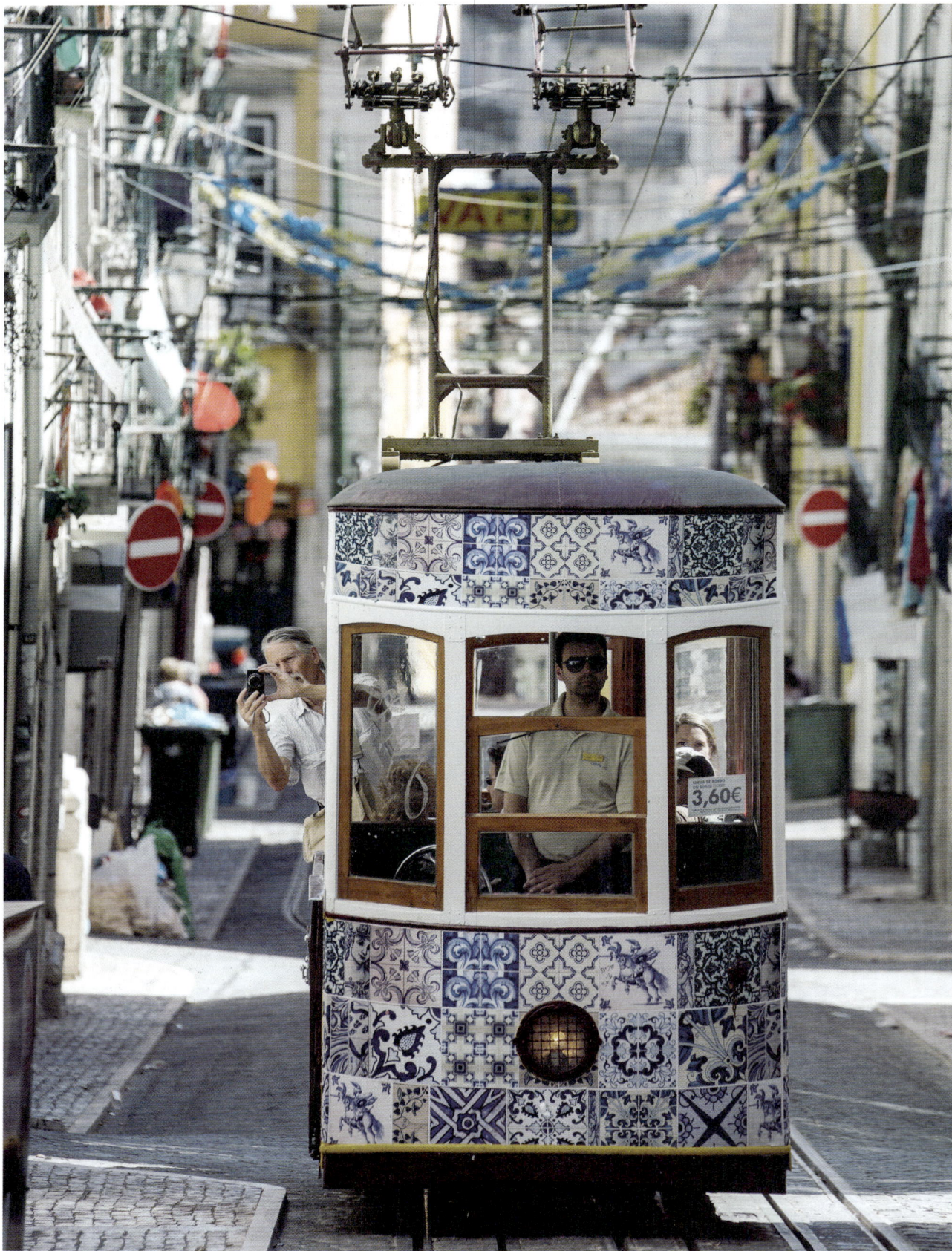

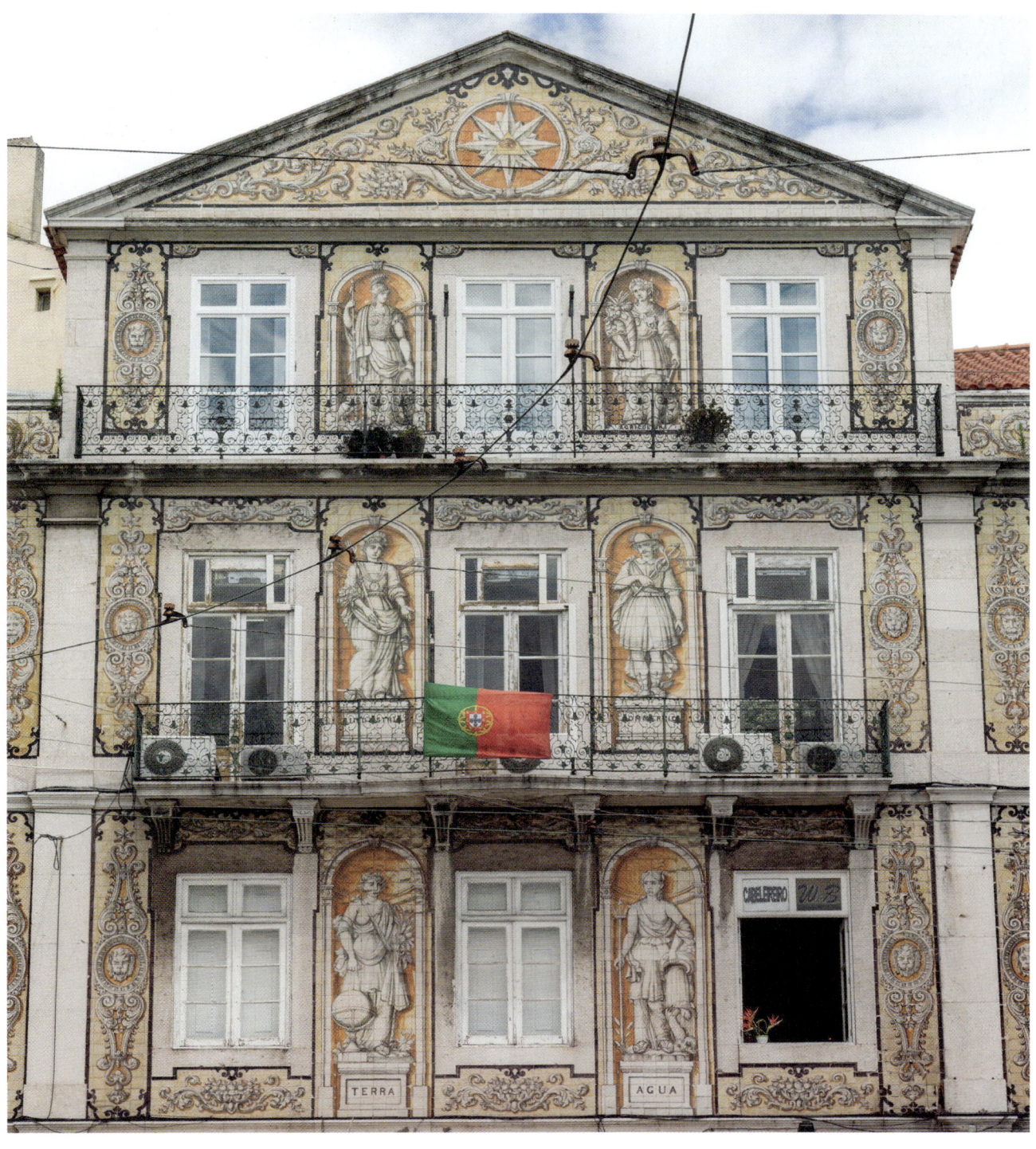

ABOVE: *Azulejos on the façade of Casa do Ferreira das Tabuletas create the illusion of three-dimensional statues. Not carvings, the allegories were hand-painted onto the tiles by the artist Luís Ferreira.*

LEFT: *Azulejos on tramcars are no surprise in Lisbon.*

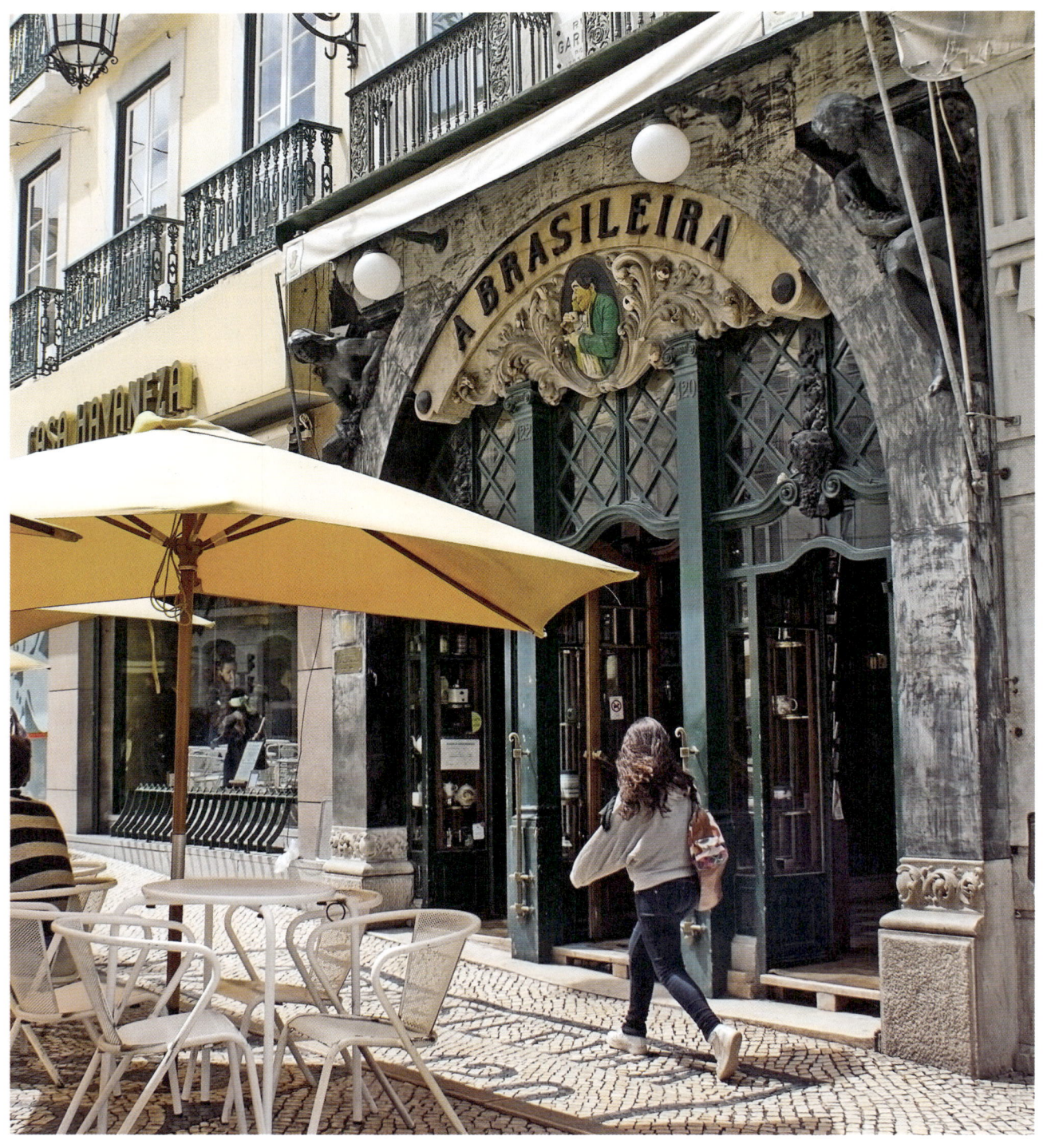

ABOVE AND RIGHT: *Café A Brasileira in the Chiado district is among Lisbon's oldest coffeehouses. Its ornate Art Nouveau entrance commands attention. To promote coffee from his own roastery, the merchant Telles once gave away freshly brewed* bica, *helping to establish espresso as part of Portugal's coffee culture.*

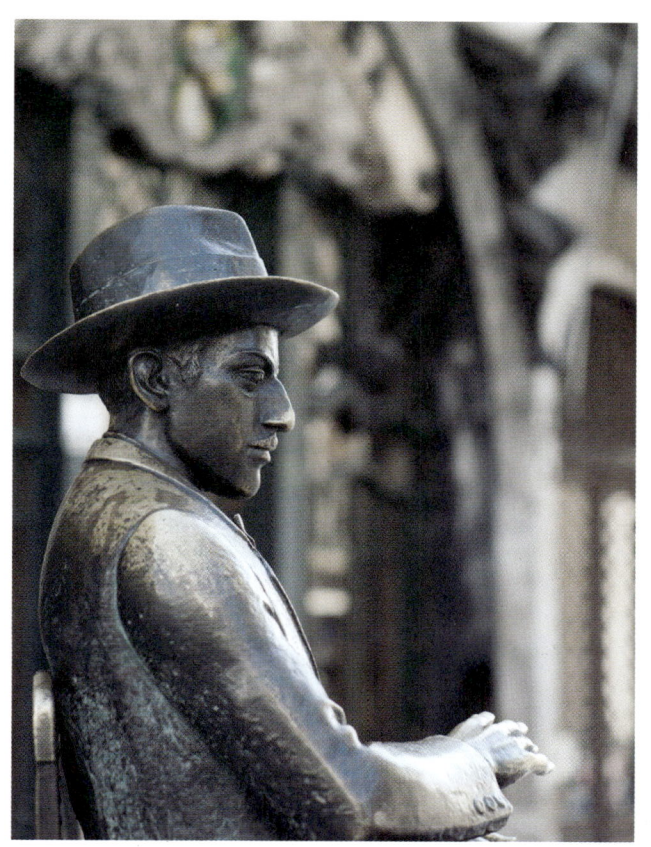
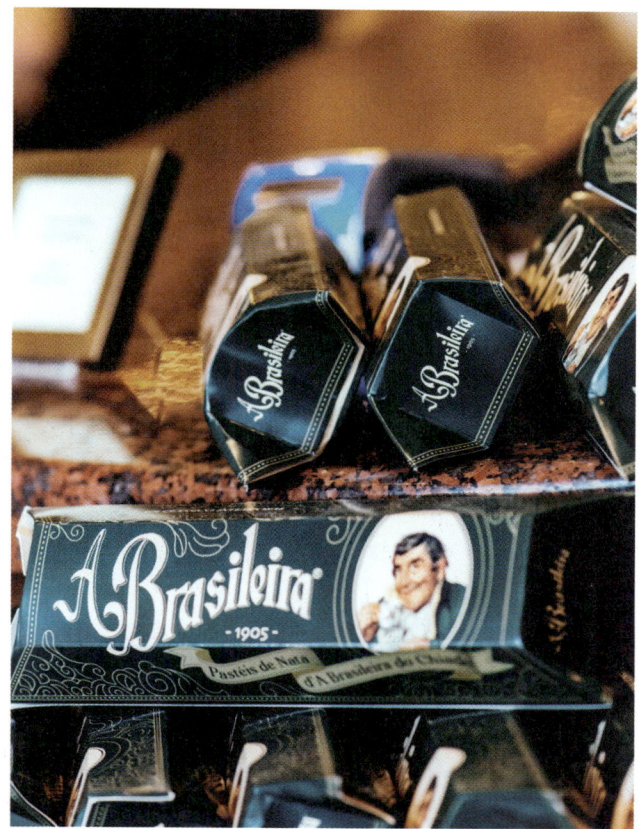
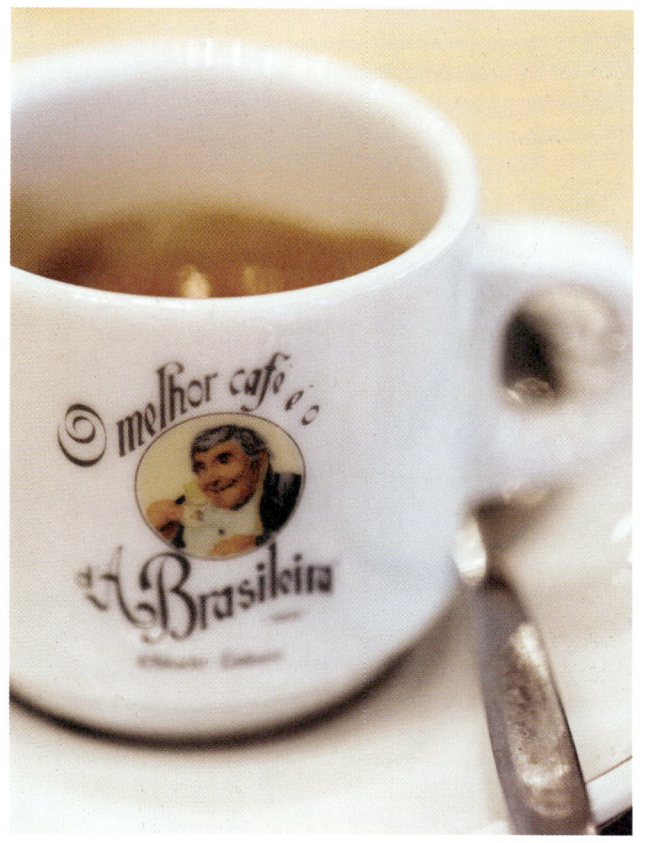
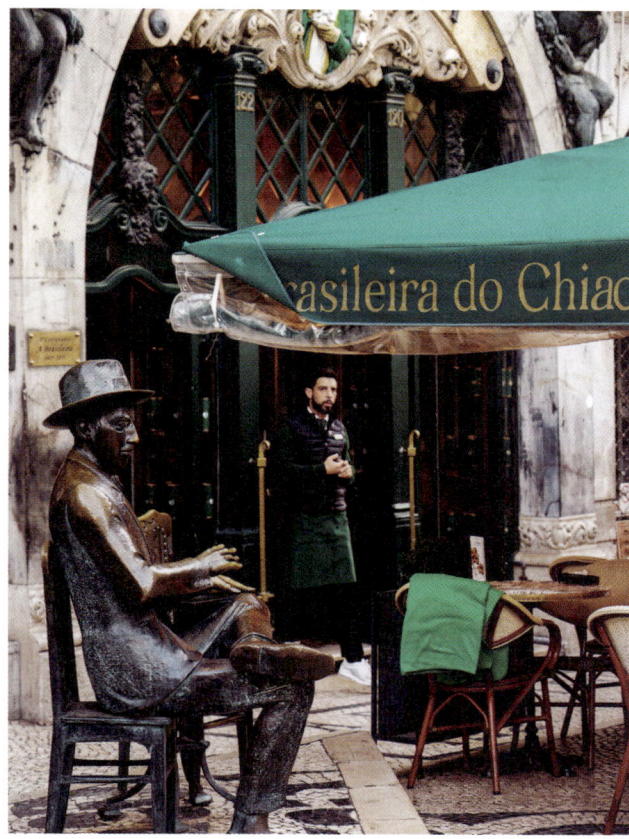

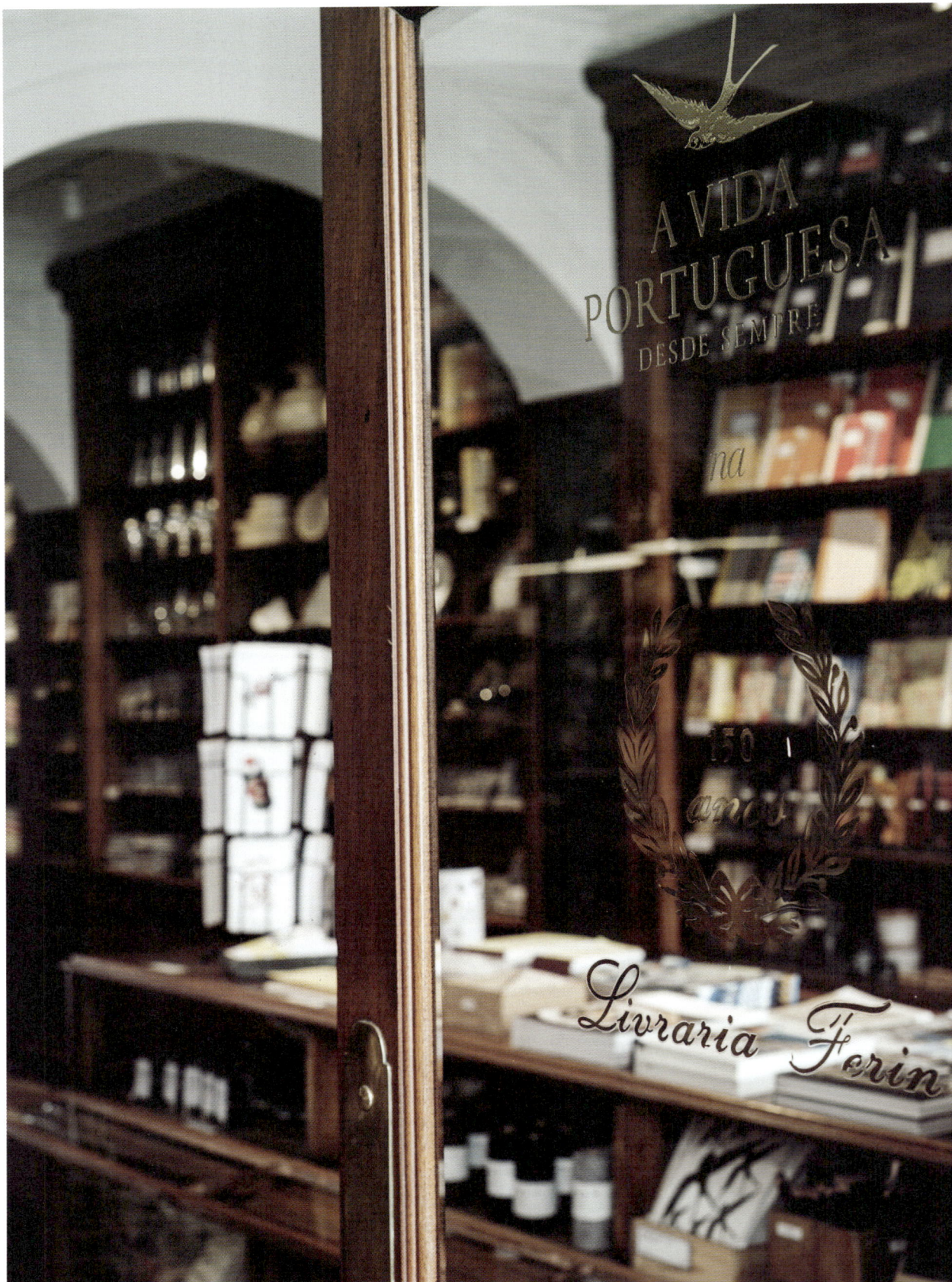

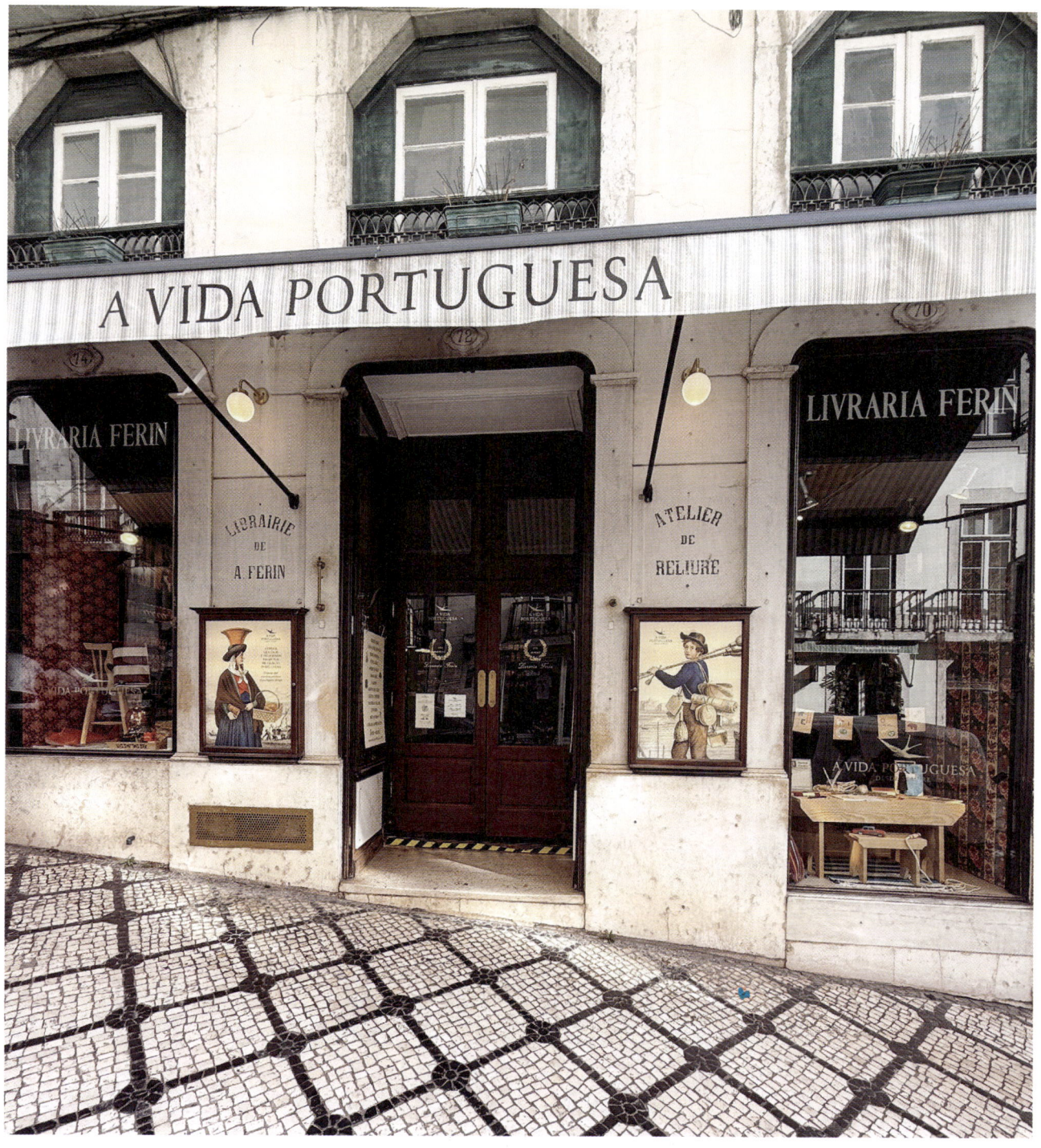

ABOVE AND LEFT: *Signature Portuguese paraphernalia on sale at the household-goods shop A Vida Portuguesa.*
Sardine tins and kitchen ceramics from an earlier generation's kitchen.

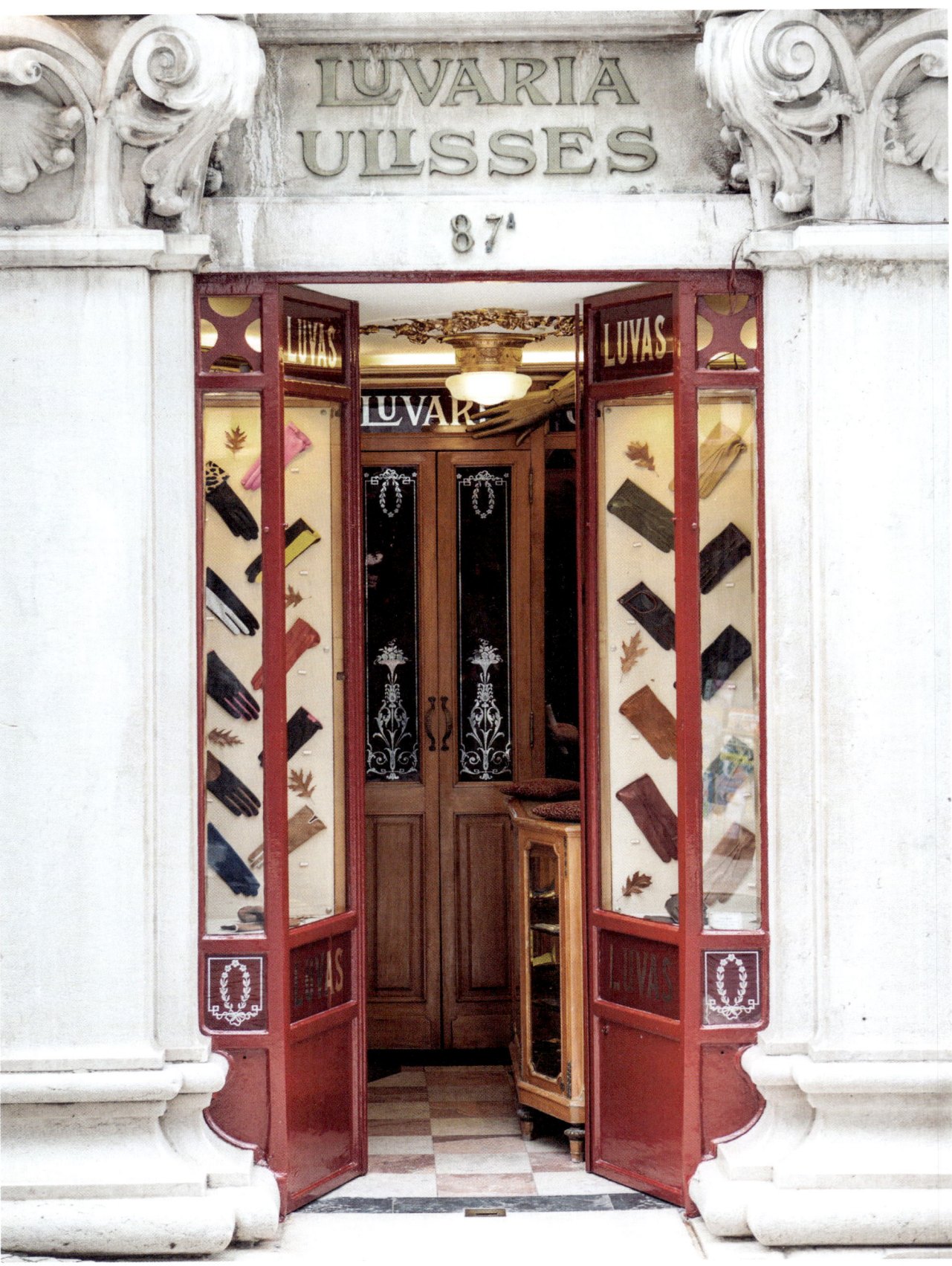

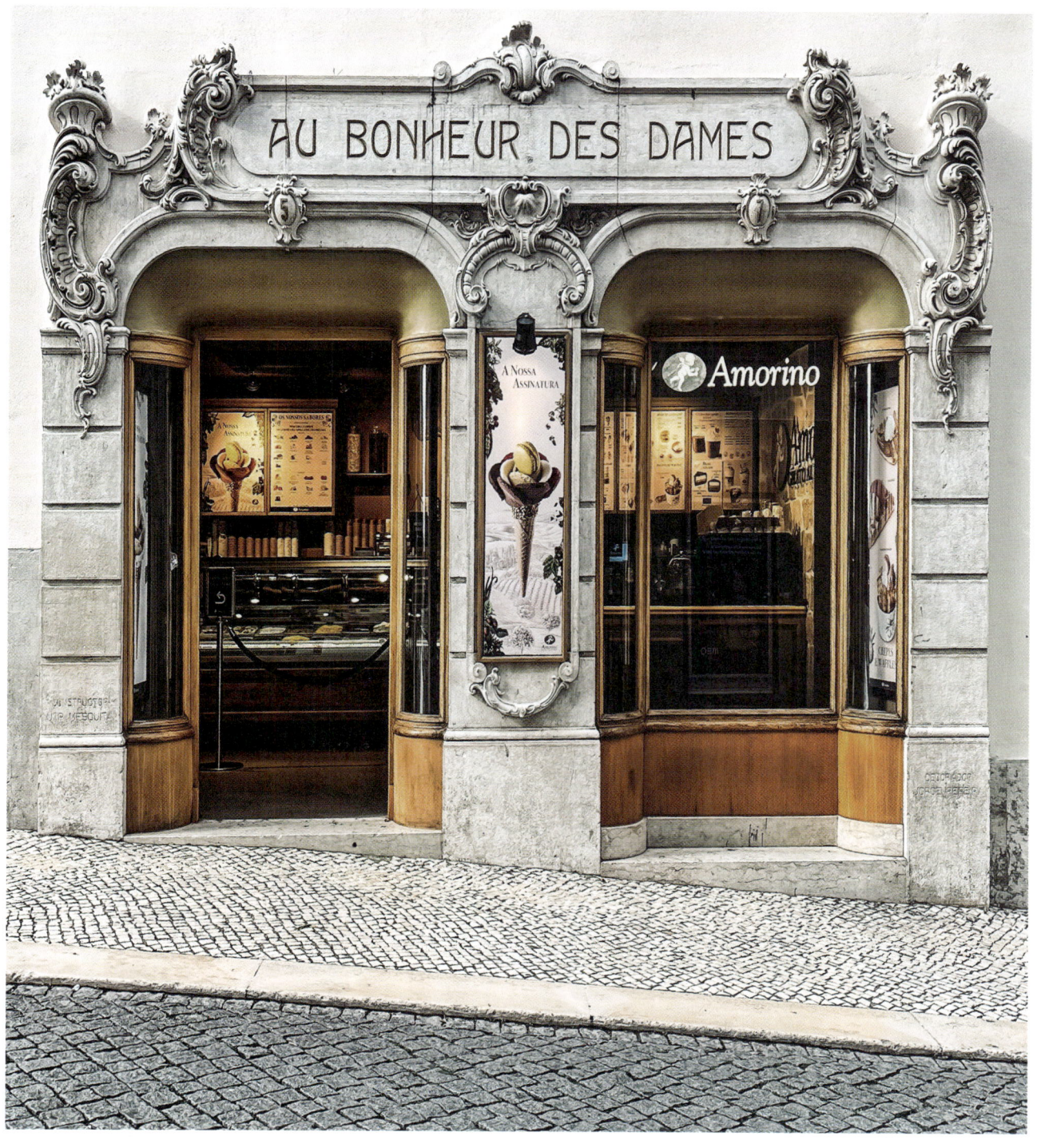

ABOVE AND LEFT: *Old establishments between Chiado and Baixa, like the glove maker Ulisses (left), with its recognizable traditional storefront. Sometimes it's only the exterior, though, like the ice-cream parlor now operating behind the ornate façade of a former luxury perfumery.*

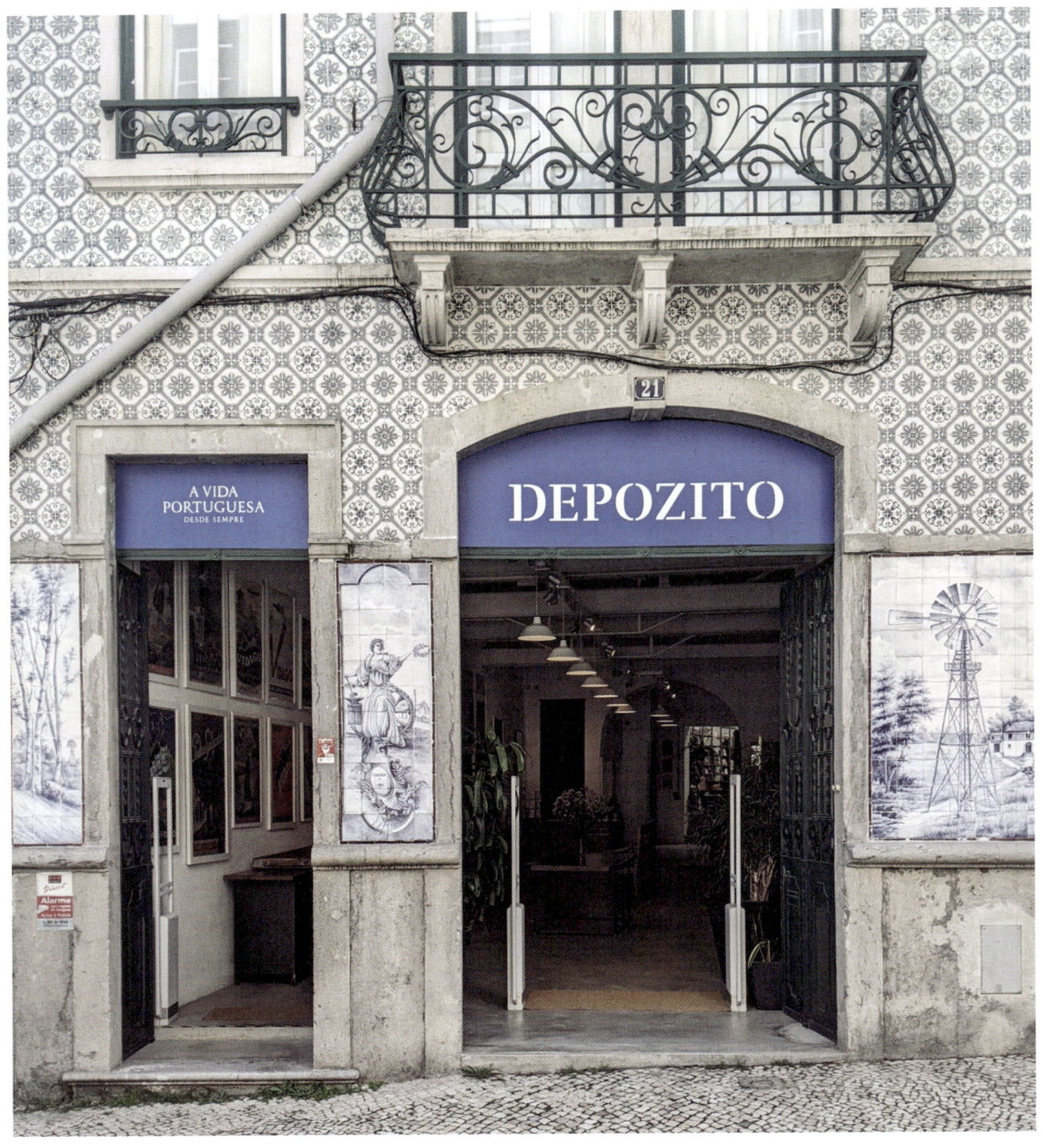

ABOVE AND RIGHT: *Sometimes the historic fabric can be retained and repurposed. In a former department store behind a façade of historic azulejos and wrought-iron gates is a branch of the household-goods store Depozito, which sells Portuguese crafts in a retro atmosphere.*

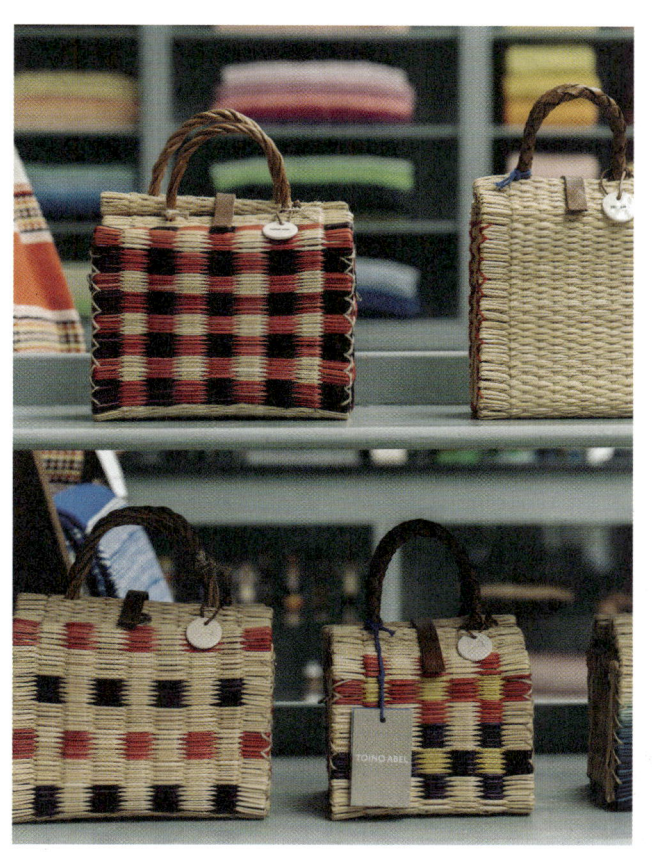
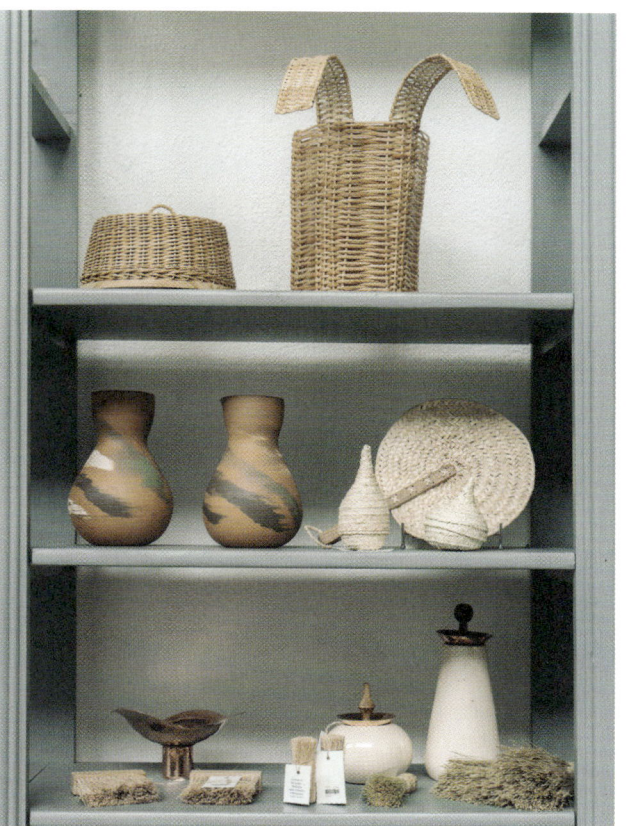

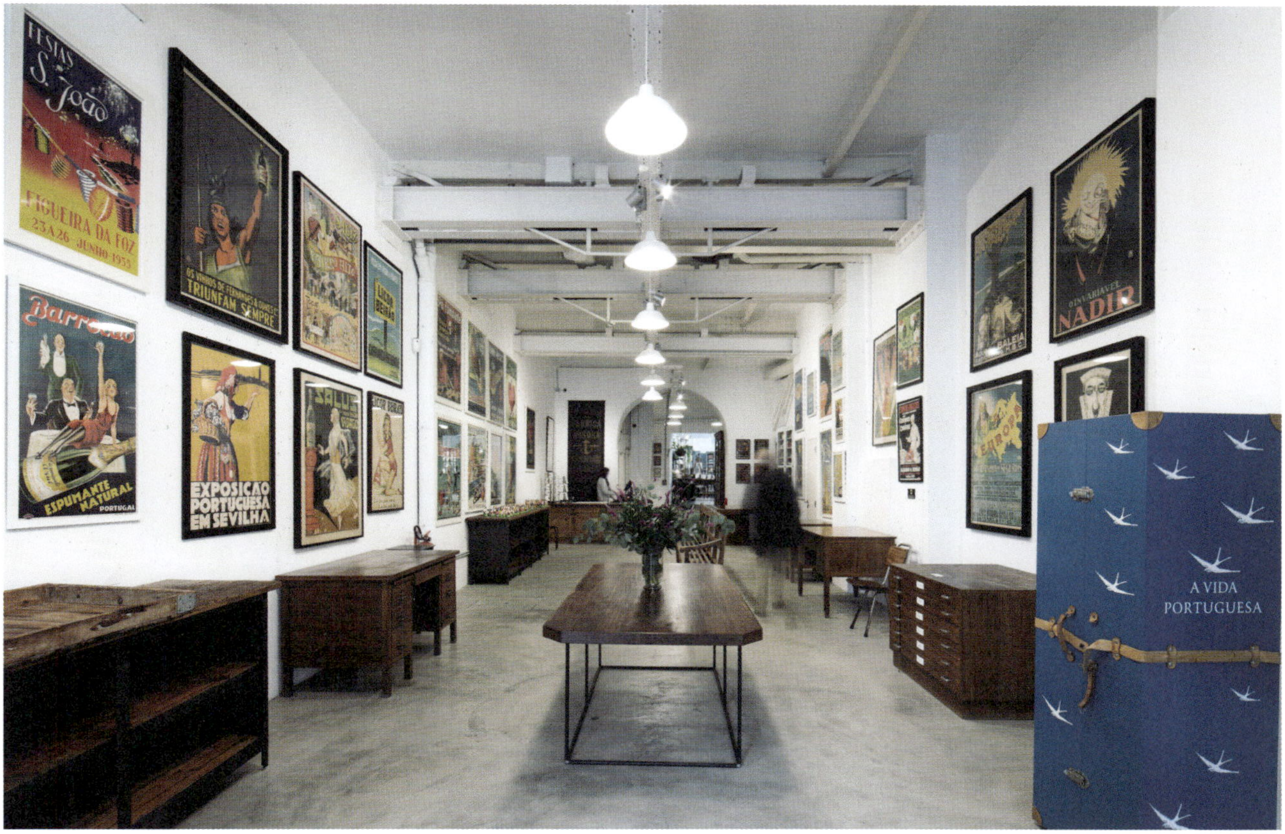

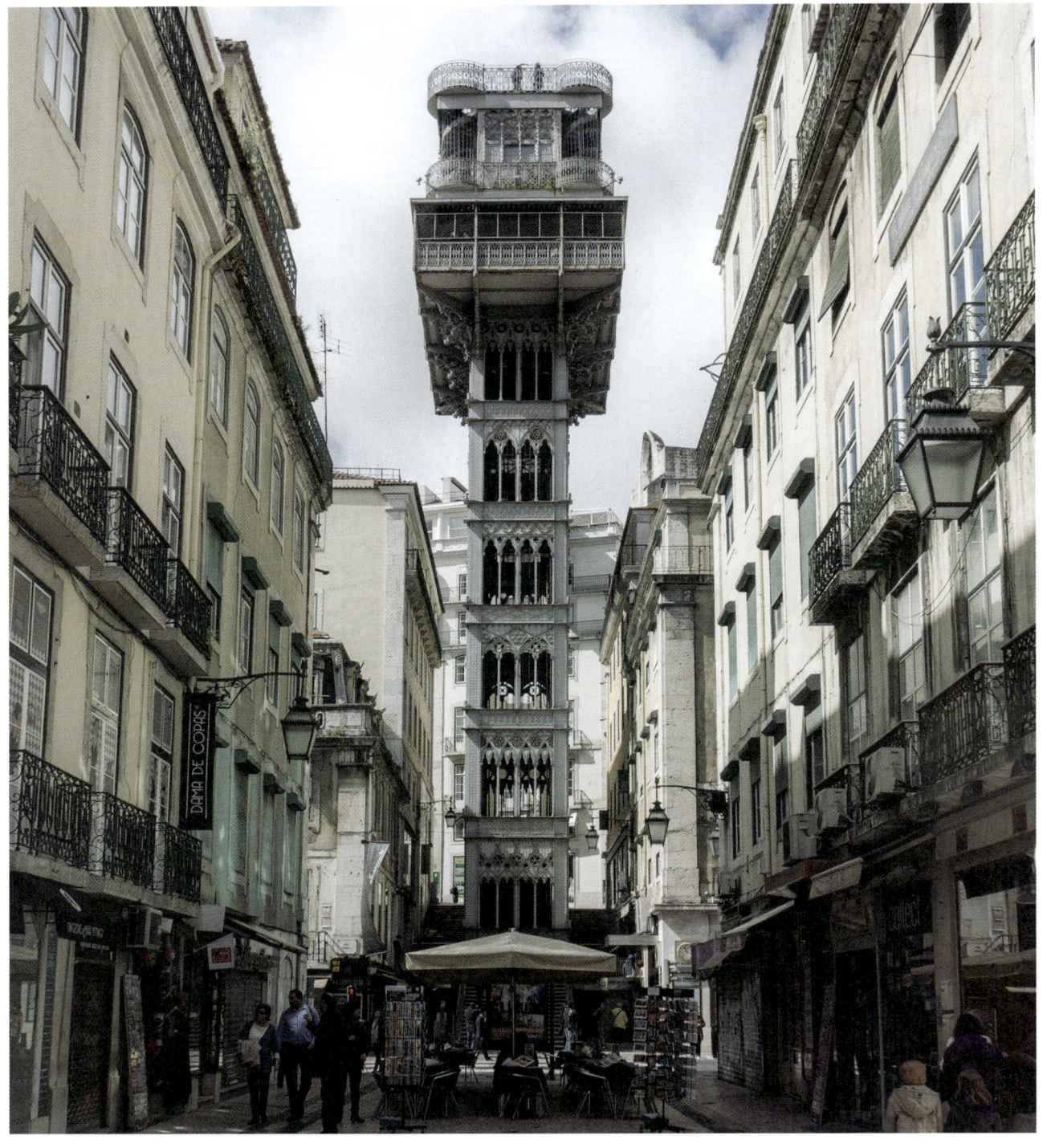

ABOVE: *The Elevador de Santa Justa links the lower city with Bairro Alto and Chiado. Its neo-Gothic structure remains striking more than 120 years after construction.*

RIGHT: *Small cafés throughout the neighborhood in Alfama. Places to break for shade and a galão or bica in an appealing interior.*

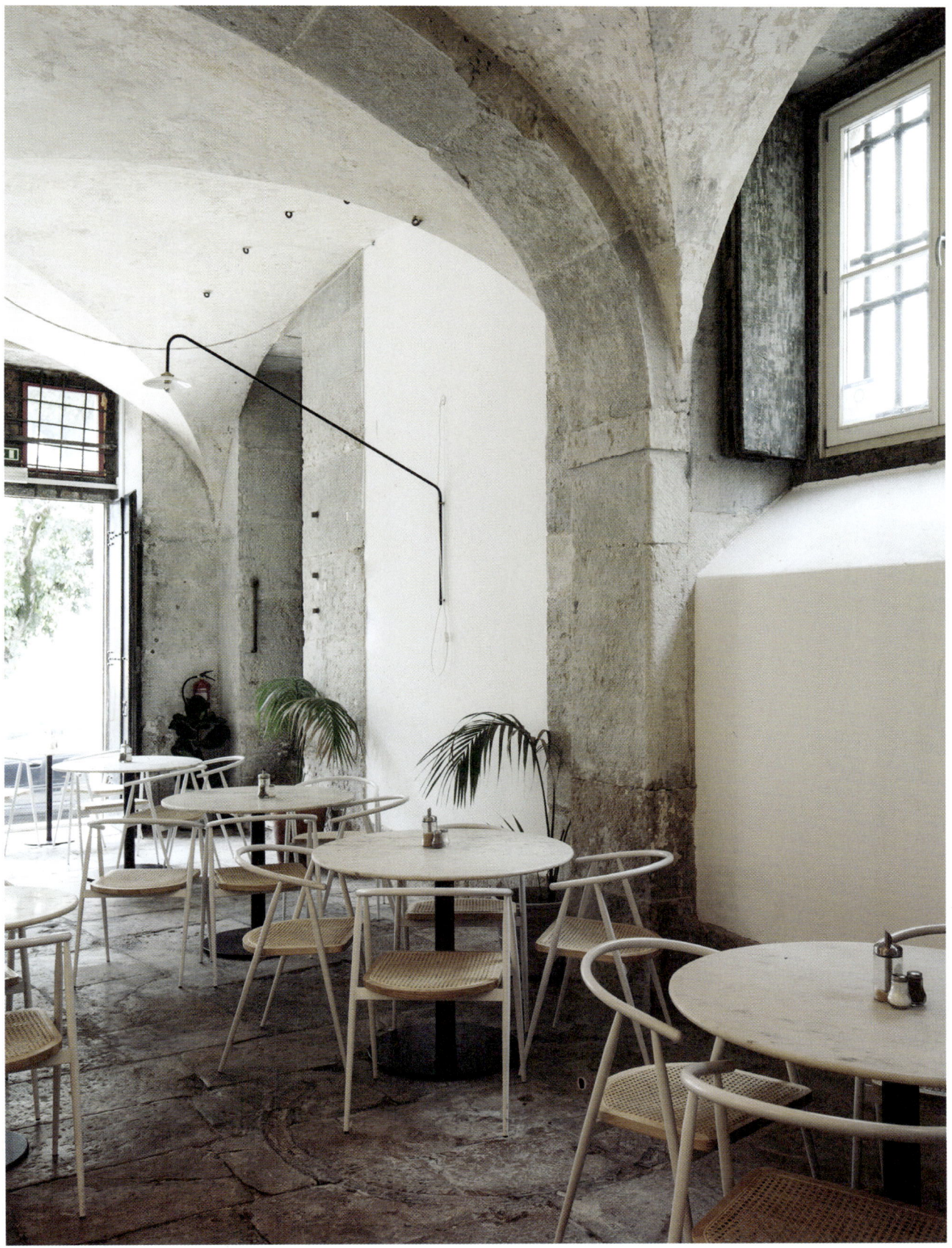

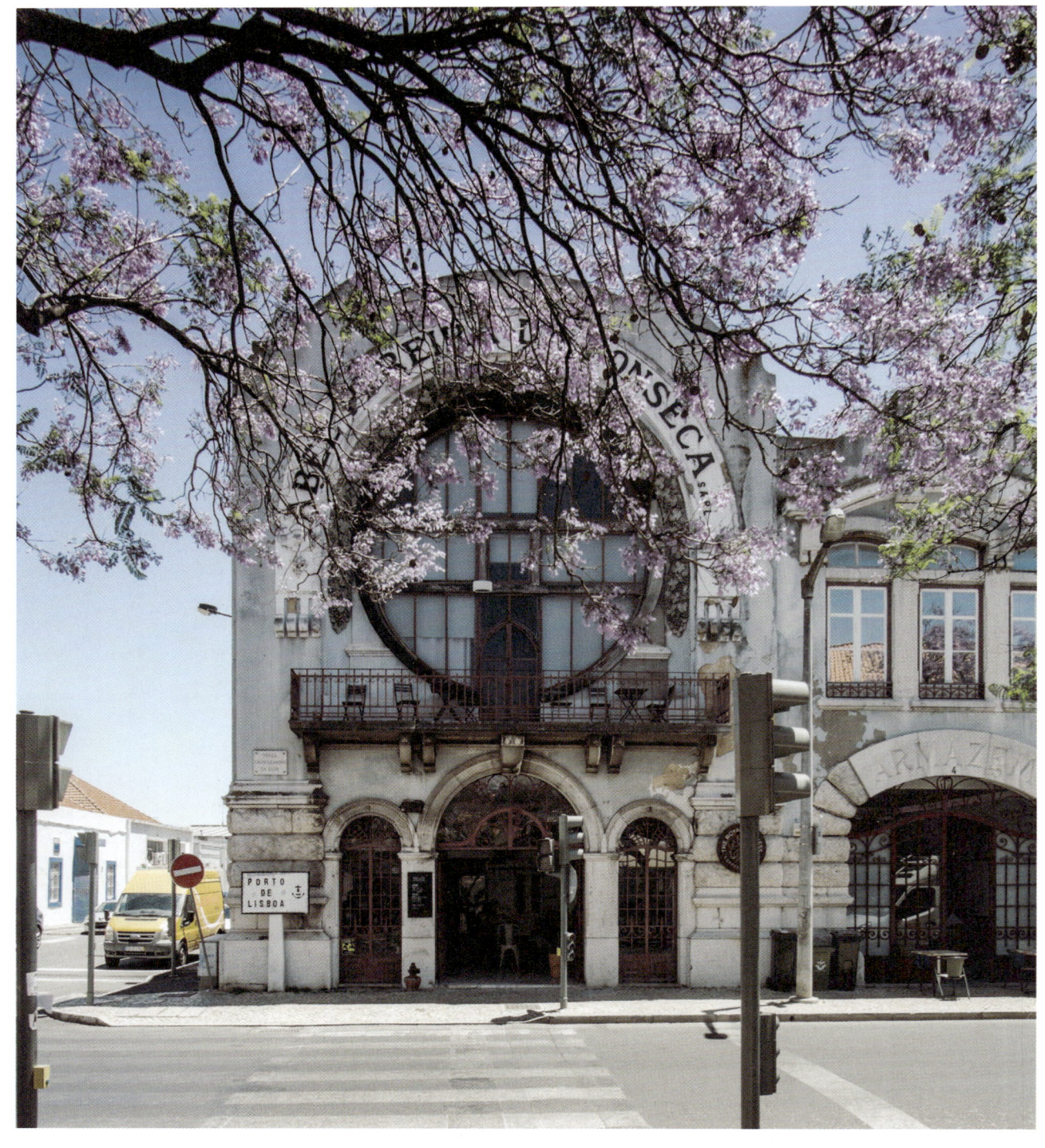

ABOVE AND RIGHT: *Past industrial uses are juxtaposed against modern culture in the Abel Pereira da Fonseca building in Marvila, an Art Nouveau warehouse from 1917 now home to a cultural center. Behind the historic façade are cafés and restaurants.*

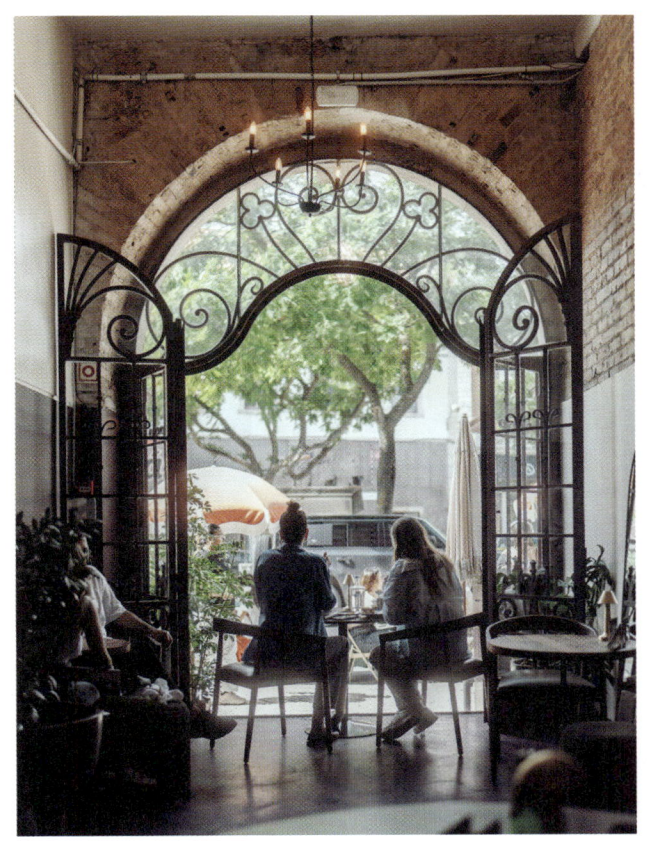
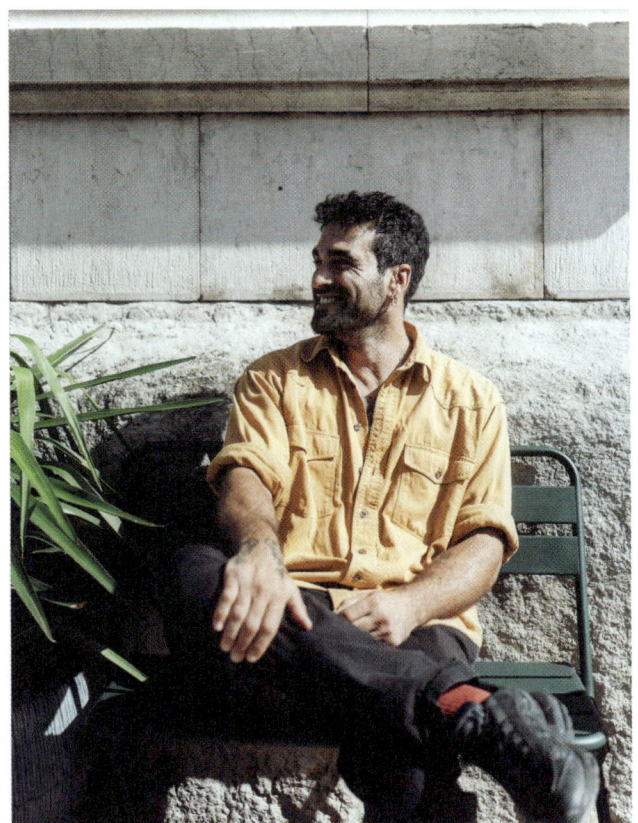
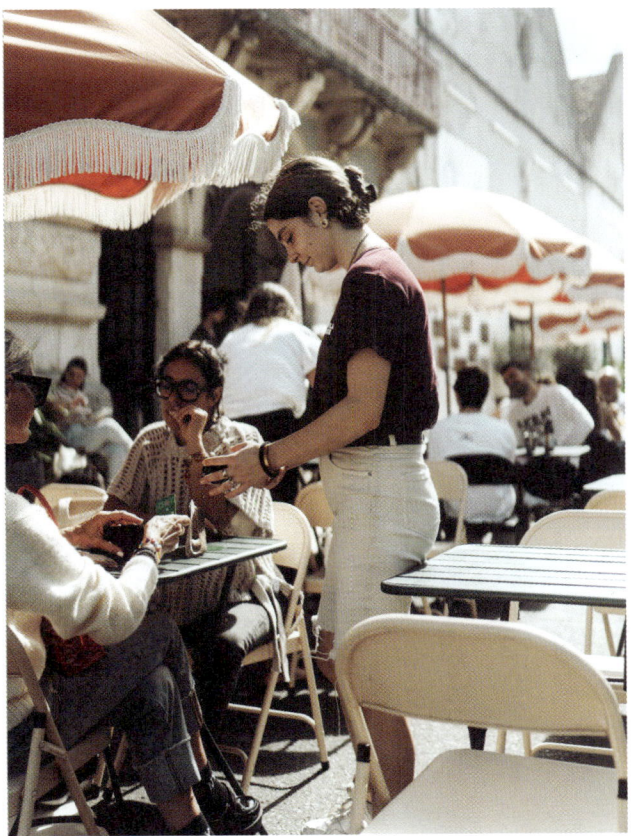
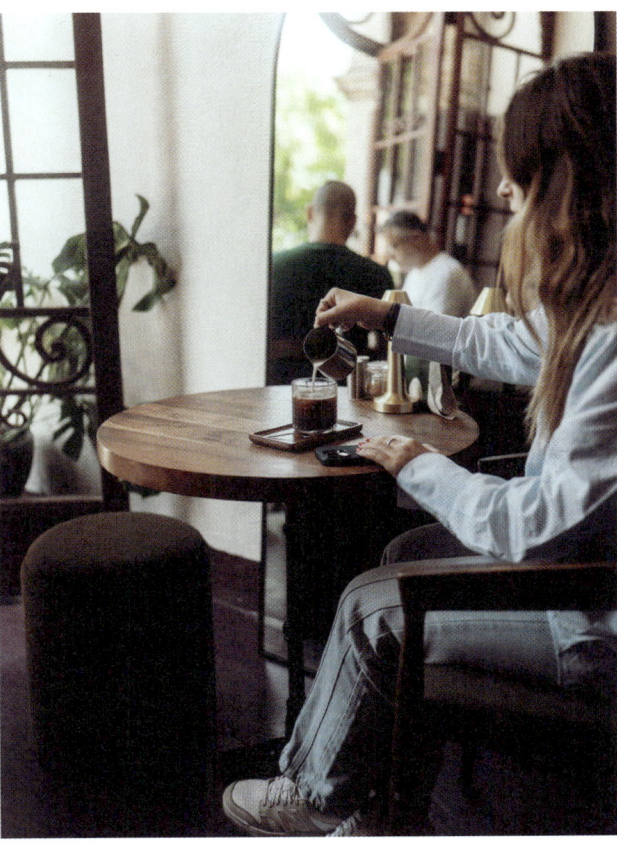

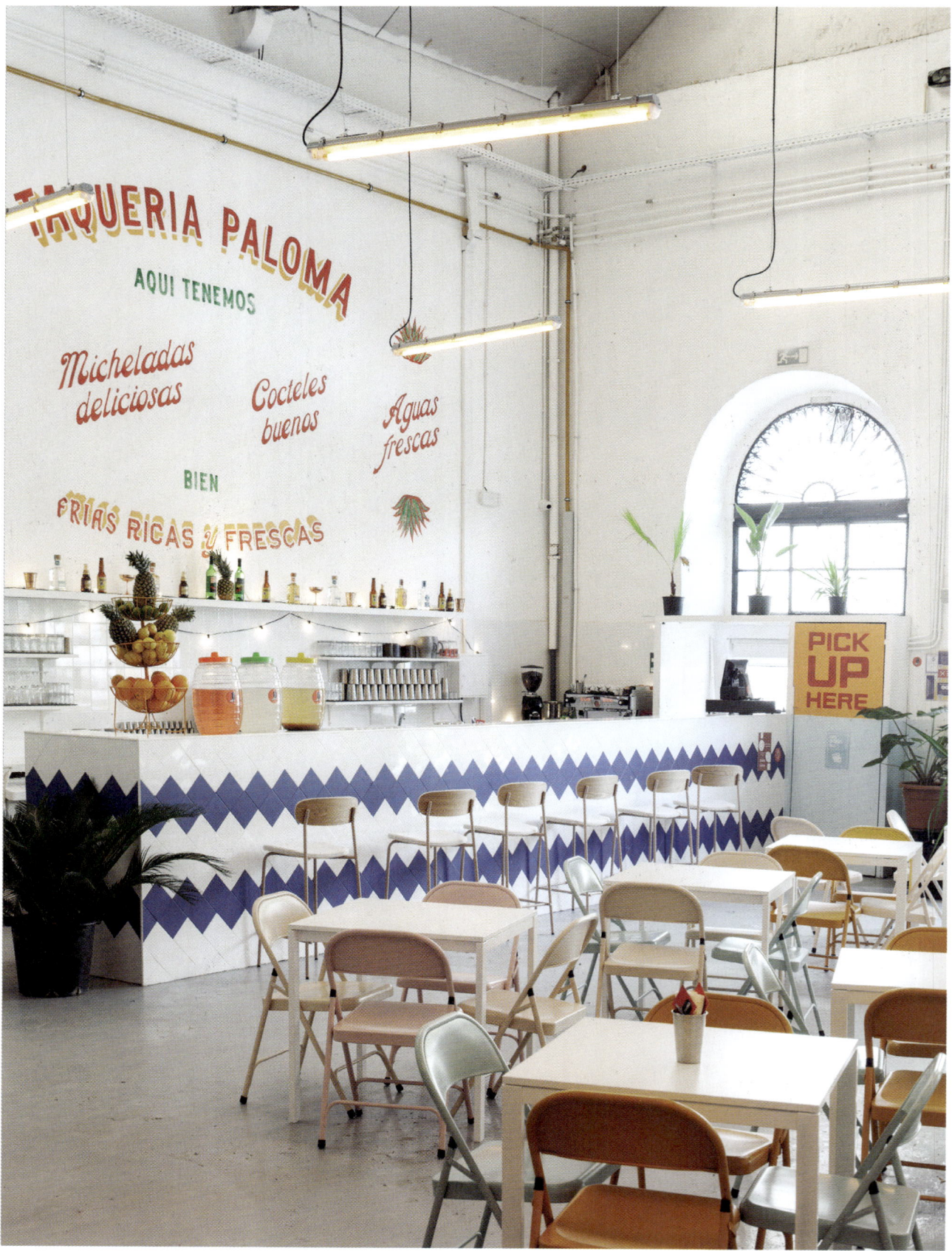

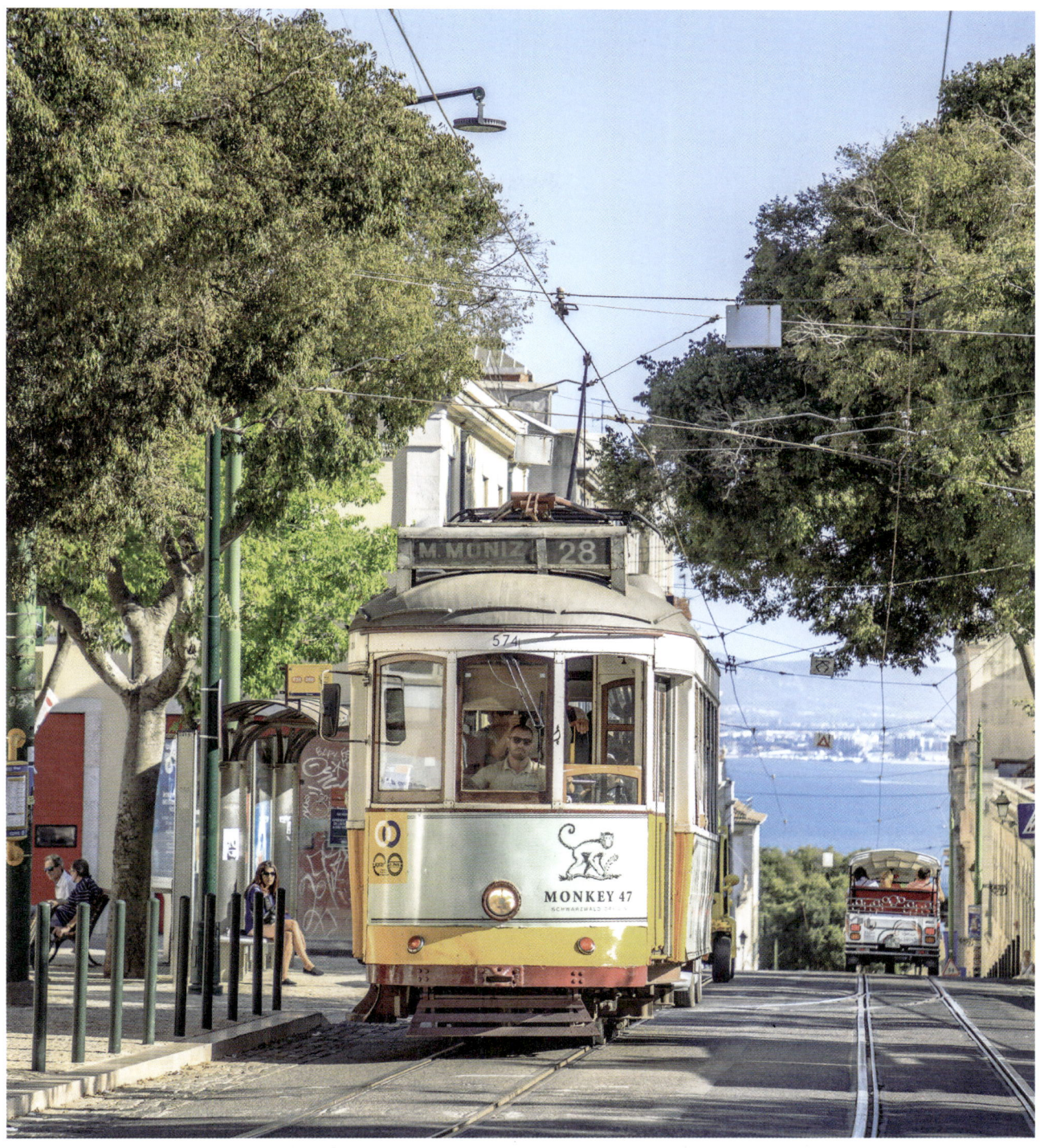

ABOVE: *Every day in Lisbon, sightseeing by tram. Line 28E threads through unusually narrow streets, passing many old-town landmarks along the way.*

LEFT: *The former warehouses of Marvila in northern Lisbon have been converted into bright gathering places with restaurants and bars. Tacos and cocktails are now served where there used to be wine by the barrel.*

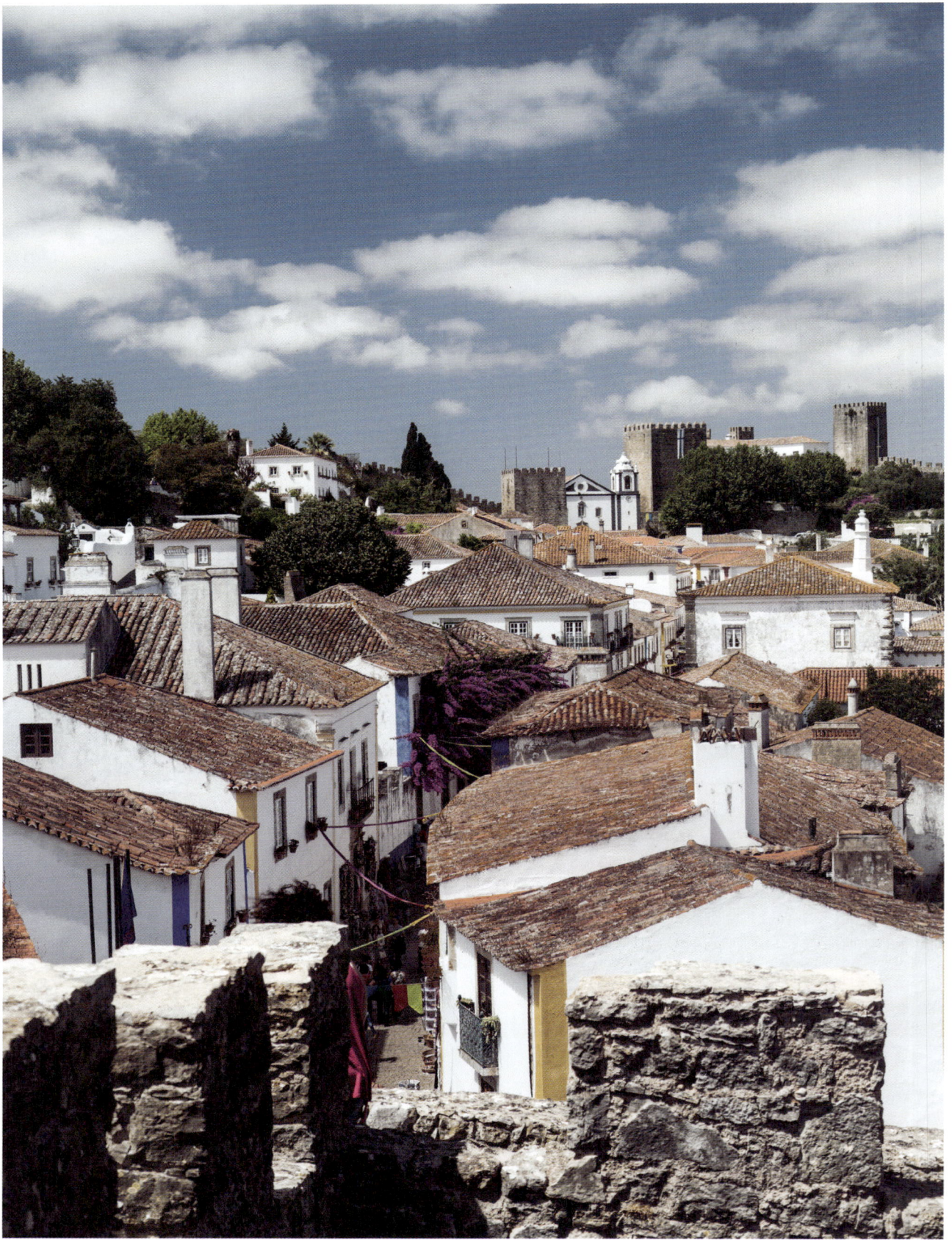

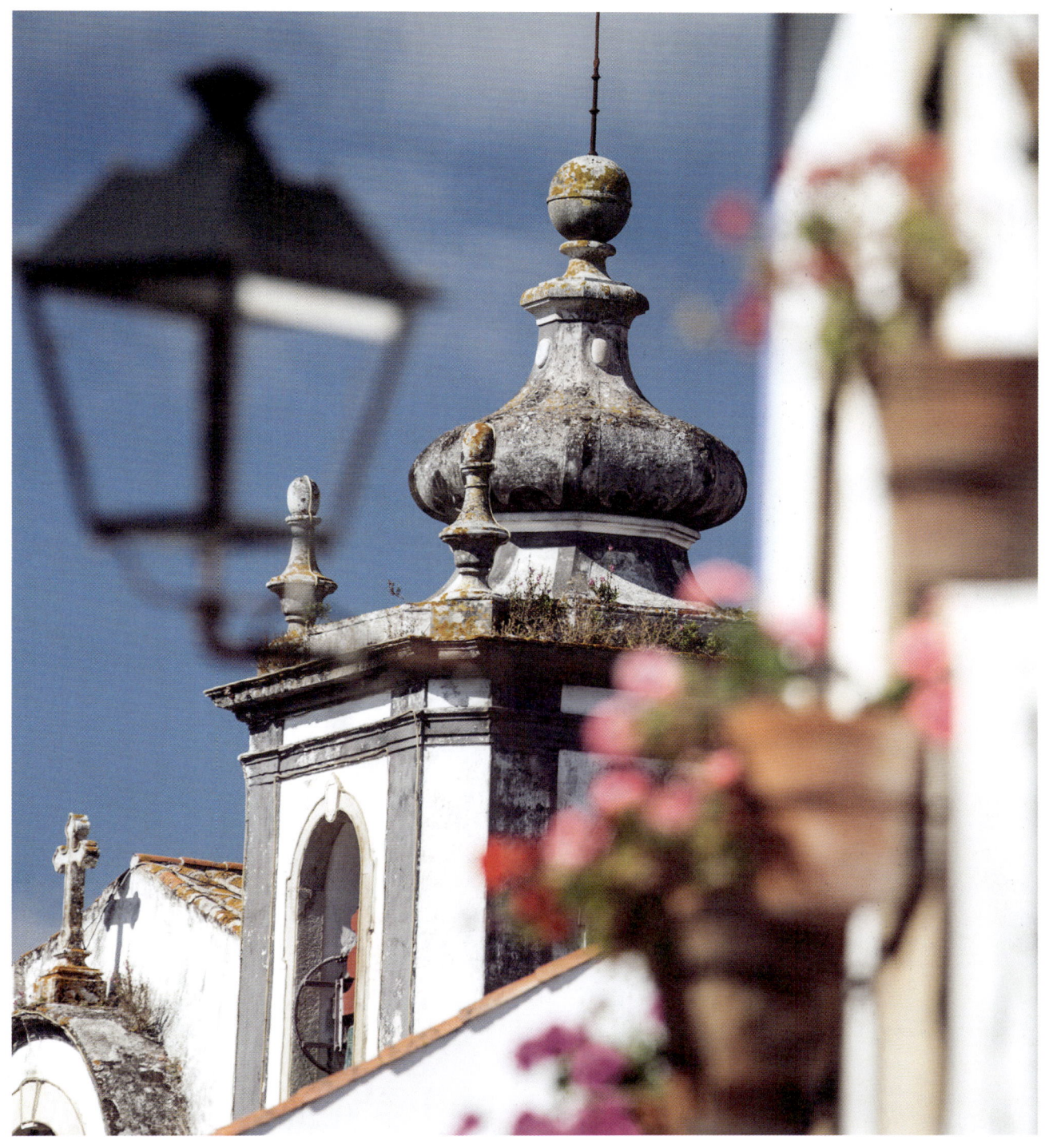

ABOVE AND LEFT: *North of Lisbon, Óbidos is completely enclosed by a ring of medieval walls. It's a tight squeeze for whitewashed houses and the Igreja de São Pedro (above).*

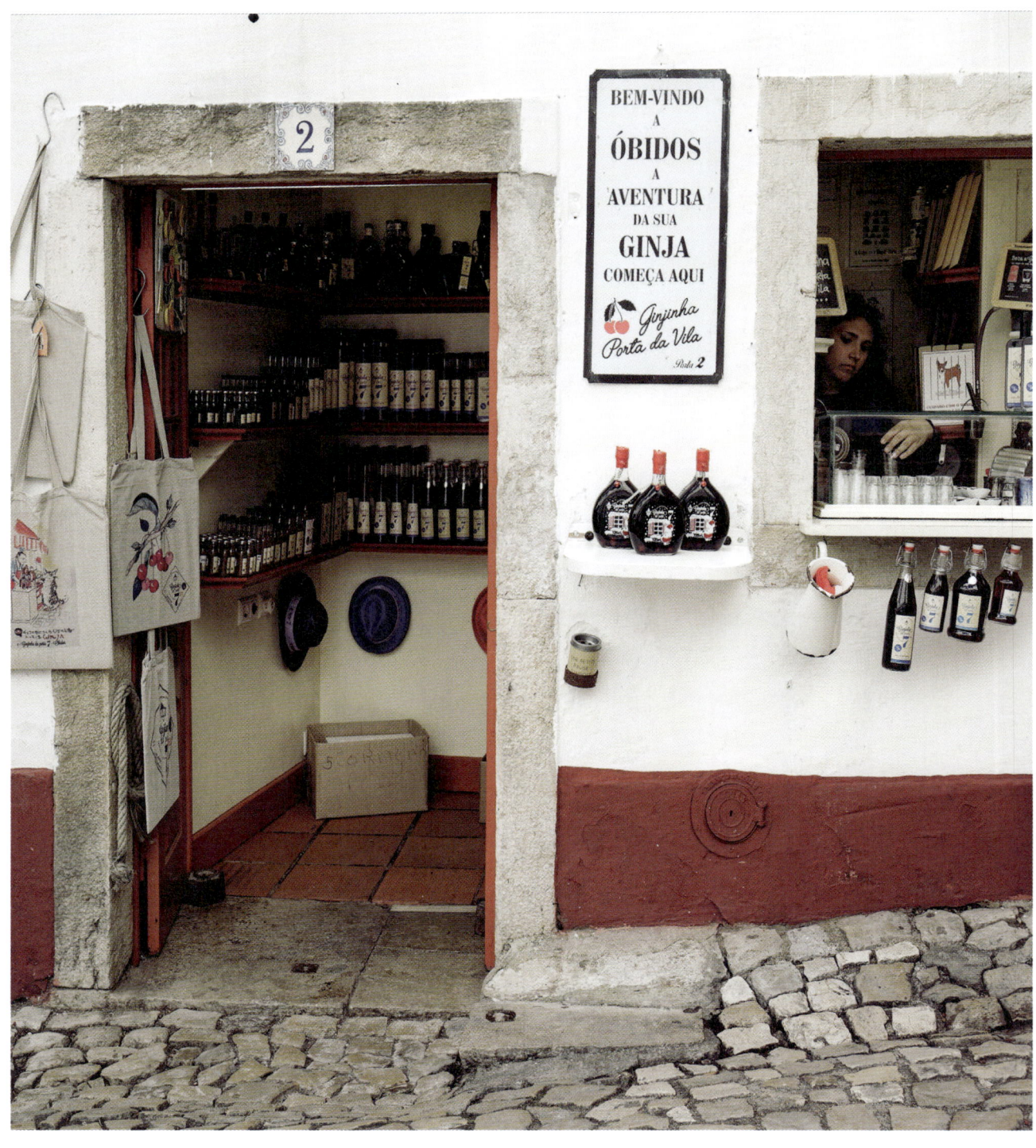

ABOVE AND RIGHT: *Óbidos has preserved its medieval character. Narrow streets contain details such as azulejos in the town gate (right, top left). For centuries, the town formed part of the queens' dowries of Portugal—making it all the more alluring.*

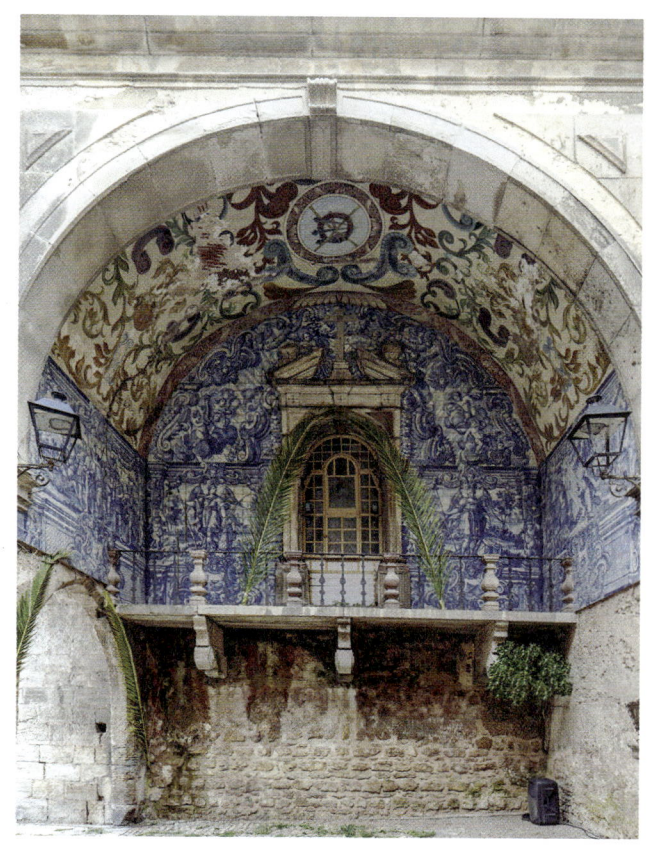
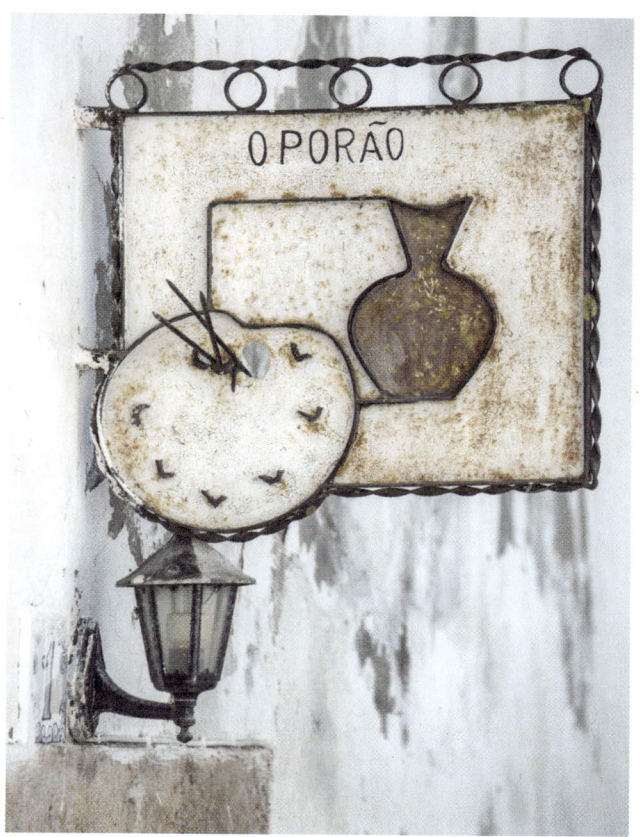
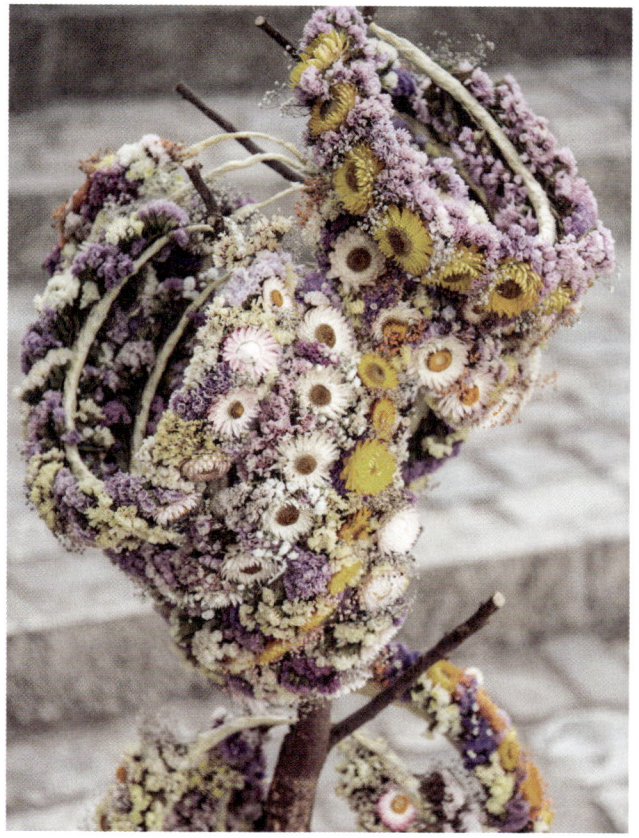
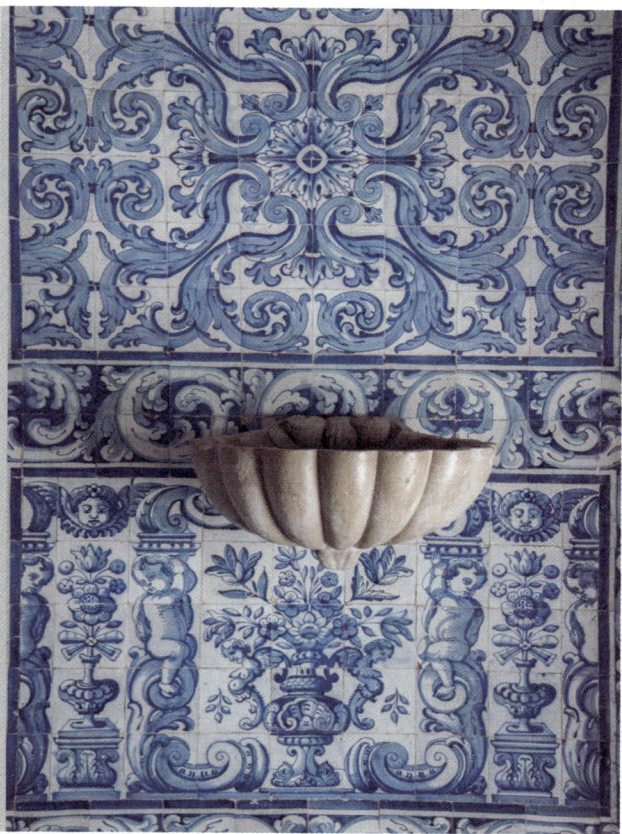

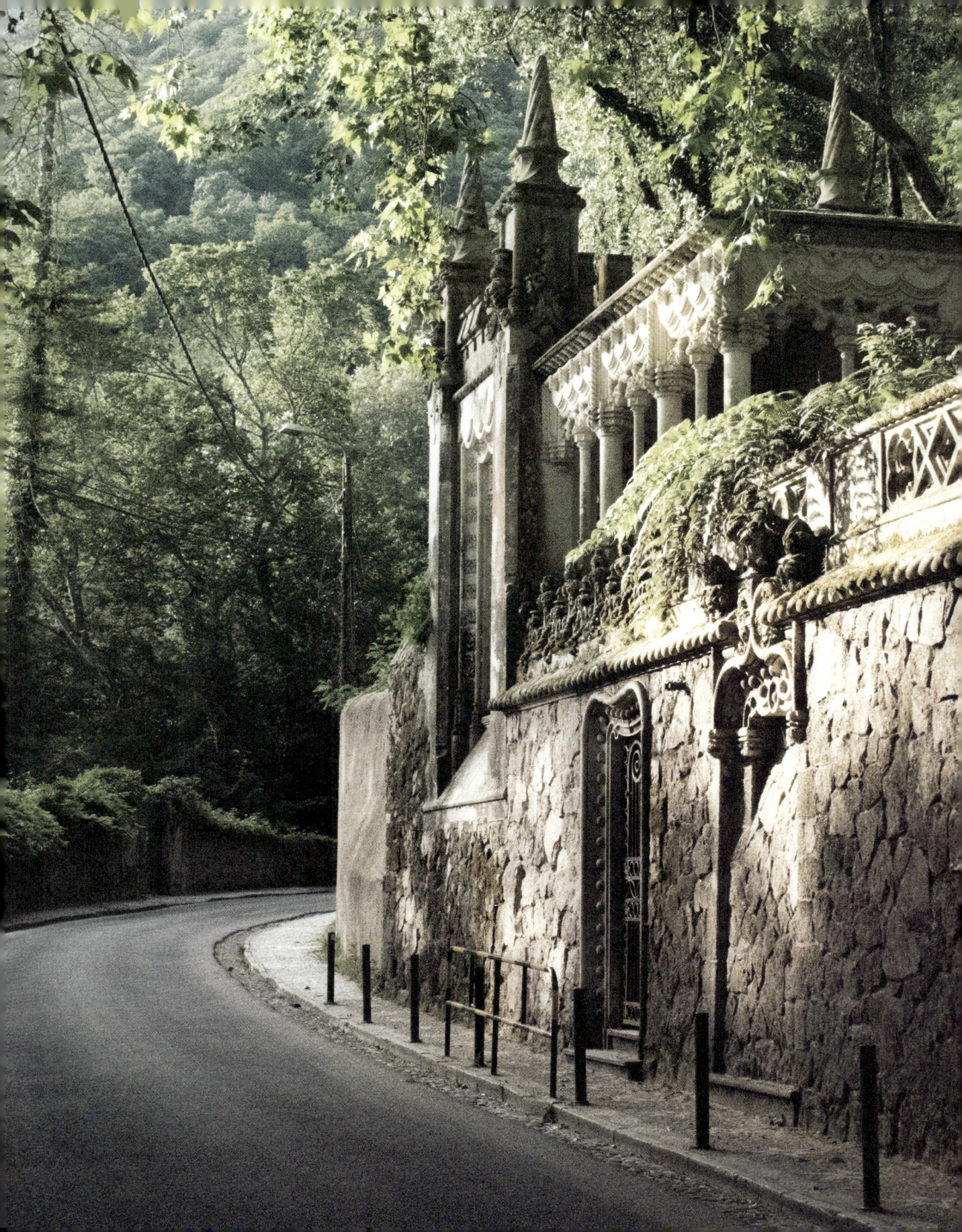

GARDENS & PARKS

PORTUGAL TELLS ITS HISTORY NOT ONLY THROUGH MONASTERIES, CATHEDRALS, AND PALACES, BUT ALSO THROUGH GARDENS AND FORESTS THAT CARRY THE PAST INTO THE PRESENT

Over the centuries, Portuguese sailors and botanists brought plants home from far-flung parts of the world. In central Portugal, more than 700 species of trees and shrubs came together to form the National Forest of Buçaco. A Carmelite monastery once enclosed the forest behind a massive wall, turning it into one of the world's earliest protected landscapes. A papal decree from 1643 forbade the felling of even a single tree—on pain of death. Prayer stations and small grottoes are still scattered through the woods. A small waterfall runs down the stonework at the center of the stepped Fonte Fria, the "Cold Spring," bringing welcome coolness on hot days. The gardens of Quinta da Regaleira in Sintra form a green fairy-tale world, carefully designed and slightly unsettling. Along winding paths stand statues and finely carved structures, and at the center a deep enigmatic well drops in a spiral like an inverted tower. It feels ancient, yet it was created only in the early twentieth century by the eccentric coffee magnate António Monteiro. Even in Portugal's dense cities, green spaces remain part of the urban fabric. In Lisbon, the jacaranda bloom plays a role similar to the cherry blossom in Japan. For a few weeks, Avenida da Liberdade and the otherwise spare Largo do Carmo, in front of the ruins of the Gothic church, turn into a haze of purple. In Porto, the Jardins do Palácio de Cristal open onto views of the Douro from the Miradouro da Ponte da Arrábida. At Serralves, garden spaces linked by paths and fountains unfold around the pink Art Deco villa, creating shifting views at every turn.

LEFT: *The gardens of Quinta da Regaleira in Sintra contain a range of symbolic structures, including a dry well, enigmatic pavilions, and chapels marked by Masonic imagery.*

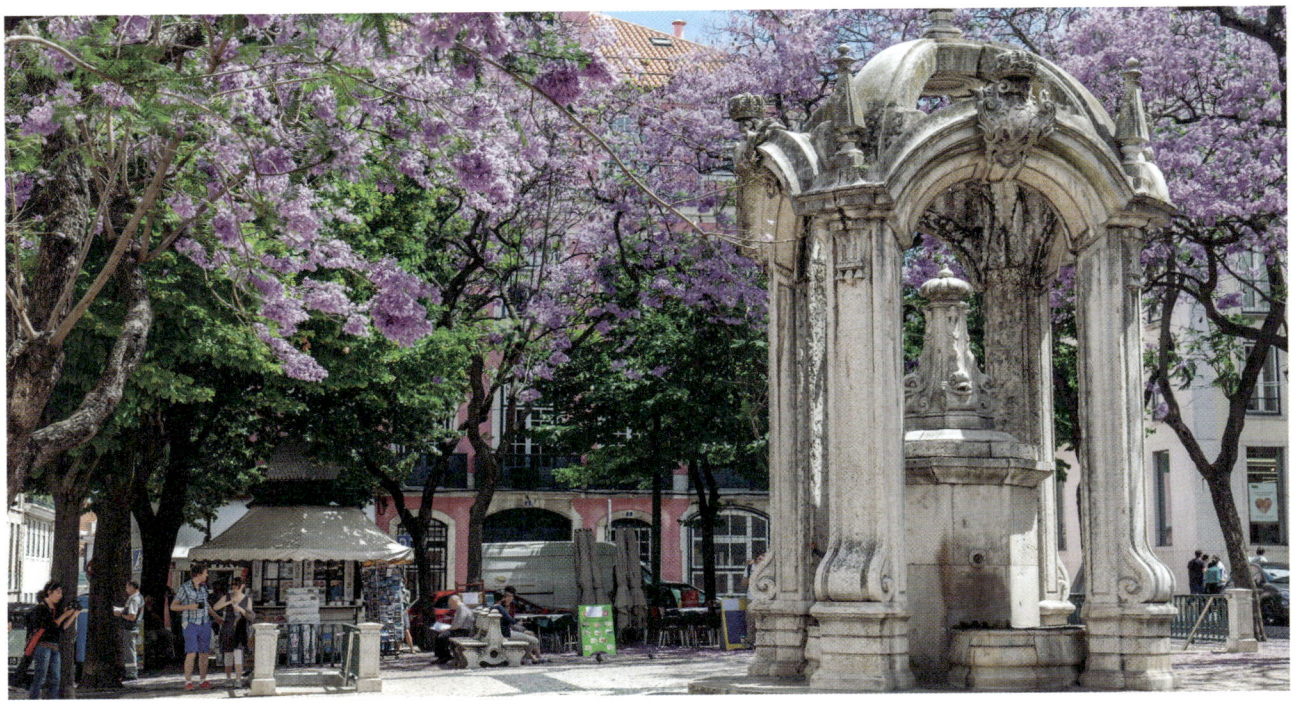

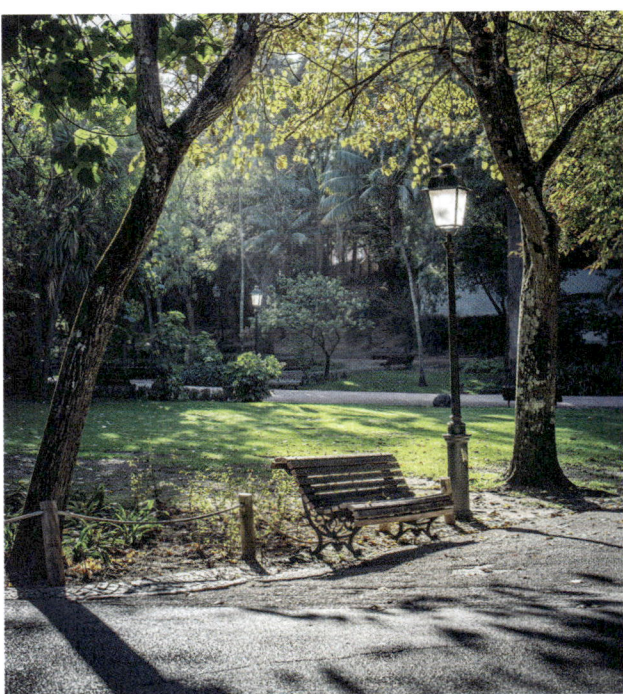

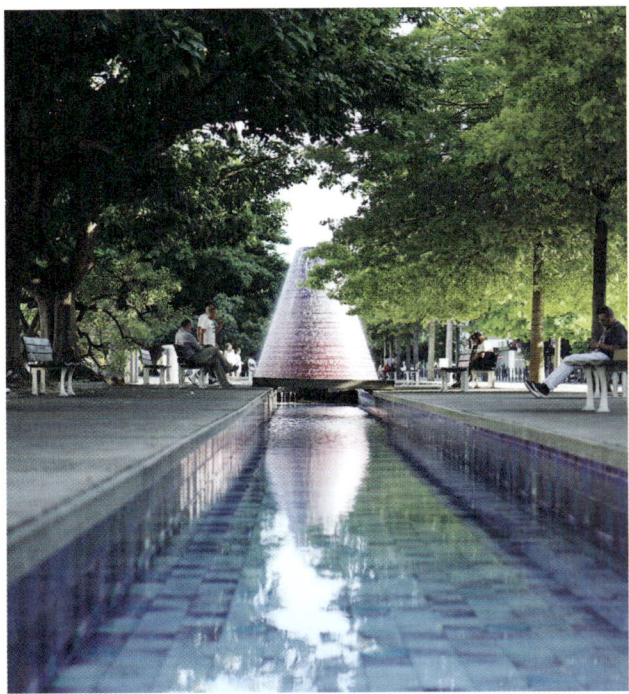

ABOVE: *Jacaranda trees surround the Largo do Carmo, casting a pale violet hue around the eighteenth-century Baroque fountain. Parque das Nações was created on the former grounds of Expo 98. One of its features is the water volcano (bottom right).*

RIGHT: *In the Buçaco National Forest, a stone staircase runs alongside dense vegetation. A small waterfall descends in shallow cascades, offering relief on hot days.*

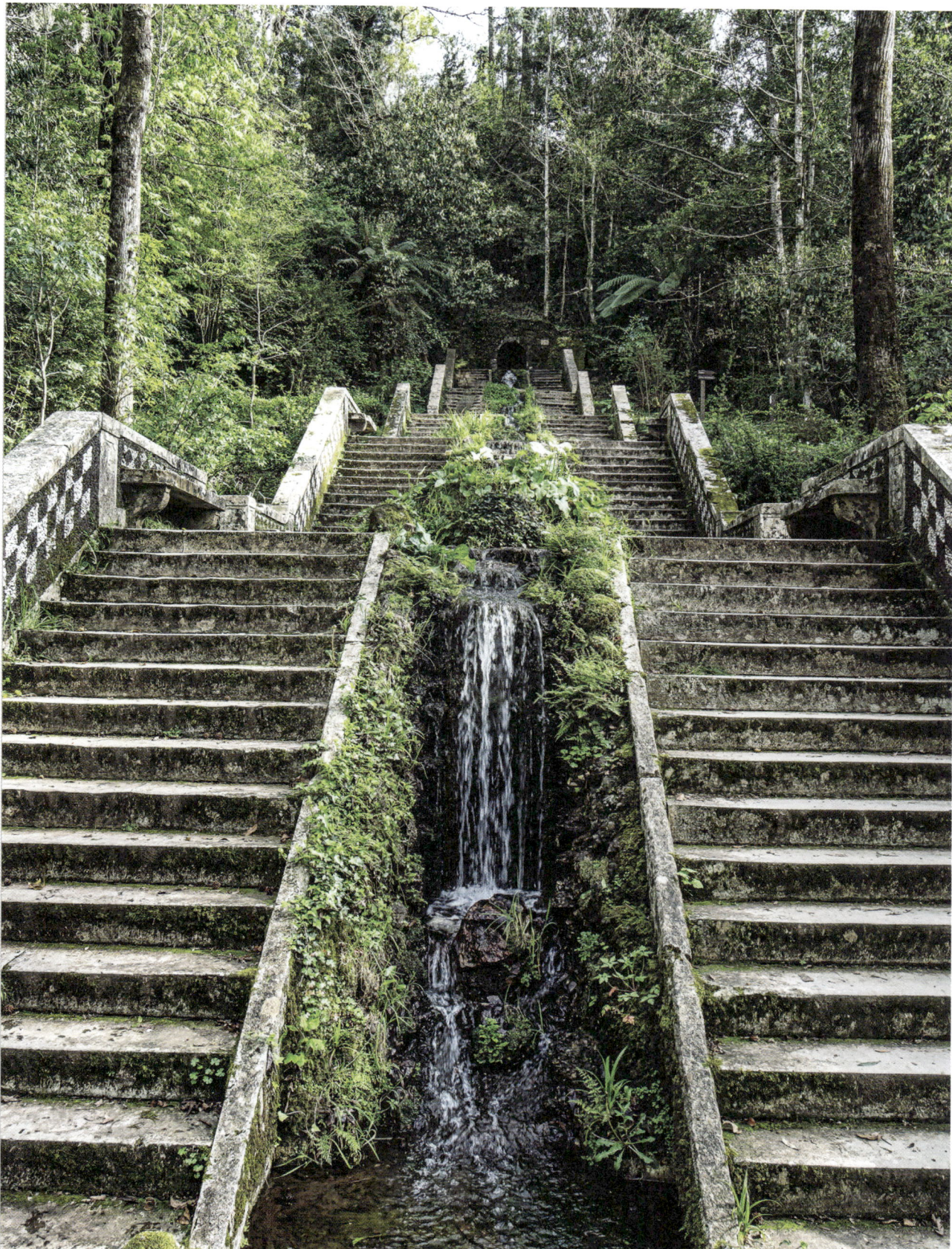

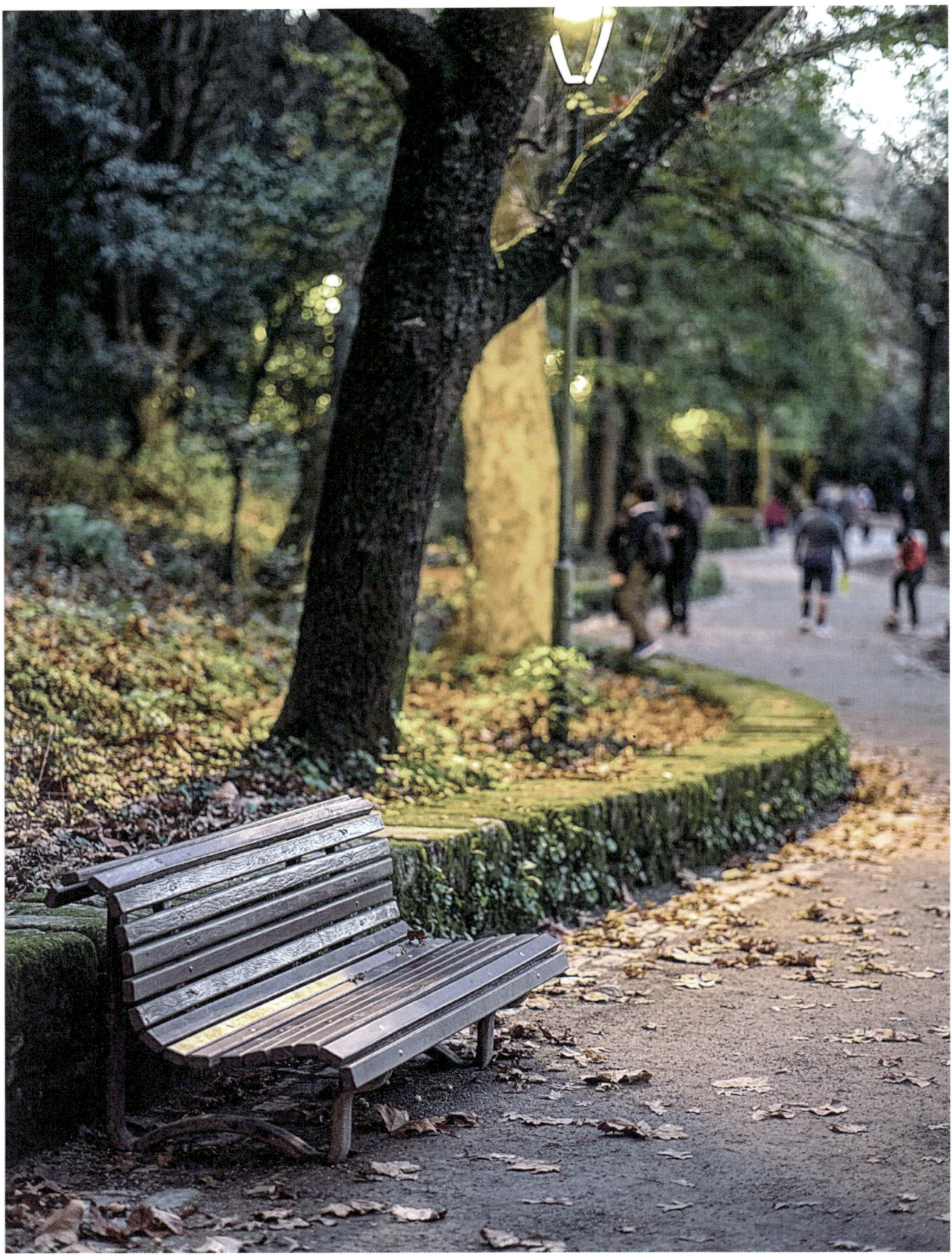

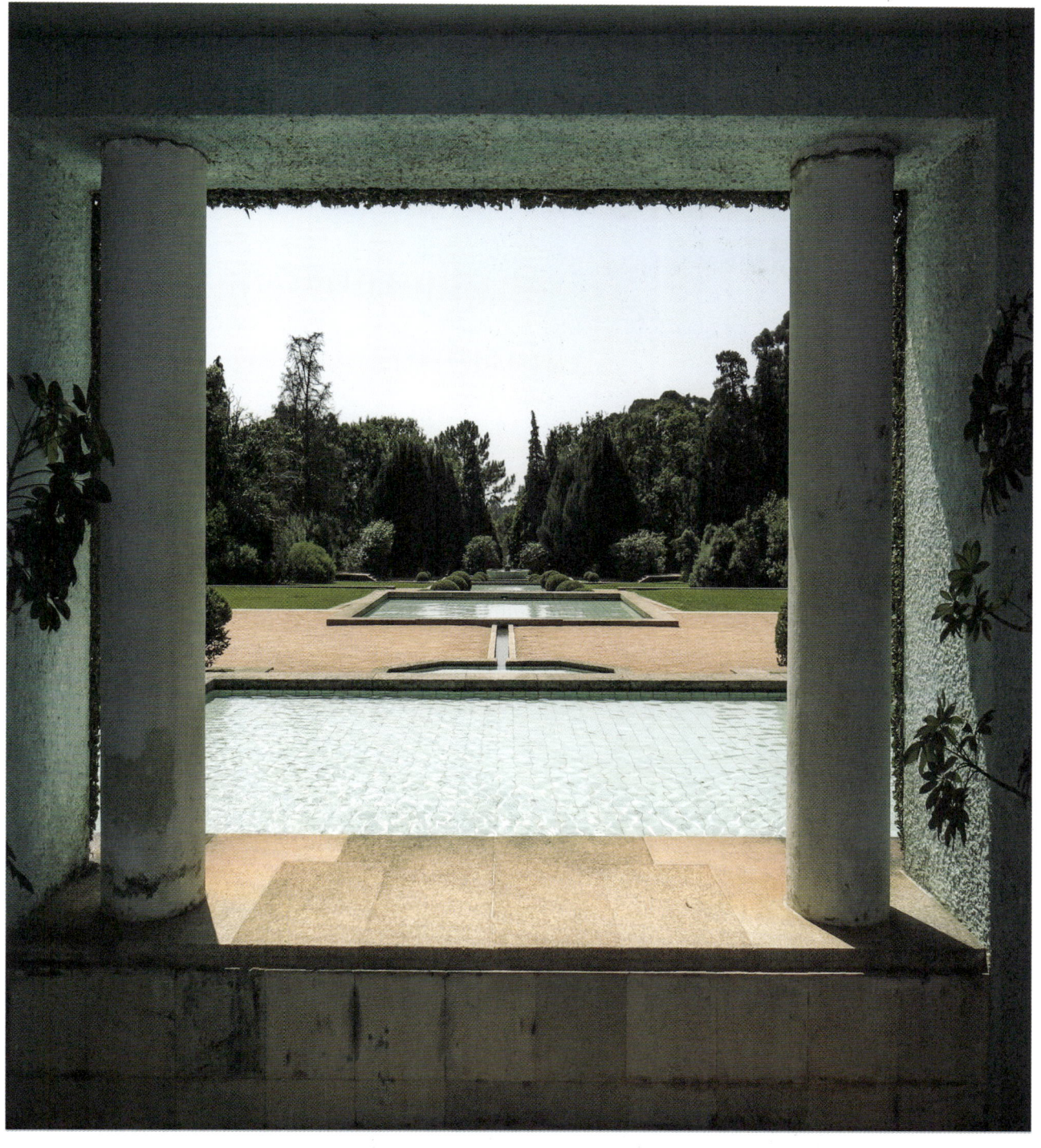

ABOVE: *The gardens surrounding Porto's Art Deco Casa Serralves, now a museum, are structured around shifting sightlines, with fountains, tree-lined paths, and labyrinthine hedges.*

LEFT: *Porto's city park, in the northern part of town, is the largest park in Portugal. Benches throughout the grounds provide shaded resting places beneath tall trees.*

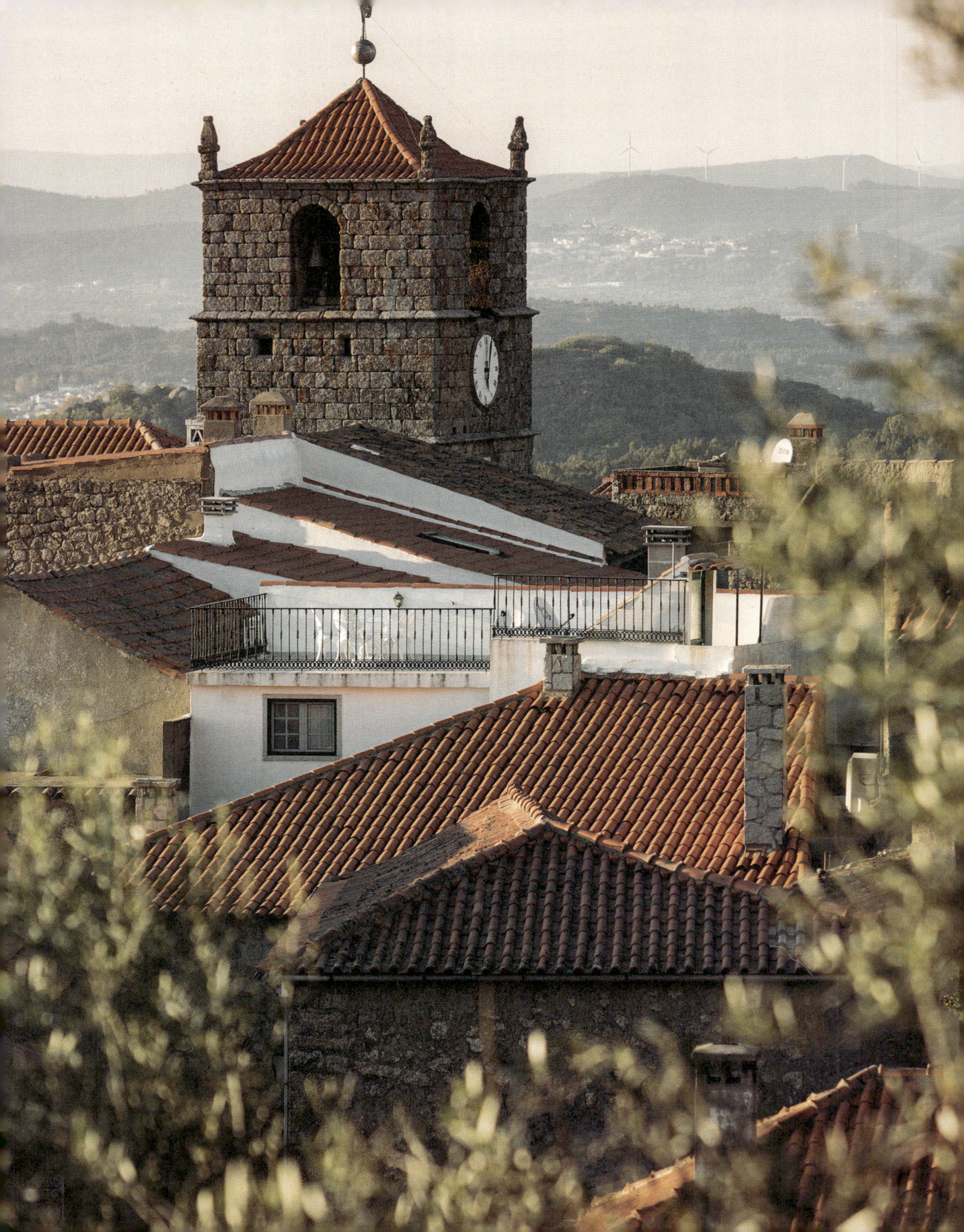

CENTRO & ALENTEJO

THE APPEAL OF PORTUGAL'S CENTRO AND ALENTEJO LIES IN THE INTERPLAY OF GENTLE HILLS, SHEER ROCK FACES, AND WIDE, QUIET EXPANSES

In remote corners, villages with long histories appear unexpectedly, their past still legible in stone and setting. Monsanto is one of them, and one of the twelve *Aldeias Históricas*. It is often described as deeply Portuguese and has served as a film location more than once. Small stone houses cluster tightly together, some appearing to grow out of the rock. Massive granite boulders form walls and roofs, as if giant children had once scattered their building blocks here and left them behind. From the ruins of Castelo de Monsanto high above the settlement, the view stretches as far as the Spanish border on clear days. In the Coimbra region, the mountain village of Piódão occupies steep terraces near the Serra do Açor. Its slate houses press close together, their dark surfaces broken by doors painted deep blue. As evening light settles in, the village grows still, briefly set apart from the present day. In Alentejo, Monsaraz stands on a hilltop beside its old castle, a place the Knights Templar likely chose for its wide views long before the Alqueva reservoir filled the valley below. Walking through uneven streets lined with whitewashed houses feels like stepping back into the Middle Ages—especially at sunset, when warm light spreads across the surrounding plains of olive groves and cork oaks. Aveiro, on the coast, offers a sharp contrast. Often called the "Venice of Portugal," the town is defined by its canals, where brightly painted *moliceiro* boats pass Art Nouveau façades reflected in the water, and everyday movement along the canals gives it a light, easy rhythm.

LEFT: *Red tile roofs, angular granite walls, and wide views over the neighboring valleys at Monsanto, one of the* aldeias históricas, *twelve towns recognized for preserving traditional architecture and practices.*

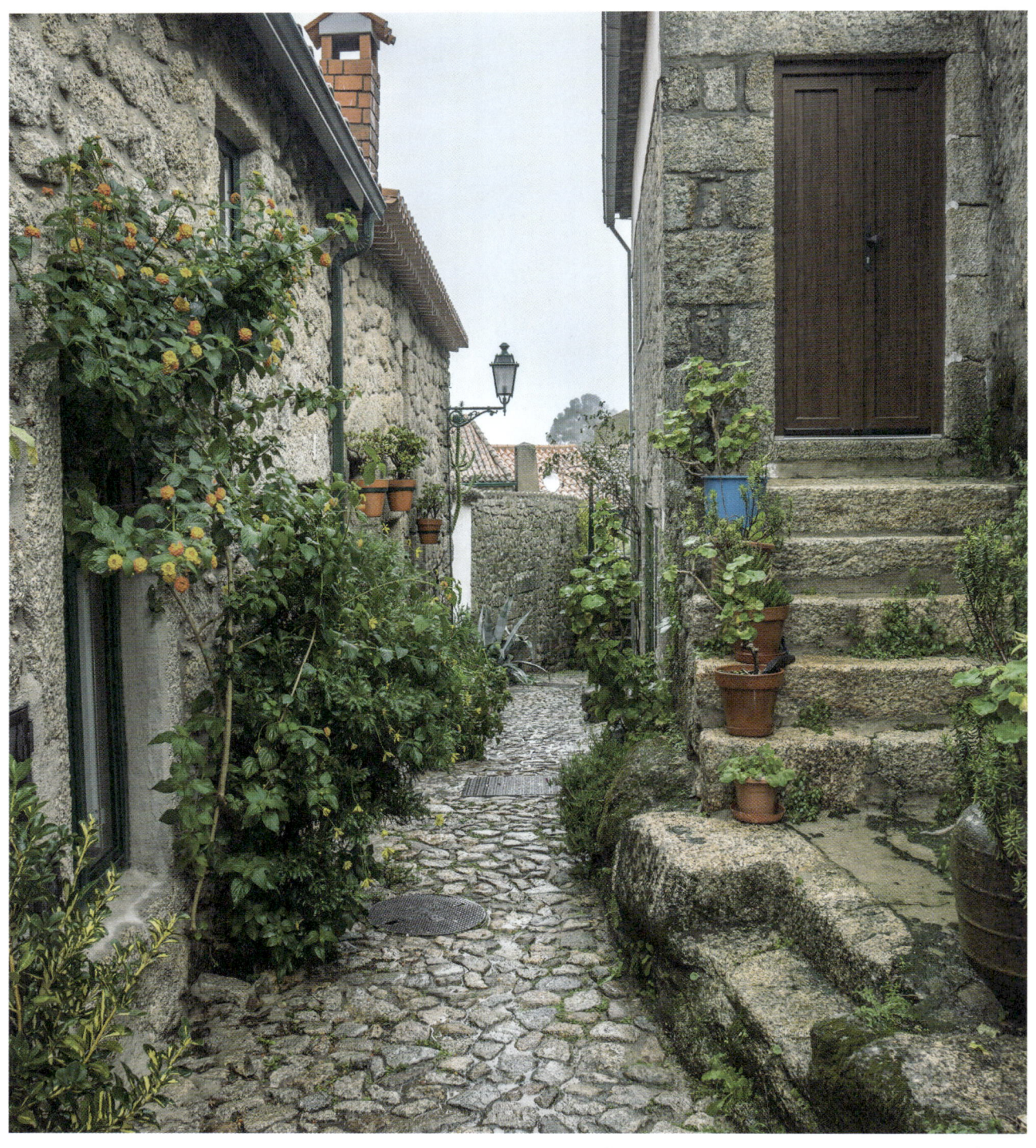

ABOVE AND RIGHT: *Houses in Monsanto, built of the granite on which the medieval village stands, seem a unique kind of outcropping.*

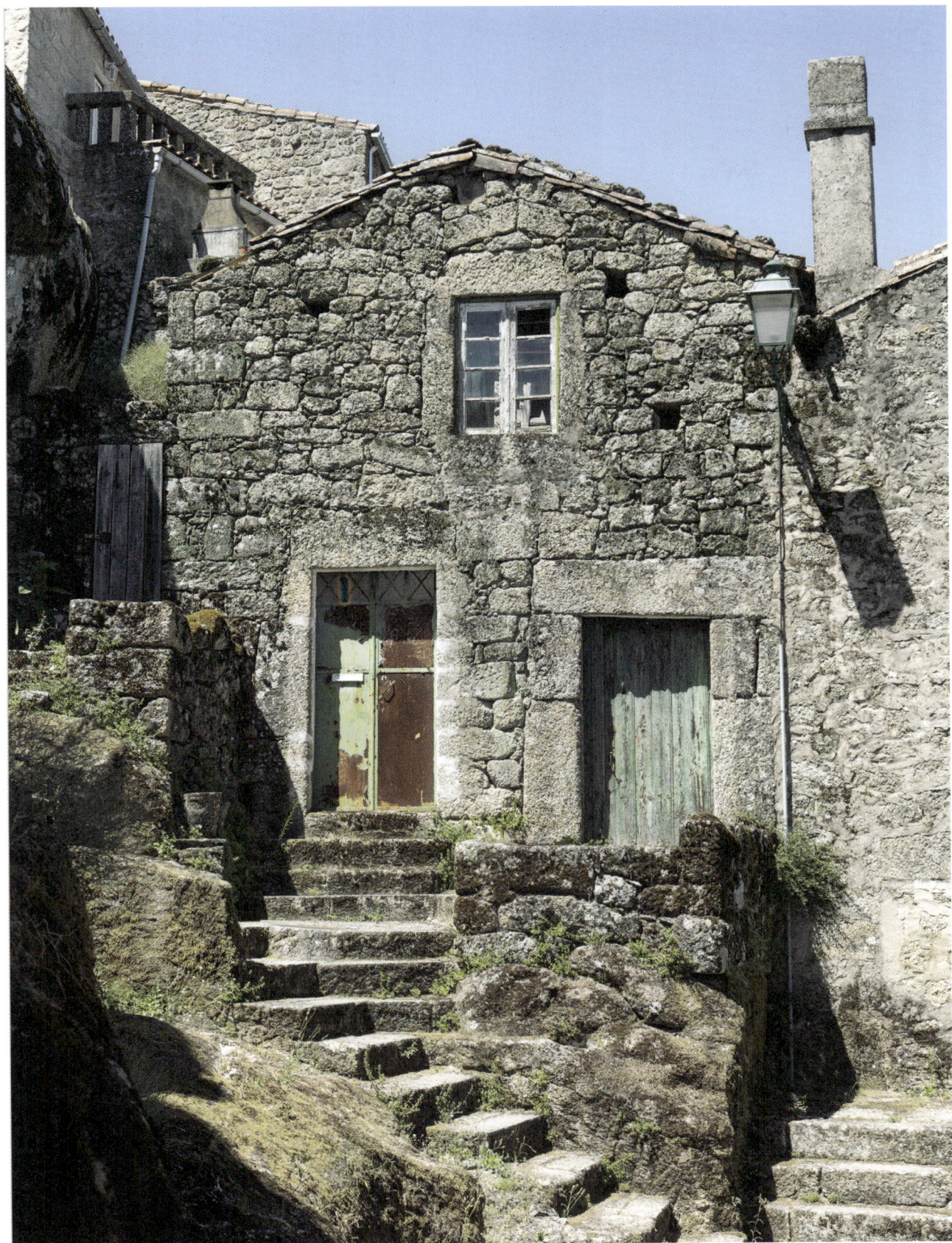

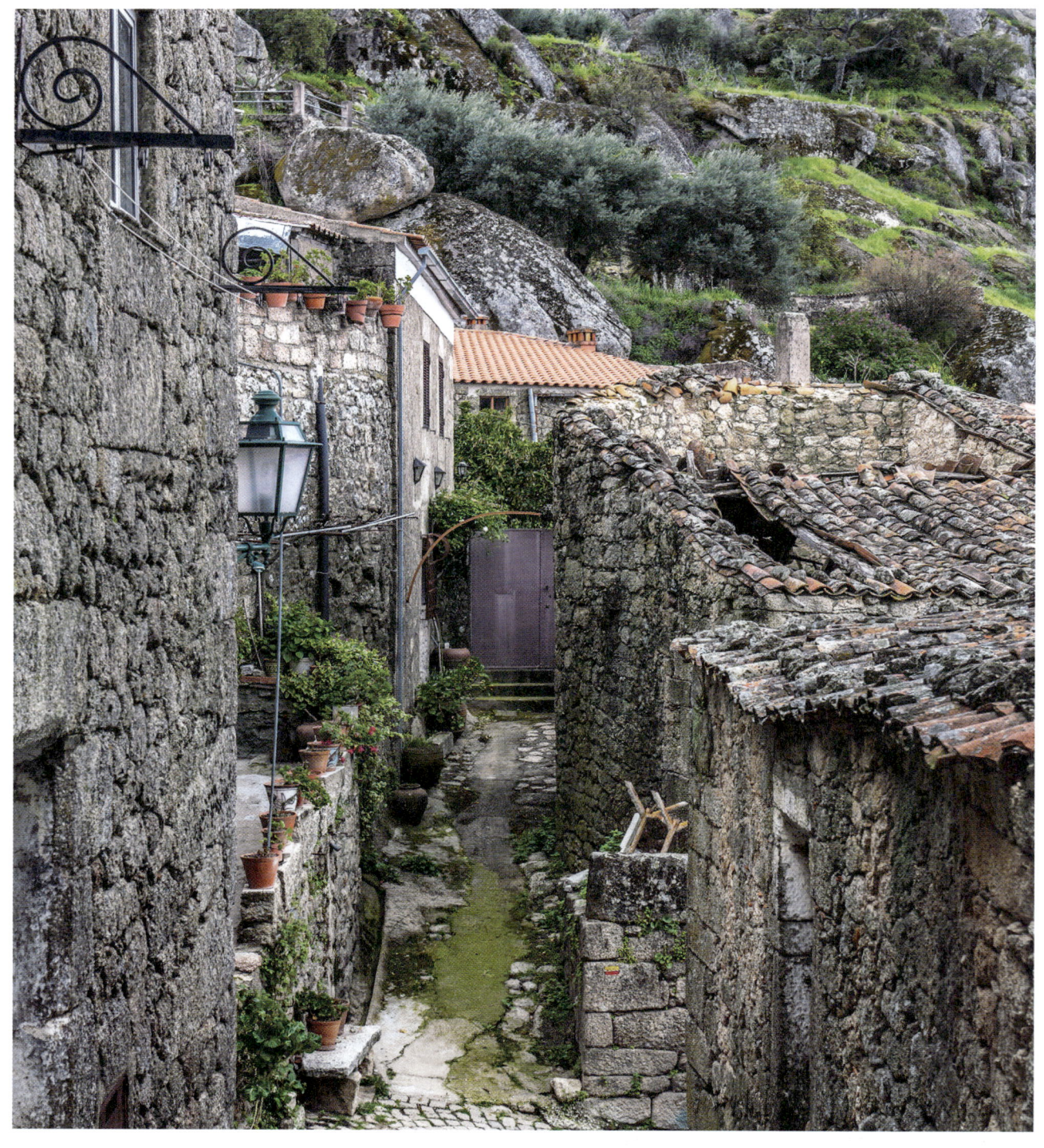

ABOVE AND RIGHT: *Construction has been dictated by the contours of rock. Steep, narrow passages, and yet a cornucopia of subtle details can be found throughout the mountain village, like granite troughs and stone benches.*

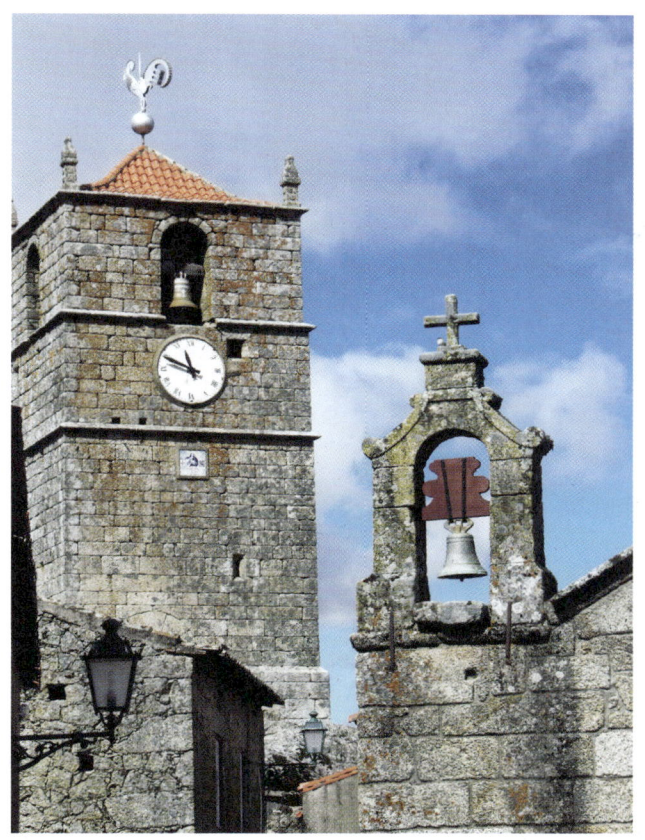
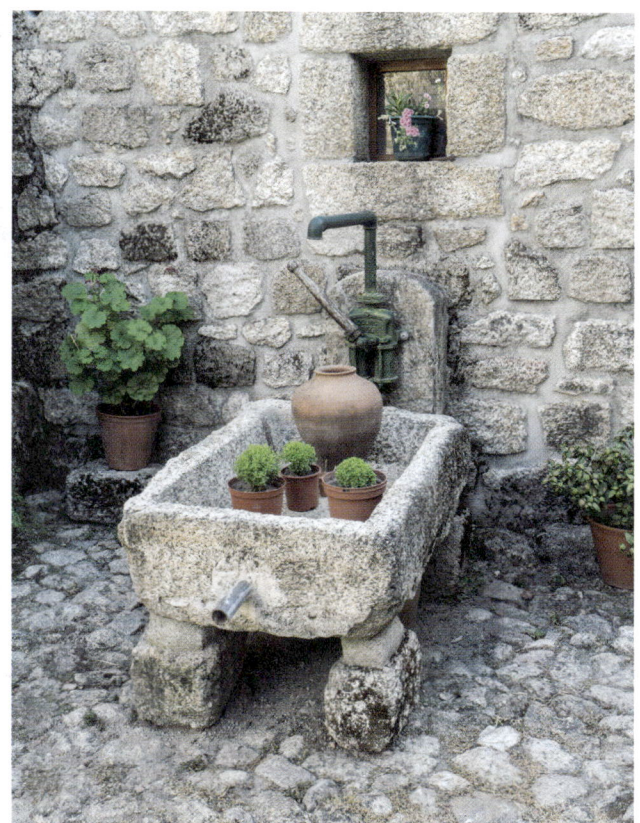
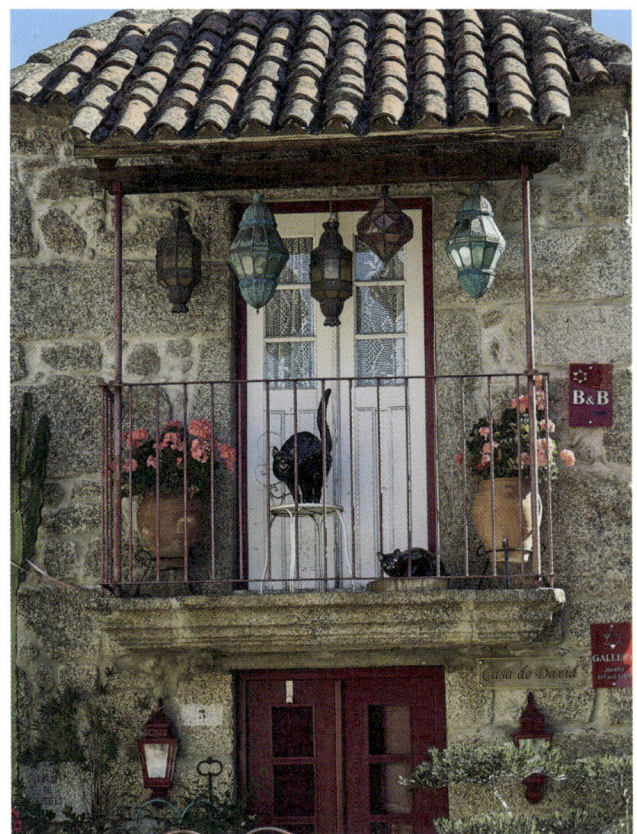
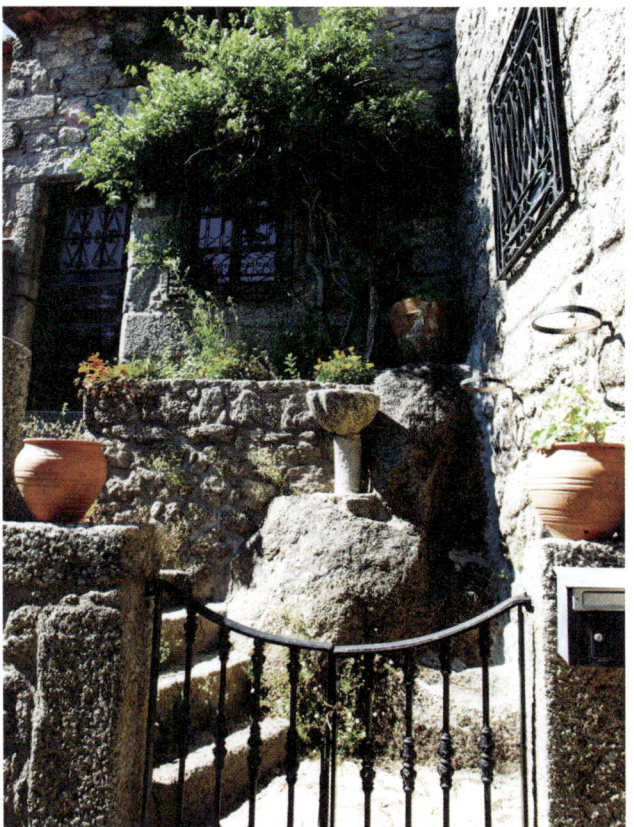

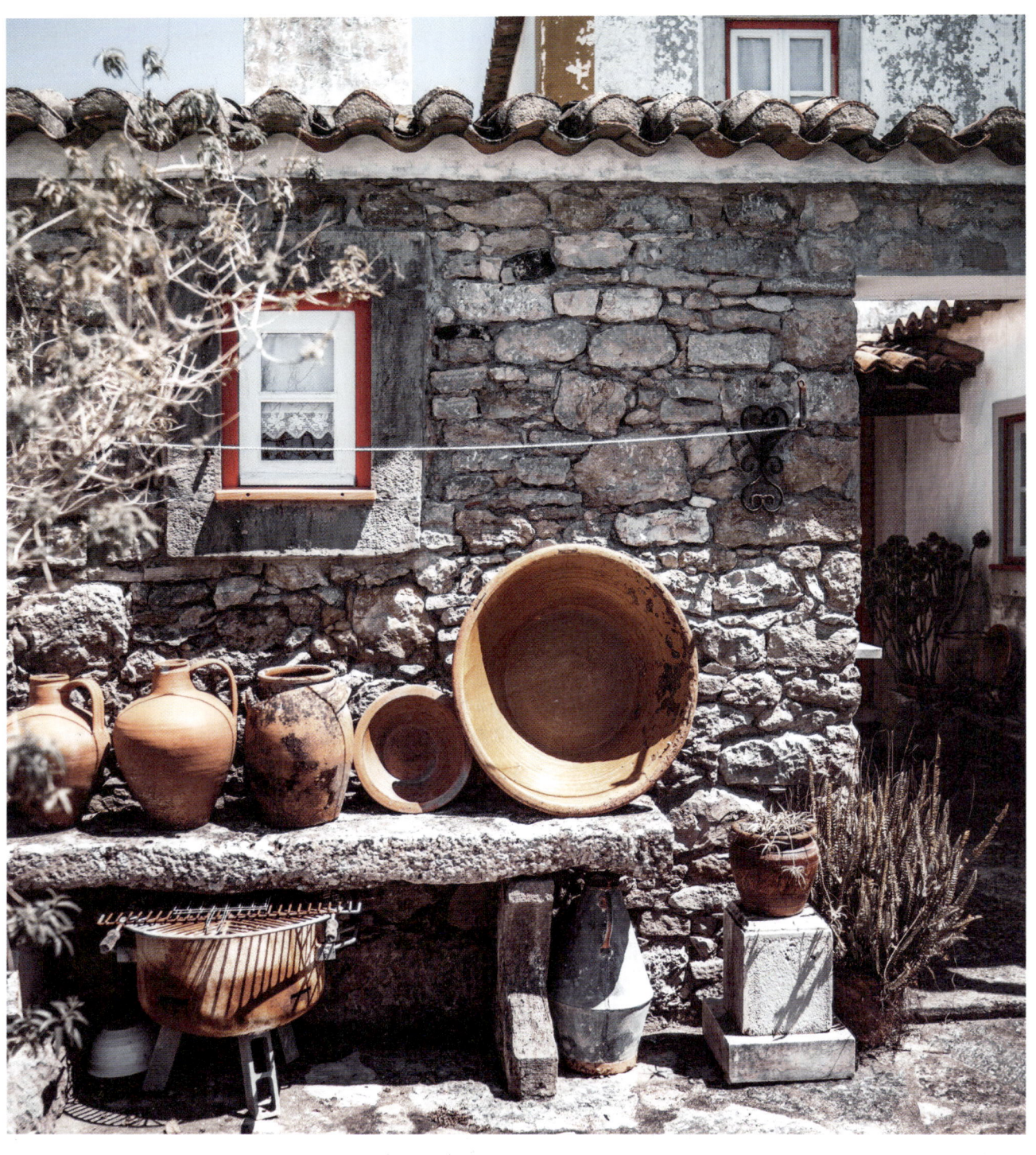

ABOVE AND RIGHT: *The old days preserved in the compact village of Aldeia da Mata Pequena, only half an hour north of Lisbon, near Mafra. The hamlet now practices low-impact tourism.*

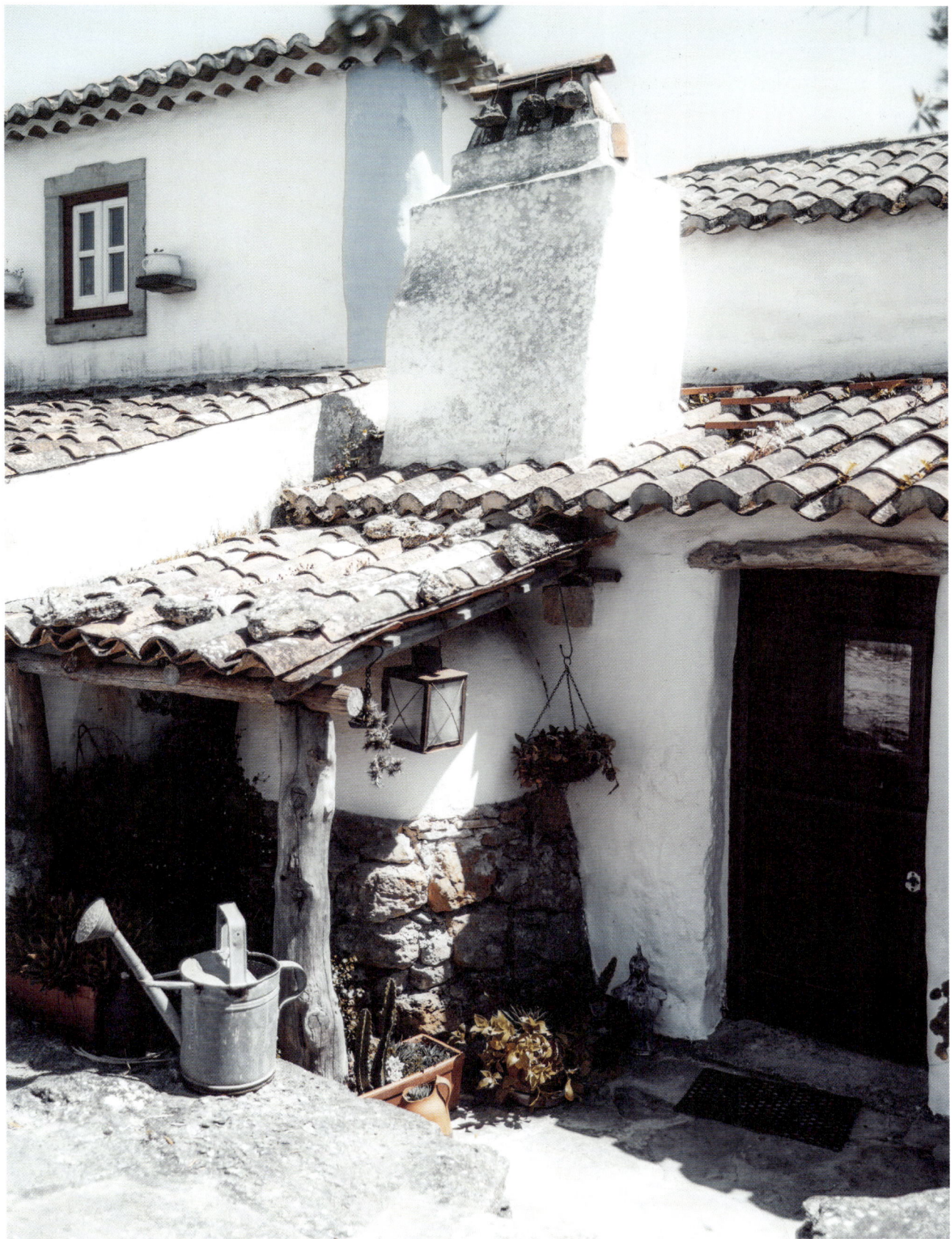

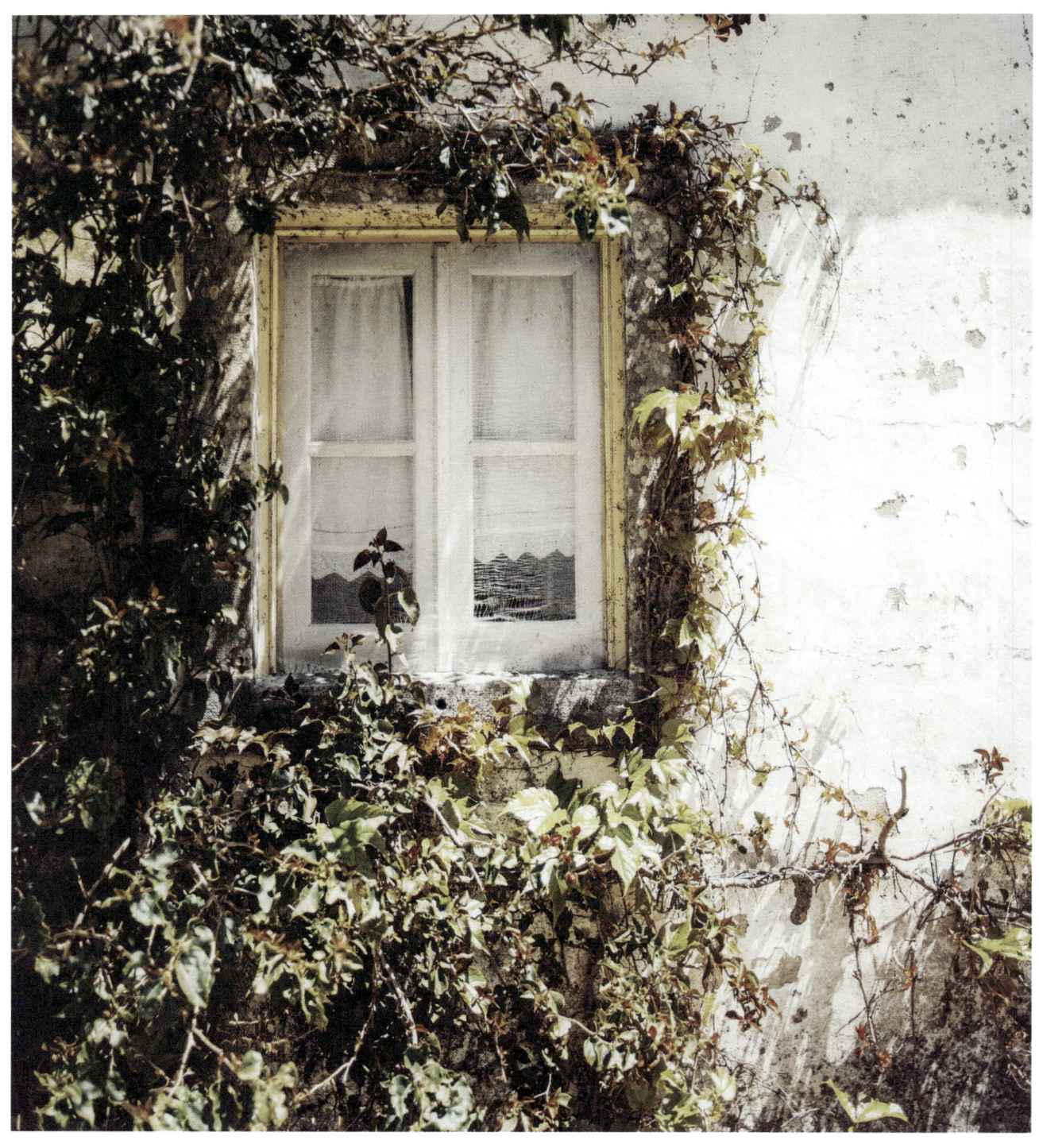

ABOVE AND RIGHT: *Old stone houses with whitewashed walls and brightly painted doors framed by ivy and mature trees. The historical fabric is kept but adapted to present use.*

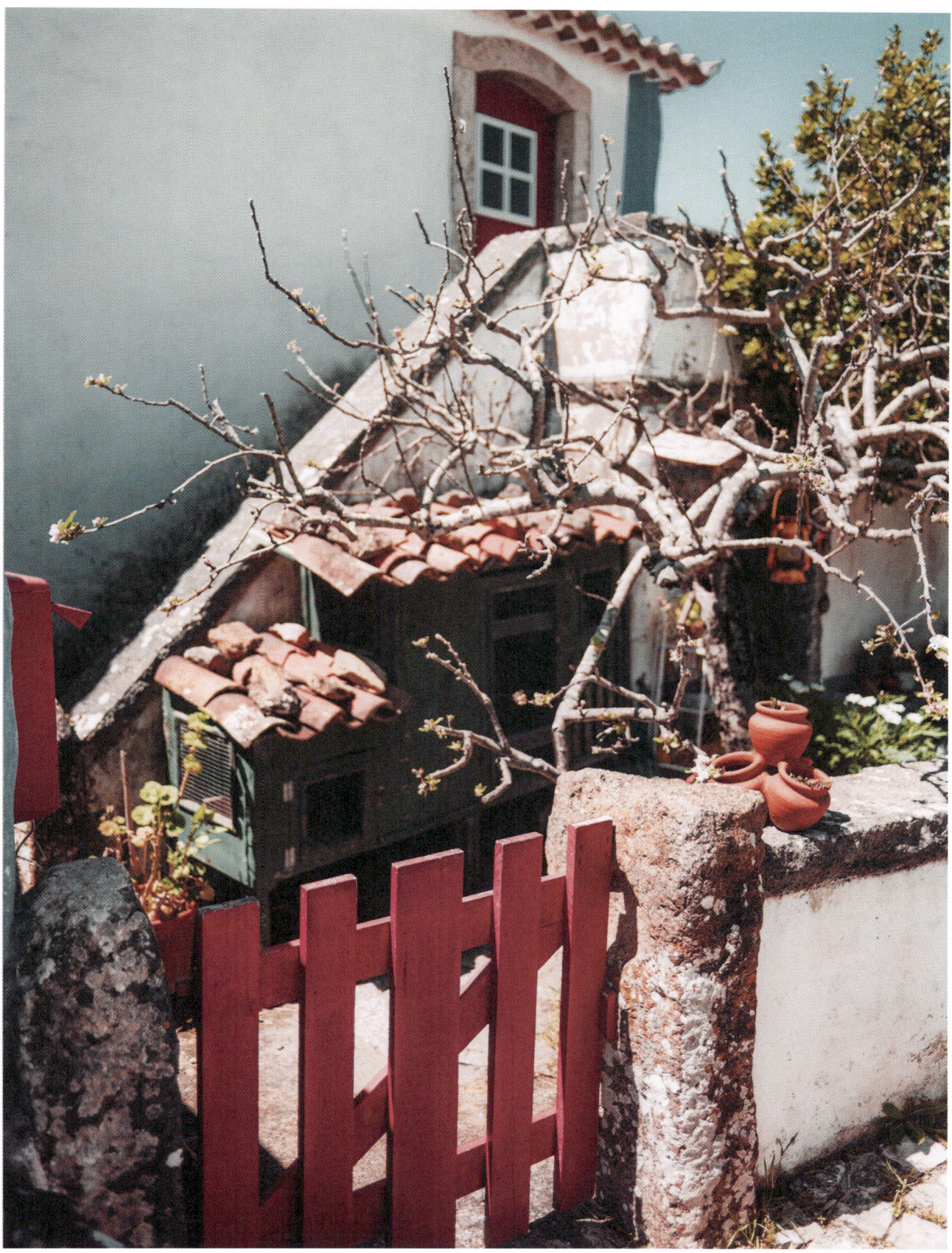

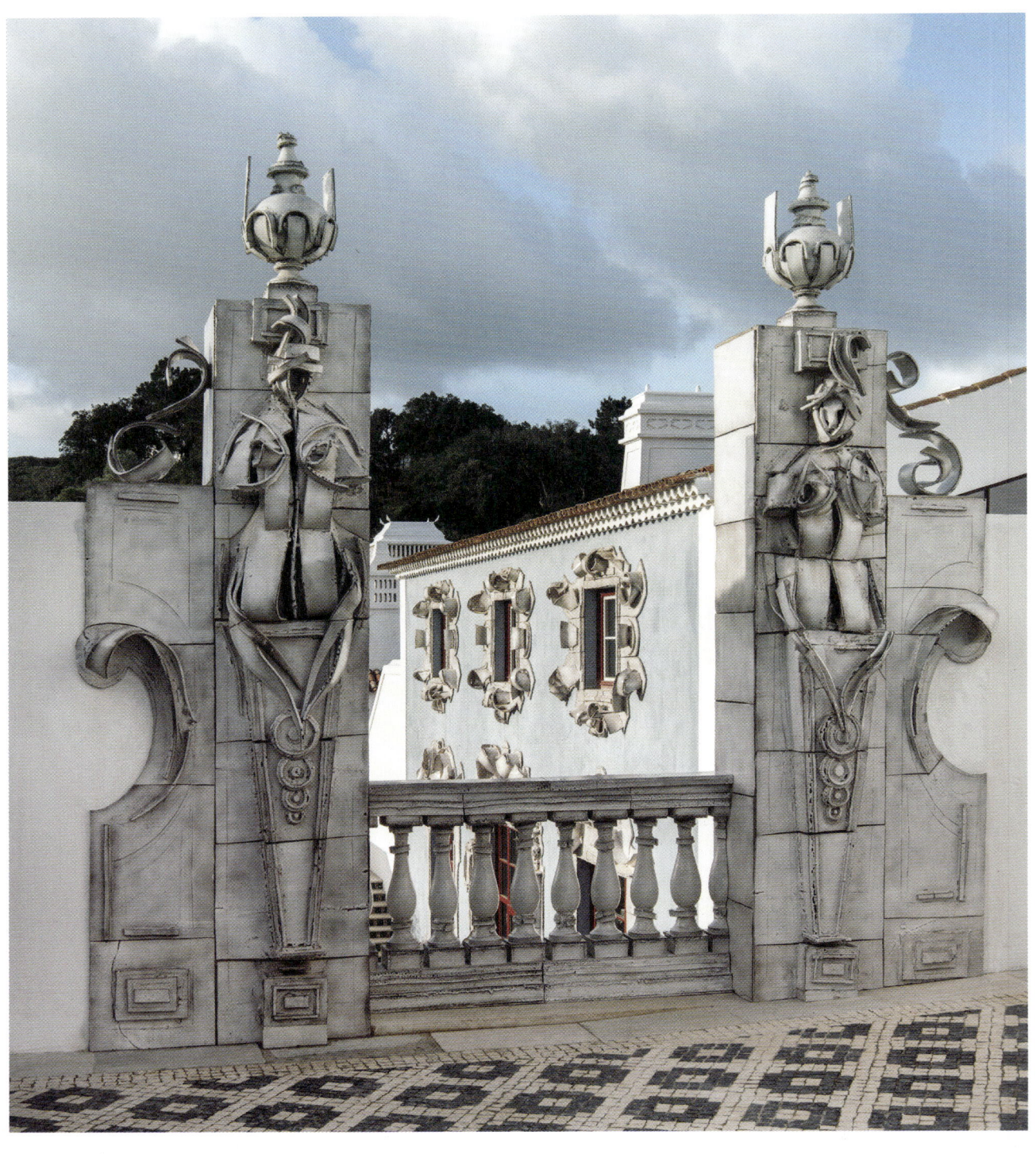

ABOVE AND RIGHT: *French shoe designer Christian Louboutin purchased land in the Alentejo. Twenty years later, he has established the boutique hotel Vermelho in the village of Melides, where Portuguese craftsmanship meets a distinct personal design language.*

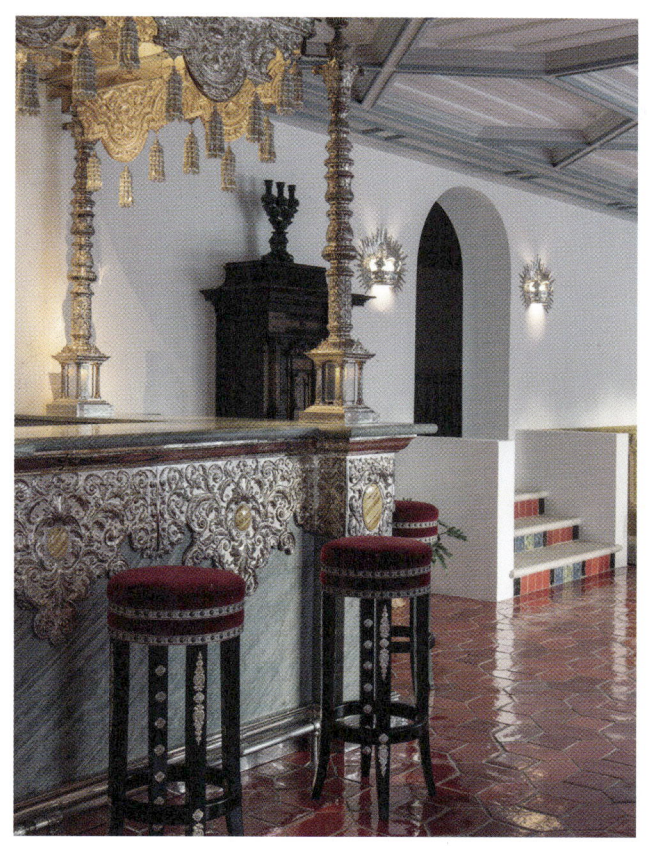
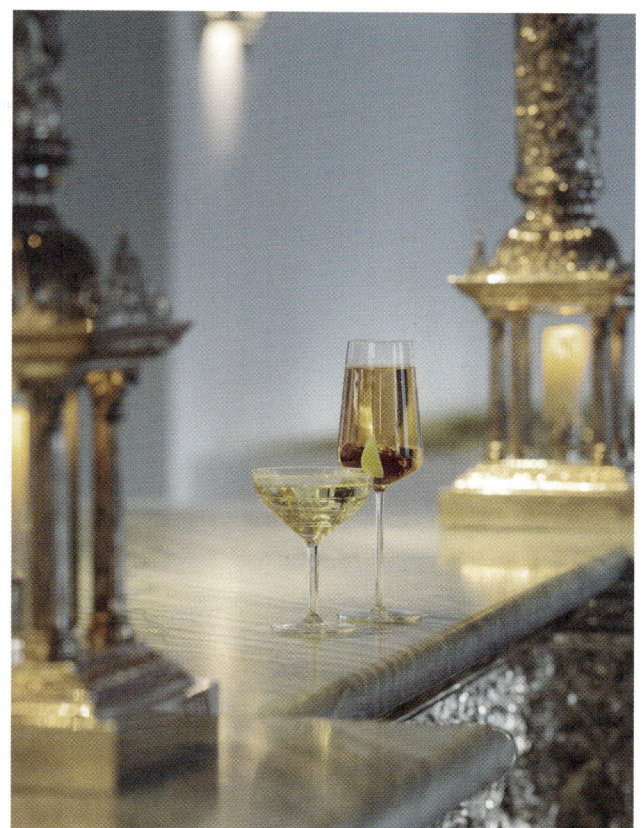
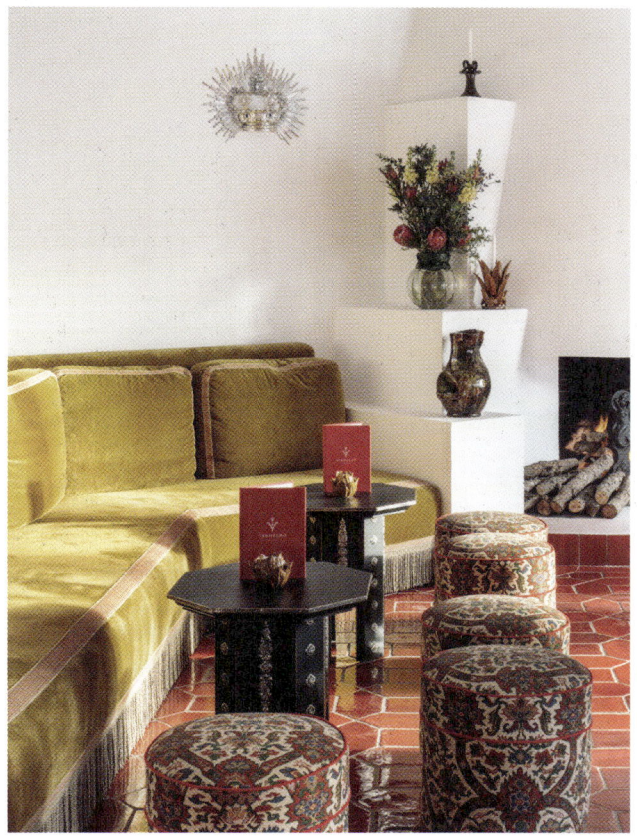
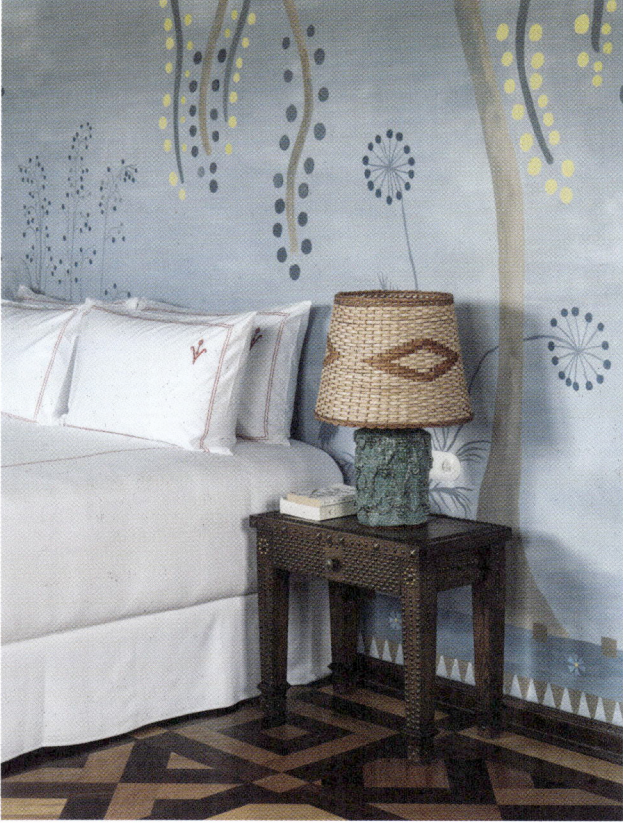

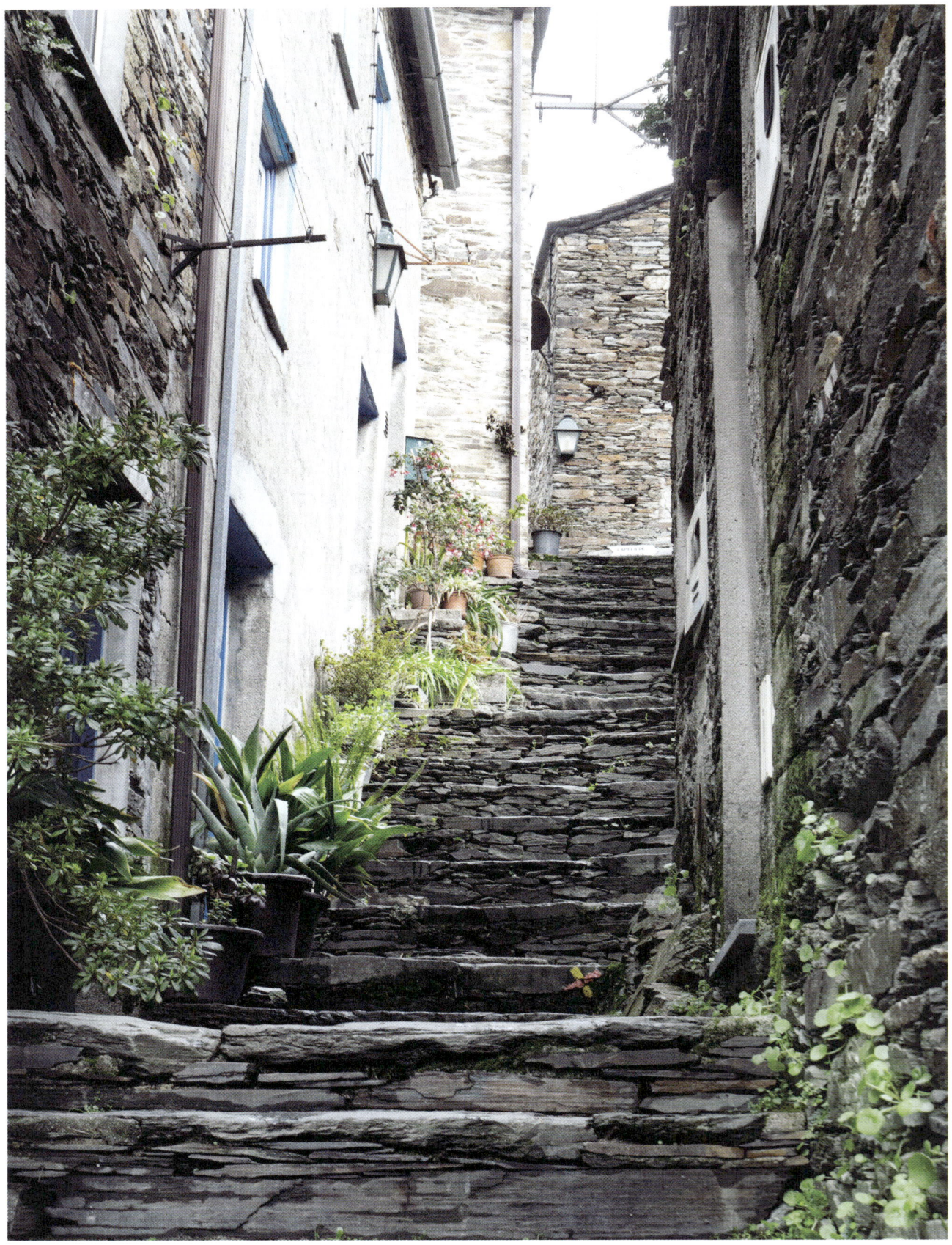

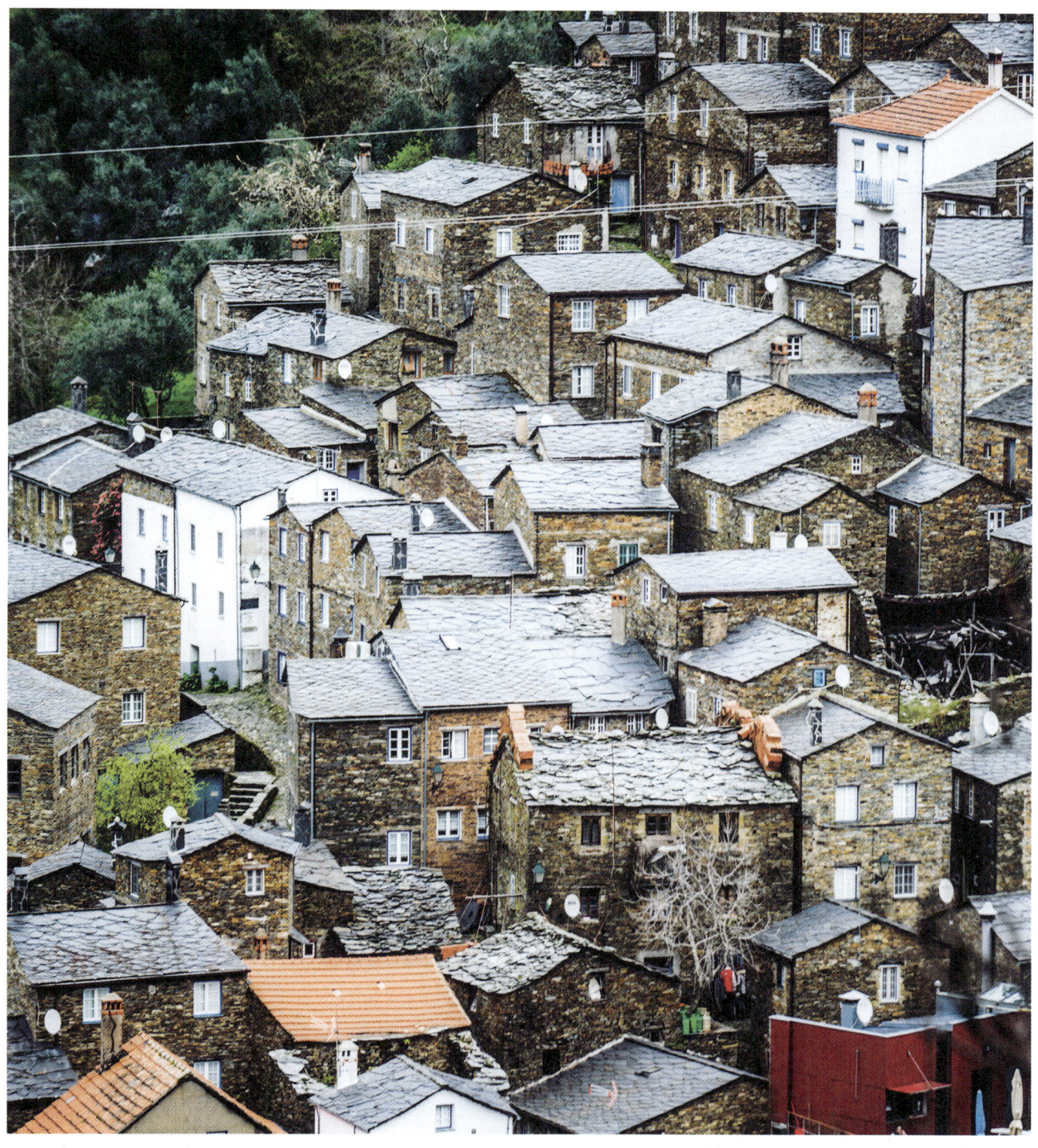

ABOVE AND LEFT: *Also one of the* aldeias históricas, *the village of Piódão in the Coimbra region is built largely from slate. Small houses wrap around the steep hillside, with many stairways for streets.*

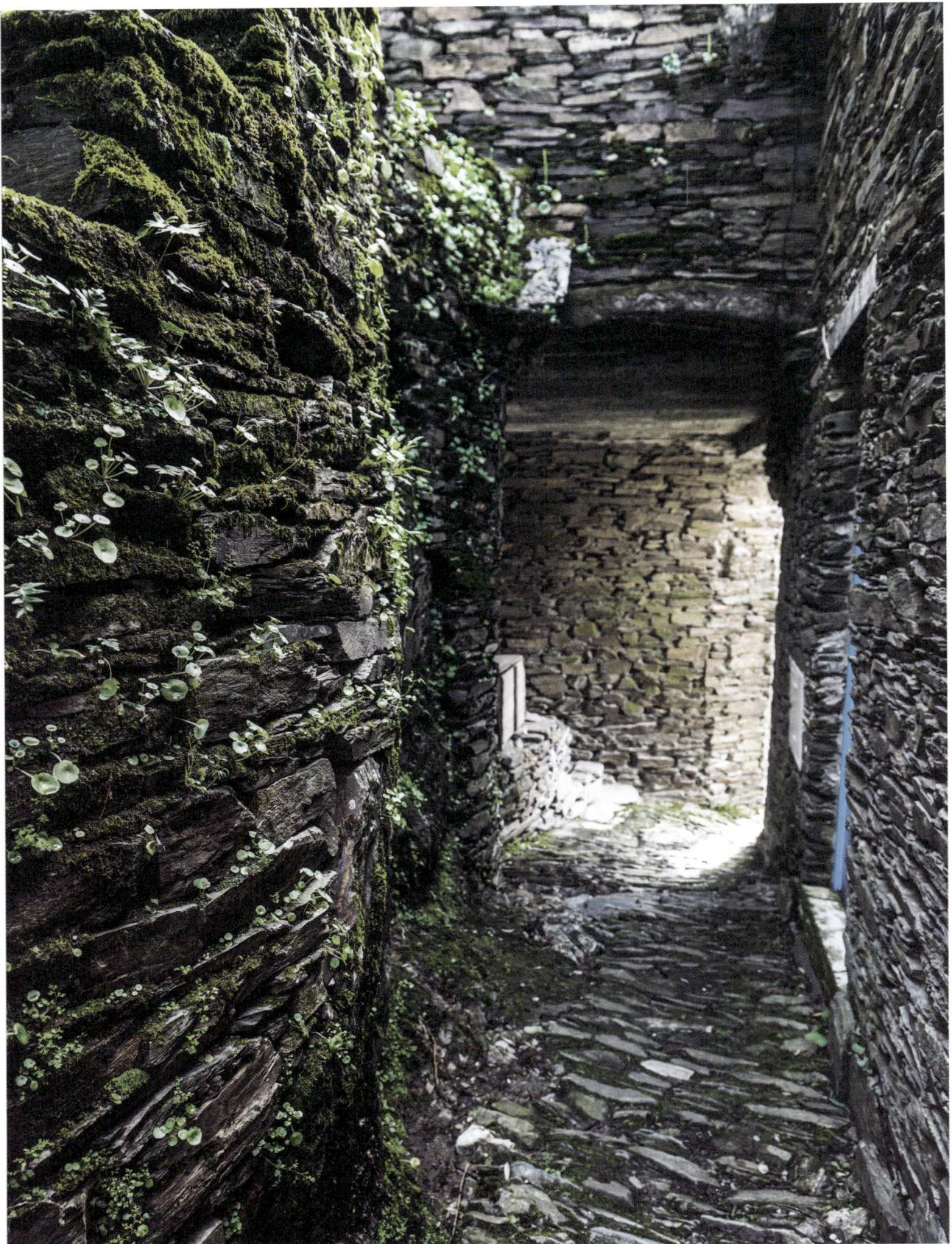

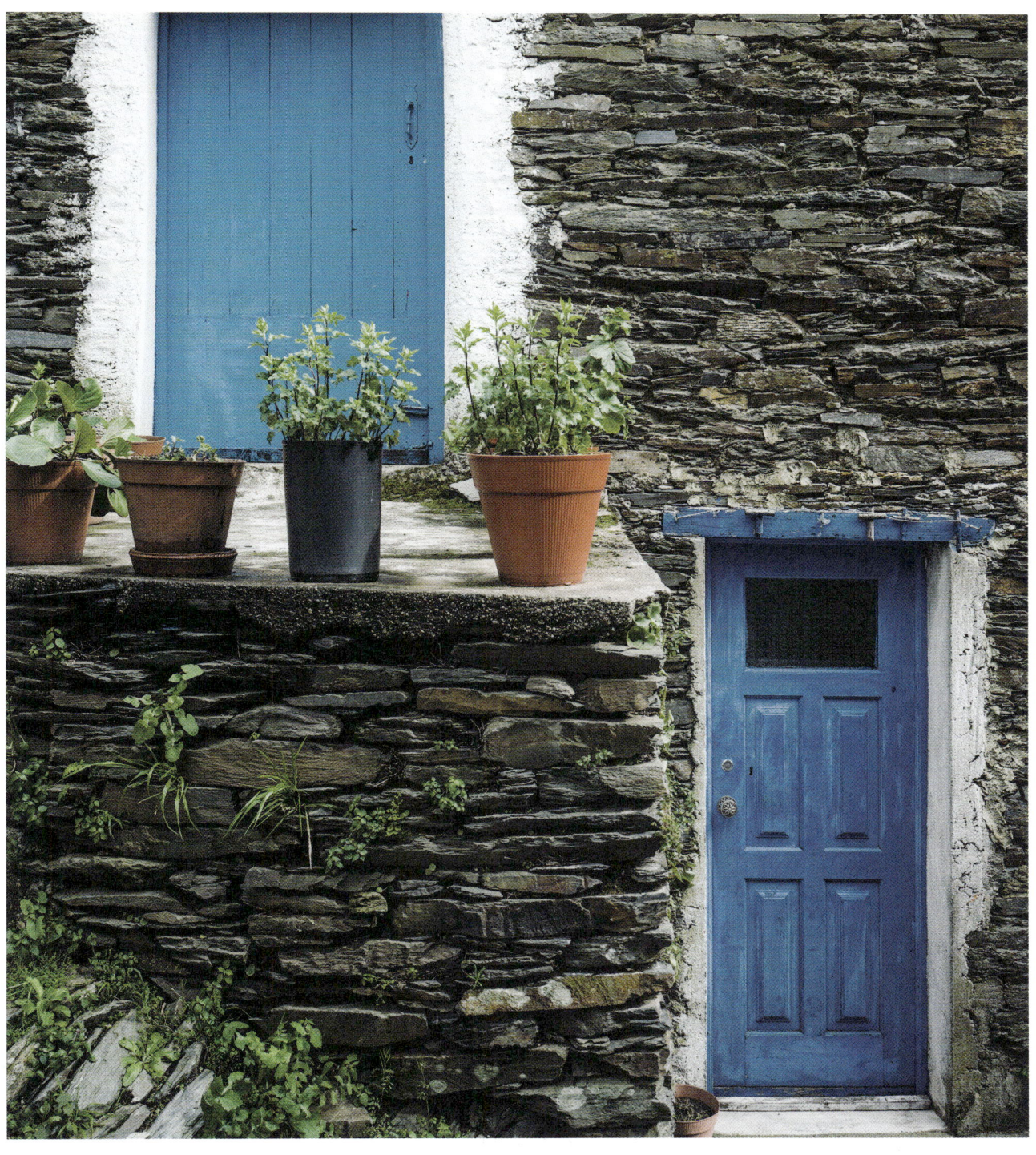

ABOVE AND LEFT: *The slate walls of Piódão seem dark and austere except for the moss and herbs pushing through narrow gaps in the stone. Brightly painted doors and windows are a source of variation.*

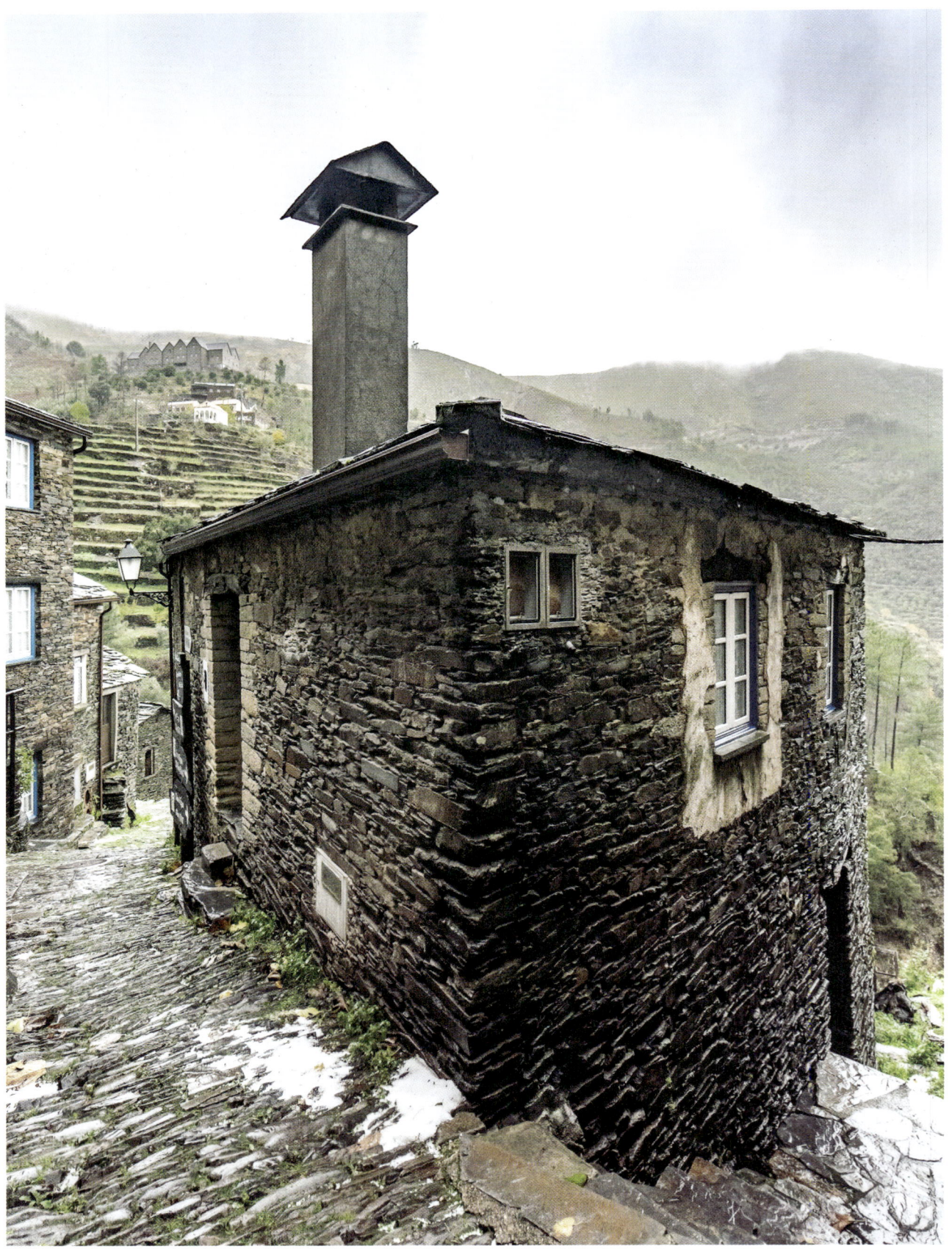

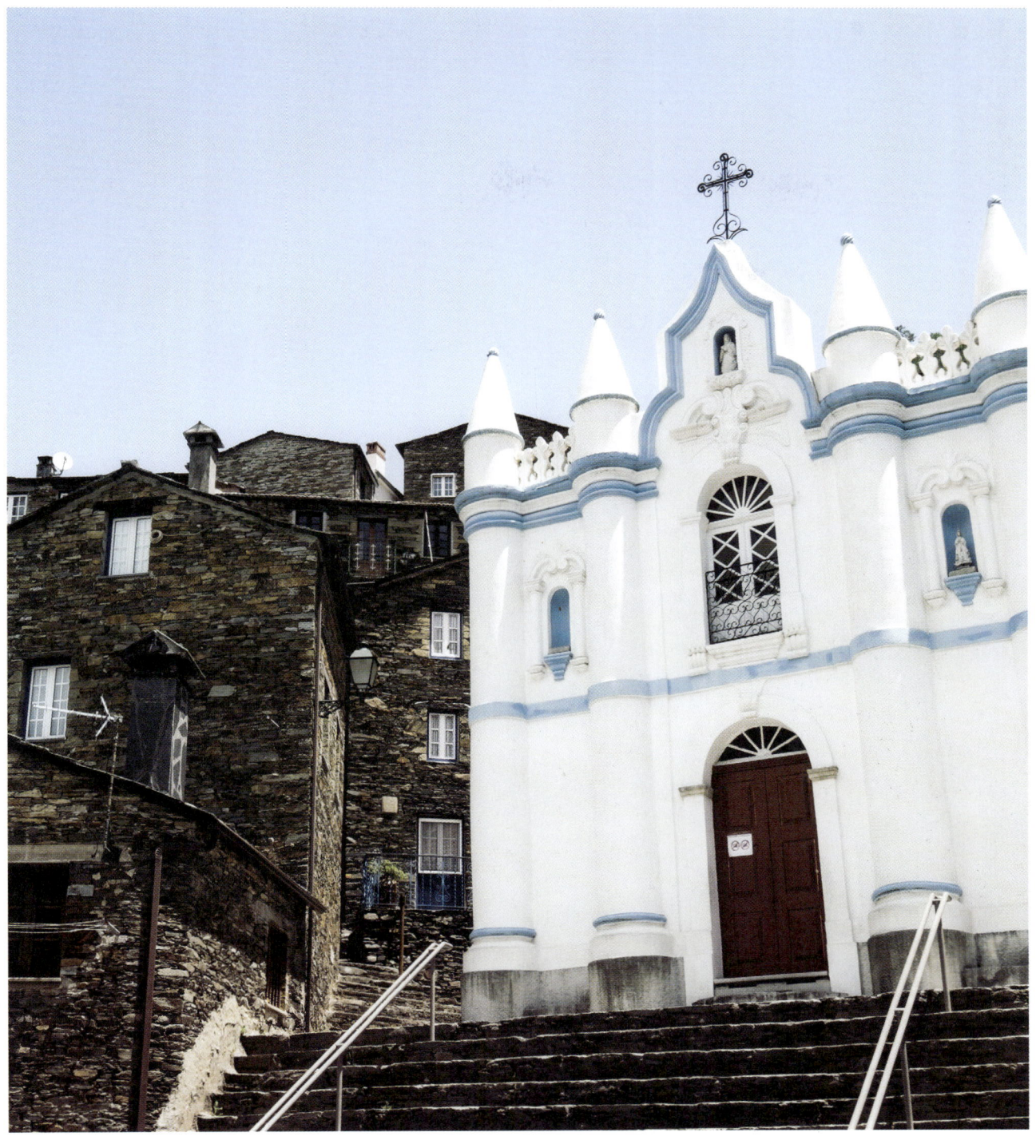

ABOVE: *The blue-accented, gleaming white village church of Piódão and its prominent portal stand out against the muted roofs of gray slate.*

LEFT: *Medieval construction techniques: Slate houses stand at all angles along the terraced slopes of the Serra do Açor.*

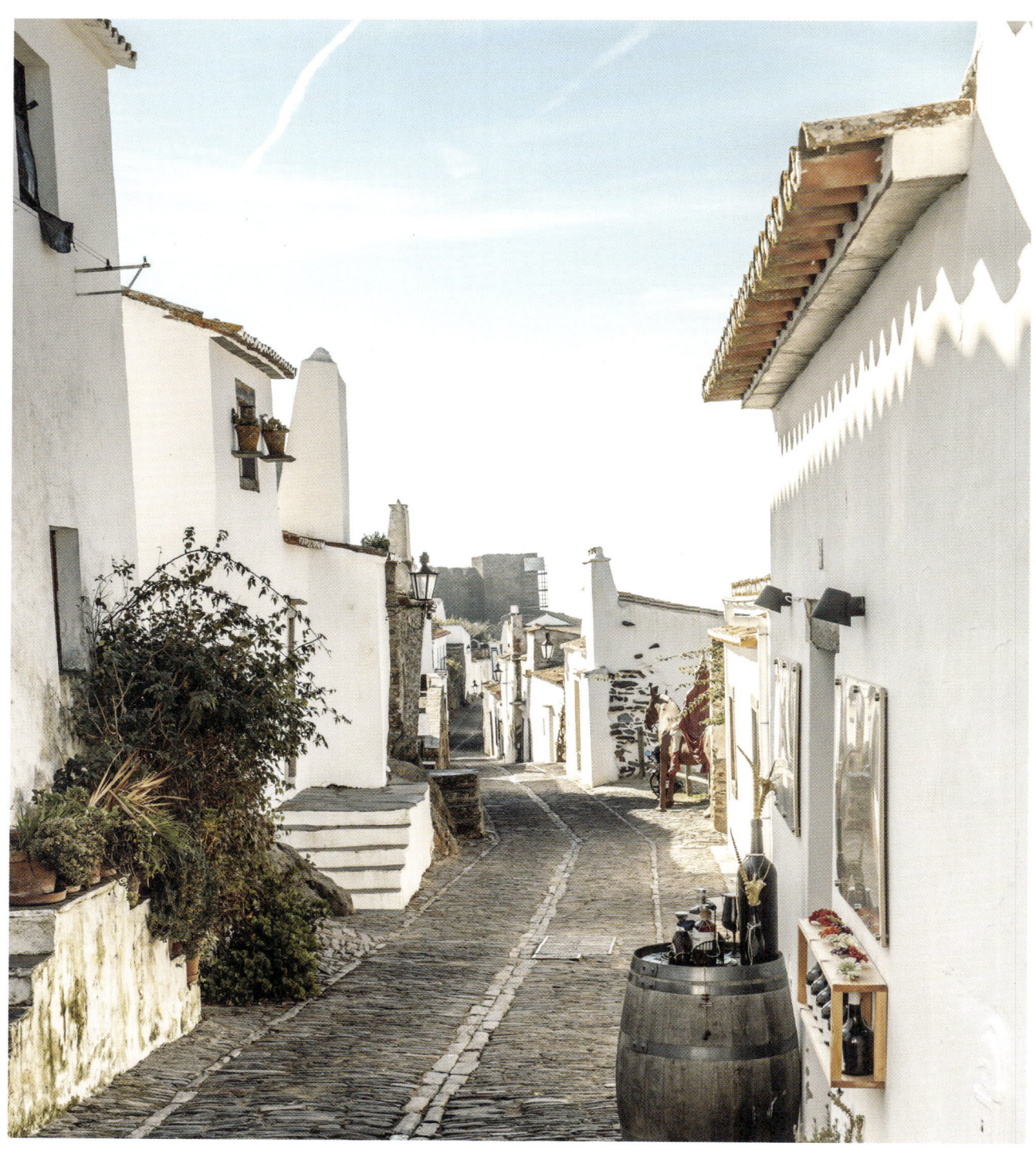

ABOVE AND RIGHT: *High on a hilltop, Monsaraz is enclosed by stout walls beside the castle. Whitewashed houses reflect the sunlight. Many quiet corners in the medieval layout of the village.*

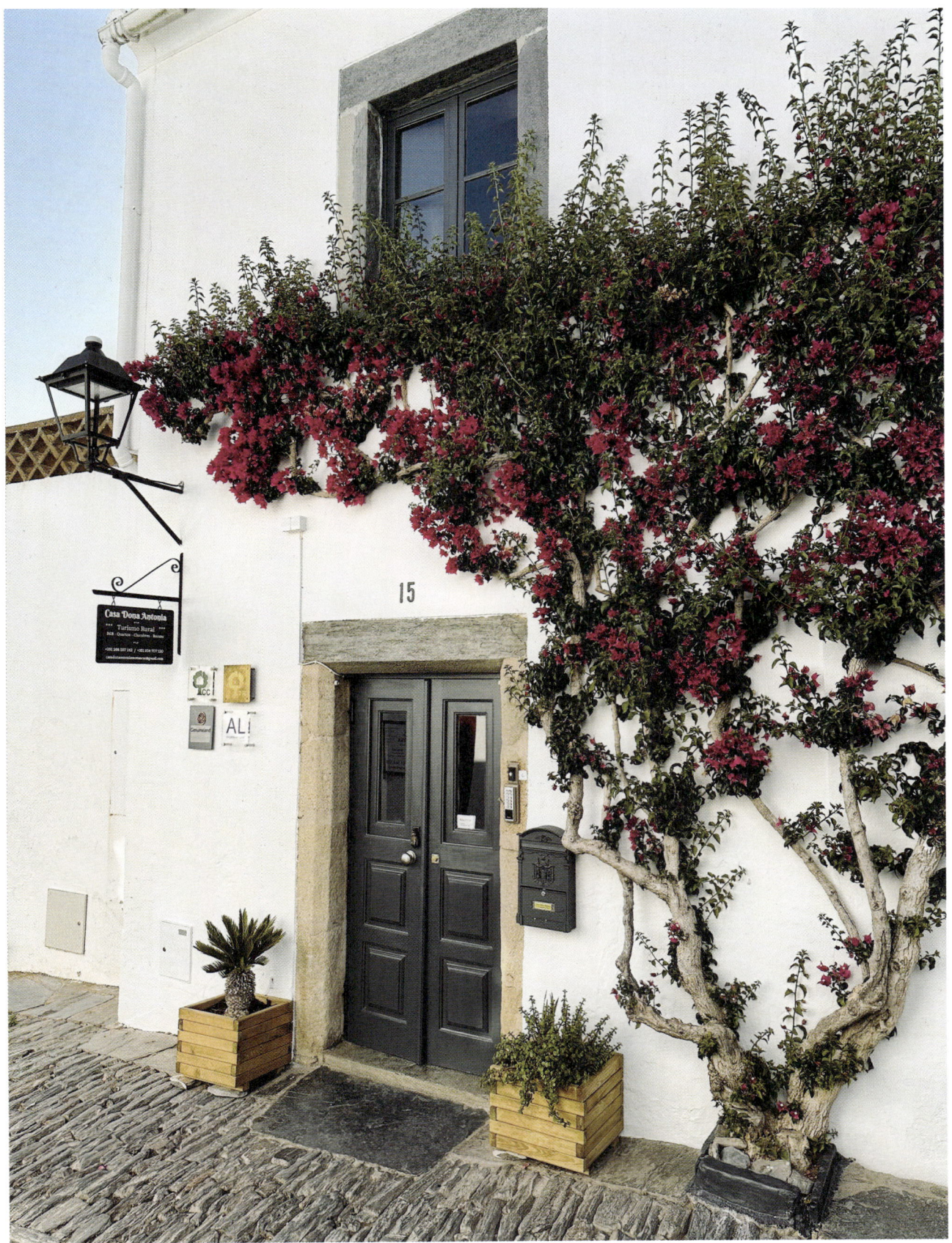

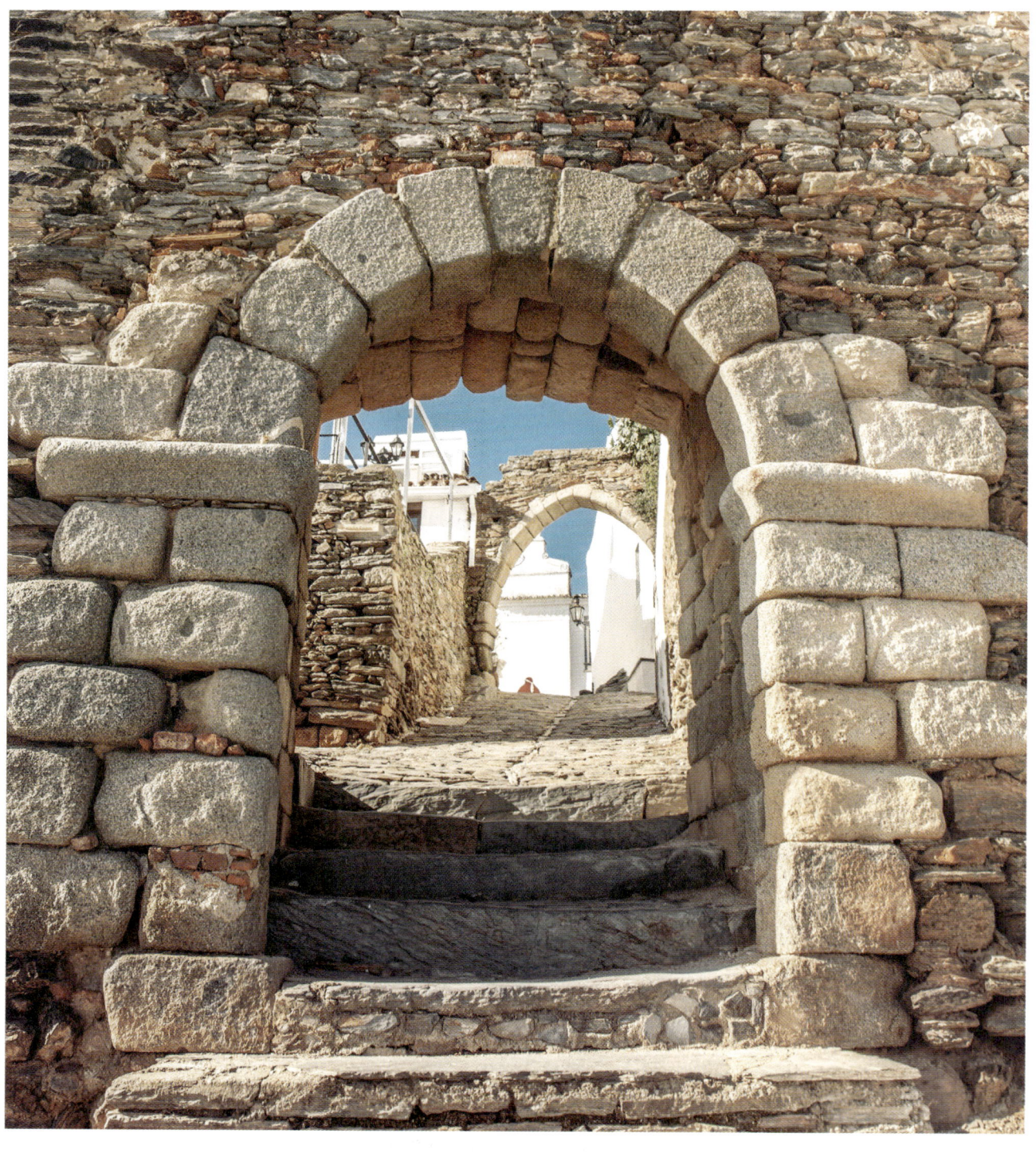

ABOVE AND RIGHT: *Stone and clay brick walls enclose the houses of Monsaraz; the church tower rises above the passageways. Views toward the nearby Spanish frontier from beneath arched gateways. The Knights Templar once battled to wrest this fortress from the Moors.*

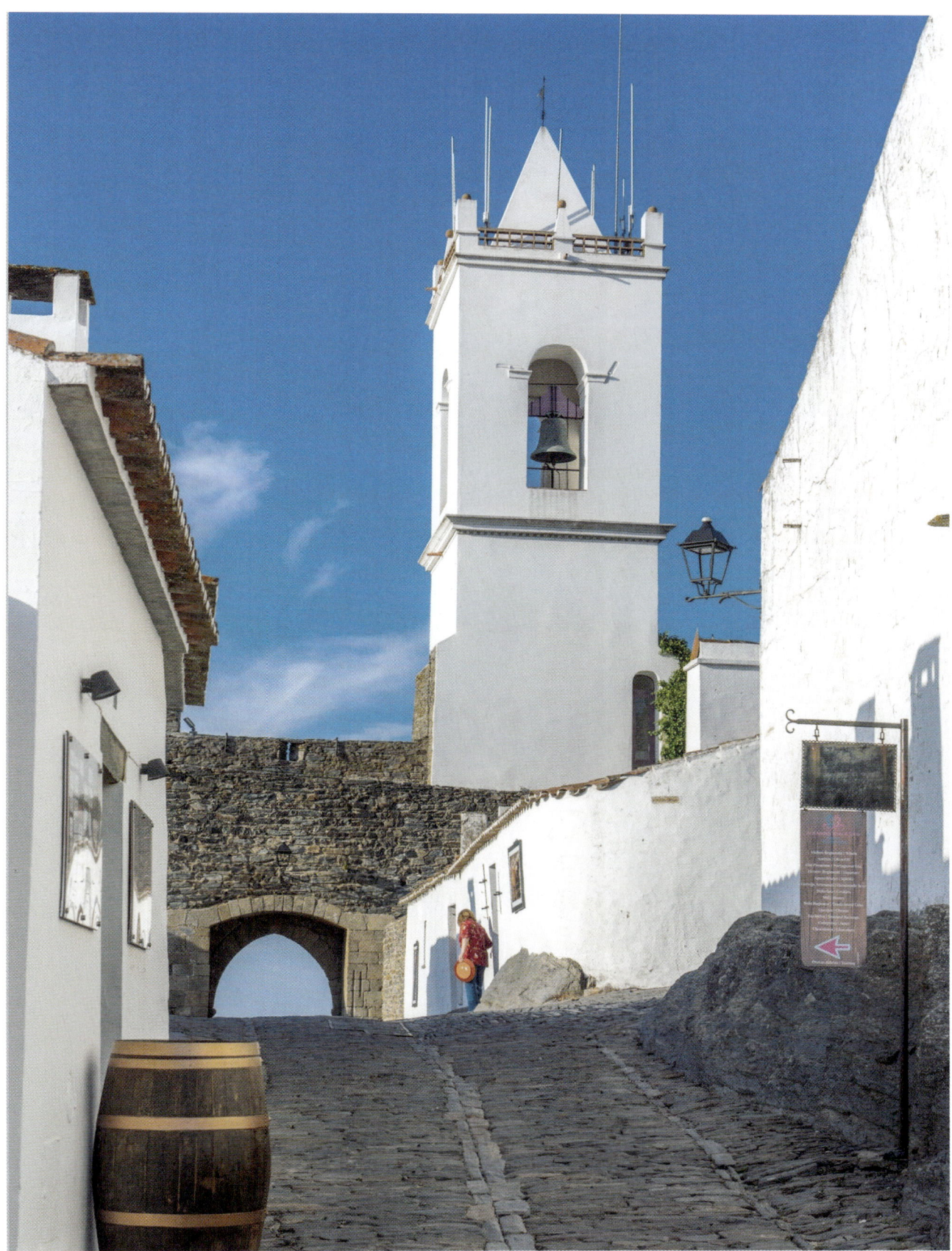

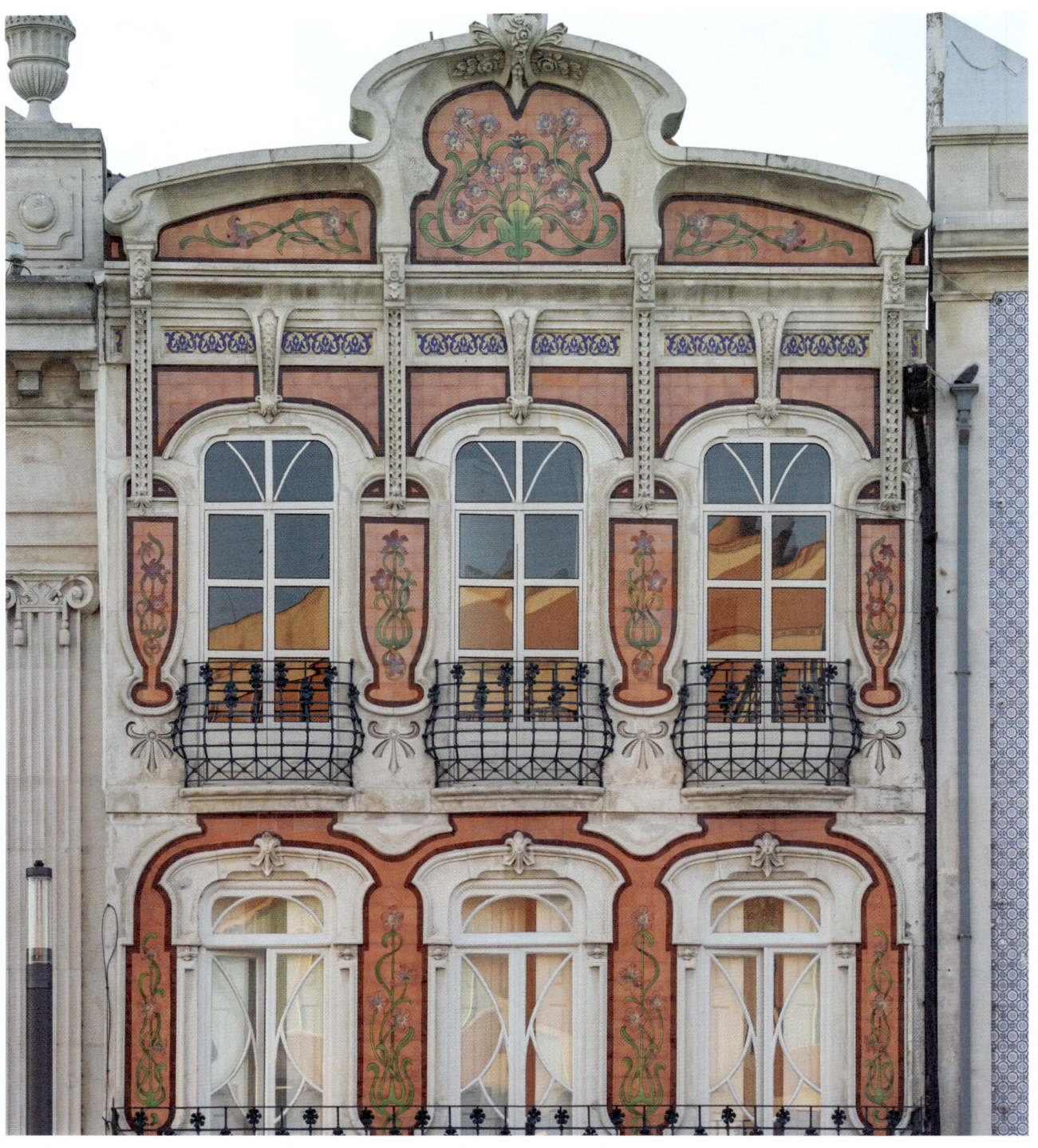

ABOVE: *Playful Art Nouveau façades bring color to the streets of Aveiro.*

RIGHT: *Moliceiro boats were once used to harvest moliço, a fertile seaweed, from the lagoon off Aveiro on Portugal's central west coast. Today, these former working boats are brightly painted and among the main attractions in the town on the lagoon.*

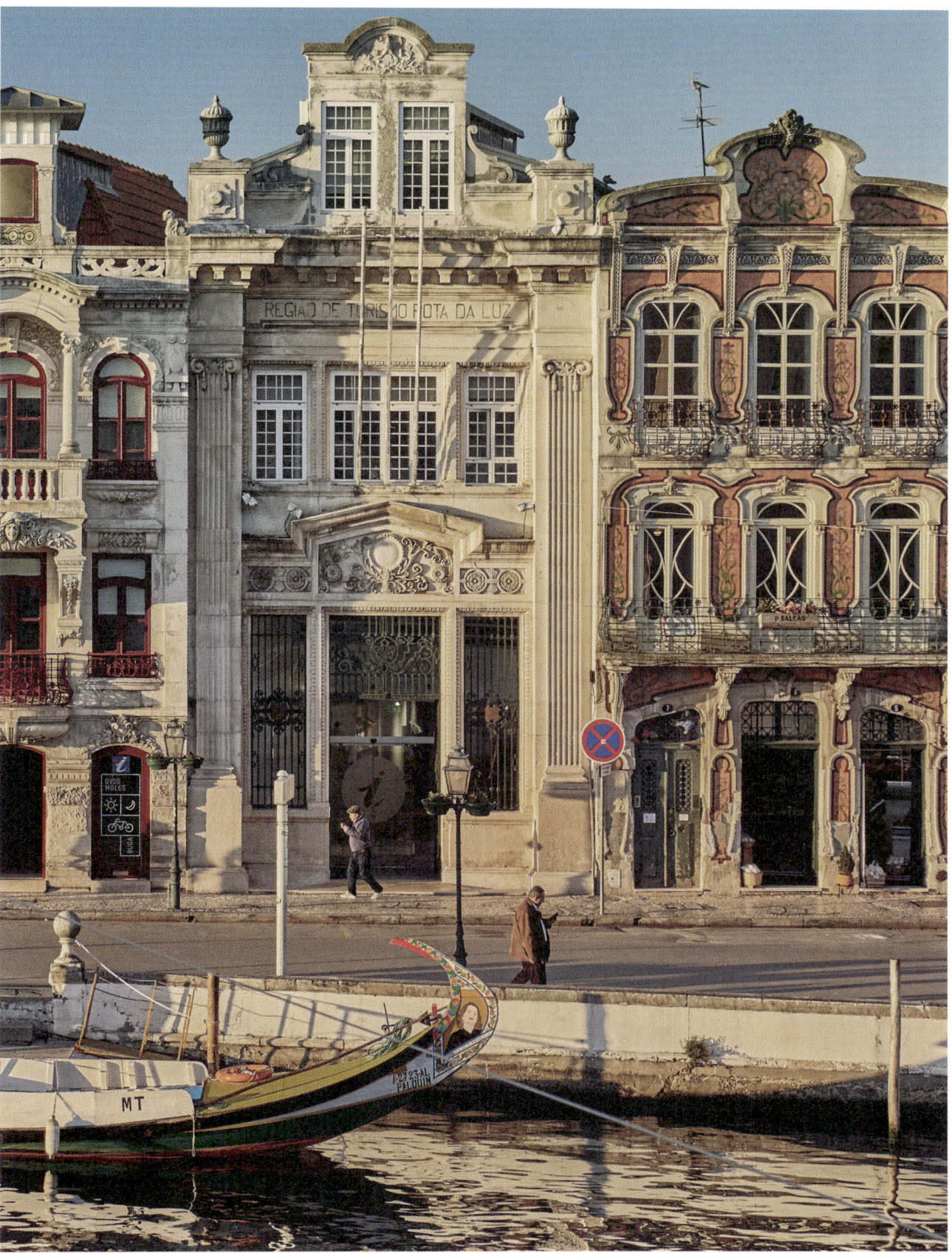

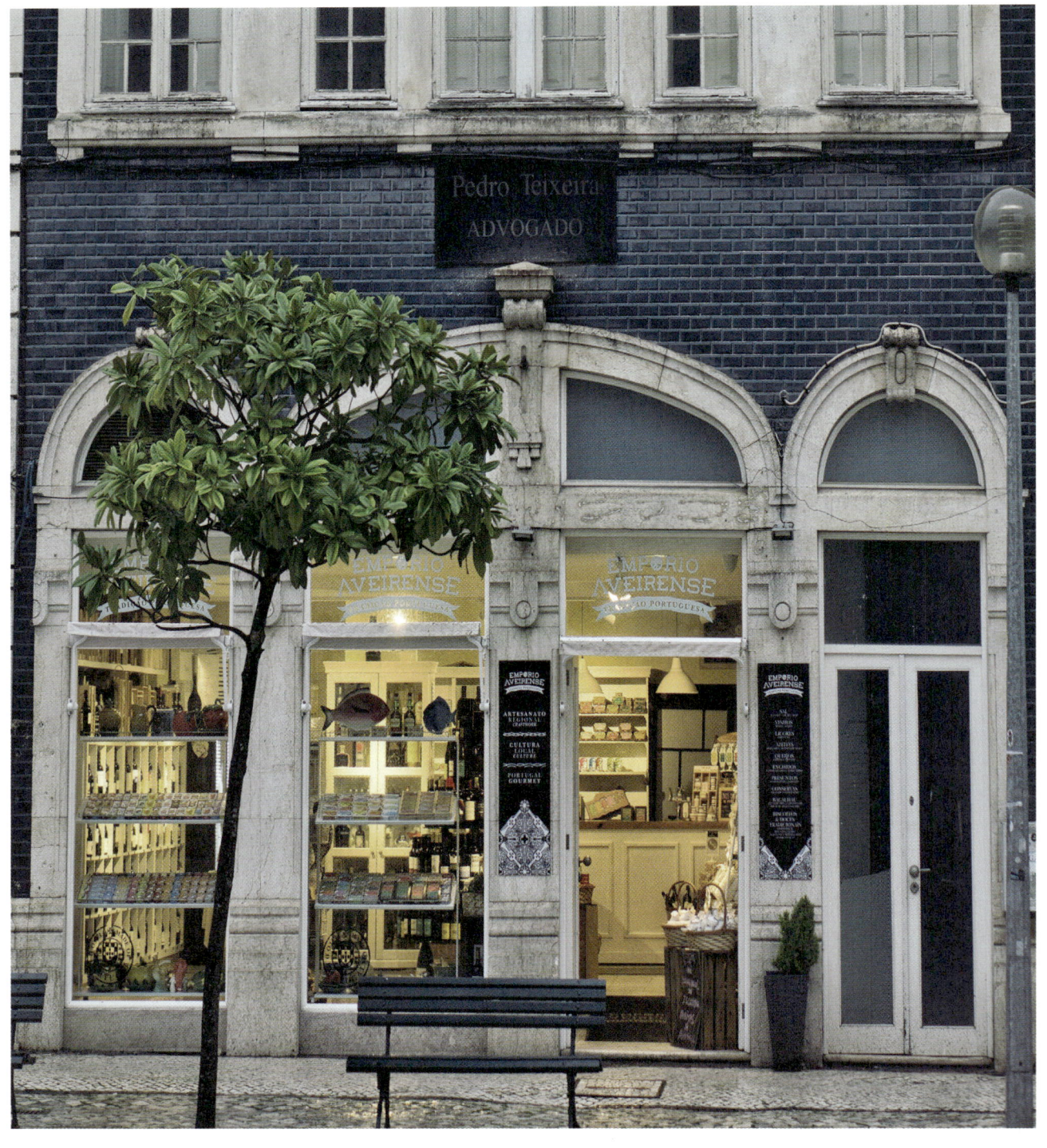

ABOVE AND RIGHT: *The façades of Aveiro's commercial buildings and restaurants still reflect the wealth generated by salt production. For centuries, salt was harvested in the surrounding lagoons. In the nineteenth century, a new canal system added to the city's prominence and led to the nickname "Venice of Portugal."*

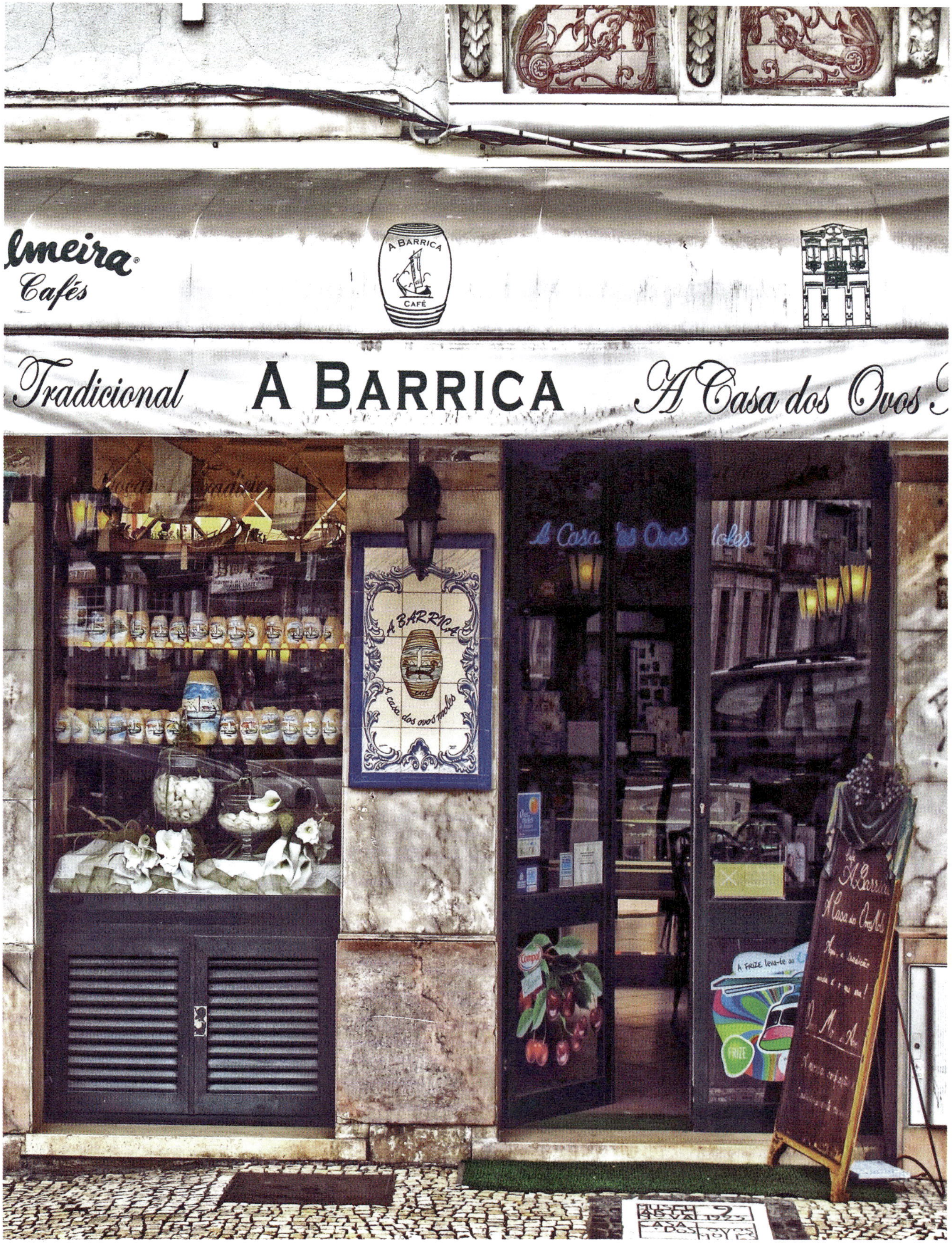

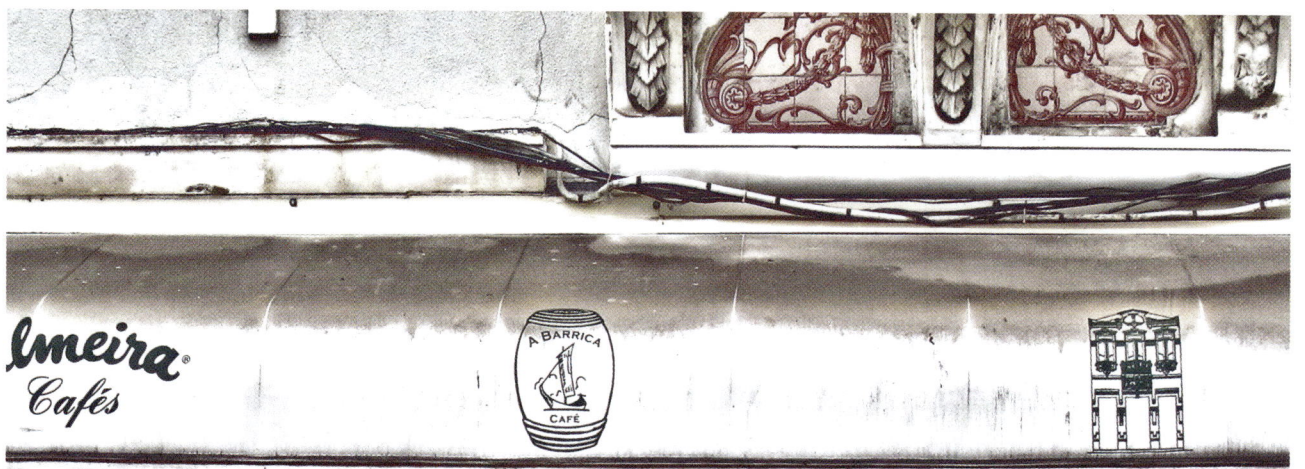

lmeira®
Cafés

A BARRICA
CAFÉ

Tradicional **A BARRICA** *A Casa dos Ovos*

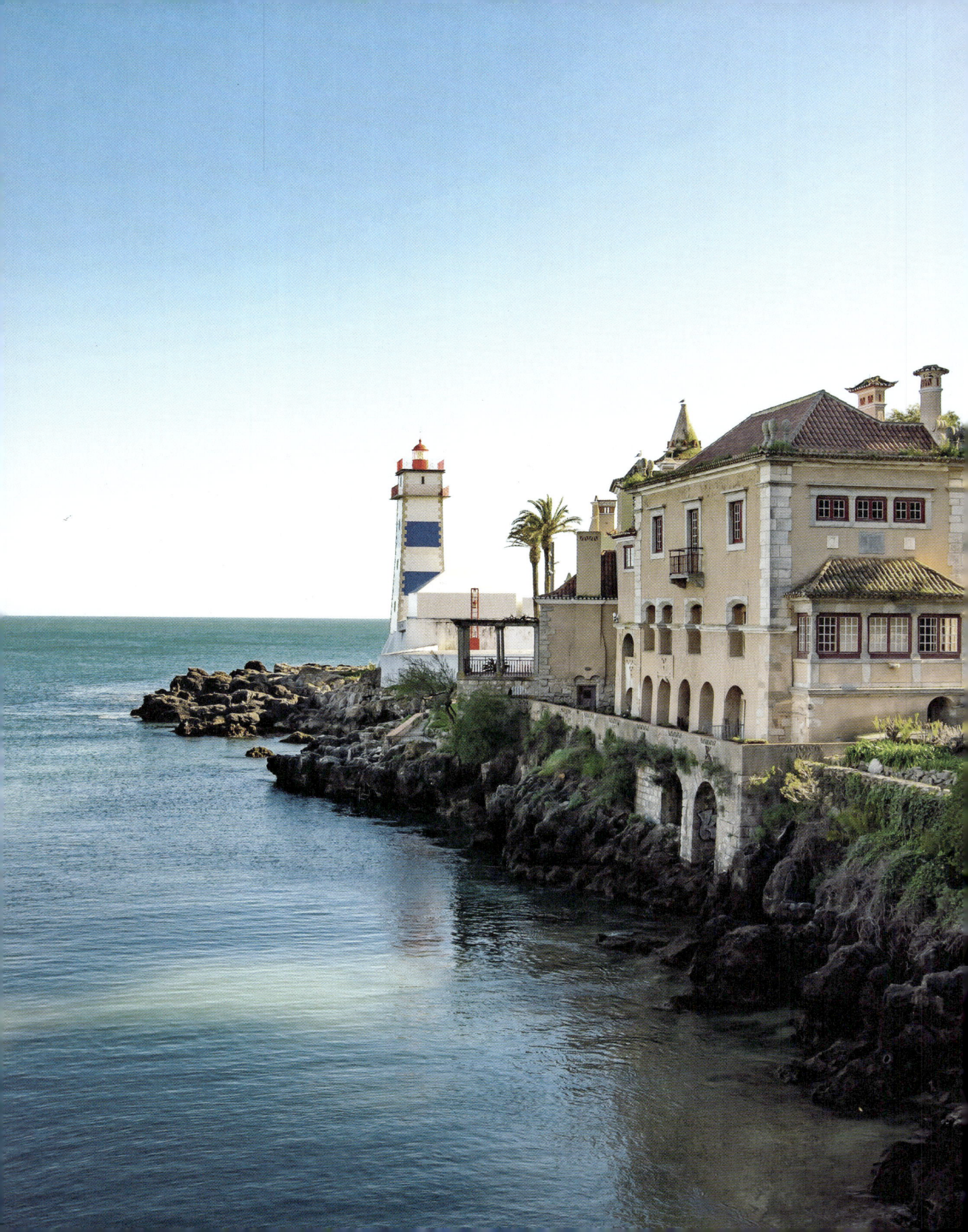

ON THE COAST

THE ATLANTIC'S CONSTANT SURGE AND STONE TRACES OF HISTORY DEFINE THE COSTA DE PRATA FROM LISBON NORTHWARD

Along Portugal's central coast, the ocean shapes daily life and sets the pace. Off the fishing town of Nazaré, summer brings calm turquoise water along wide sandy beaches. In winter, storms create a spectacle best seen from the small red lighthouse on the fortified cliffs, as surfers from around the world confront waves that rise to 30 meters, their faces streaked with silver foam. Earlier generations of pilgrims traveled instead to Sítio, high above the cliffs, to venerate the Black Madonna in the Church of Nossa Senhora da Nazaré. Since 1889, a funicular has linked the lower town to this major pilgrimage site atop a steep slope. Below, the lower town belongs equally to visitors and local fishermen, whose brightly painted boats line the shore. Inland, following the Alcobaça River leads to one of Portugal's largest and oldest monasteries, now a UNESCO World Heritage site. In the fourteenth century, its Cistercian abbots—close advisors to the royal court—were drawn into the tragic story of Pedro I and Inês de Castro. Murdered for political reasons to block her marriage to the heir to the throne, Inês was later proclaimed queen by Pedro after his accession. Their tombs remain in the monastery today. Cascais, just outside Lisbon, also carries royal associations, having once served as a summer retreat for the Portuguese court. A walk through streets lined with pastel houses leads to the blue-and-white Santa Marta lighthouse overlooking the coast, and the neighboring museum, which records the area's maritime past.

LEFT: *An easy feeling in the resort of Cascais along the Portuguese Riviera, not far from central Lisbon. Once a fishing village, later a summer residence for the Portuguese royal family—a veritable jewel in the crown.*

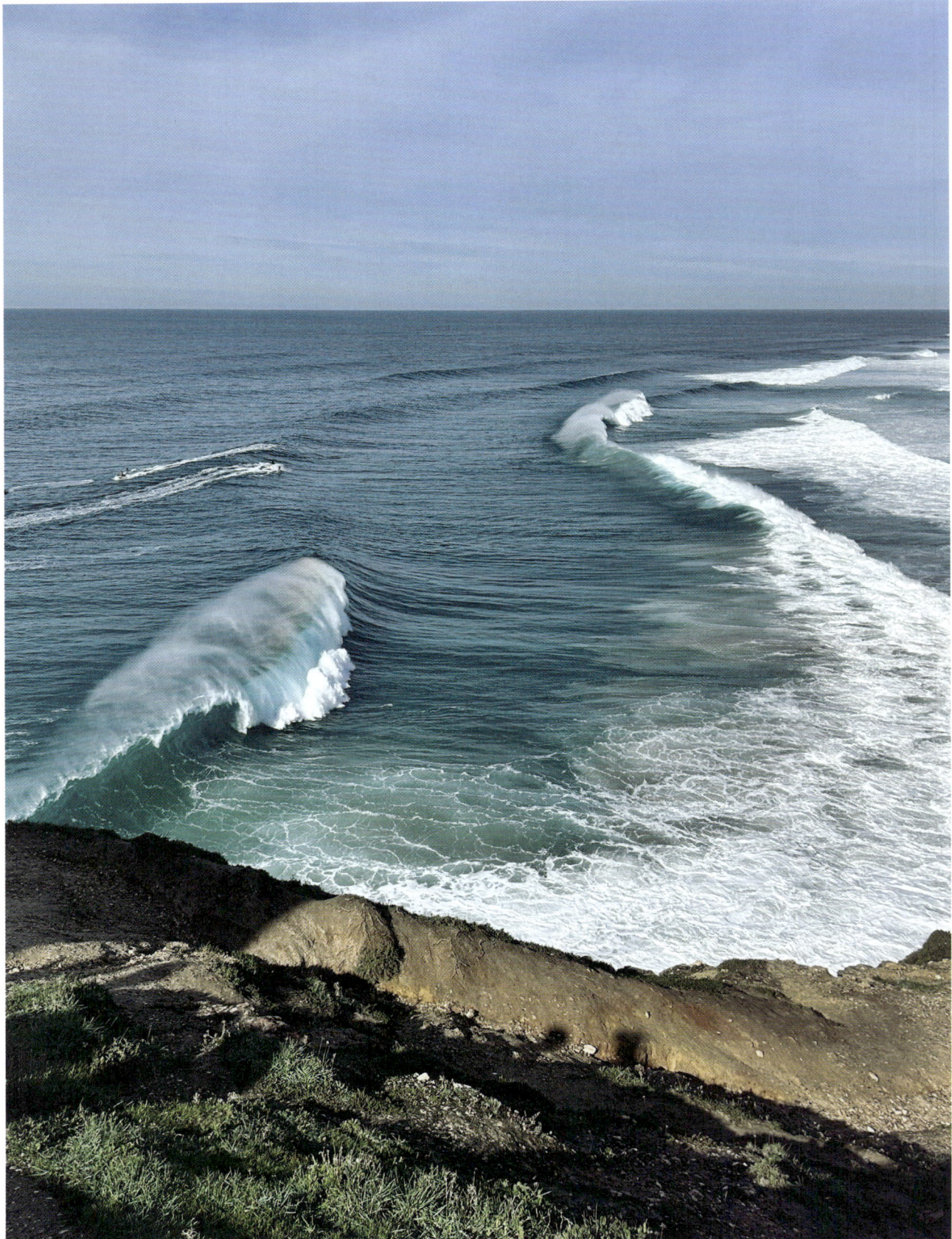

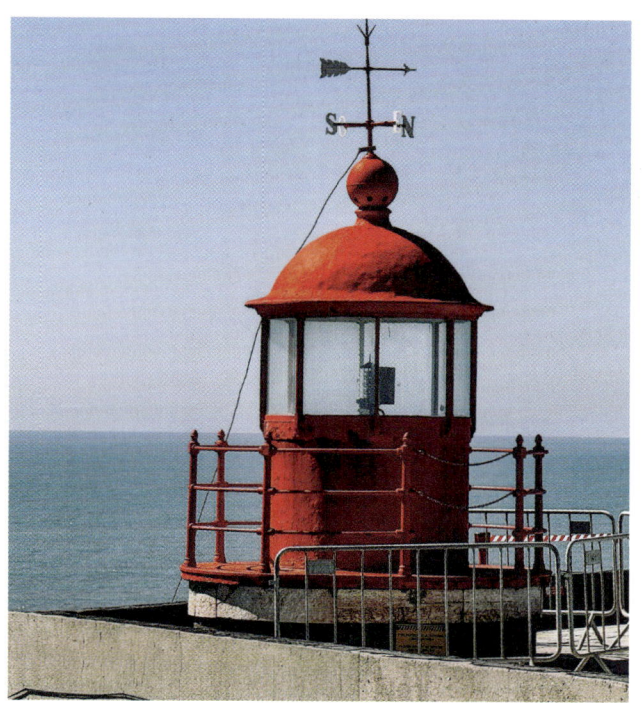

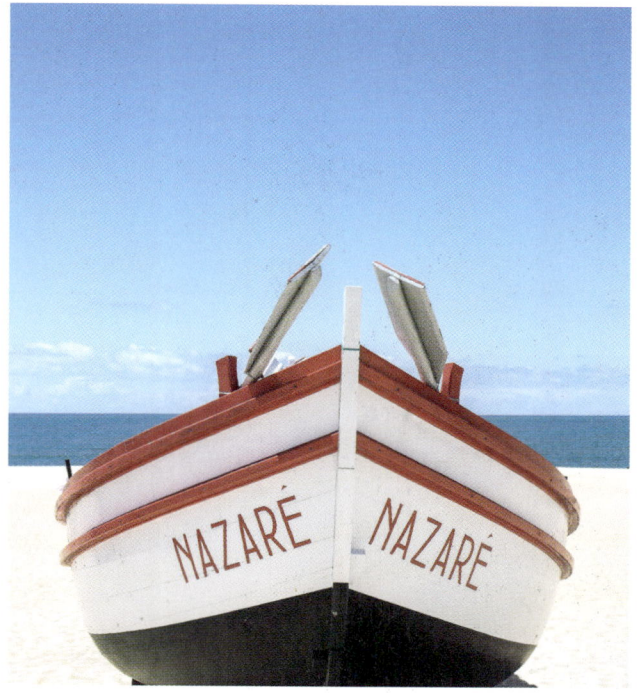

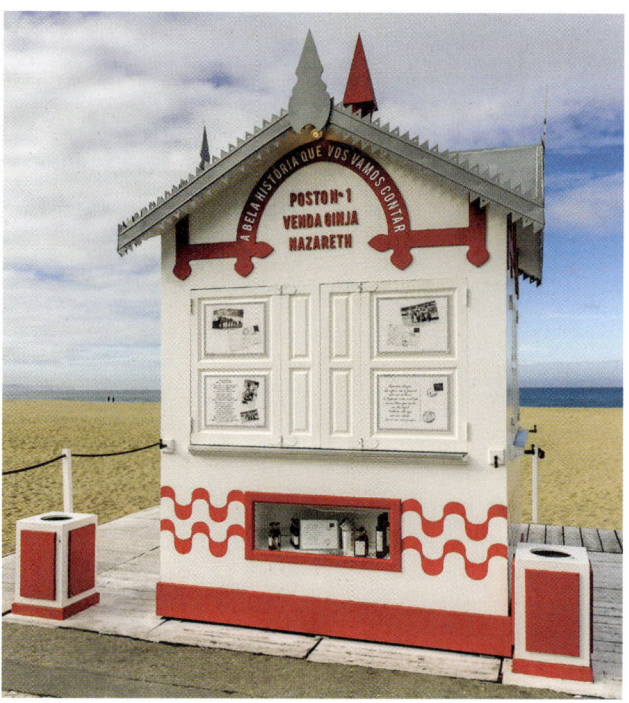

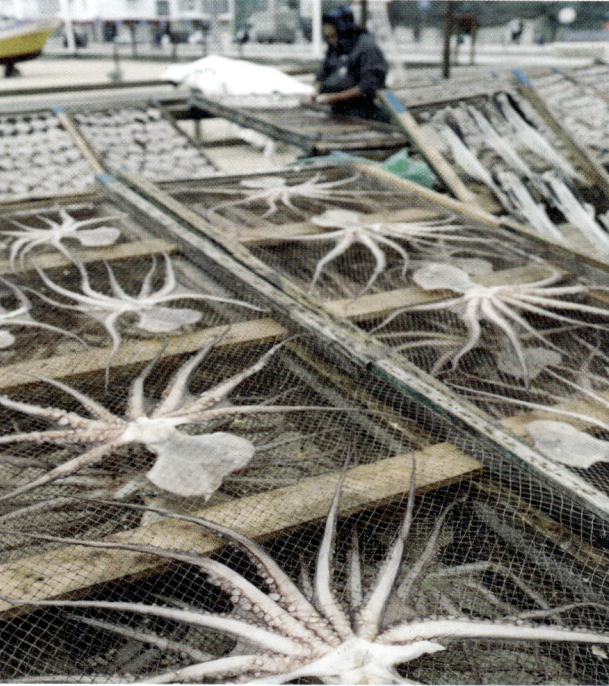

ABOVE AND LEFT: *There are many broad, sandy bays along the Atlantic coast, but Nazaré gets towering winter surf.*
Before the surfers arrived, fishermen in red-and-white boats were the only ones who would venture out.

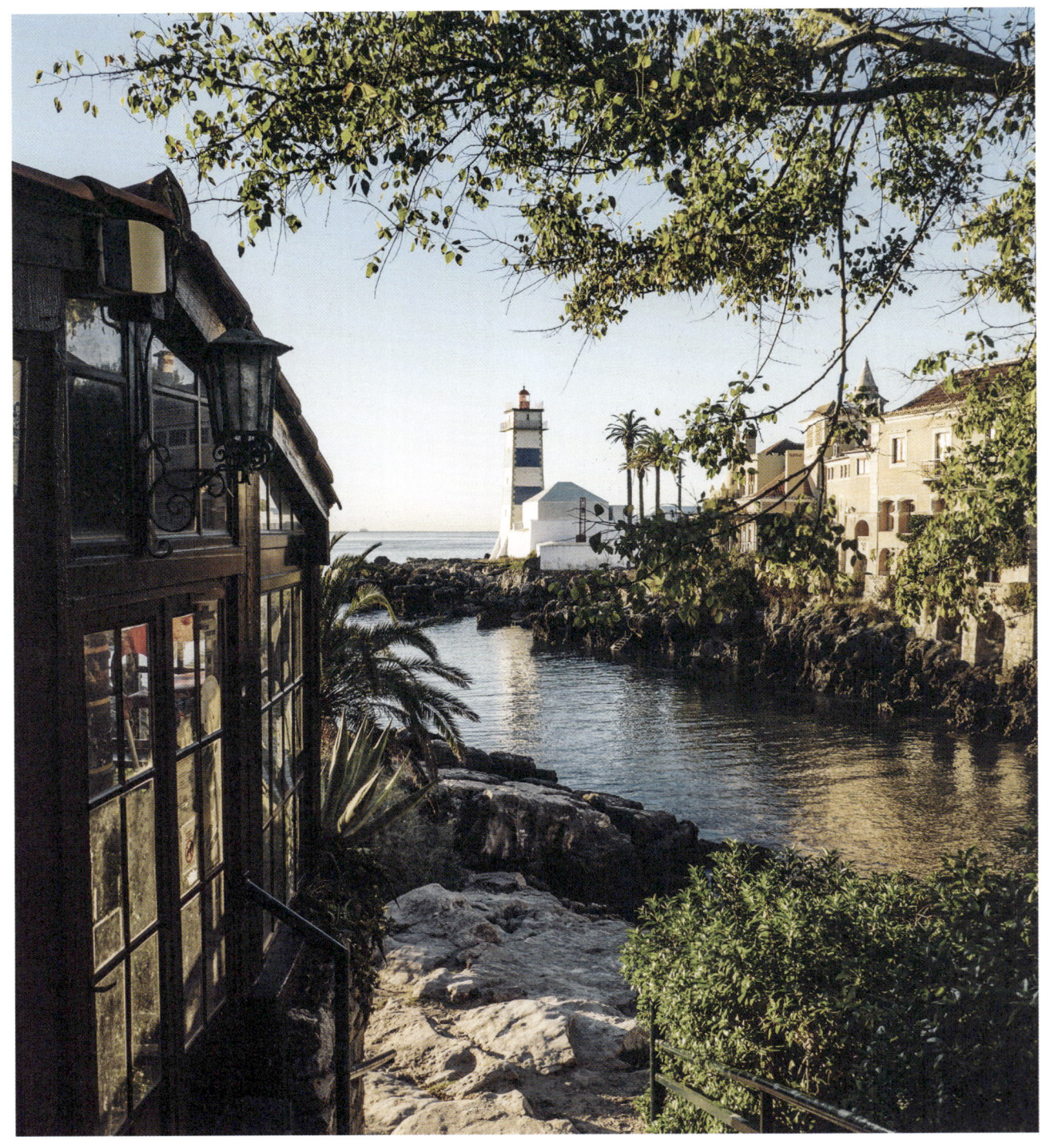

ABOVE: *Cascais's lighthouse seen from the former Palace of the Condes de Castro Guimarães. The white-and-blue lighthouse of Santa Marta is now a museum.*

RIGHT: *Built around 1900 as a summer residence, the eclectic Palace of the Counts of Castro Guimarães has been an art museum since 1931.*

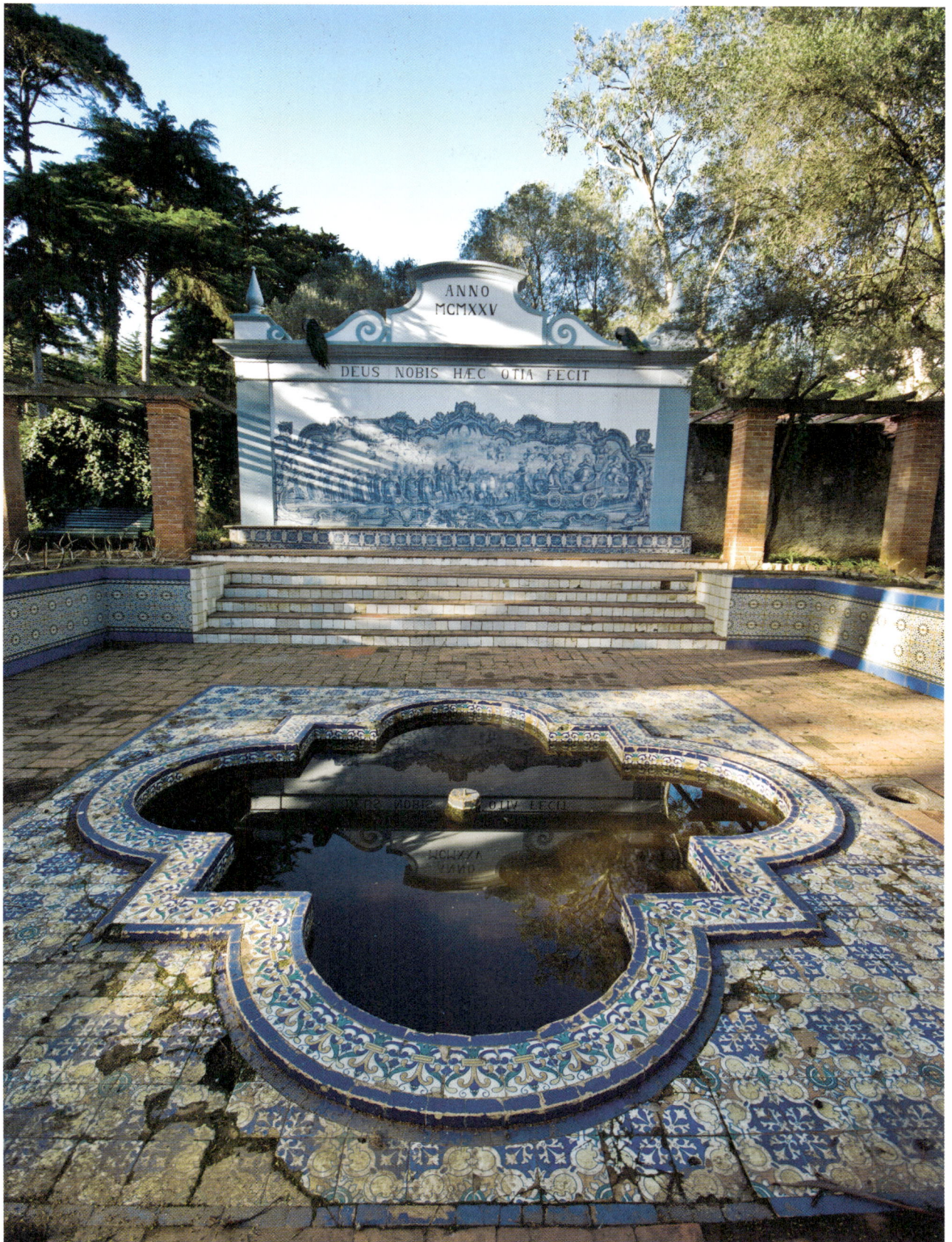

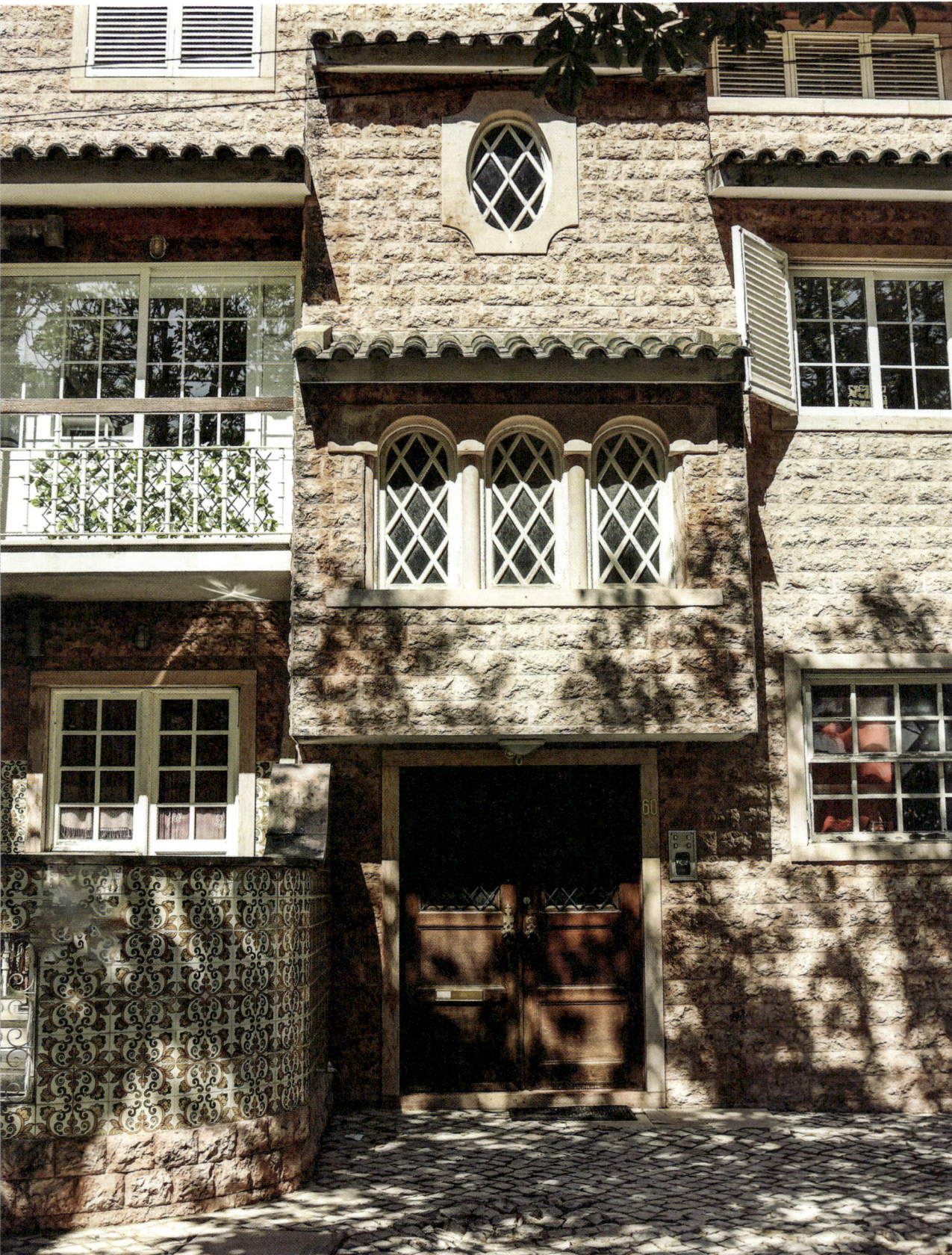

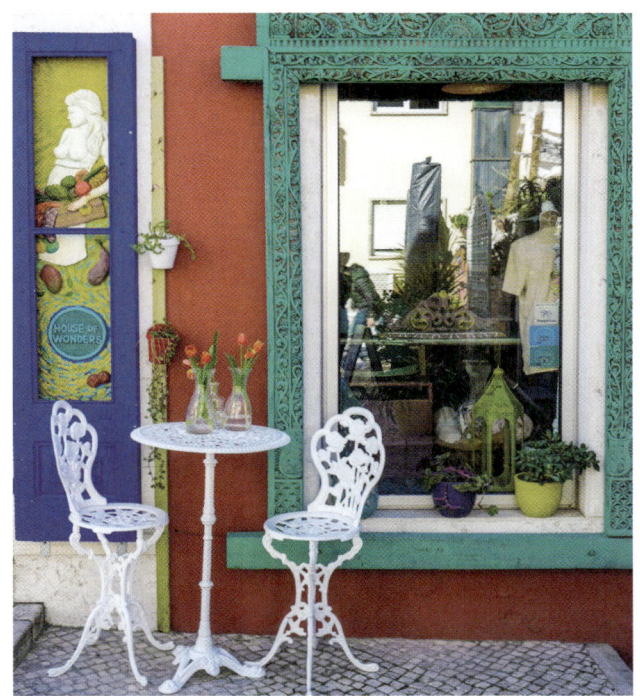

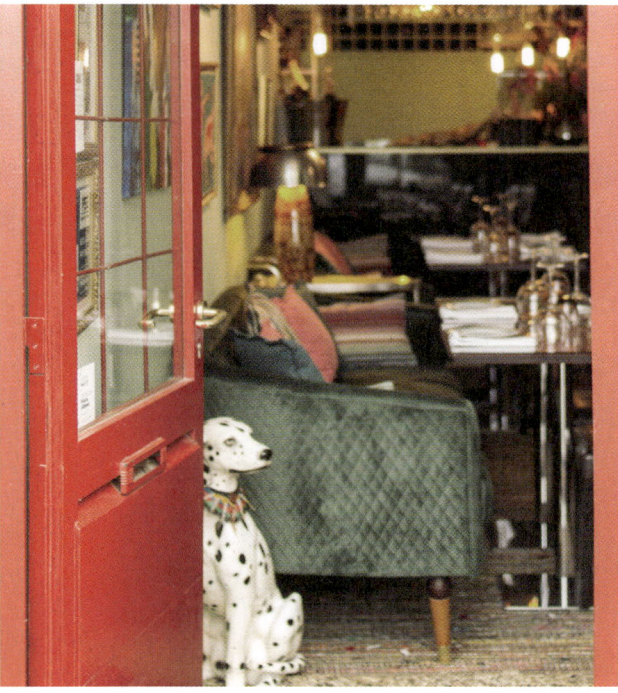

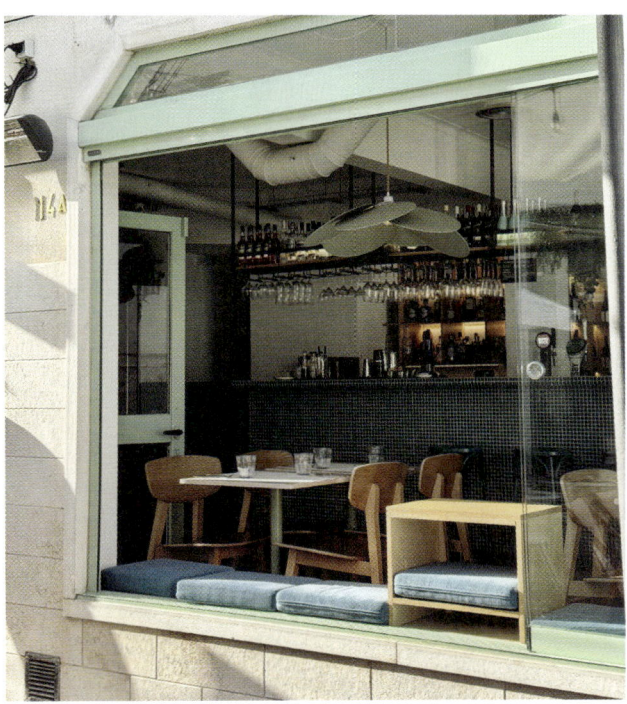

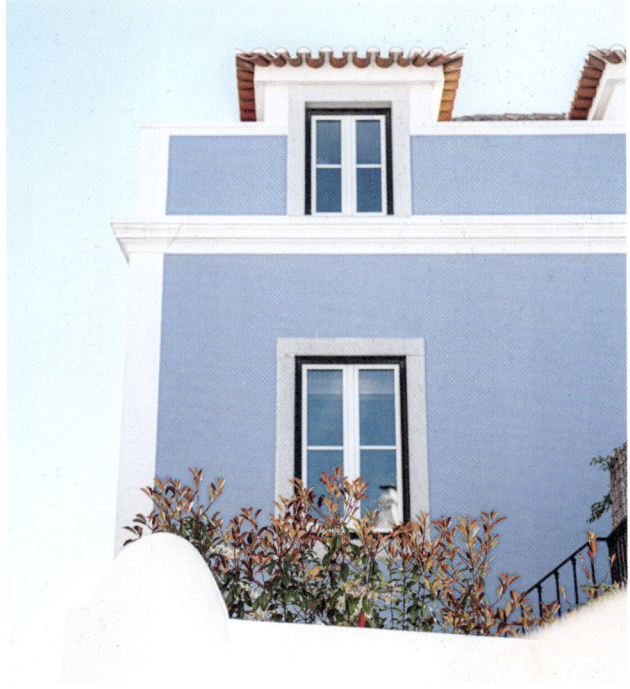

ABOVE AND LEFT: *Bright, richly detailed façades along the harbor and in the old town of Cascais range from ornate and formal to light and playful. Narrow streets packed with cafés and bars fill up on summer evenings.*

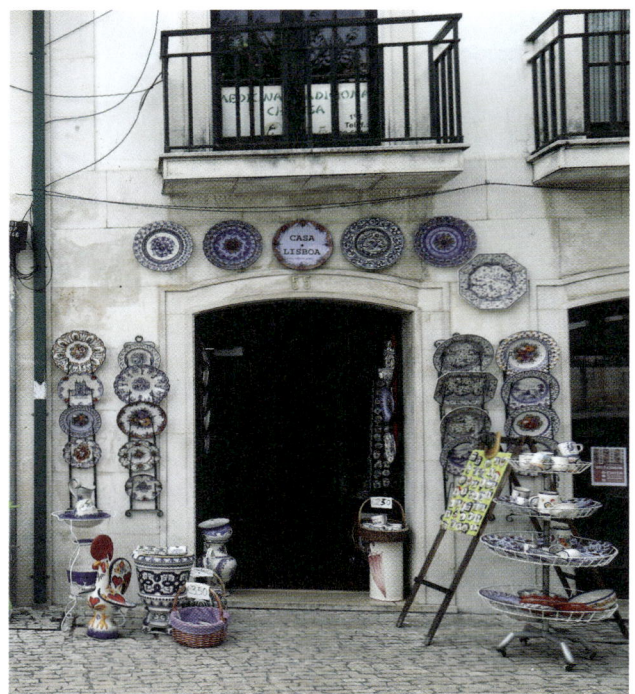

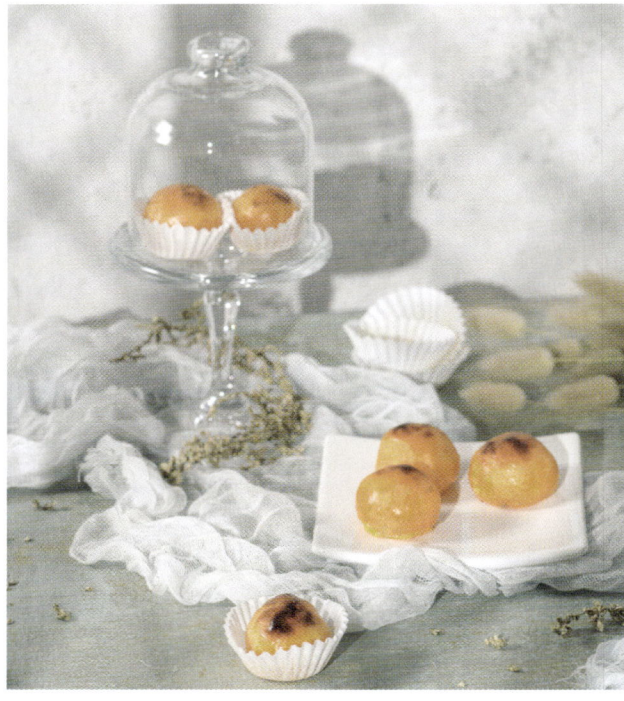

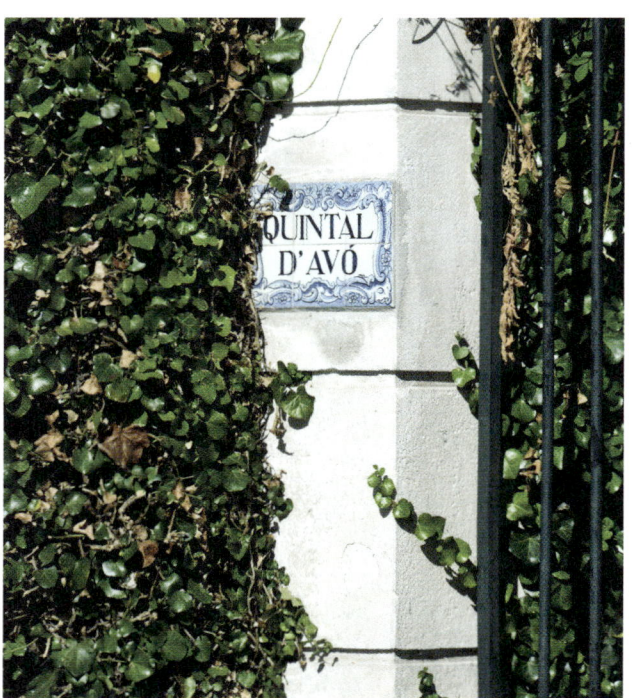

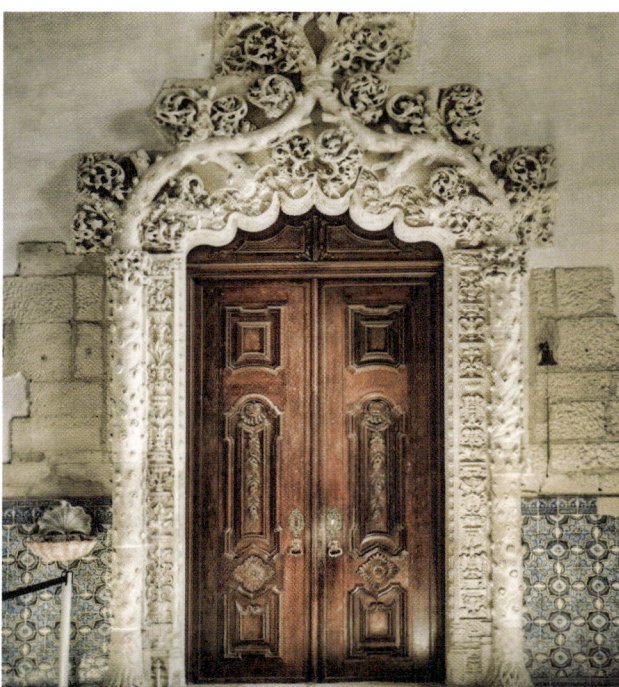

ABOVE AND RIGHT: *Founded in 1153 by Portugal's first king, Afonso, the Cistercian monastery of Alcobaça is among the country's largest monastic complexes. The fourteenth-century cloister brings together Gothic and Manueline elements.* Castanhas de ovo, *a local pastry (top right) is sold at the* pastelaria *across from the church.*

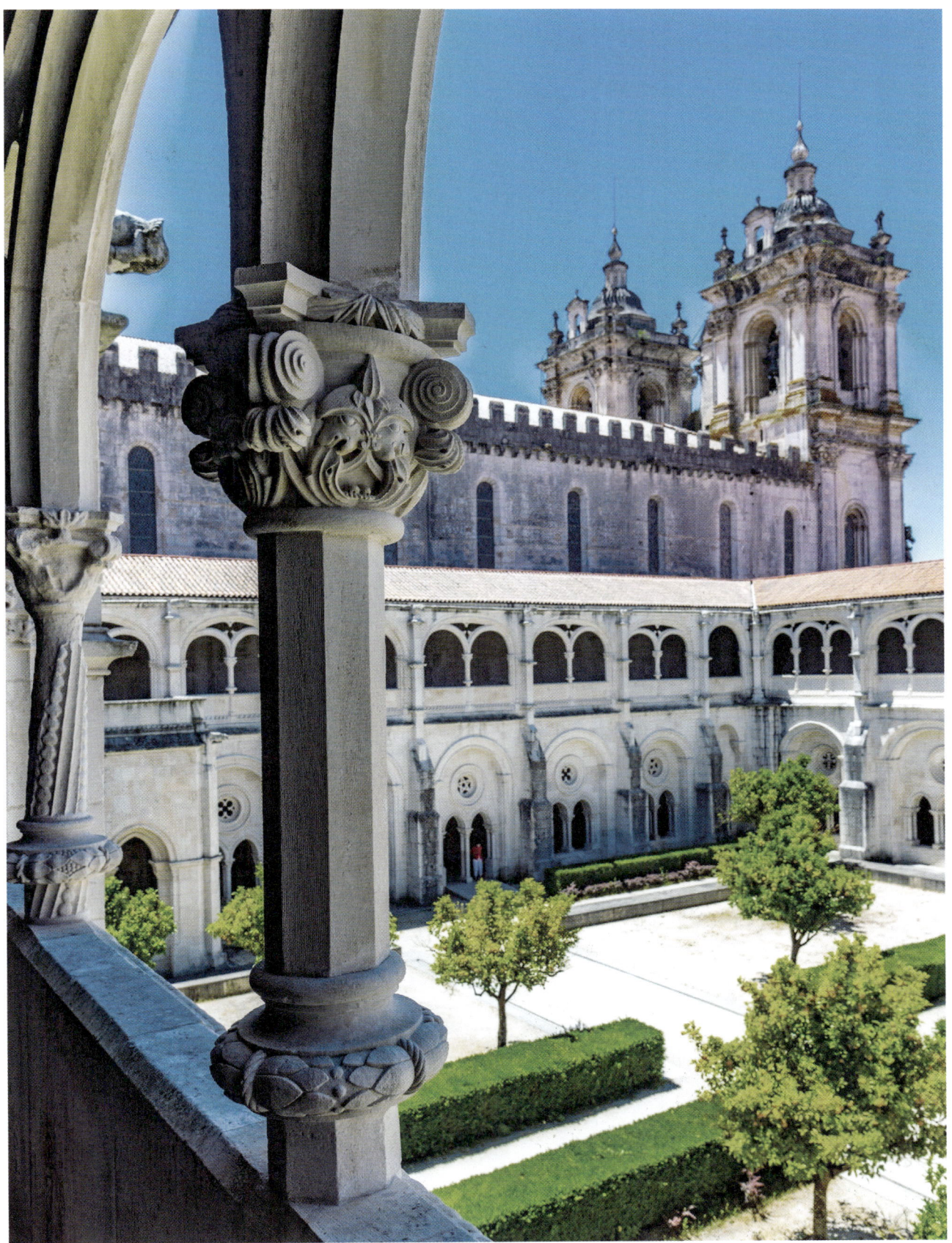

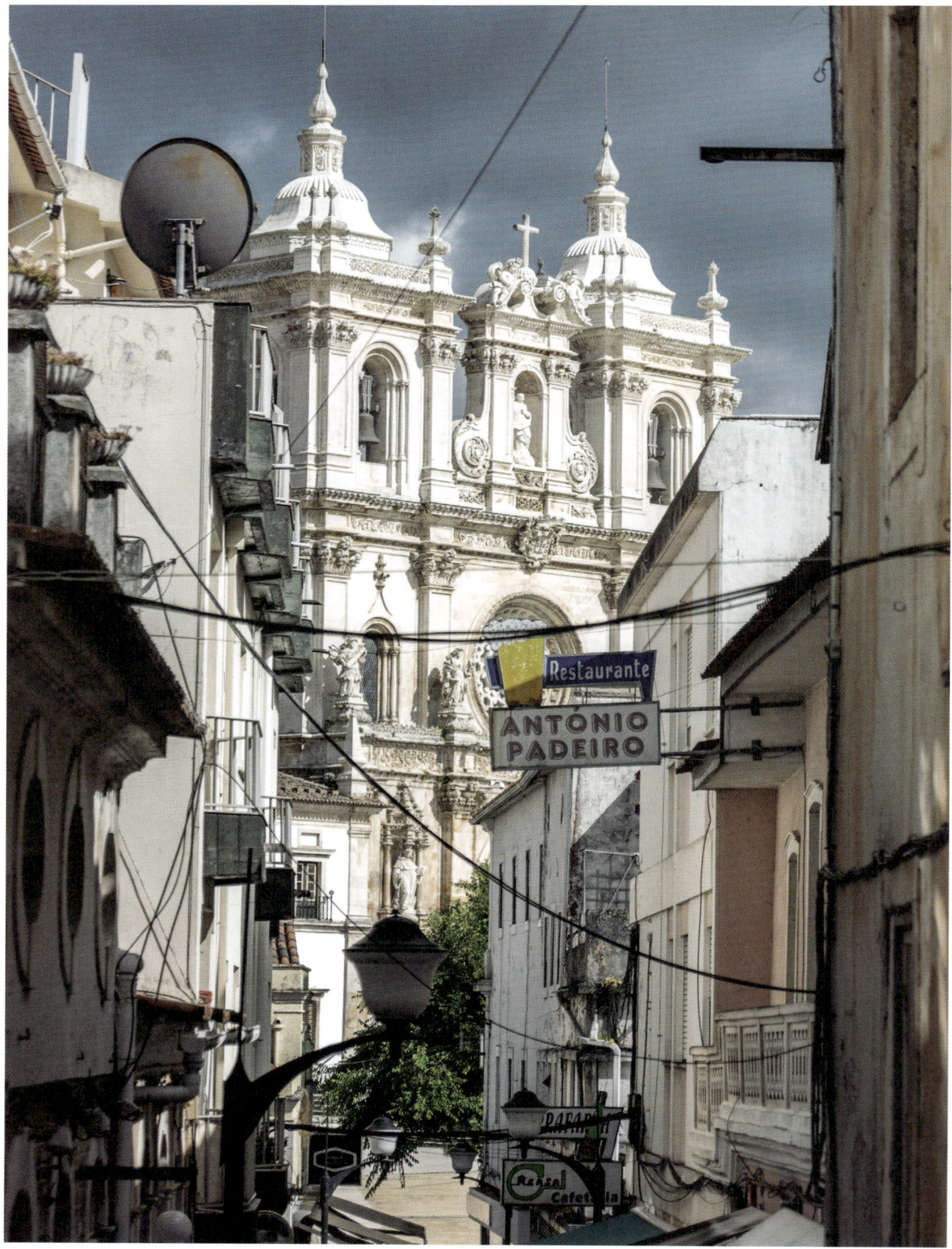

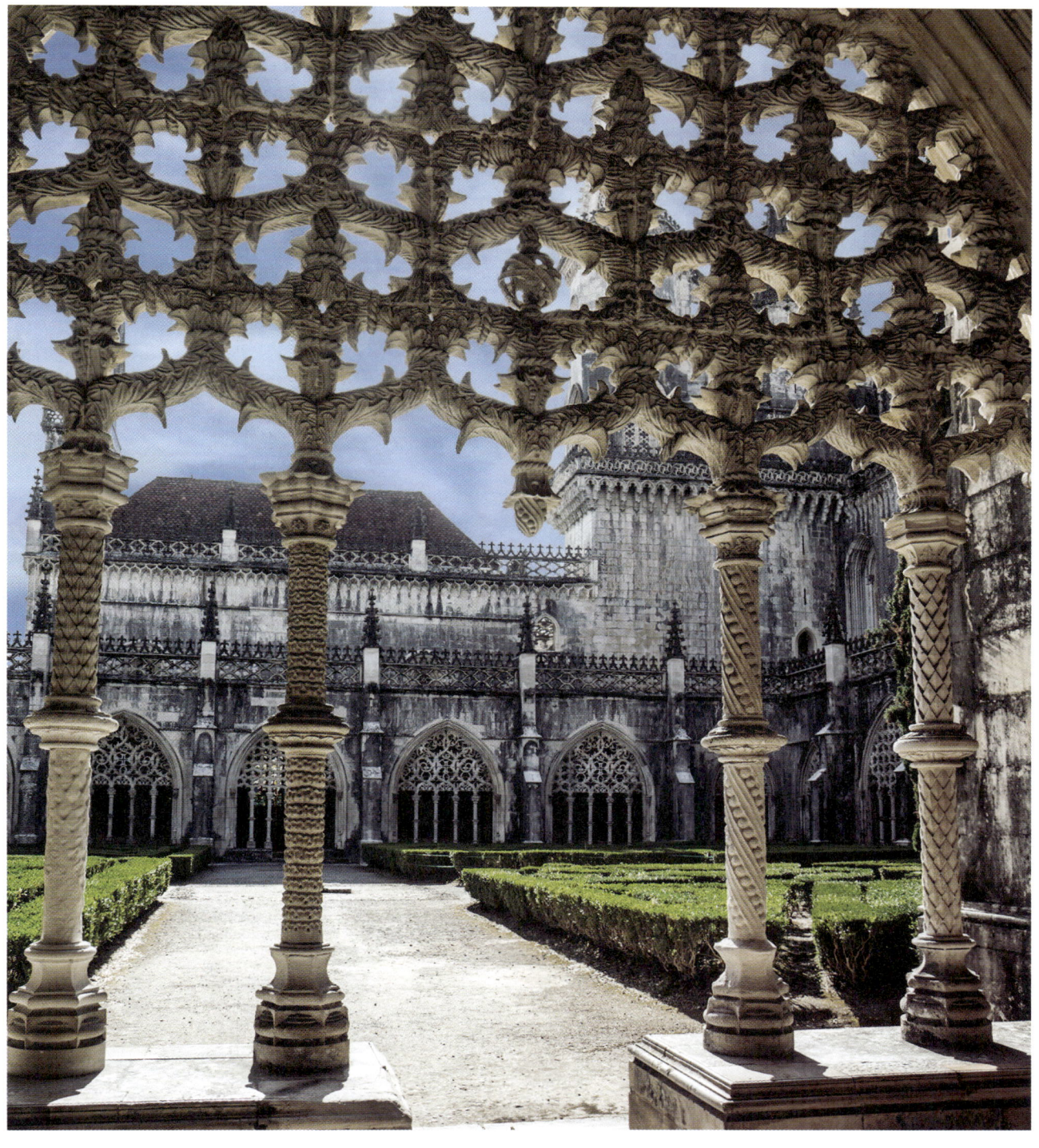

ABOVE: *Another example of sacred architecture in the monastery at Batalha. Fascinating details on the carved stone cloister.*

LEFT: *Alcobaça monastery church looks like a small palace with its Baroque façade.*

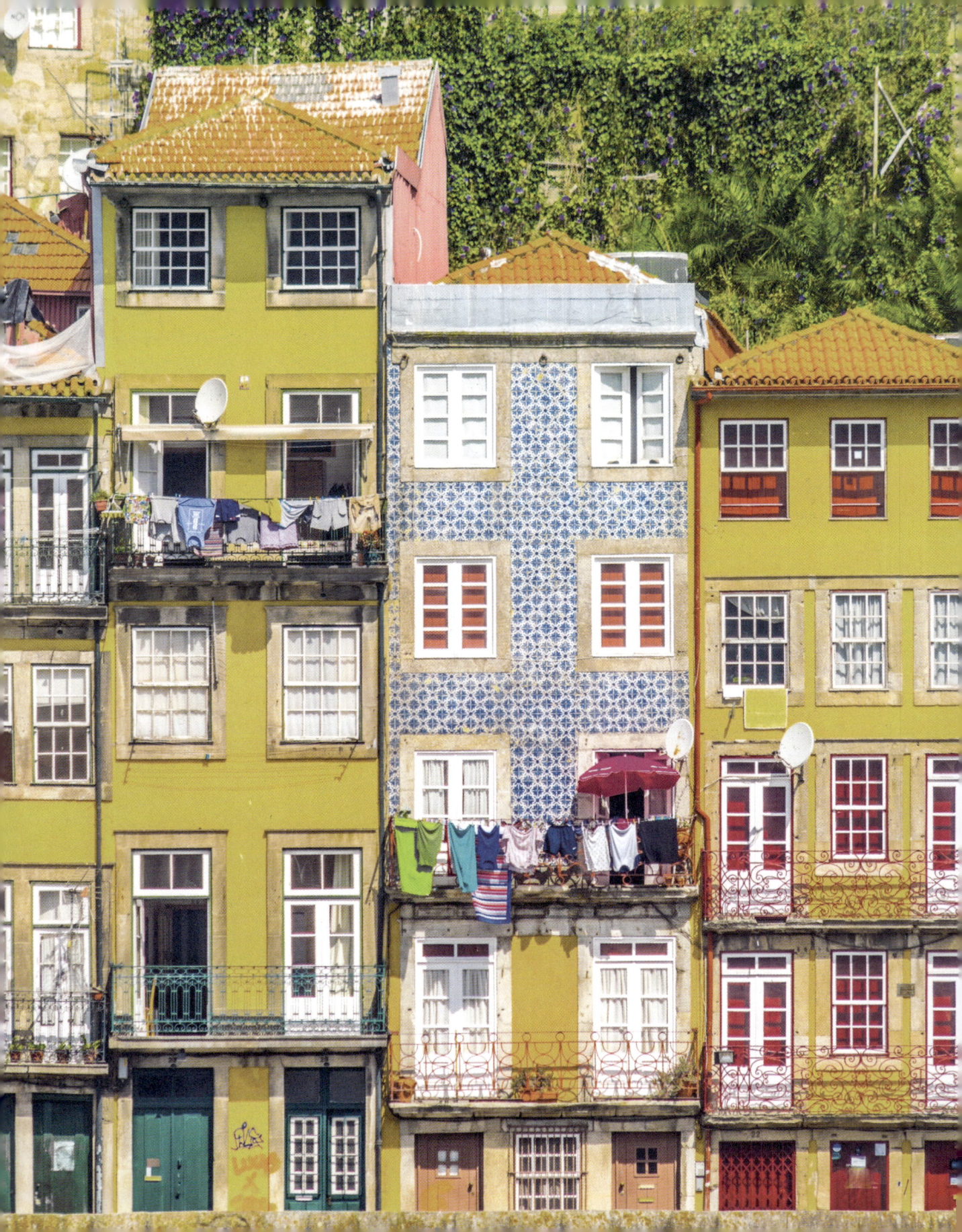

PORTO

PORTO, A CITY OF LIGHT AND NARROW LANES, RISES IN STEEP TIERS ABOVE THE DOURO, AND THE ATLANTIC AIR CARRIES BOTH SALT AND AGE

An old saying captures the city's self-image: money is made in Porto and spent in Lisbon. It's a point of pride for residents of Portugal's second-largest city on the north bank of the Douro. That confidence is most visible in Ribeira, the former fishing quarter that climbs from the riverfront toward the bishop's palace and the twelfth-century cathedral. Its houses stand tall and narrow, painted in soft pastels and pressed close together along stairways that double as streets, where clotheslines are stretched between wrought-iron balconies that seem to span the vertical space above. Even here, everyday life claims its place, with café tables set in passages barely wide enough to walk through. At intervals the tight corridors open onto small squares such as Largo da Pena Ventosa. These pockets of space still recall a time when the colorful surrounding houses were occupied only by fishermen and their families. A quieter sort of elegance, with the added appeal of reminiscence, takes hold near the university. Between Praça da Liberdade and the baroque Igreja do Carmo, with its azulejo-covered façade, long-established shops and cafés line the streets, many dating from the Art Nouveau era. One of them is Livraria Lello, which opened in 1906 and is often listed among the world's most beautiful bookstores. Its sweeping staircase and carved wood interior are said to have inspired the Hogwarts of the Harry Potter novels. Whether or not that claim holds, the place makes an immediate impression. So does São Bento station, often described as Portugal's most beautiful, its main hall lined with more than twenty thousand azulejo tiles presenting a sweeping chronicle of Portuguese history.

LEFT: *Along the Ribeira quay, tall and narrow fishermen's houses with painted façades. Ribeira is Porto's oldest district.*

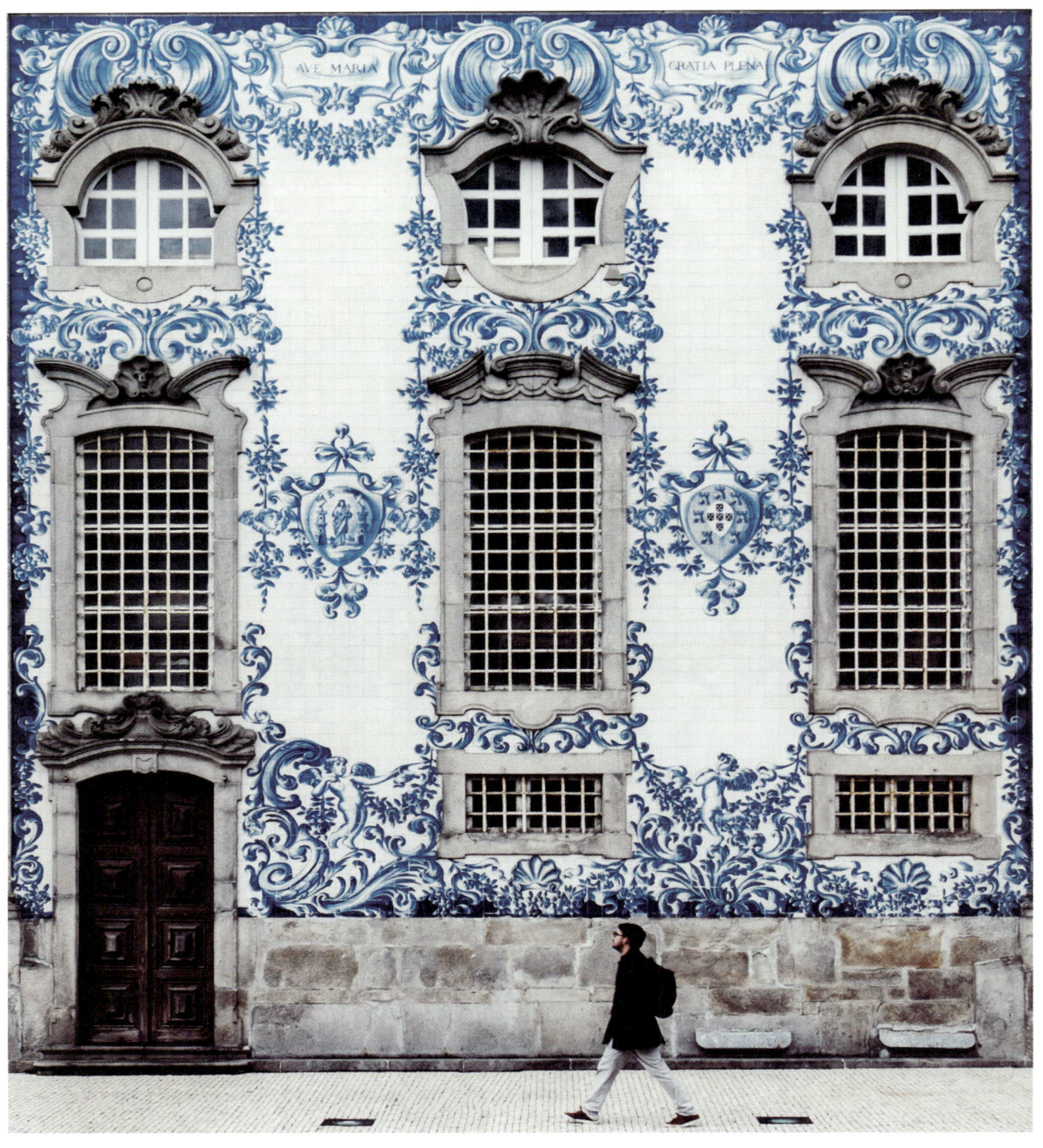

ABOVE AND RIGHT: *In Porto, azulejos appear throughout the city, from the façade of the Igreja do Carmo to the colorful houses of Ribeira.*

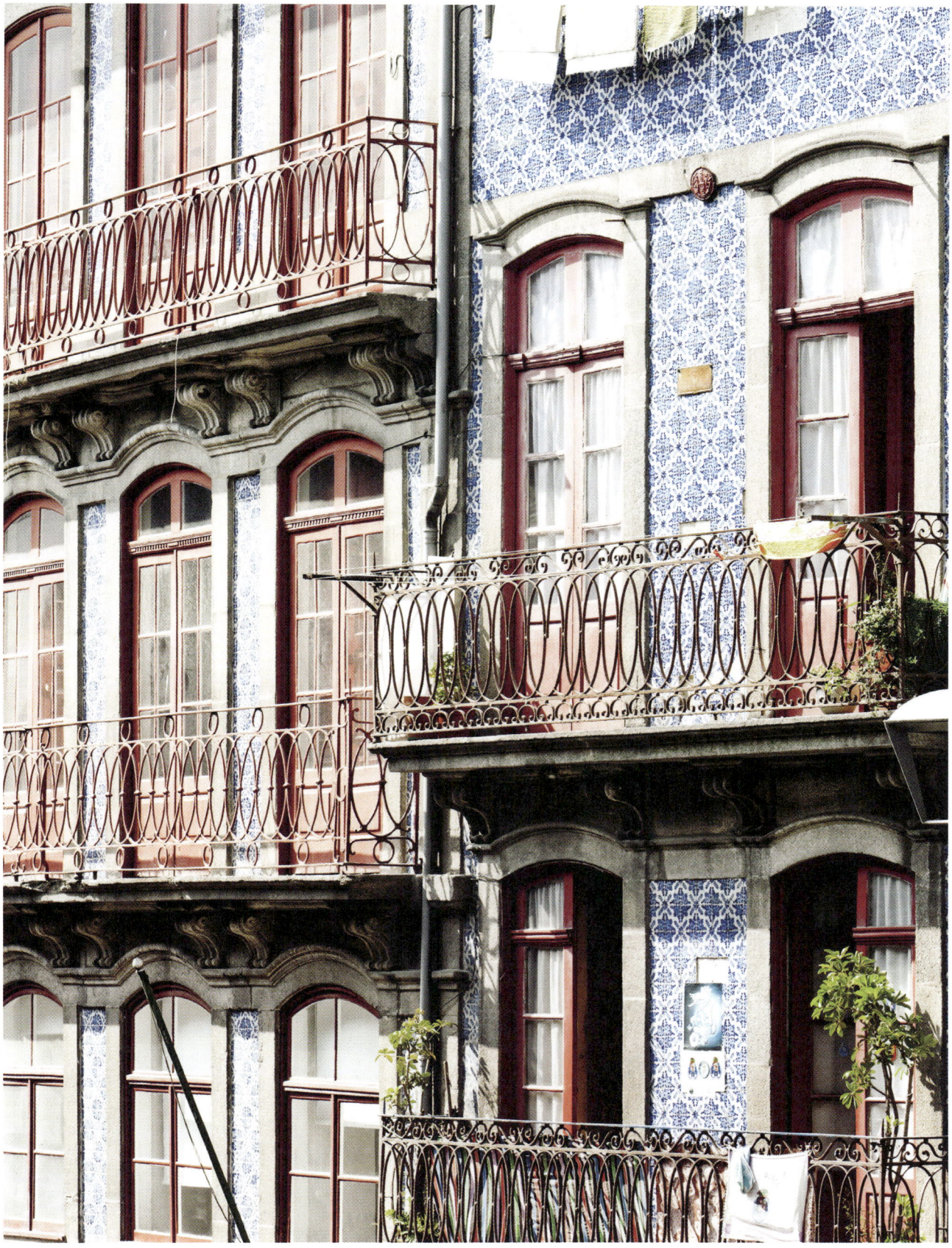

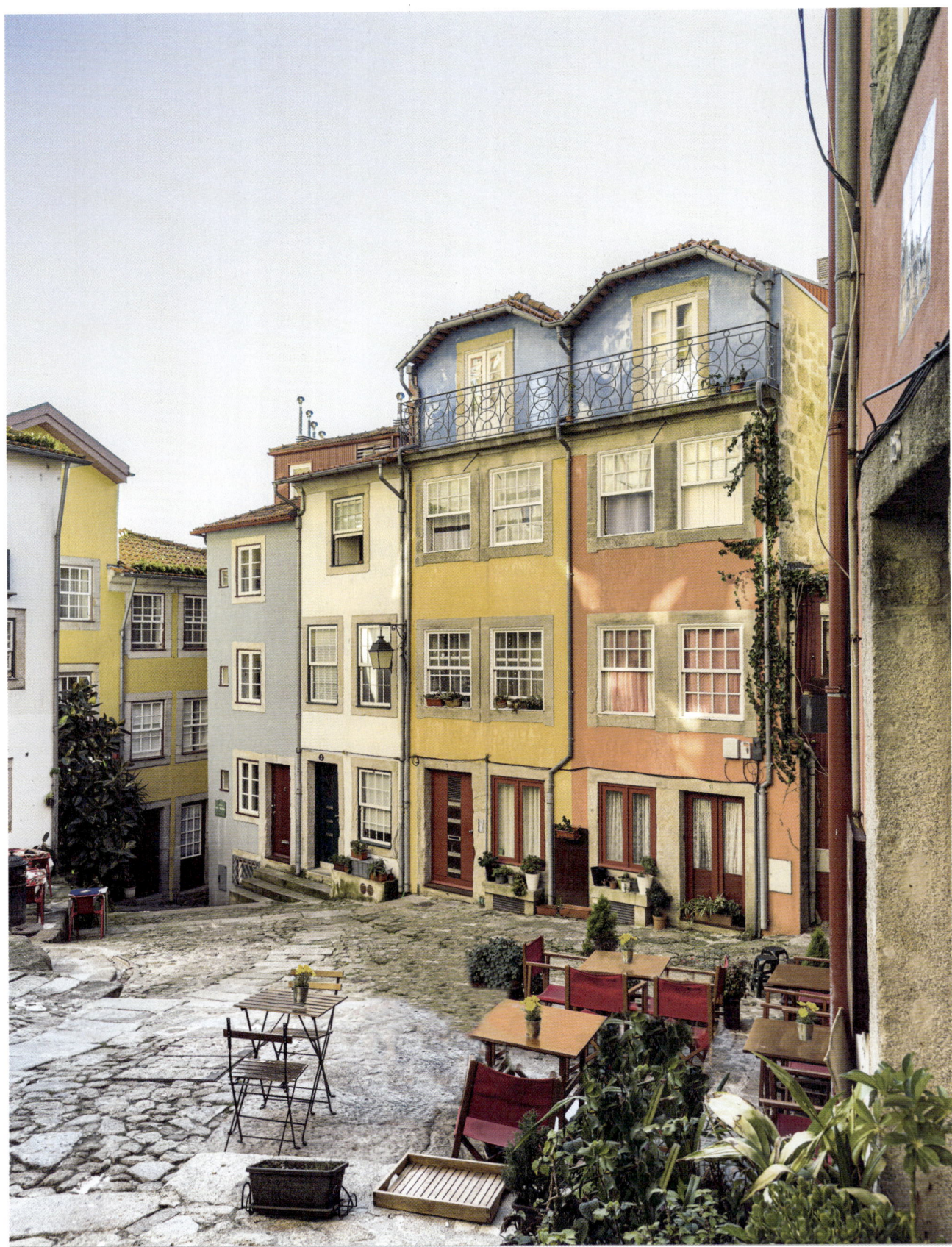

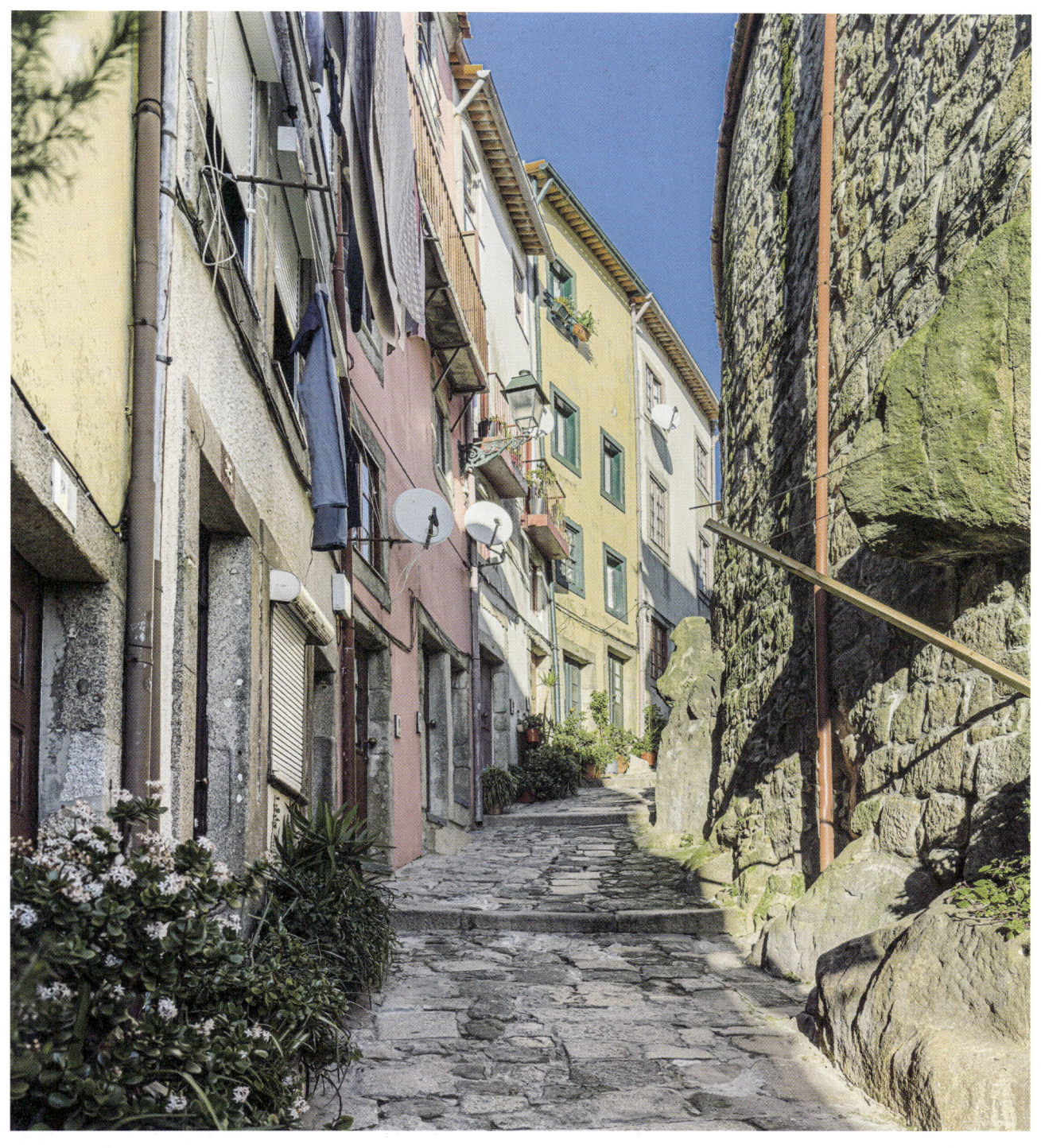

ABOVE AND LEFT: *Largo da Pena Ventosa lies within the tight network of passageways in Ribeira. The colorful buildings, now home to small cafés, retain their historic appearance.*

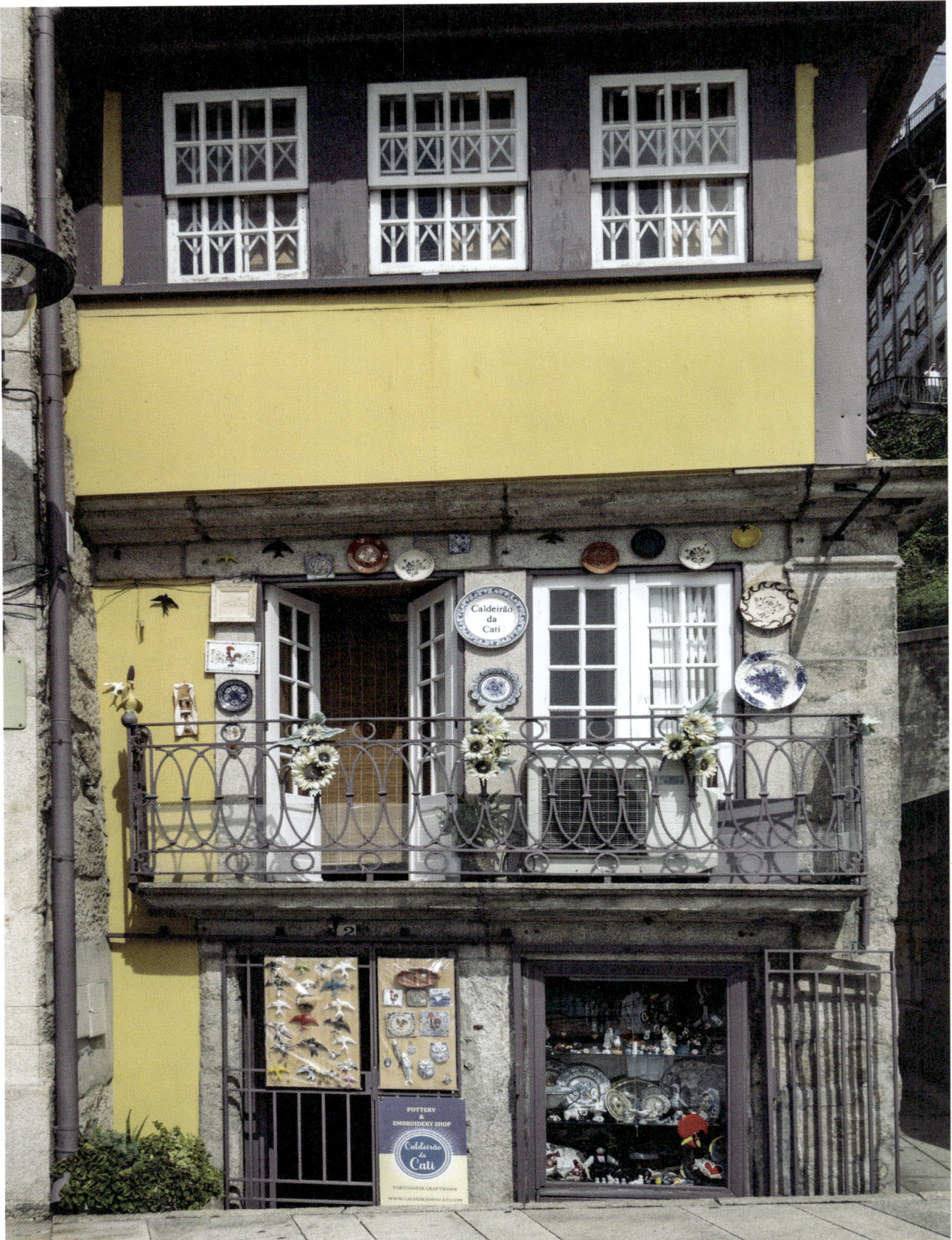

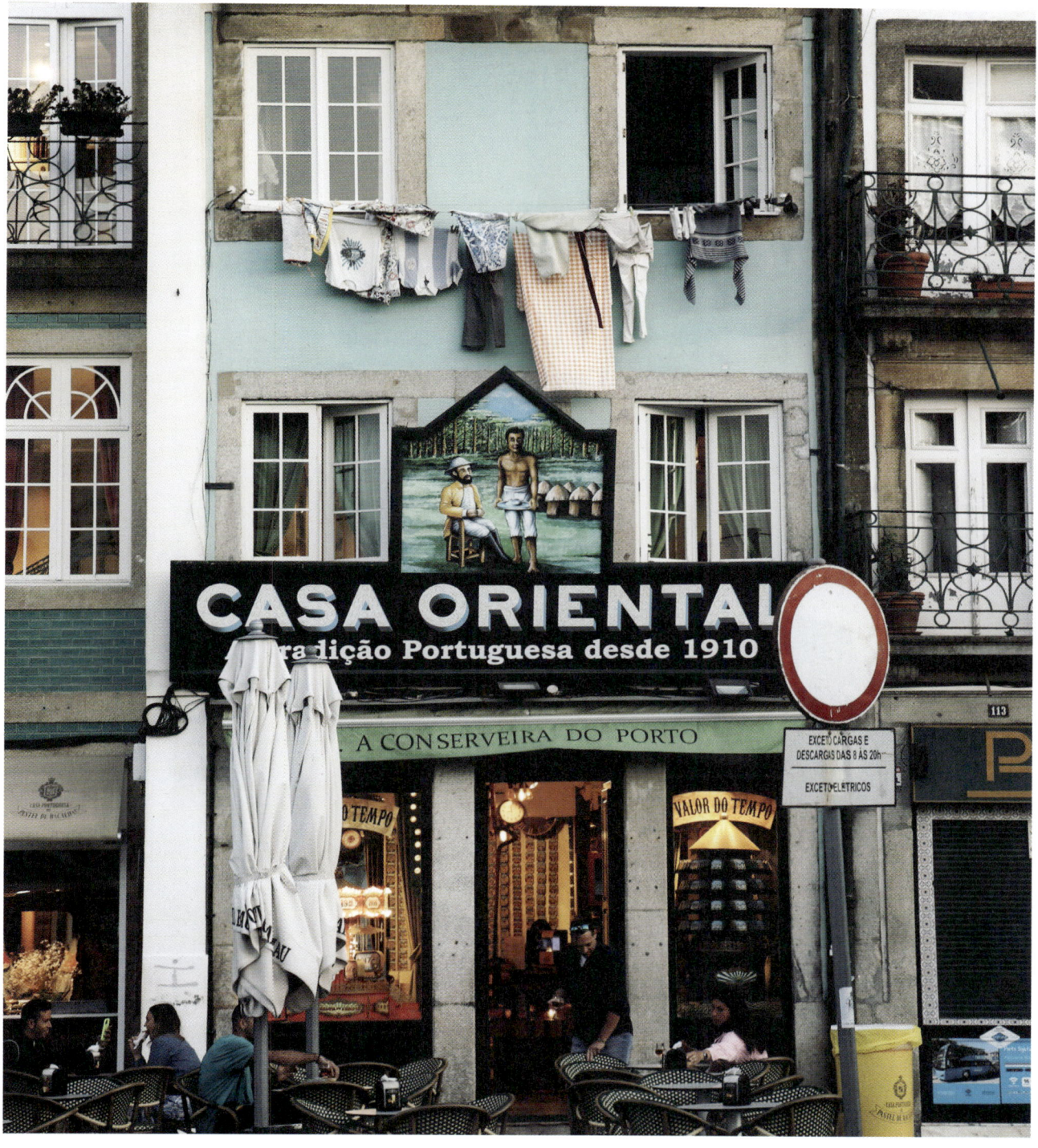

ABOVE AND LEFT: *Houses around Ribeira once belonged to fishermen and traders. Today, craft traditions continue in souvenir shops and small workshops. Ceramics and local specialties such as* sardinhas em azeite *are readily available.*

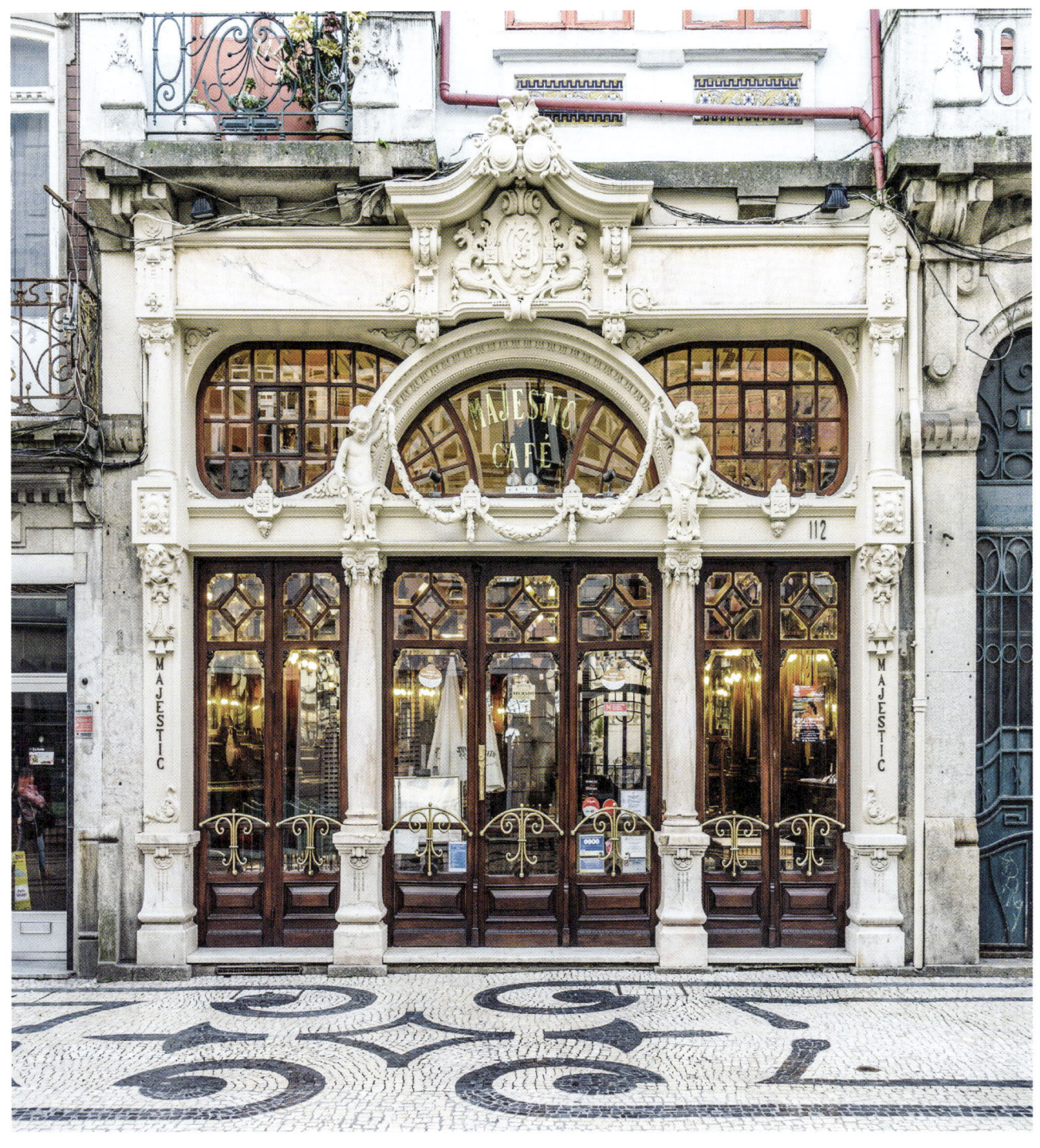

ABOVE AND RIGHT: *Café Majestic preserves Portuguese coffee traditions within an Art Nouveau interior.*
The café once served as a meeting place for writers and intellectuals, and they have managed to keep it alive.

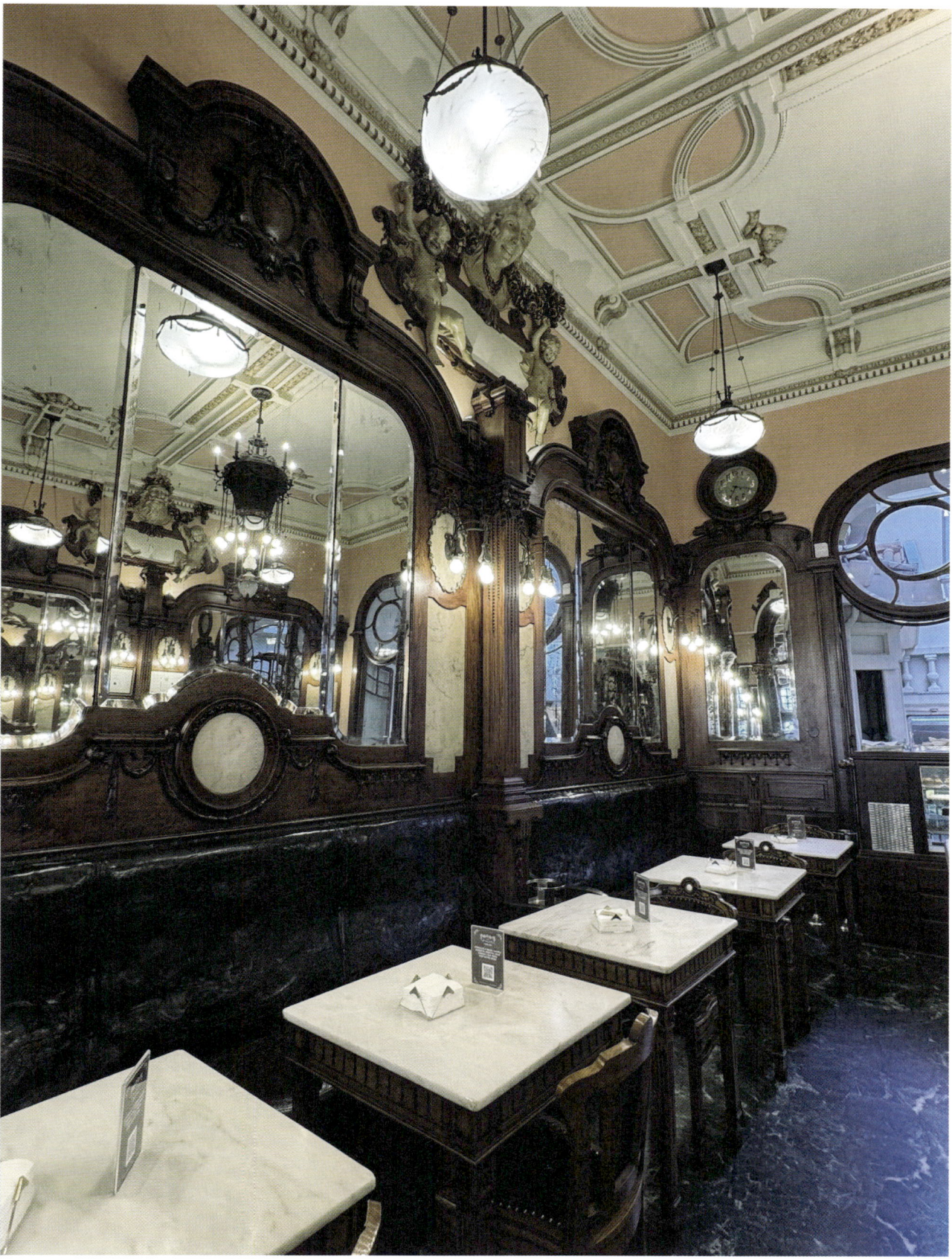

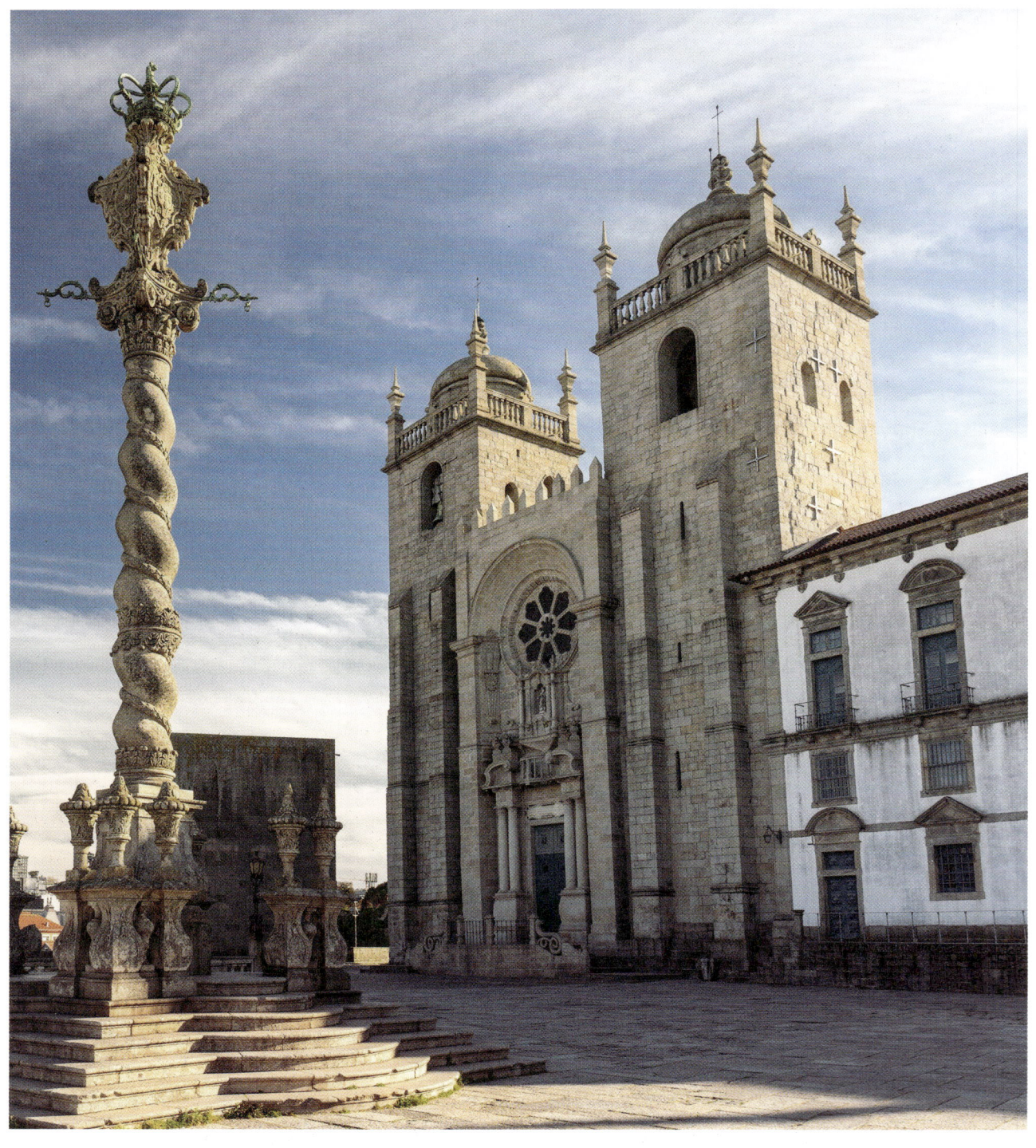

ABOVE: *The Pelourinho pillory near Porto Cathedral dates to the twelfth century but was reconstructed in 1945 based on historical drawings. So, old, but not that old.*

RIGHT: *Porto Cathedral's fourteenth-century Gothic cloister. Four centuries later, the azulejo artist Valentim de Almeida added large religious scenes.*

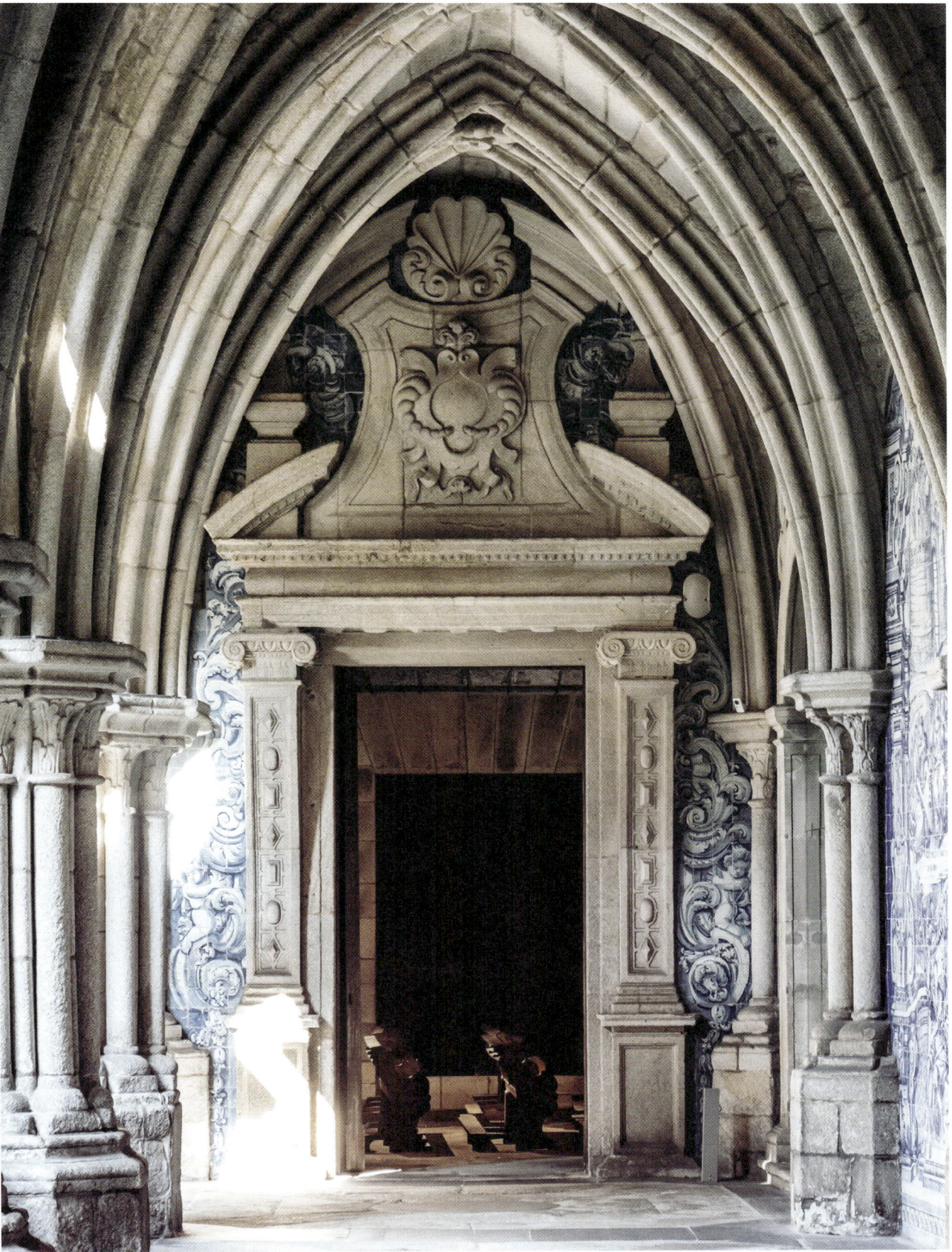

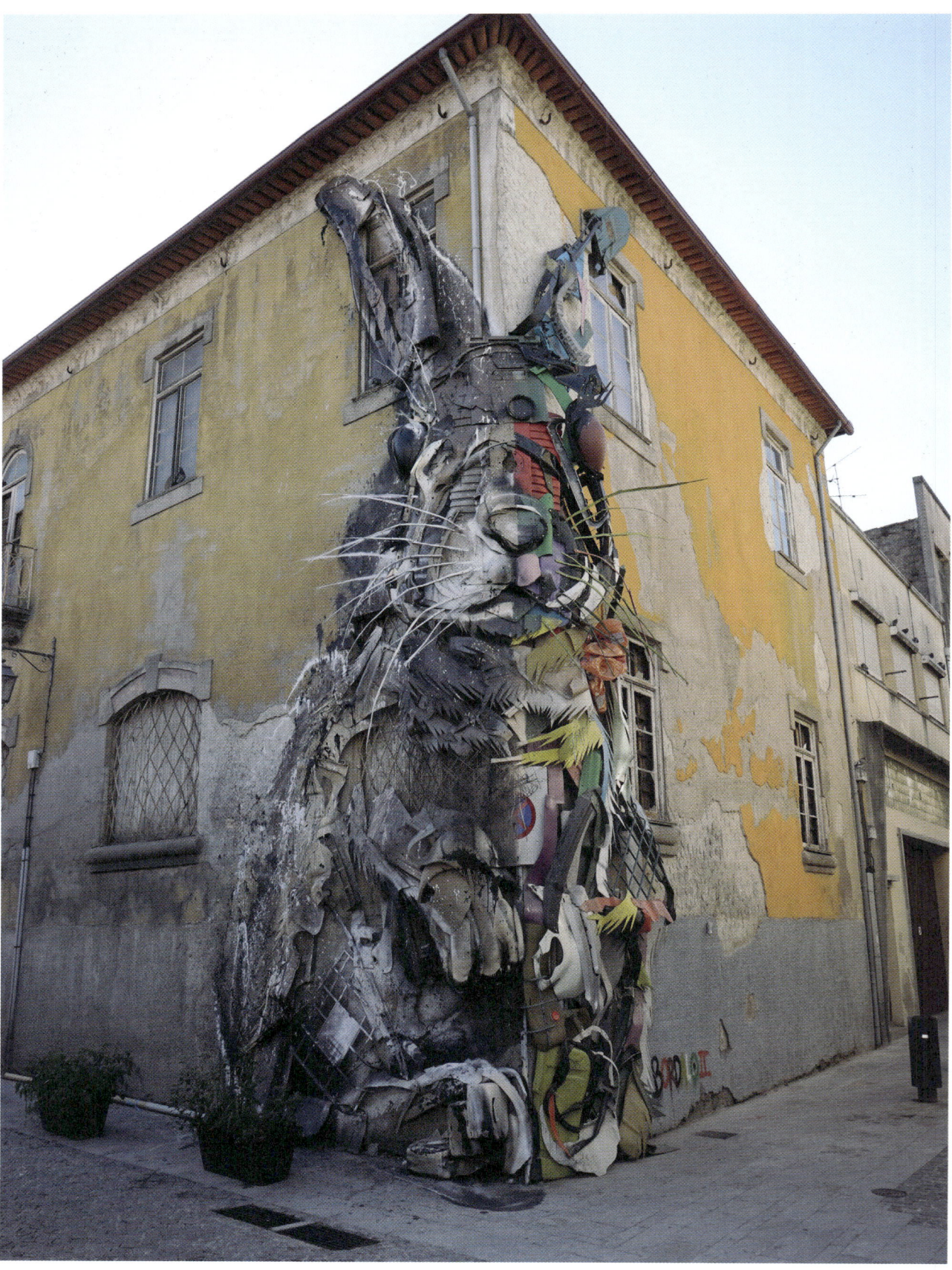

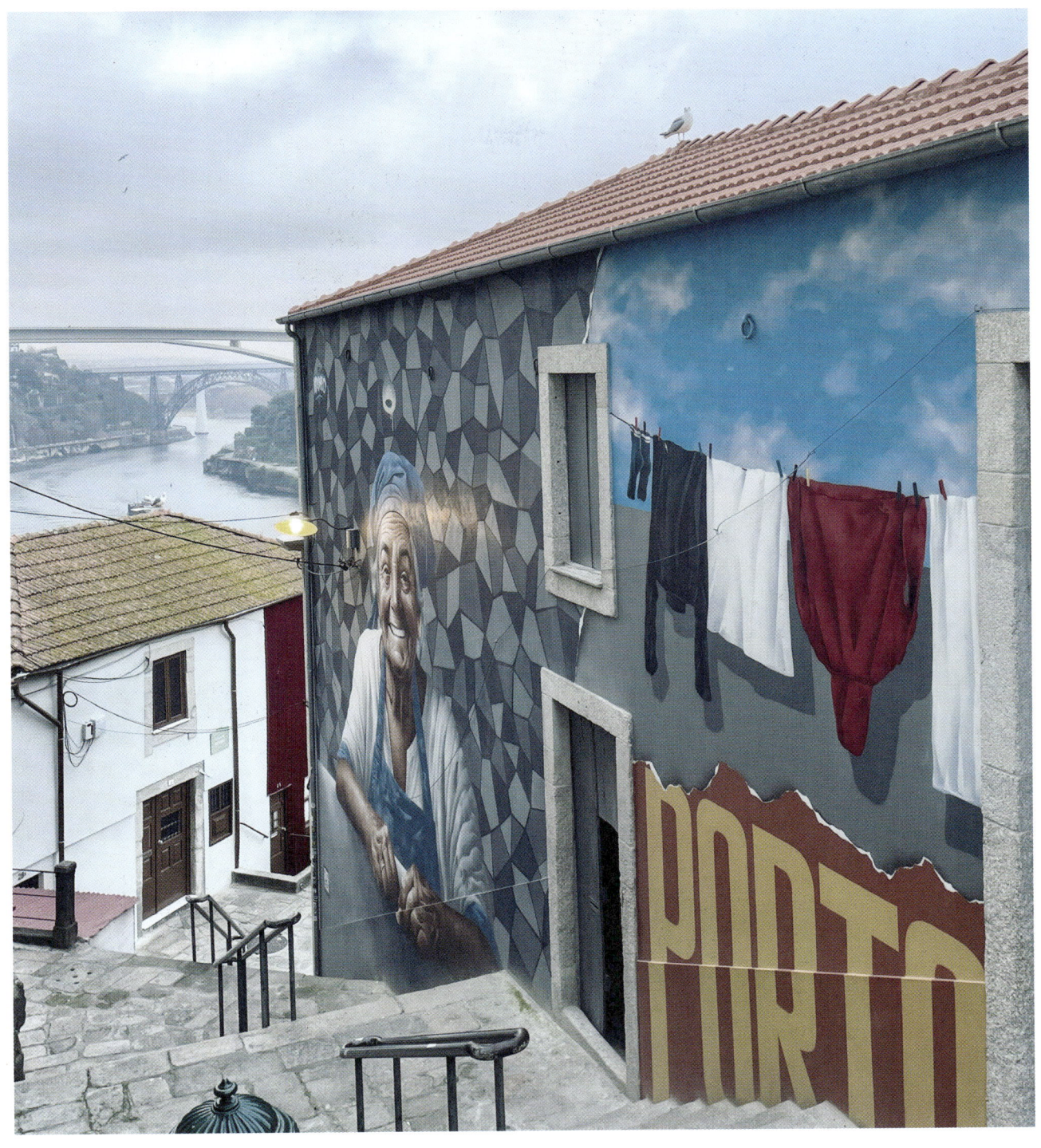

ABOVE: *The steep steps of Guindais in Porto's old town are good for street art. Dona Rosa, by Mr. Dheo, is a tribute to the women of Porto.*

LEFT: *In Vila Nova de Gaia, street artist Bordalo II created the three-dimensional installation* Half Rabbit *from recycled materials. The work calls out environmental destruction.*

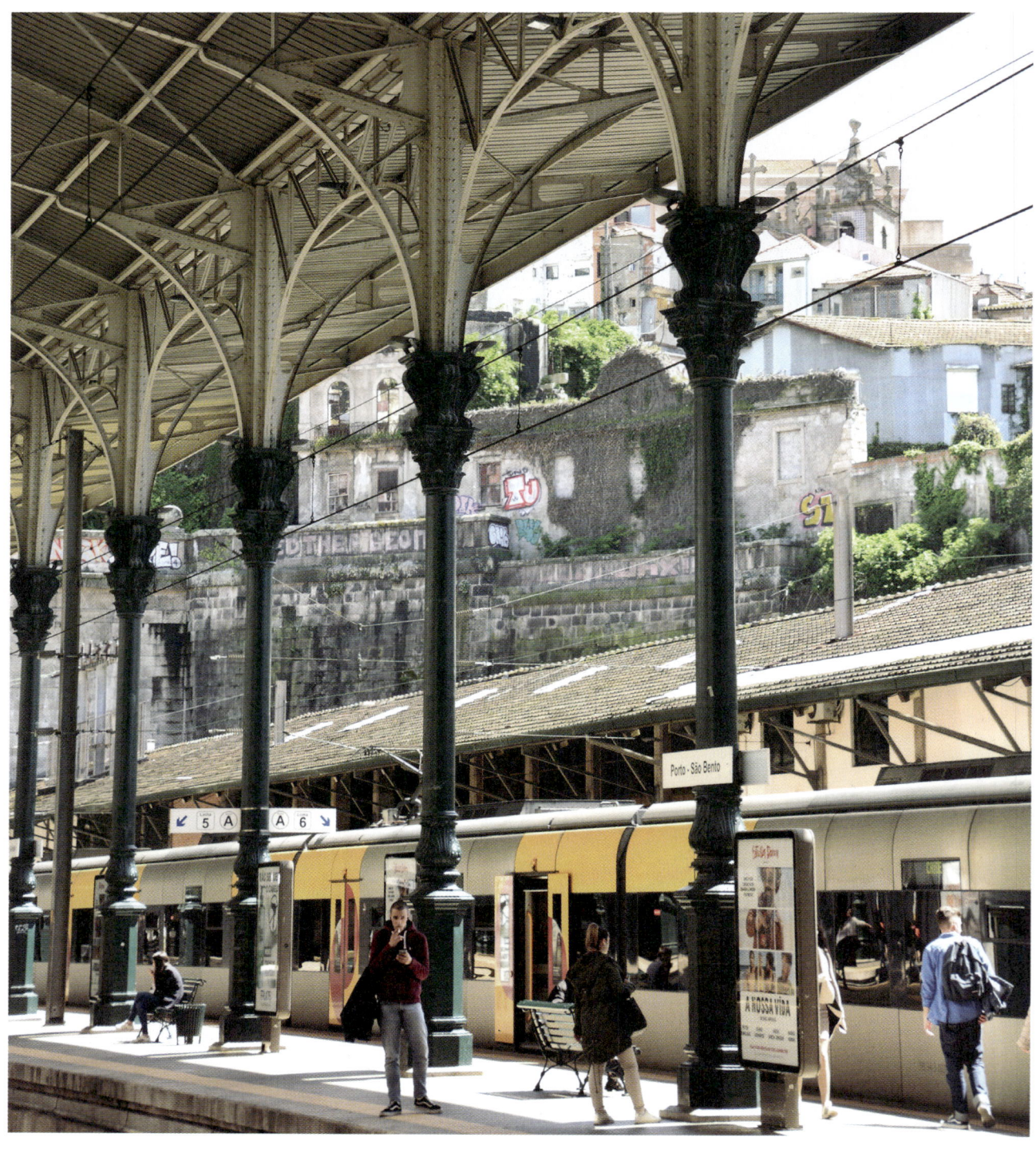

ABOVE AND RIGHT: *São Bento station, an everyday landmark in the center of Porto. Between 1905 and 1916, the artist Jorge Colaço condensed Portuguese history onto more than 20,000 tiles.*

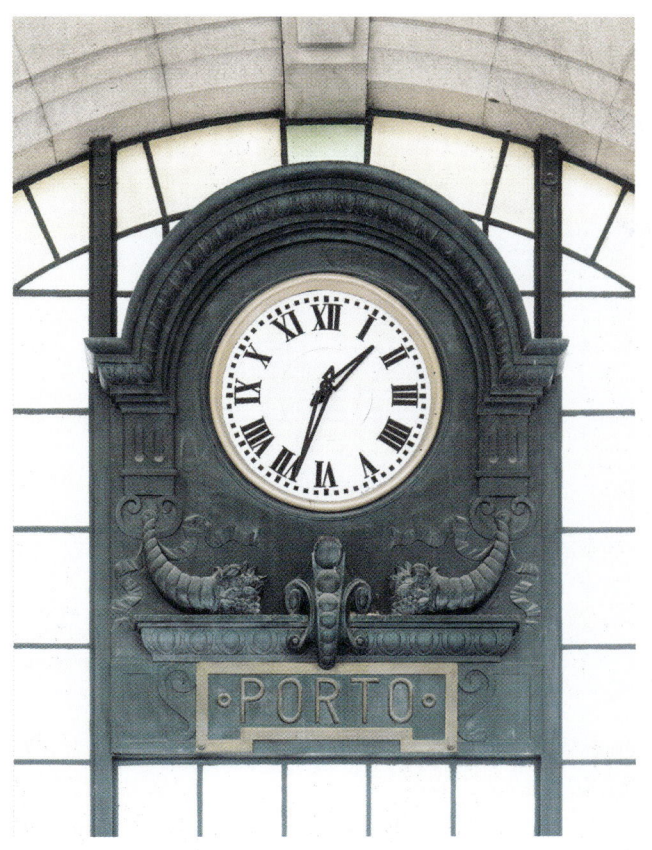

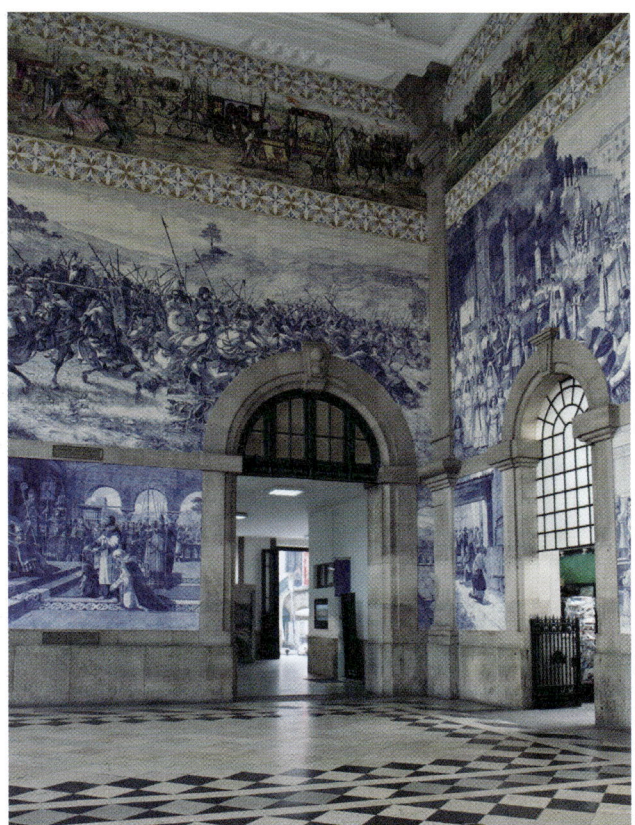

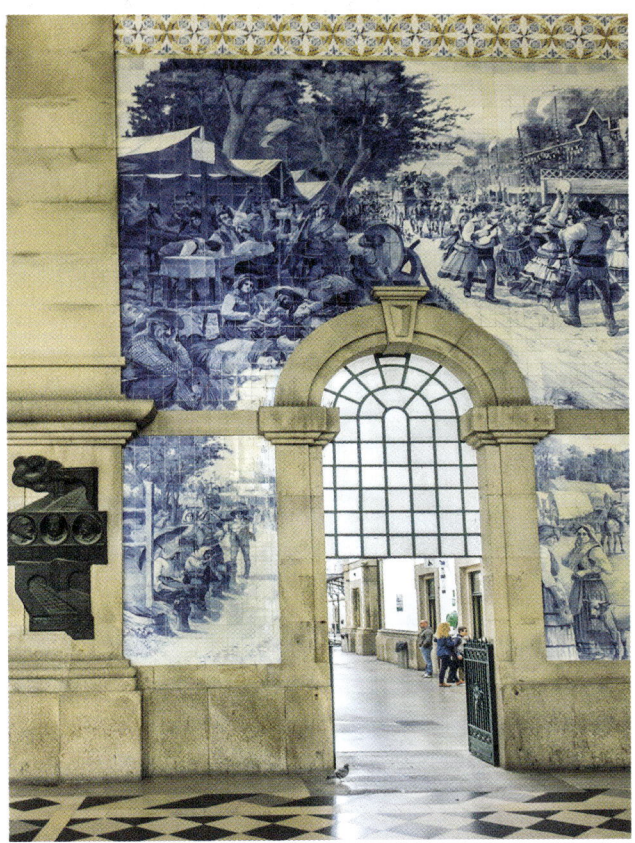

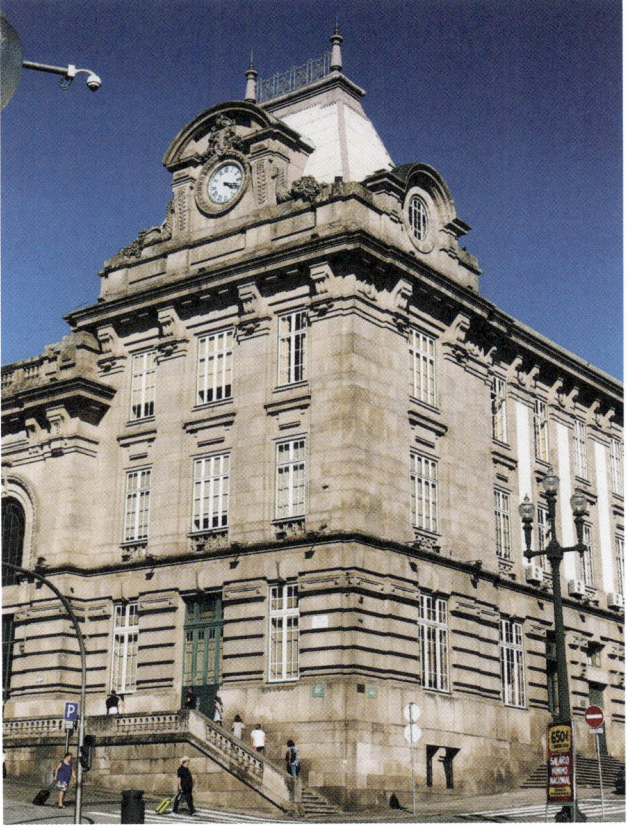

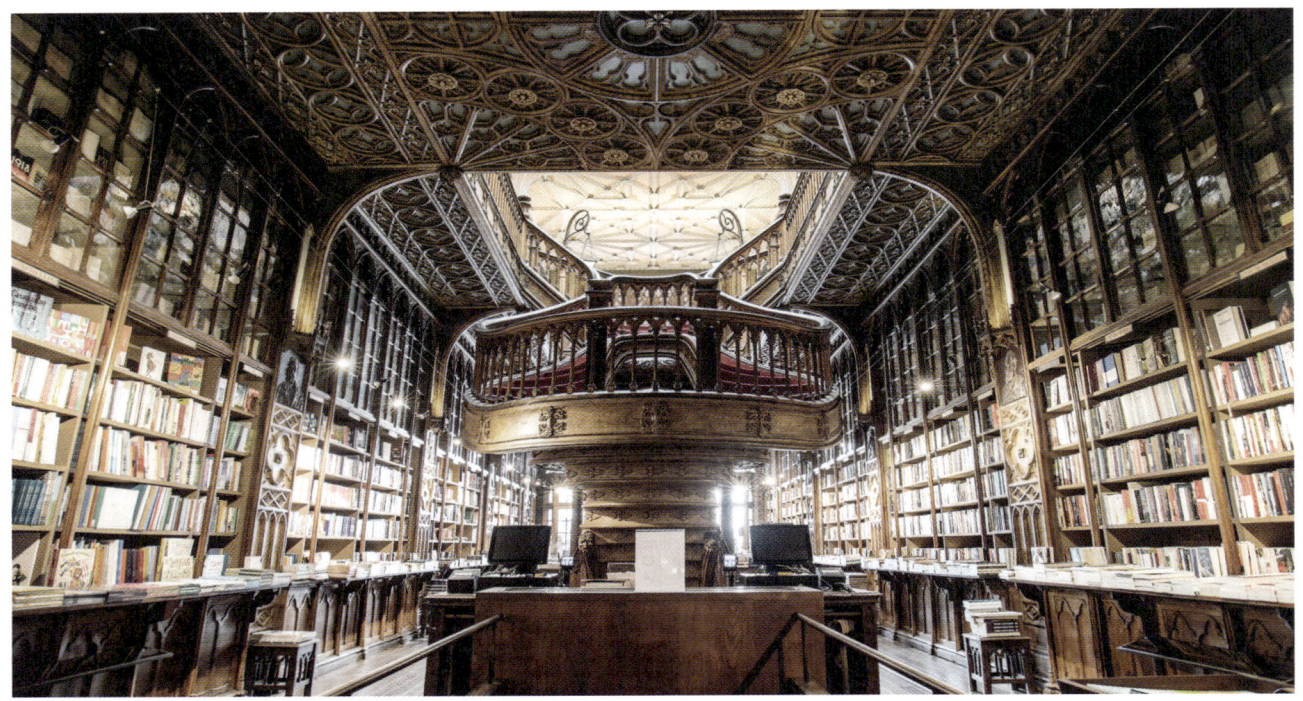

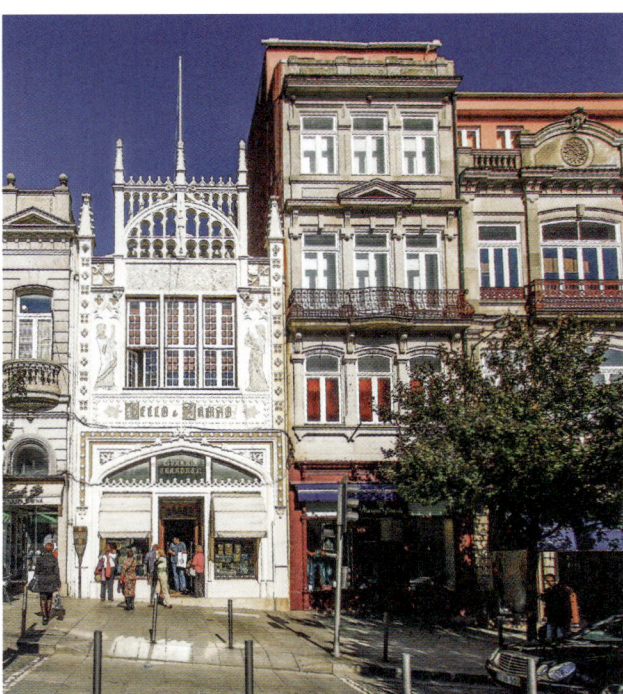

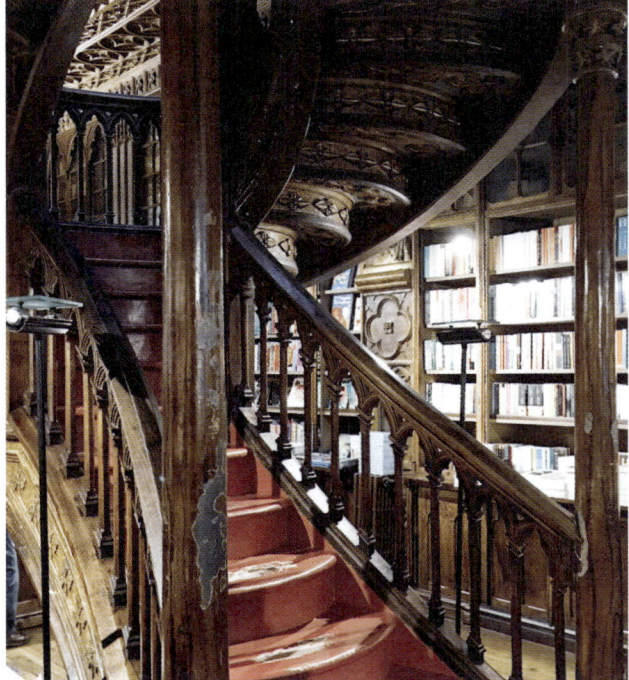

ABOVE AND RIGHT: *Livraria Lello is widely regarded as Portugal's oldest bookstore and is so famous they had to start charging people to enter. Ornate balustrades, coffered ceilings, and a sweeping staircase define the Art Nouveau interior, a frequent point of comparison with fantasy film scenery.*

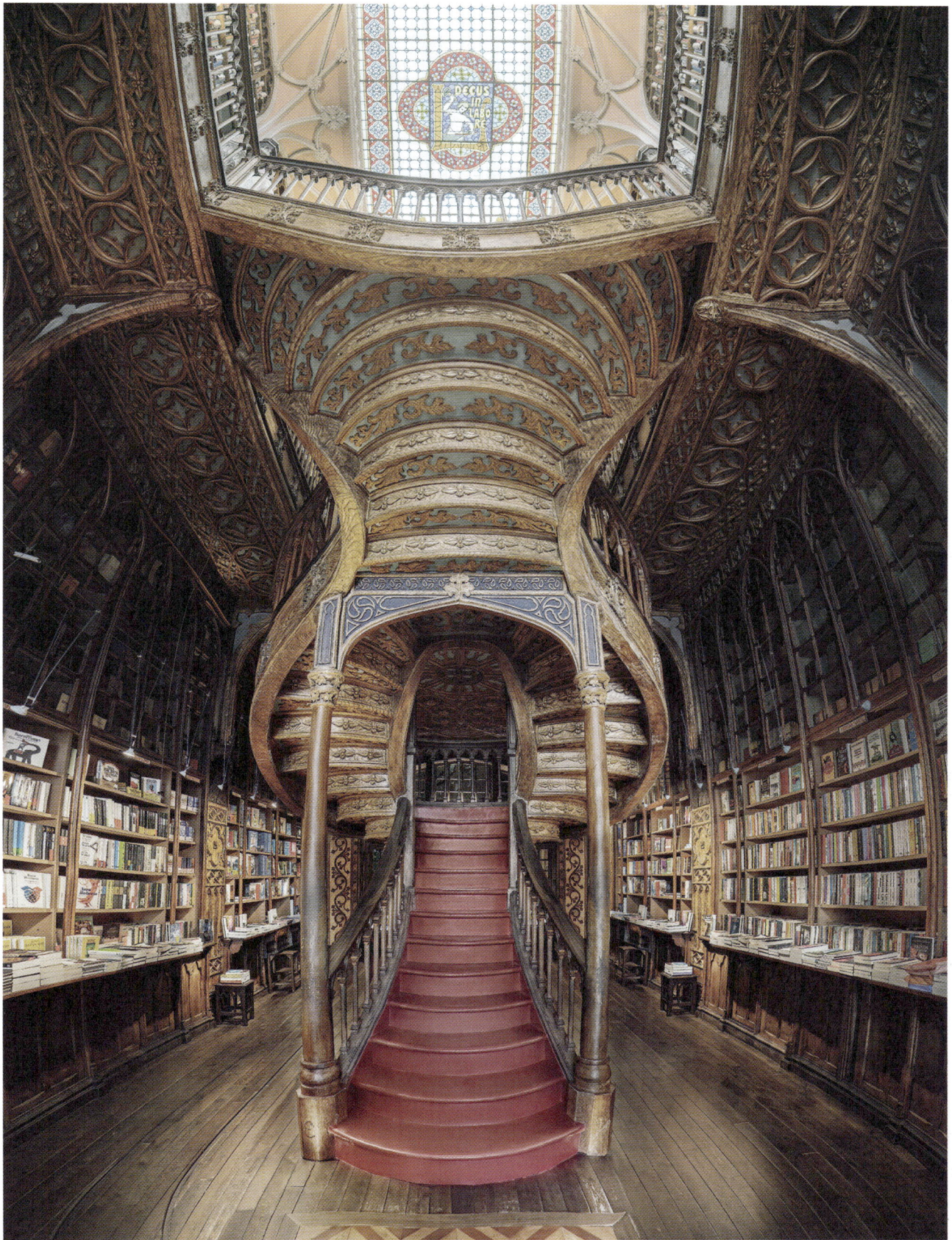

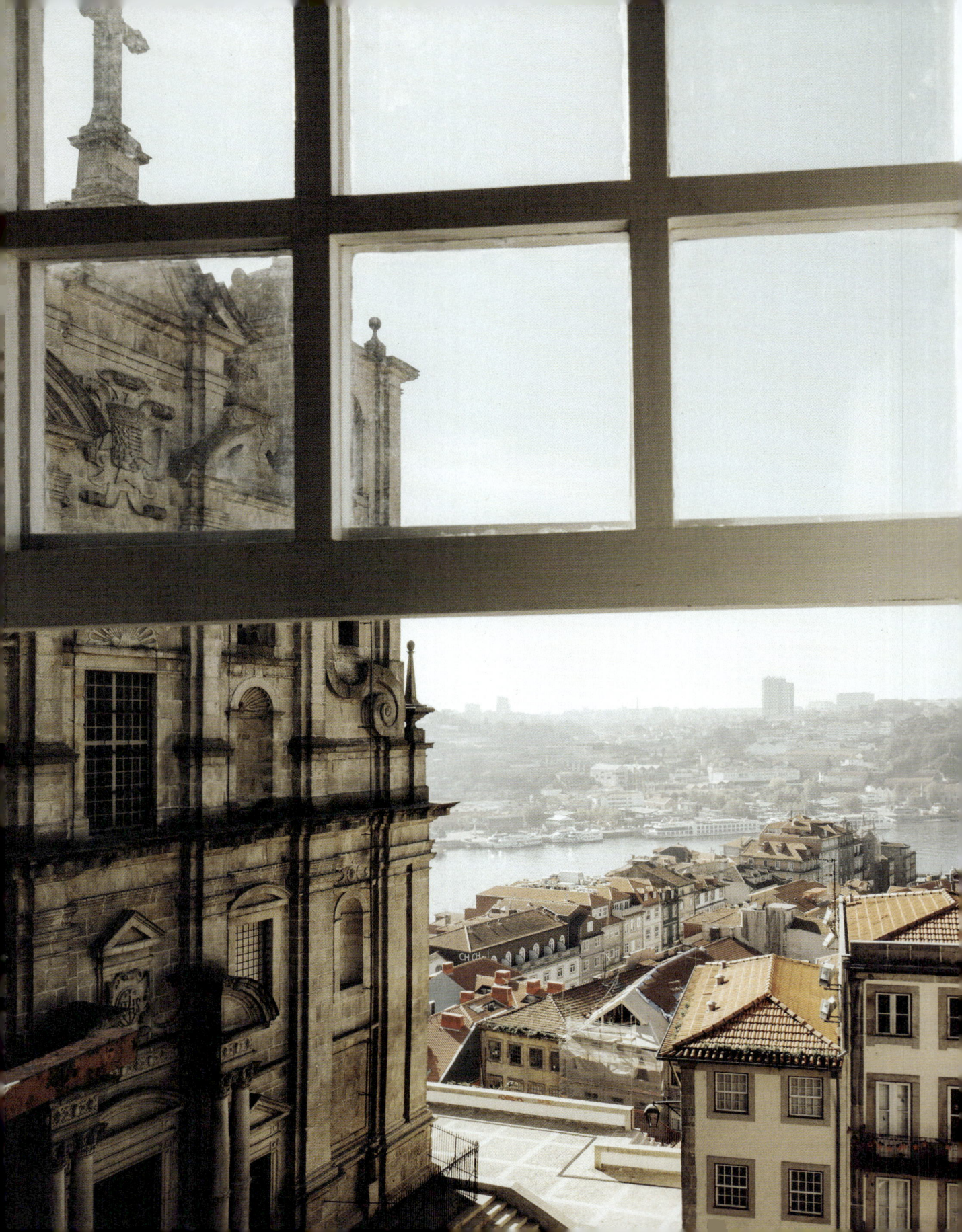

MIRADOUROS

THE NUMBER OF MIRADOUROS IN LISBON AND PORTO IS NO ACCIDENT. BOTH CITIES GREW ON STEEP HILLS SHAPED BY THE STRATEGIC IMPORTANCE OF THE TAGUS AND THE DOURO, AND BY ATLANTIC LIGHT THAT FAVORS LONG, OPEN SIGHTLINES

As the cities rose, these high points took on the deliberate purpose of keeping views of river and harbor clear. The earliest *miradouros* were working look-out posts from which approaching ships could be seen well before they reached port and threats could be spotted from a distance. In Porto, one of the most striking viewpoints is the Miradouro da Rua das Aldas. Set high above the Ribeira quarter near the cathedral, it looks across the Douro to the Ponte Dom Luís I and the rooftops of Vila Nova de Gaia. On the opposite bank, evenings draw people to the Jardim do Morro. A small park near the Gaia cable car station offers a wide view and is a favorite spot to watch the sun set. Lisbon offers its own chain of *miradouros* overlooking the Tagus. The Miradouro das Portas do Sol projects outward like a balcony above Alfama, historically one of the best spots to watch ships leave the harbor. Just a short walk away, the pergola of the Miradouro de Santa Luzia, wrapped in bougainvillea, offers a quieter setting. For Portugal, a country shaped by the sea, the horizon once carried very real hopes of distant return. People gathered at these overlooks to scan the water, waiting for a ship that might bring someone home, a loved one. Over time, miradouros also became meeting places. Paths and terraces formed around them, as at the Miradouro de São Pedro de Alcântara, where a wide view can be had with a walk through the adjoining garden. When evening light settles on rooftops and glints off the river and sea, few places in Lisbon and Porto draw more people than these terraces above the city, whether for a date or simply to close out the day.

LEFT: *Near the Miradouro da Rua das Aldas, a view across Porto to the Douro. In the foreground is the Igreja dos Grilos. Visitors to the Museum of Sacred Art can climb the church tower for an incredible view.*

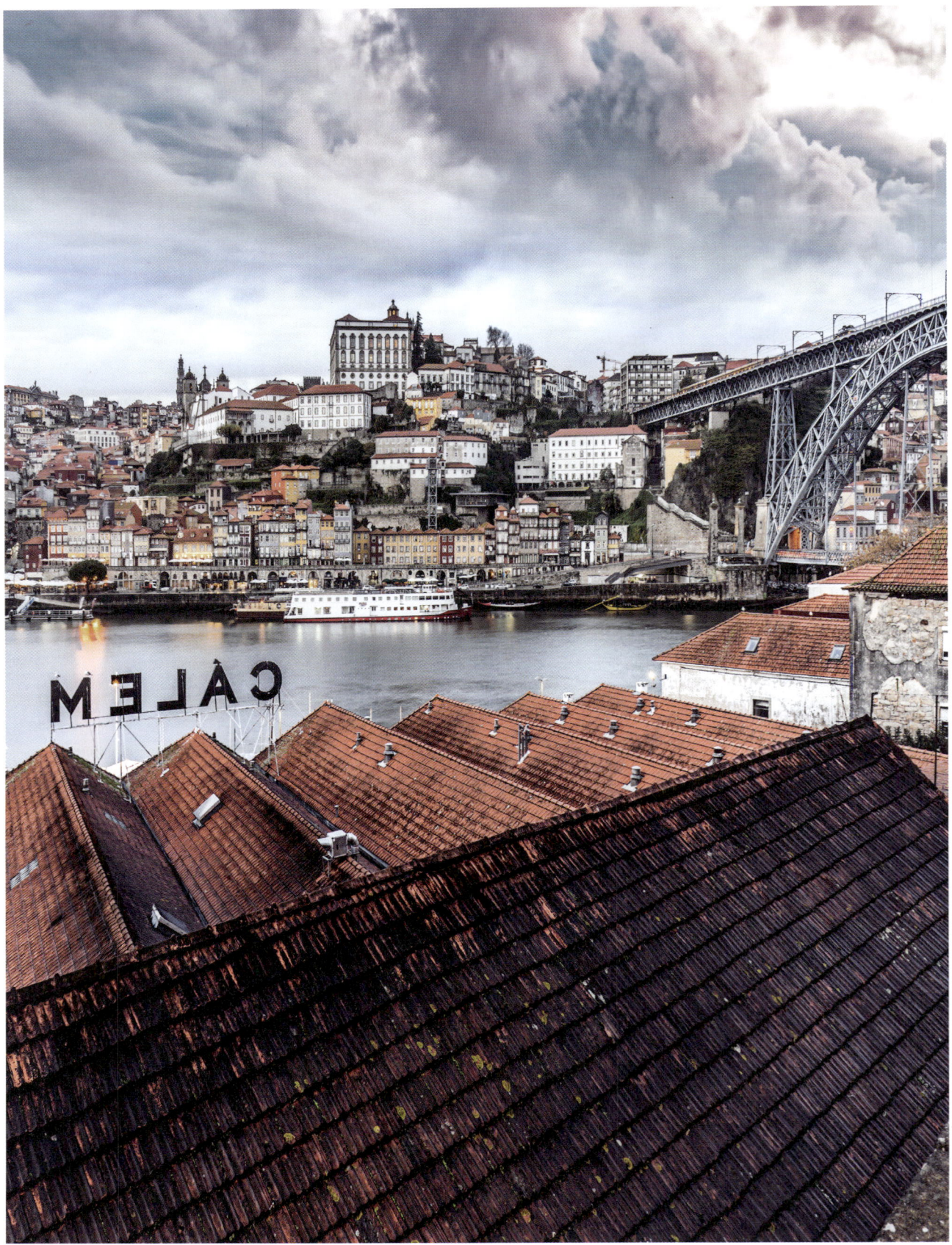

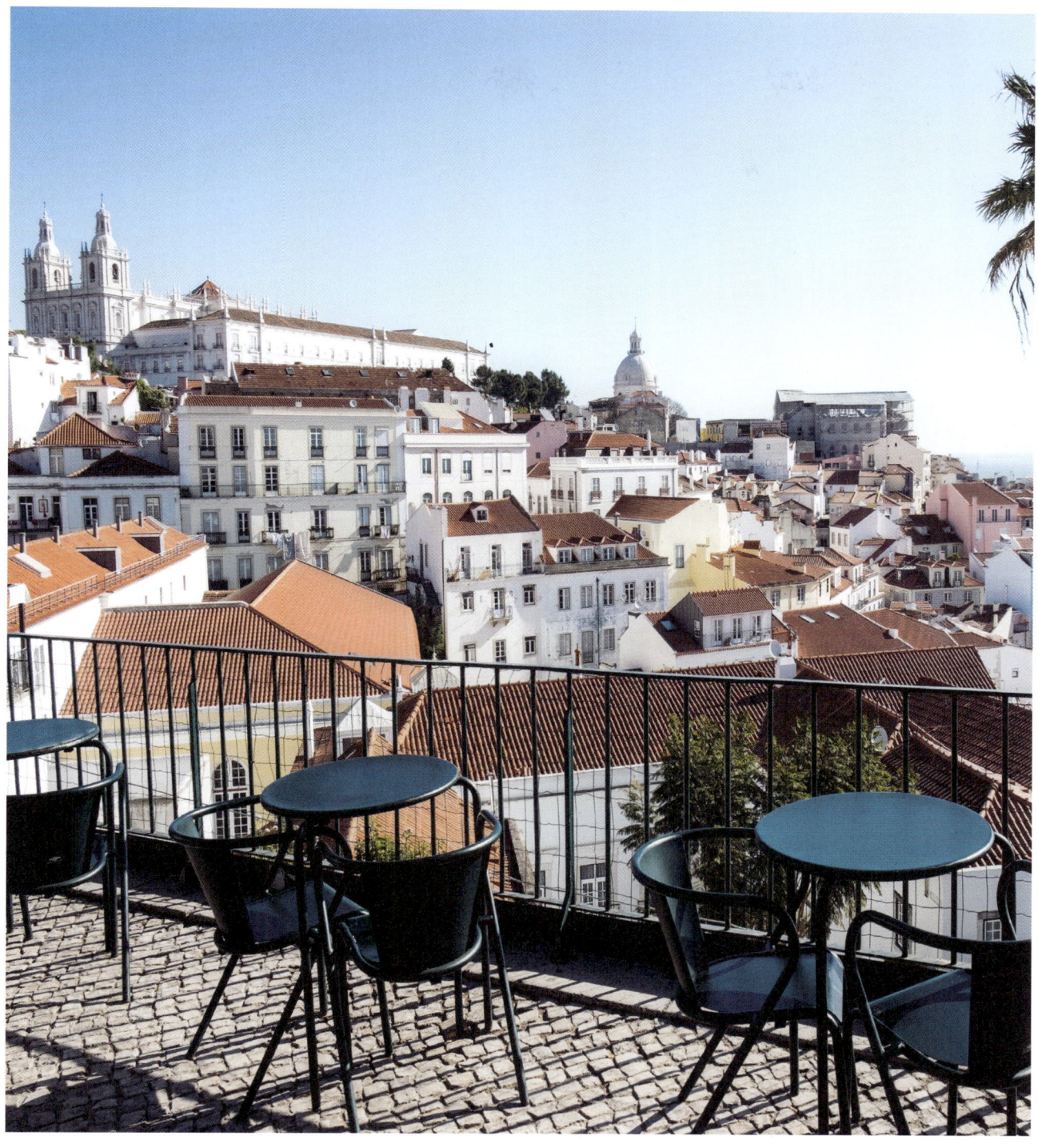

ABOVE: *The Monastery of São Vicente de Fora from the Miradouro das Portas do Sol in Lisbon's Alfama district. A nearby terrace offers space for a galão, a Portuguese café au lait.*

LEFT: *The steel arch of the Ponte Dom Luís I frames Ribeira, Porto's old town. Scene from the hills of Vila Nova de Gaia on the south bank of the Douro. Great views from the park above the Gaia cable-car station.*

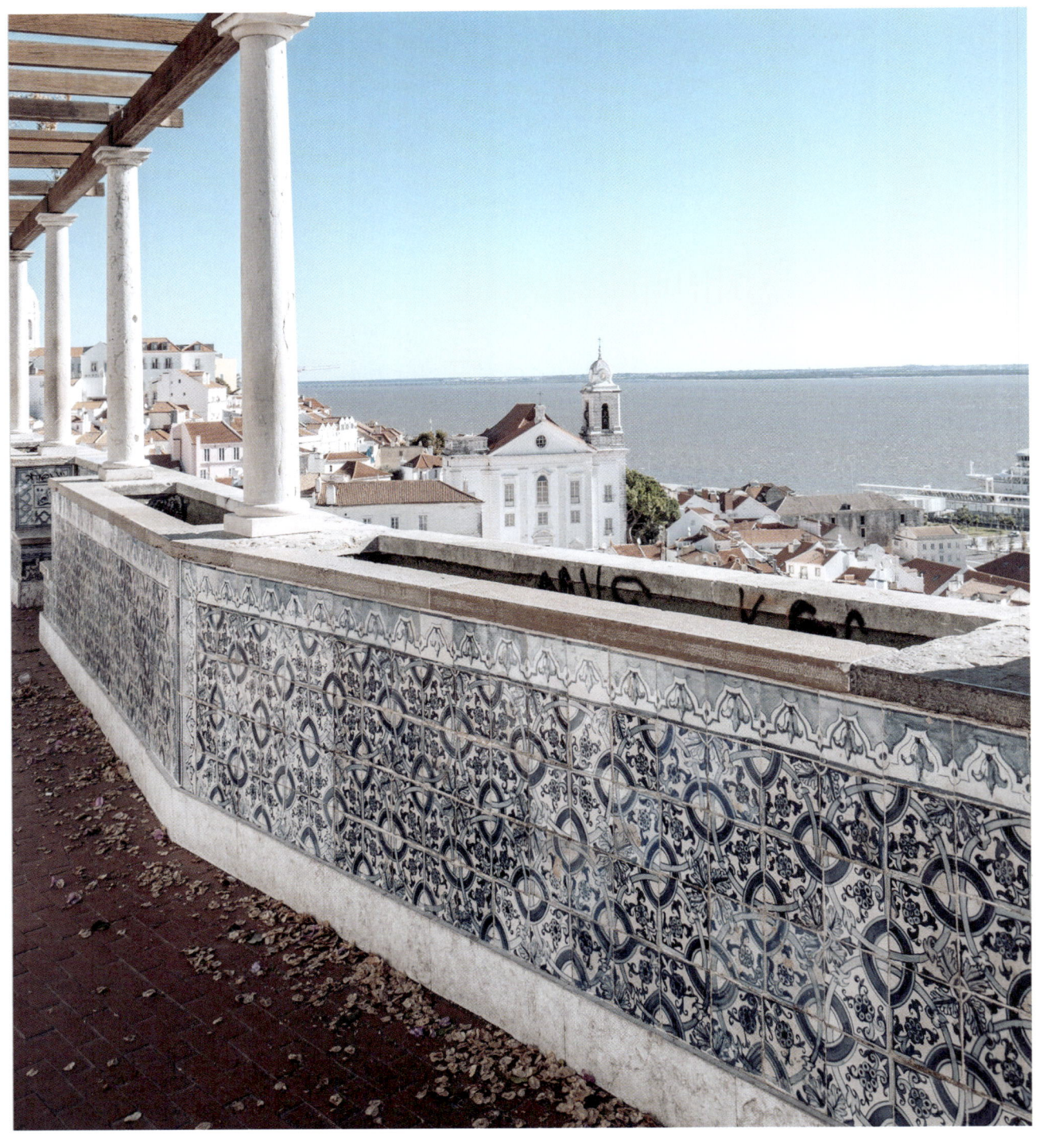

ABOVE: *At the Miradouro de Santa Luzia, tiled panels compete visually with the open view across the Tagus.*

RIGHT: *Restaurants near Lisbon Cathedral, including Chapitô à Mesa. Dining with a view.*

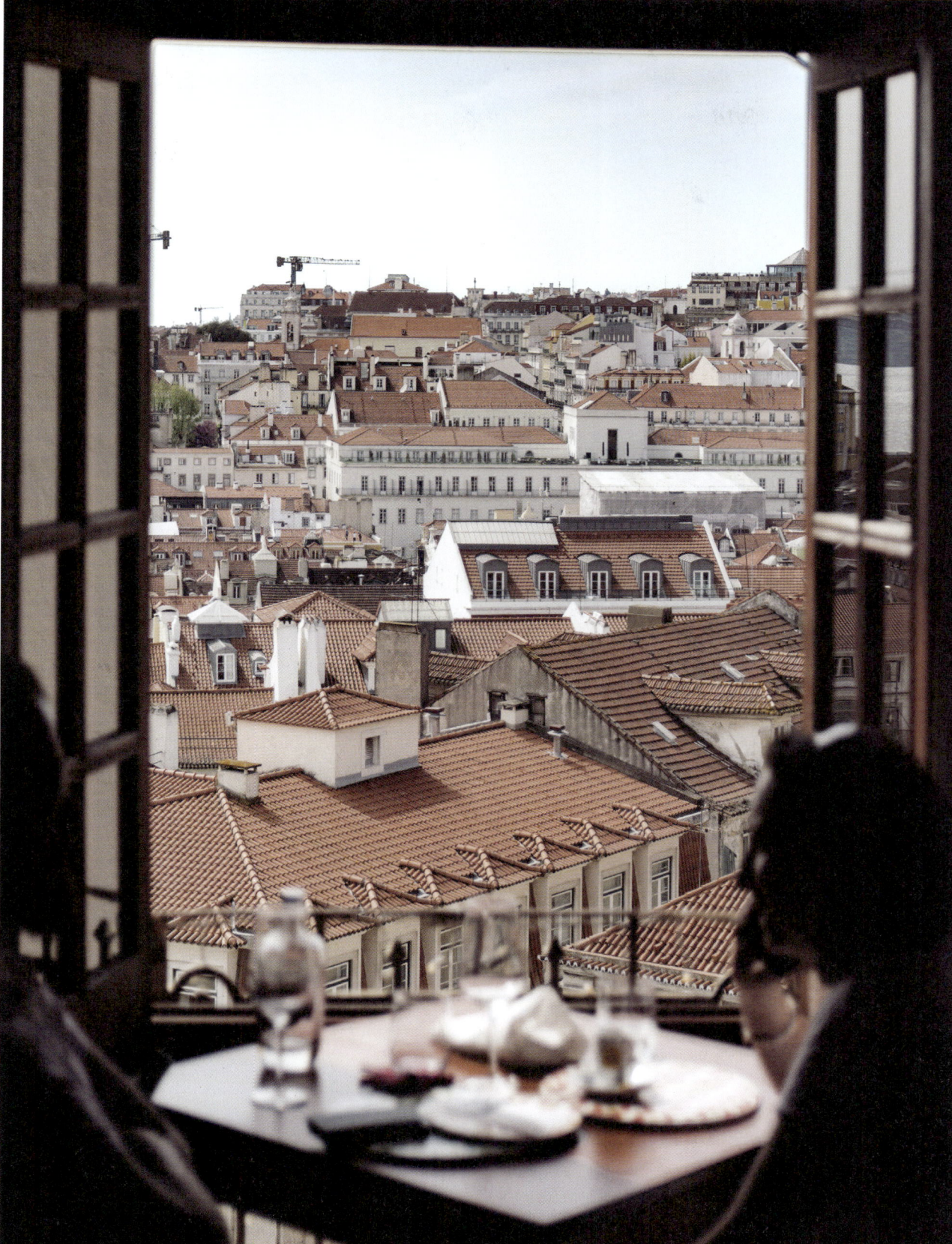

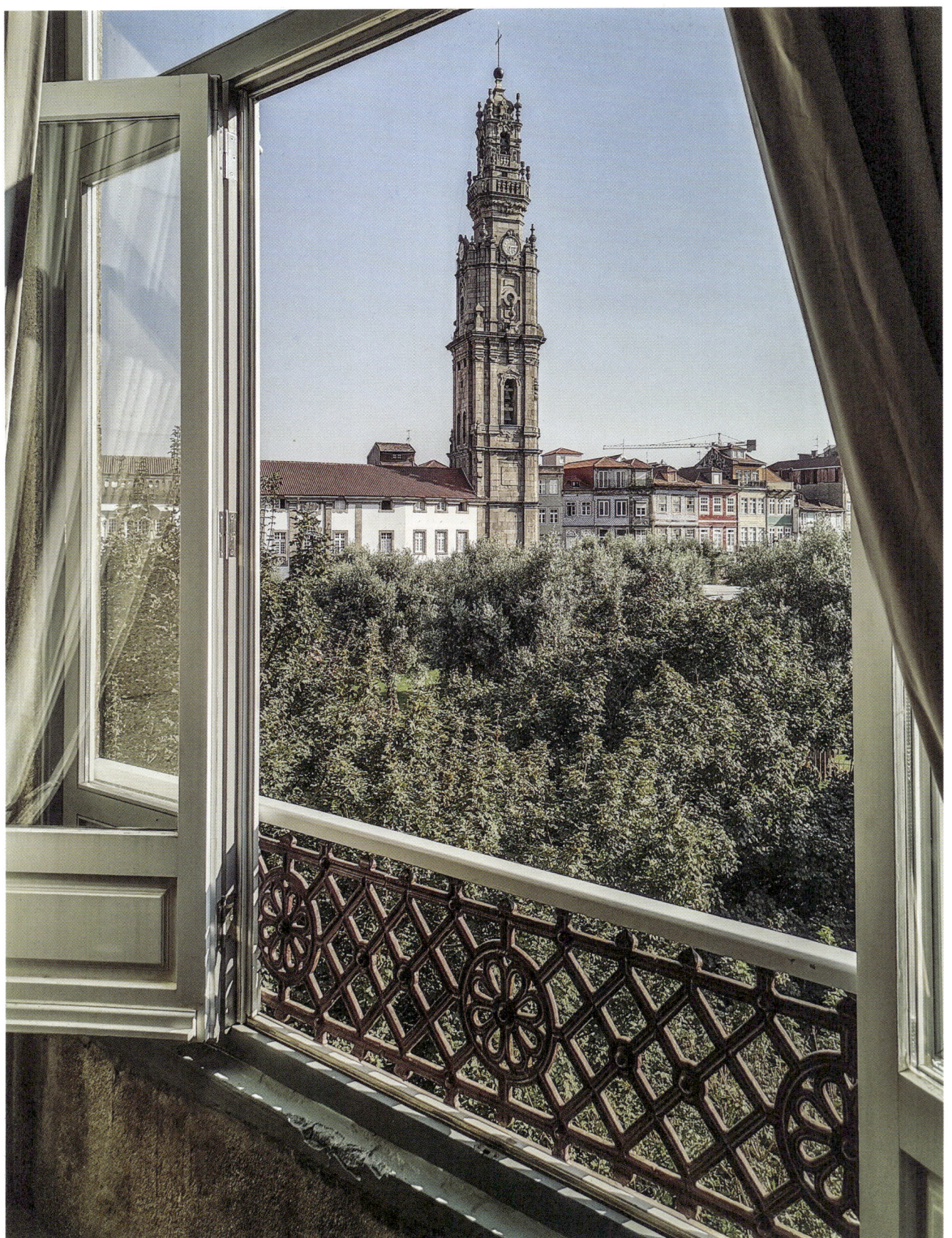

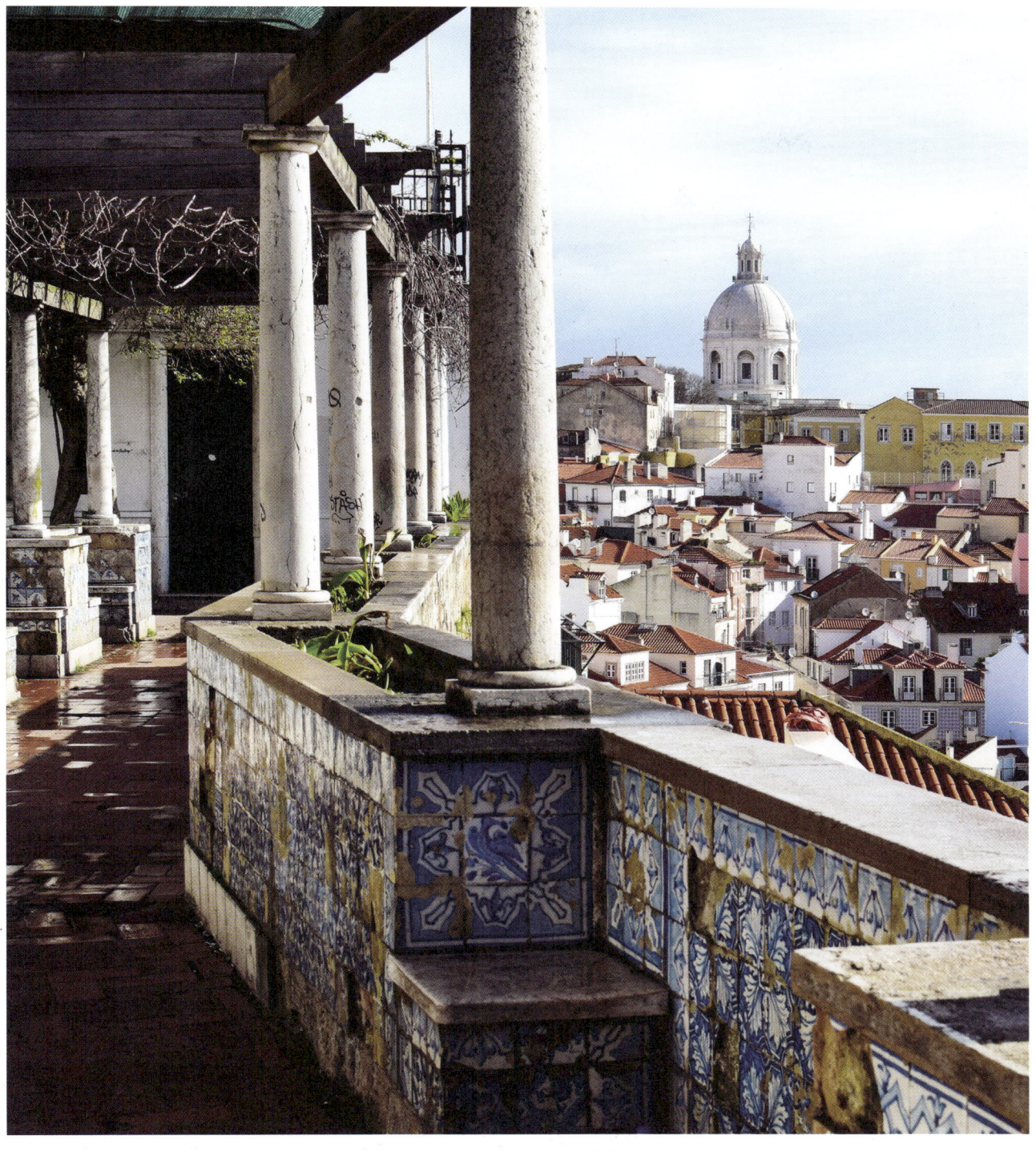

ABOVE: *The pergola at the Miradouro de Santa Luzia overlooks the rooftops of Alfama. The bougainvillea is striking at sunset.*

LEFT: *Great views from the upper floors of the older townhouses in Porto's historic center. Here, a view of the Torre dos Clérigos near Livraria Lello, the famous bookstore.*

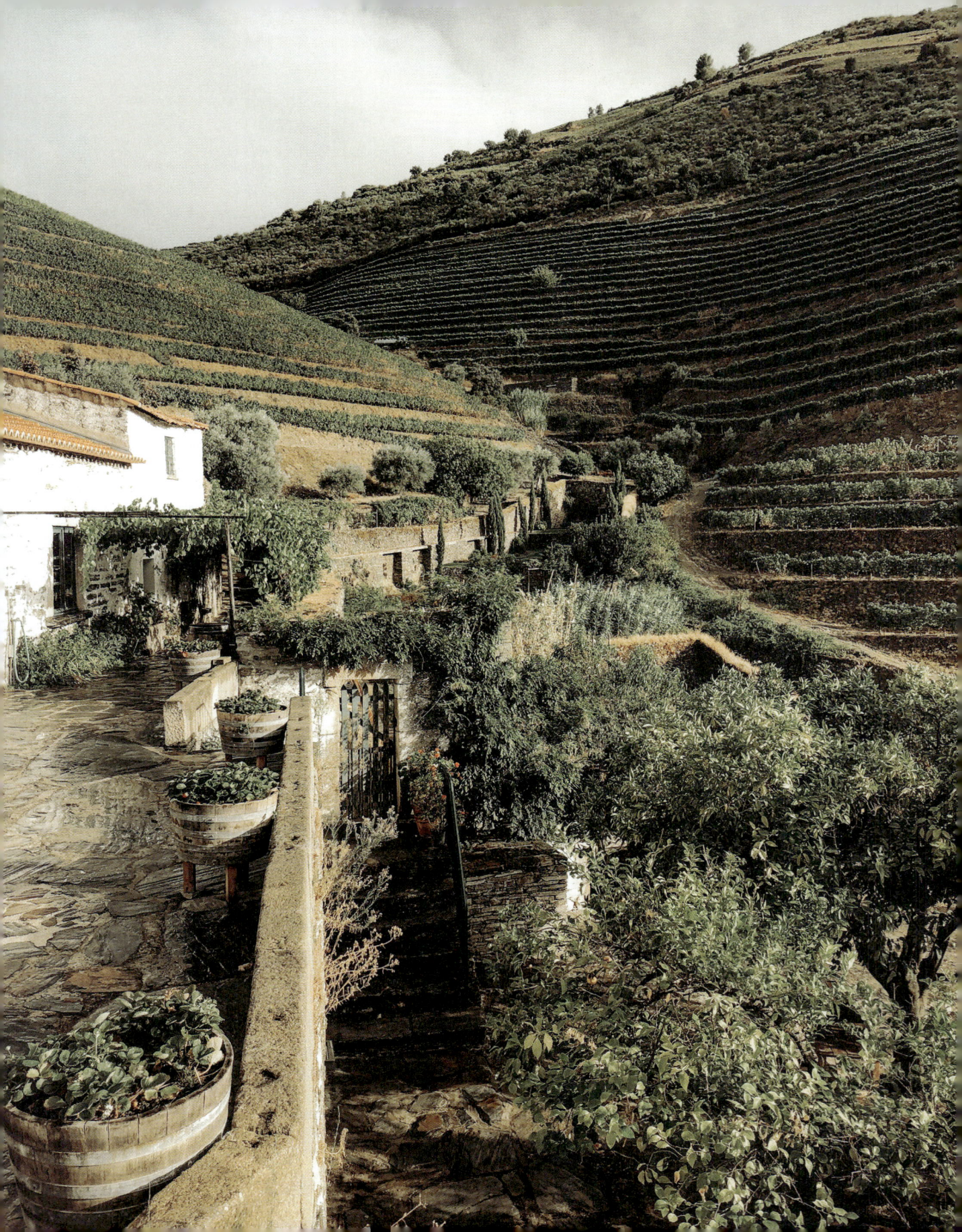

THE NORTH

PORTUGAL'S NORTH HAS LONG BEEN DESCRIBED AS THE COUNTRY'S WINE CELLAR. IT COMBINES RUGGED TERRAIN WITH A LANDSCAPE OF HISTORIC TOWNS, STEEP VALLEYS, AND A DEEP TRADITION OF FOOD AND WINE

Northern Portugal rewards slow travel like an old wine rewards patience. The region is sparsely populated, with towns and villages spread far apart, each with its own history. Pinhão lies in the Douro Valley, where many of the country's best-known wines are produced. Sunlit slate terraces line the hillsides, creating conditions well suited to port. At Pinhão's old railway station, azulejo panels depict the years before the railway, when barrels were taken downstream to Porto on traditional *rabelo* boats. Further north lies Guimarães, often described as the birthplace of the nation. Portugal's first king, Dom Afonso I, was born here, and the city's historic center still reflects that legacy. Narrow streets run between stone façades, many accented with azulejos, while wrought-iron balconies recall earlier centuries. Street cafés provide a place to stop and watch daily life unfold. If Guimarães represents Portugal's dynastic origins, Braga plays a different role. Long regarded as country's religious center, it is home to around thirty churches, including the eleventh-century Sé de Braga, often cited as Portugal's oldest cathedral. Just outside the city stands the church of Bom Jesus do Monte. Many who visit it are pilgrims who, having ascended the monumental staircase of 581 steps leading up to the church, are rewarded with sweeping views across Braga.

LEFT: *Terraced vineyards on the hills above the Douro. Some of Portugal's best-established* quintas *are near Pinhão.*

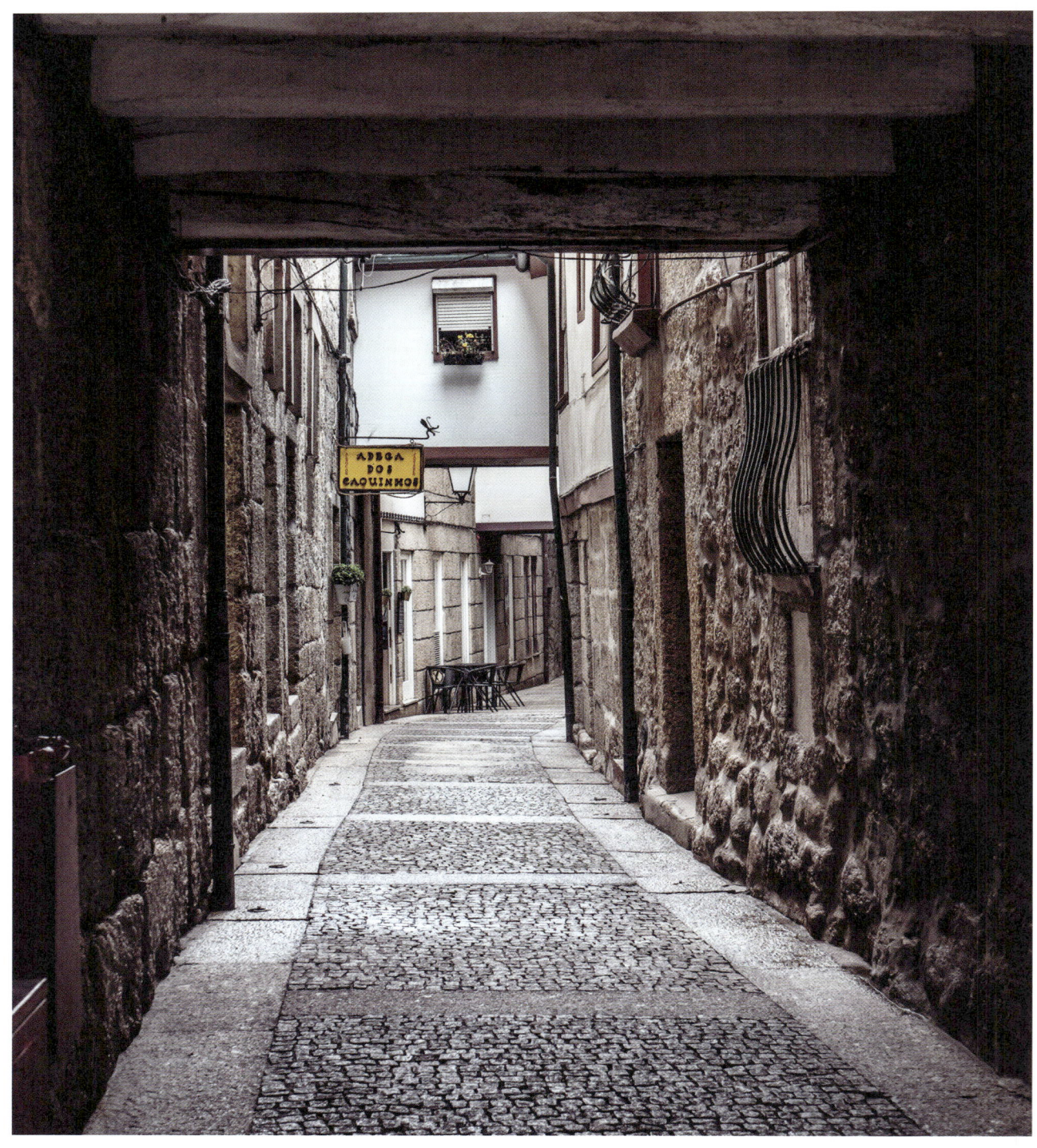

ABOVE, RIGHT, AND FOLLOWING: *Around the walls of the tenth-century castle, narrow townhouses with wrought-iron balconies line cobbled streets. Guimarães's old town retains its medieval layout and proportions.*

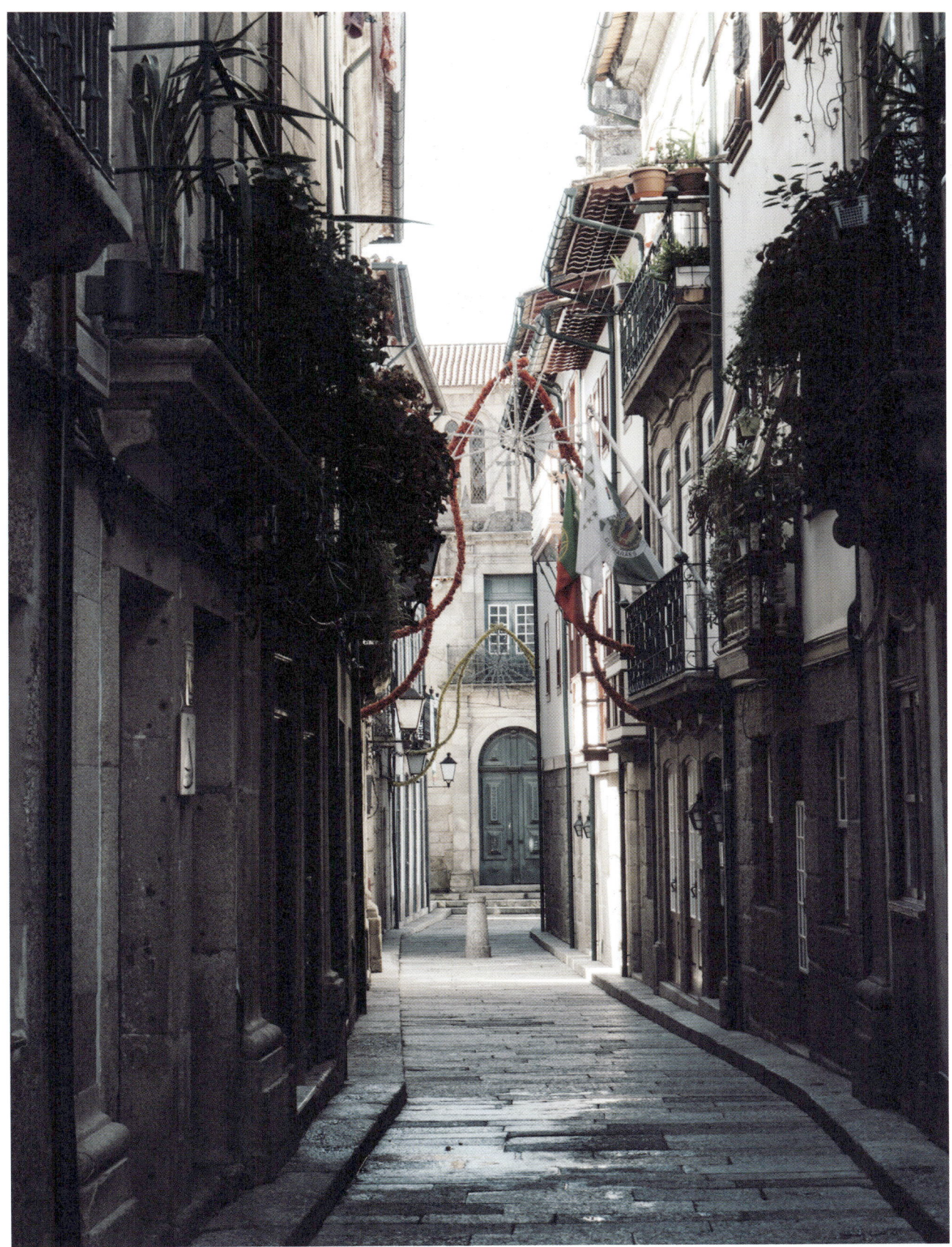

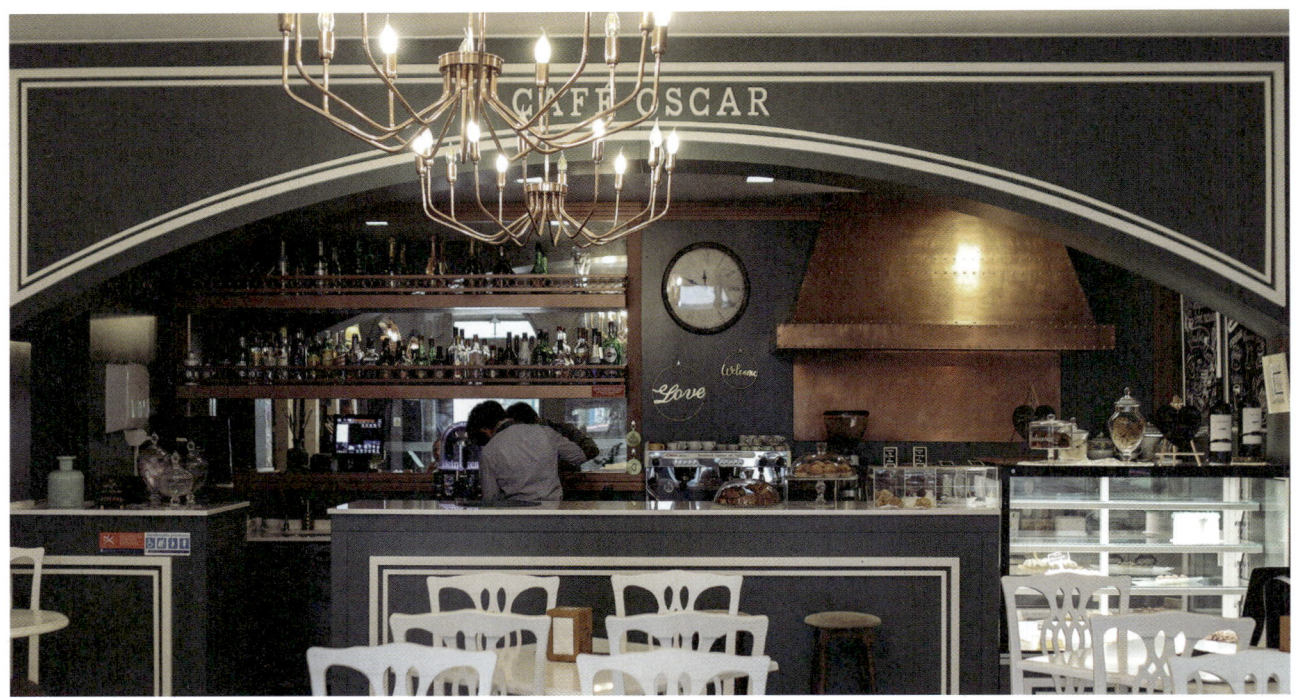

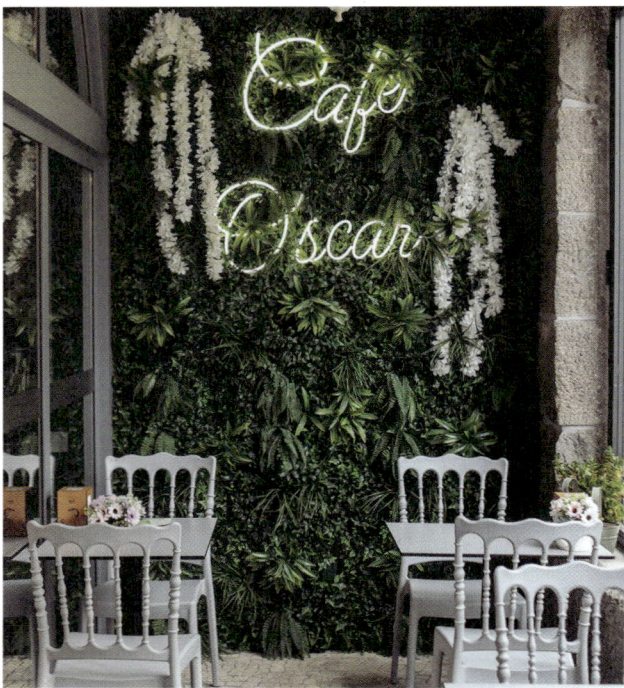

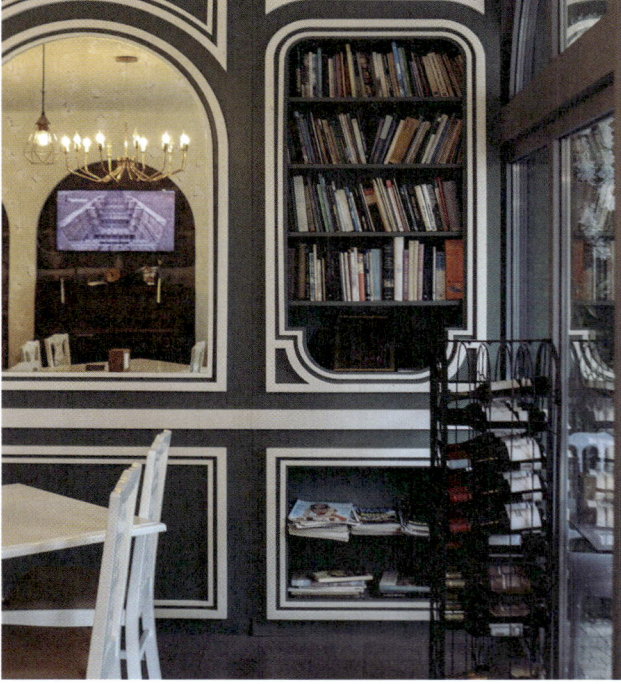

ABOVE: *In Guimarães, cafés and restaurants fill streets and squares throughout the historic center. The city was the cultural capital of Europe in 2012 and its old town is a UNESCO World Heritage Site.*

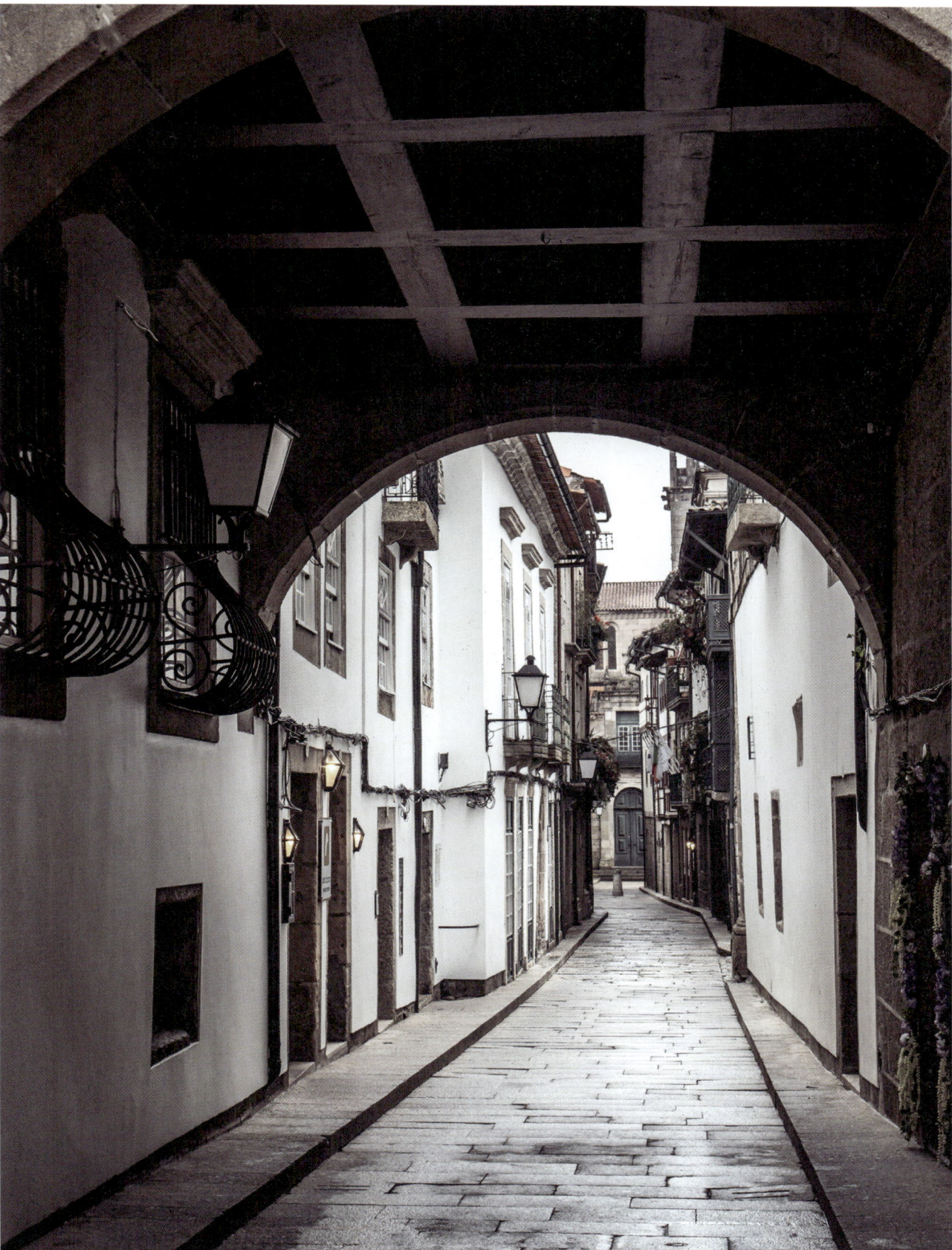

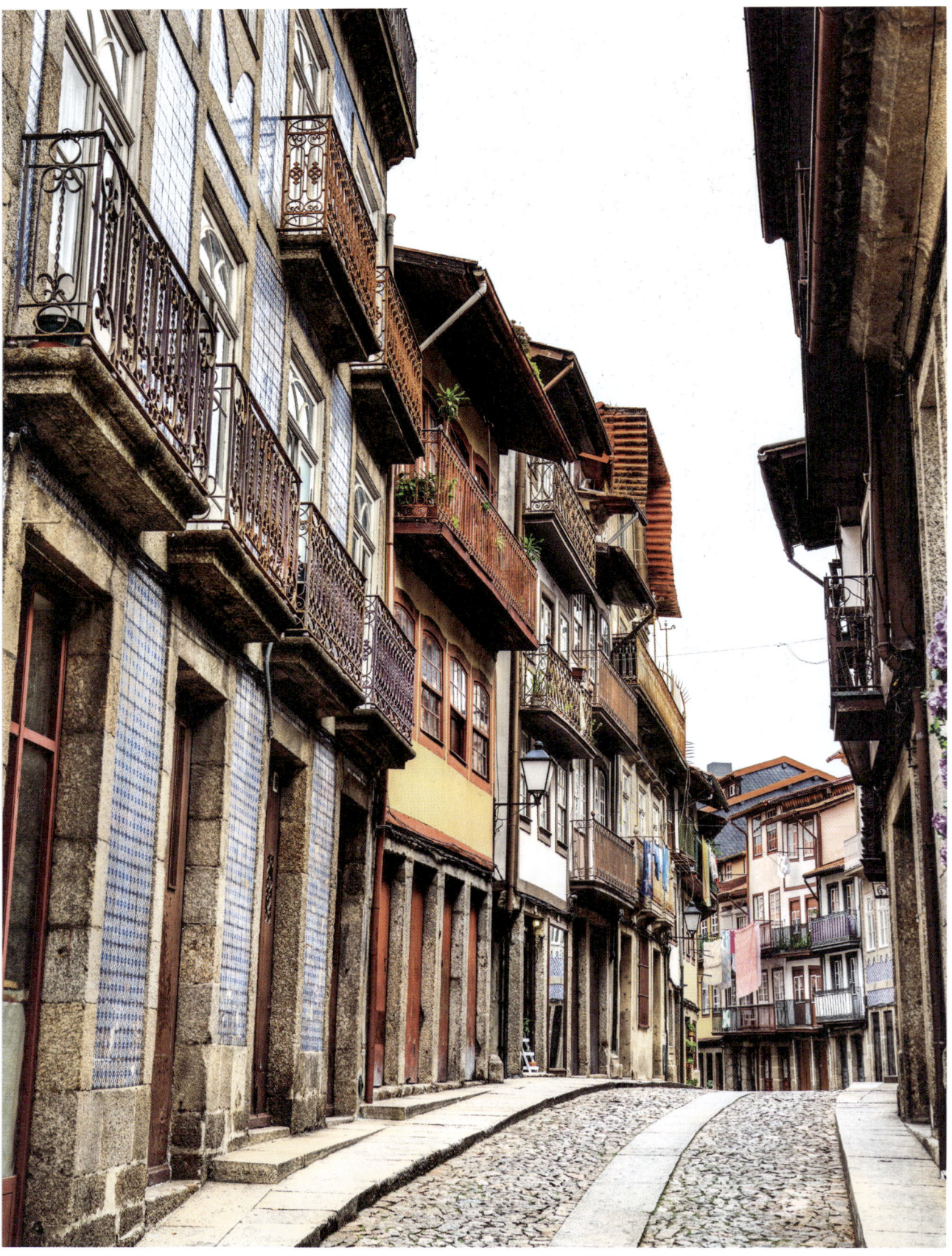

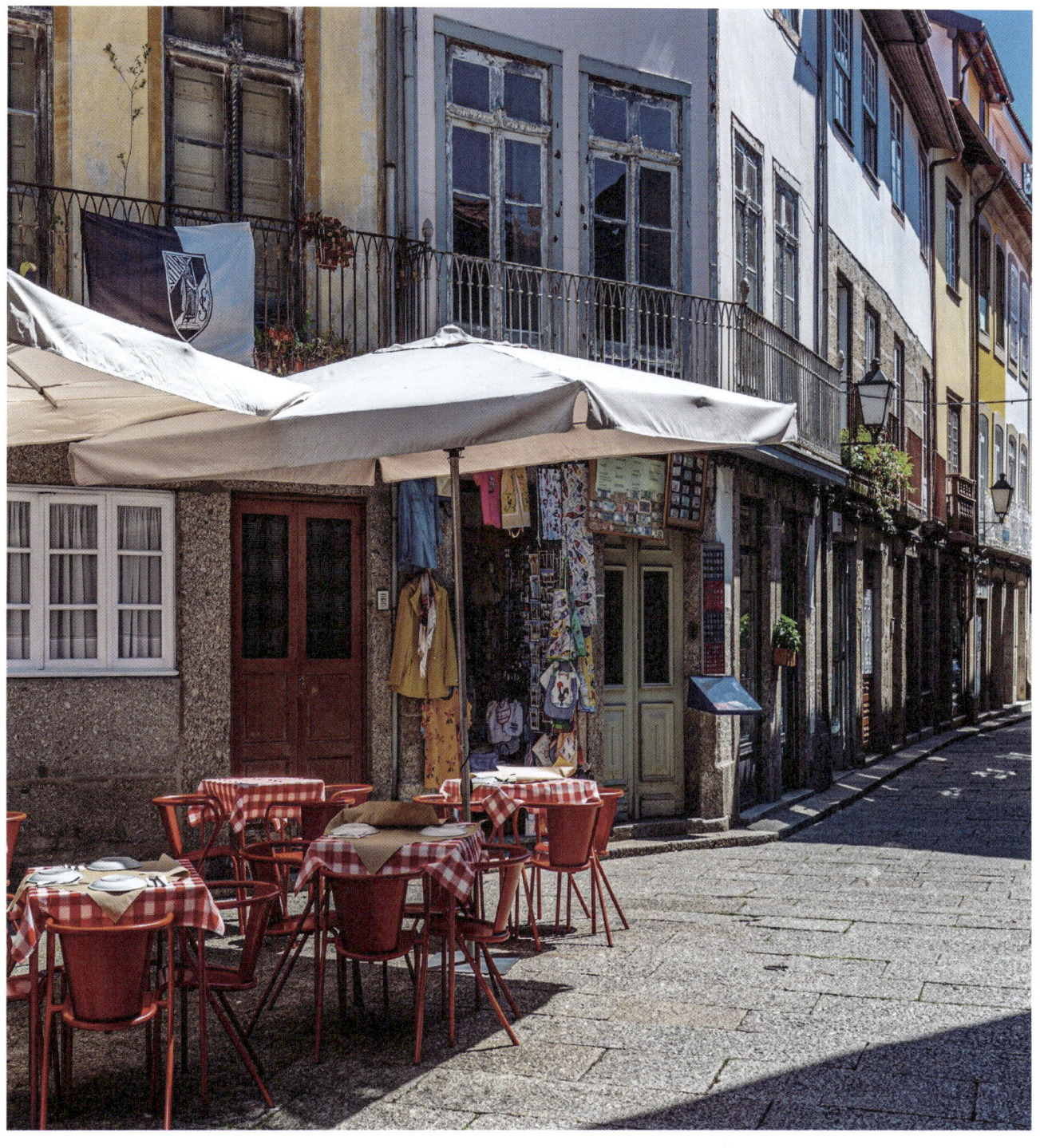

ABOVE AND LEFT: *Medieval architecture and modern urban life intersect in Guimarães. The colors all come from street cafés, small boutiques, workshops, and azulejos.*

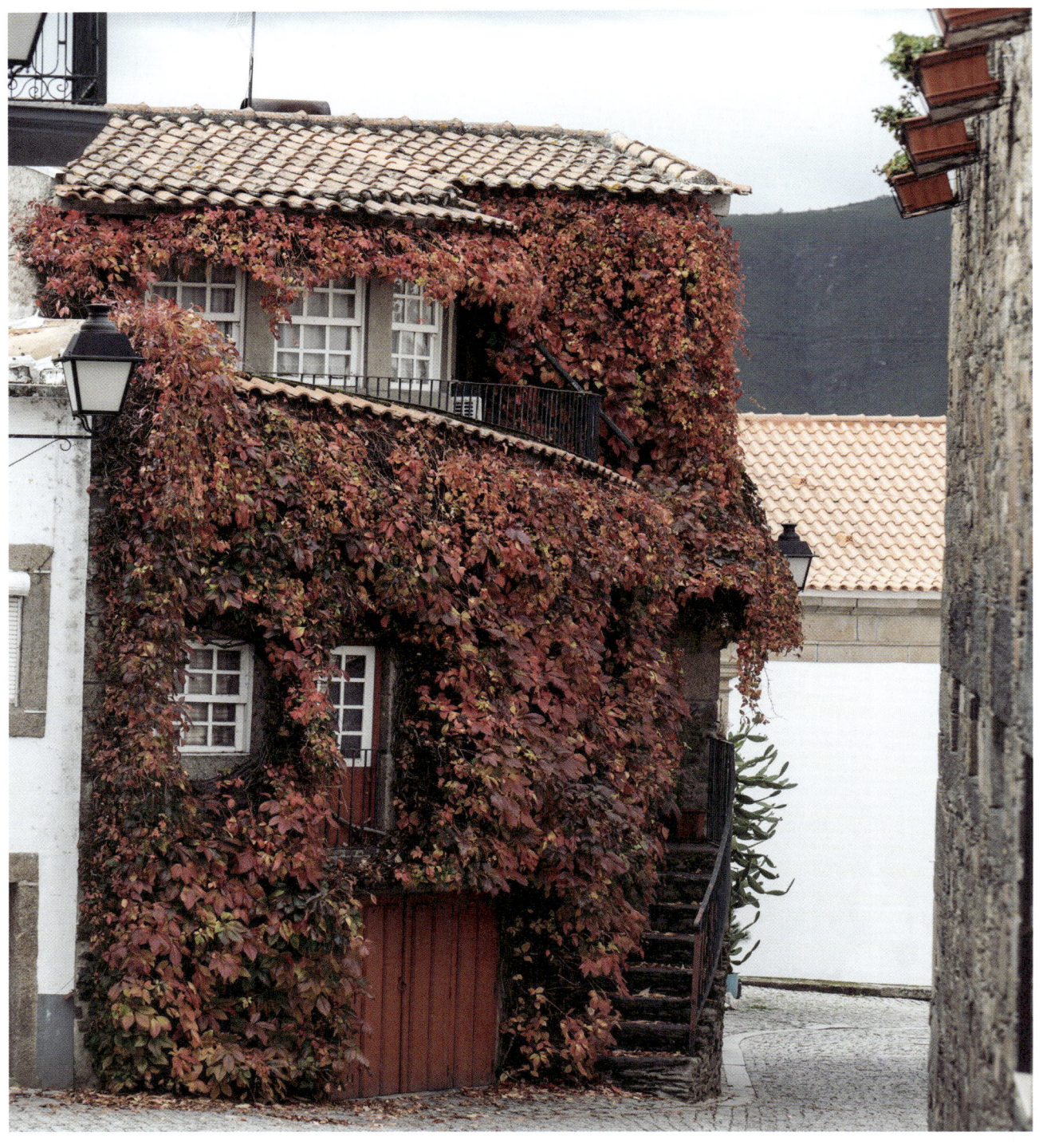

ABOVE: *Villages such as Provesende nestle among vineyards and estates called* quintas *across the Douro Valley near Pinhão. The landscape remains sparsely settled.*

RIGHT: *Larger cities like Braga also have their narrow side streets, quiet and village-like.*

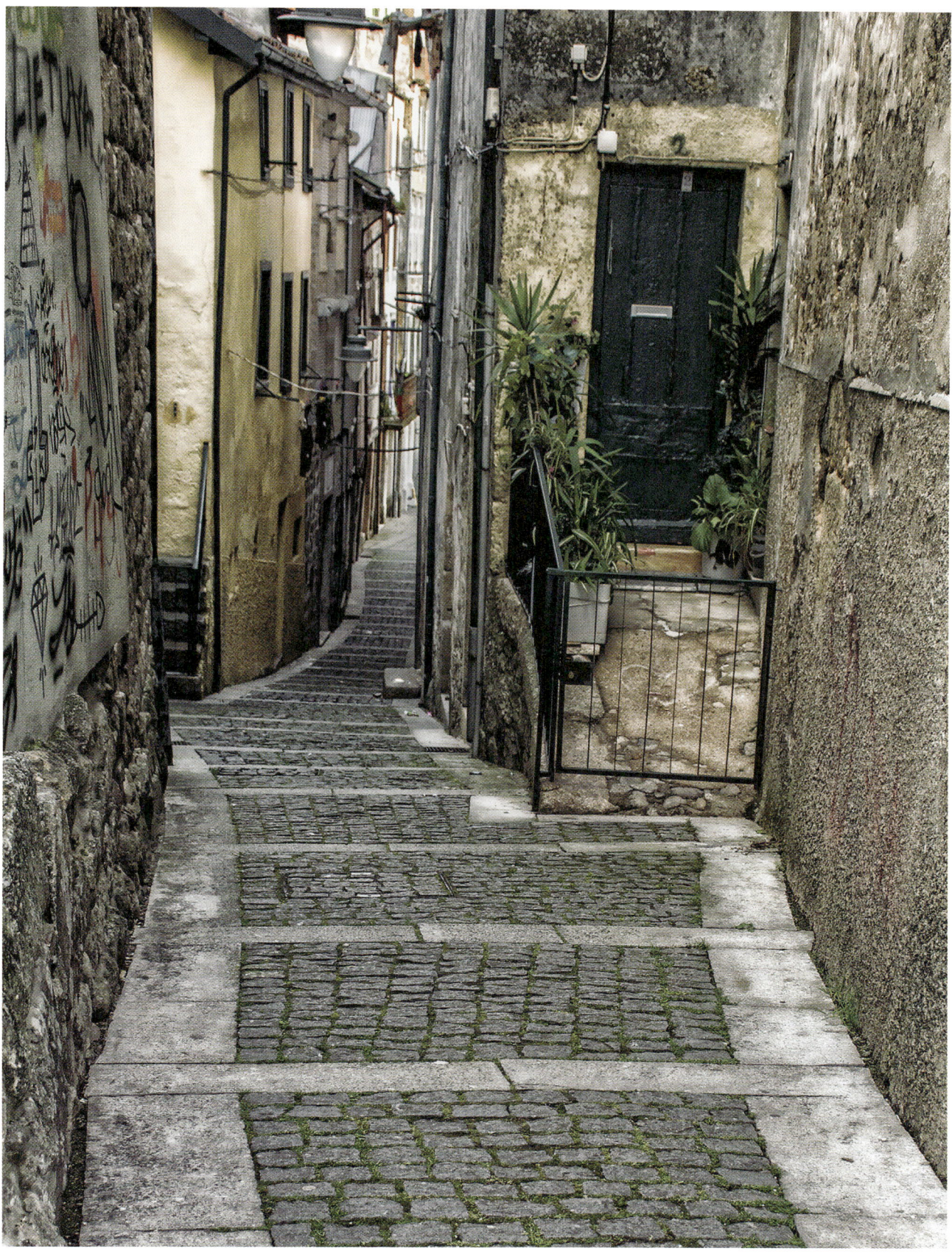

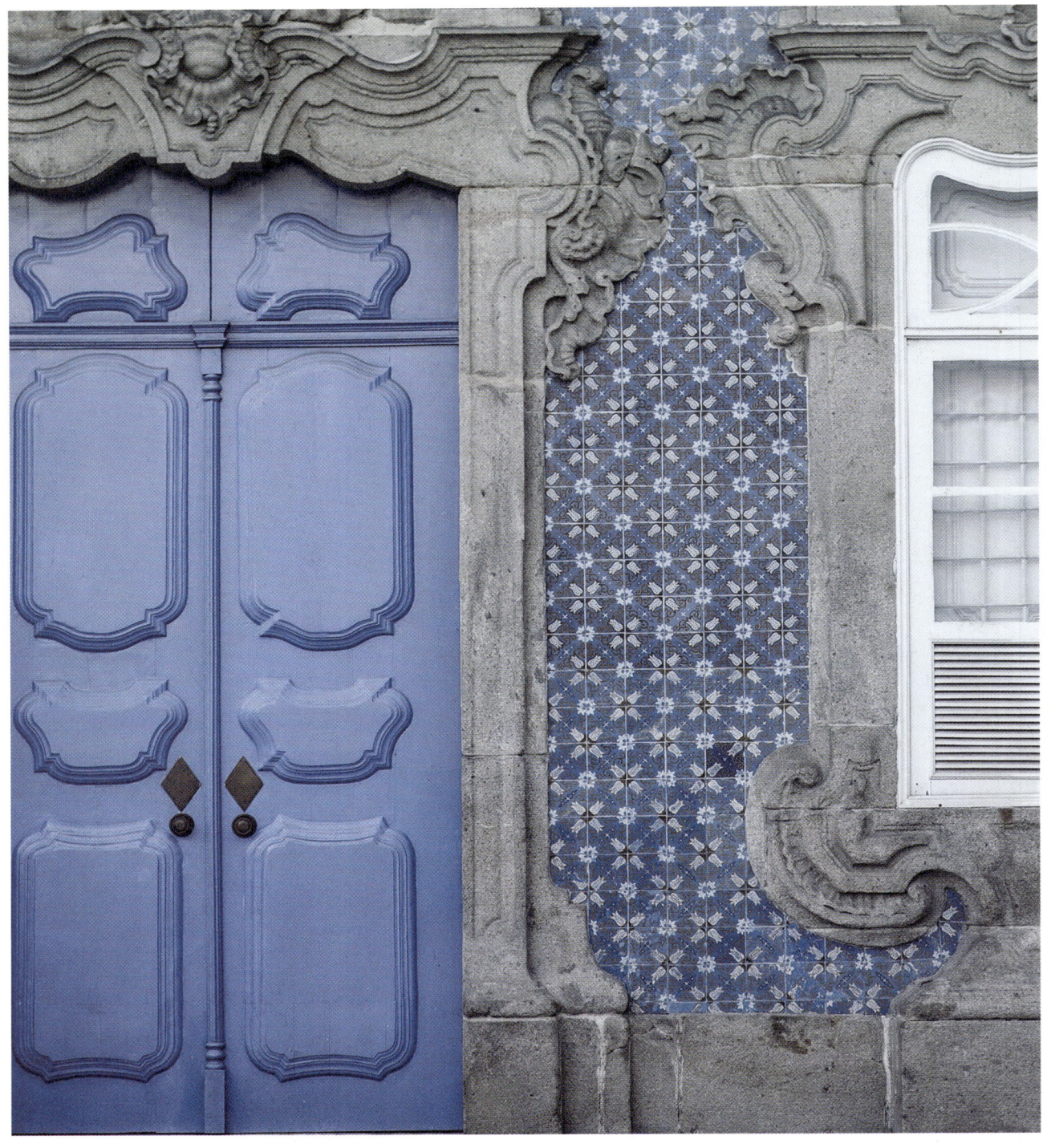

ABOVE: *The Palácio do Raio in Braga with tiled façade and Baroque ornamentation. Door and window frames reflect the style of architect André Soares, a famous city native.*

RIGHT: *Braga's Câmara Municipal, the old town hall, matches the city's sacral buildings in both scale and ornament. It too is attributed to André Soares.*

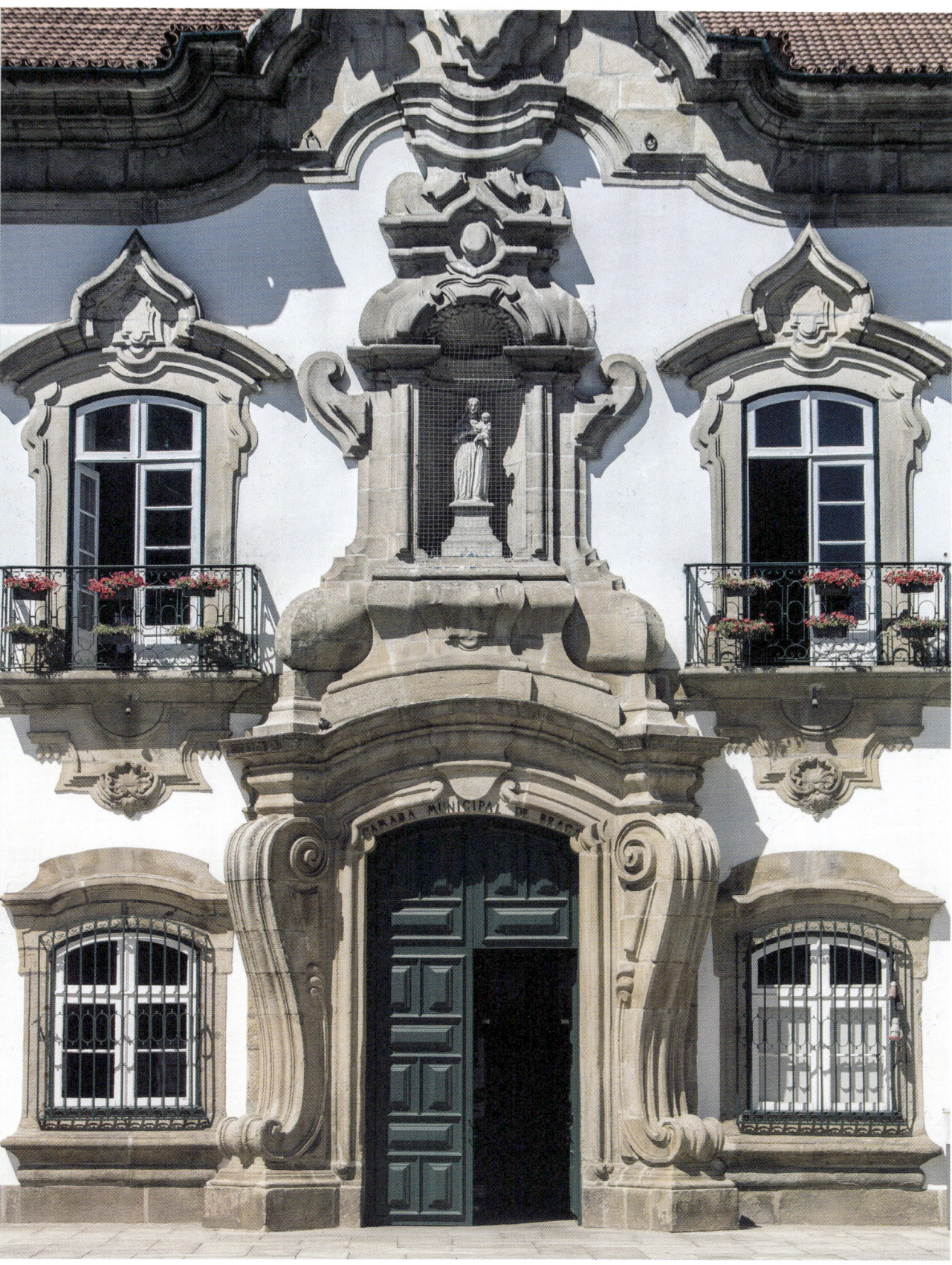

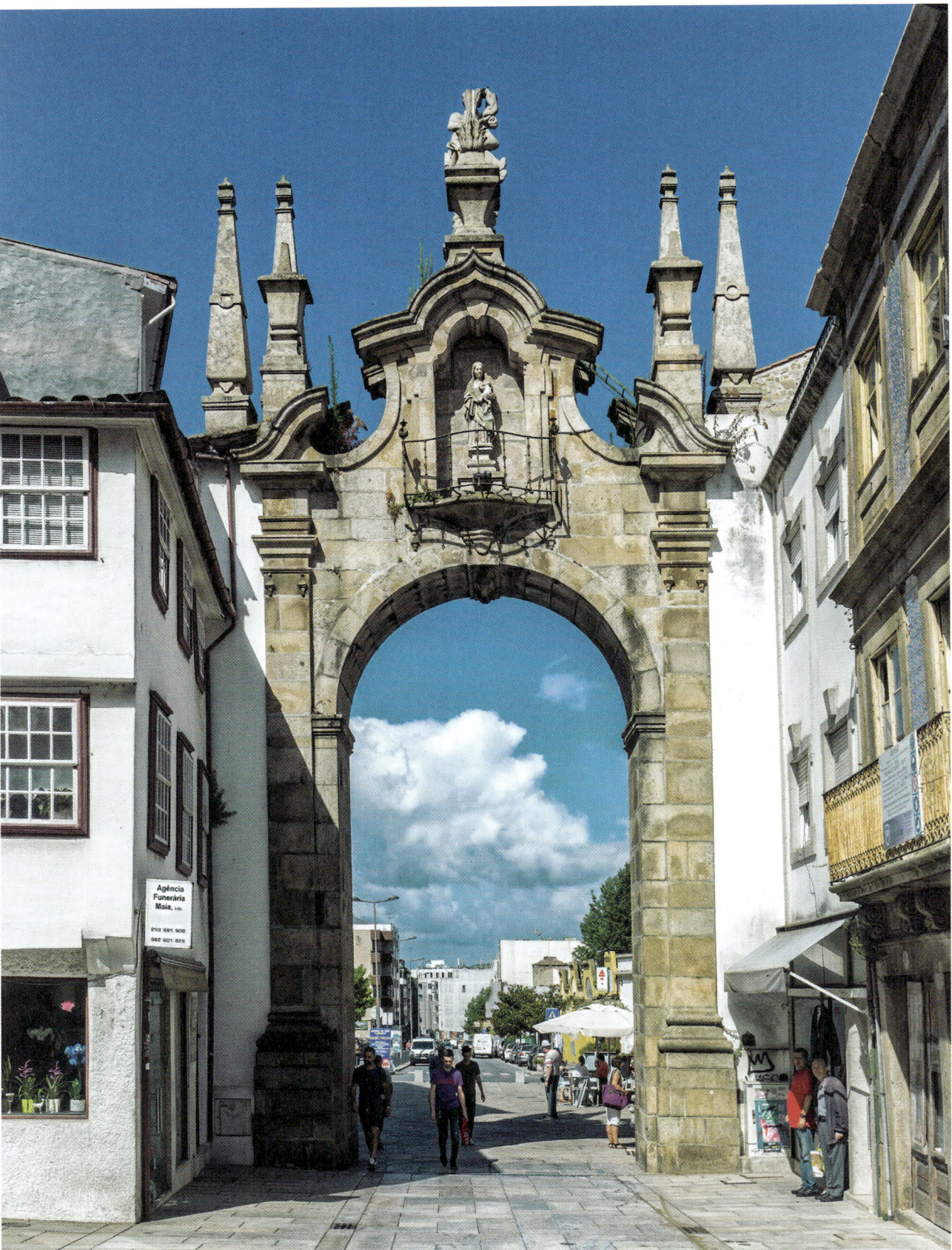

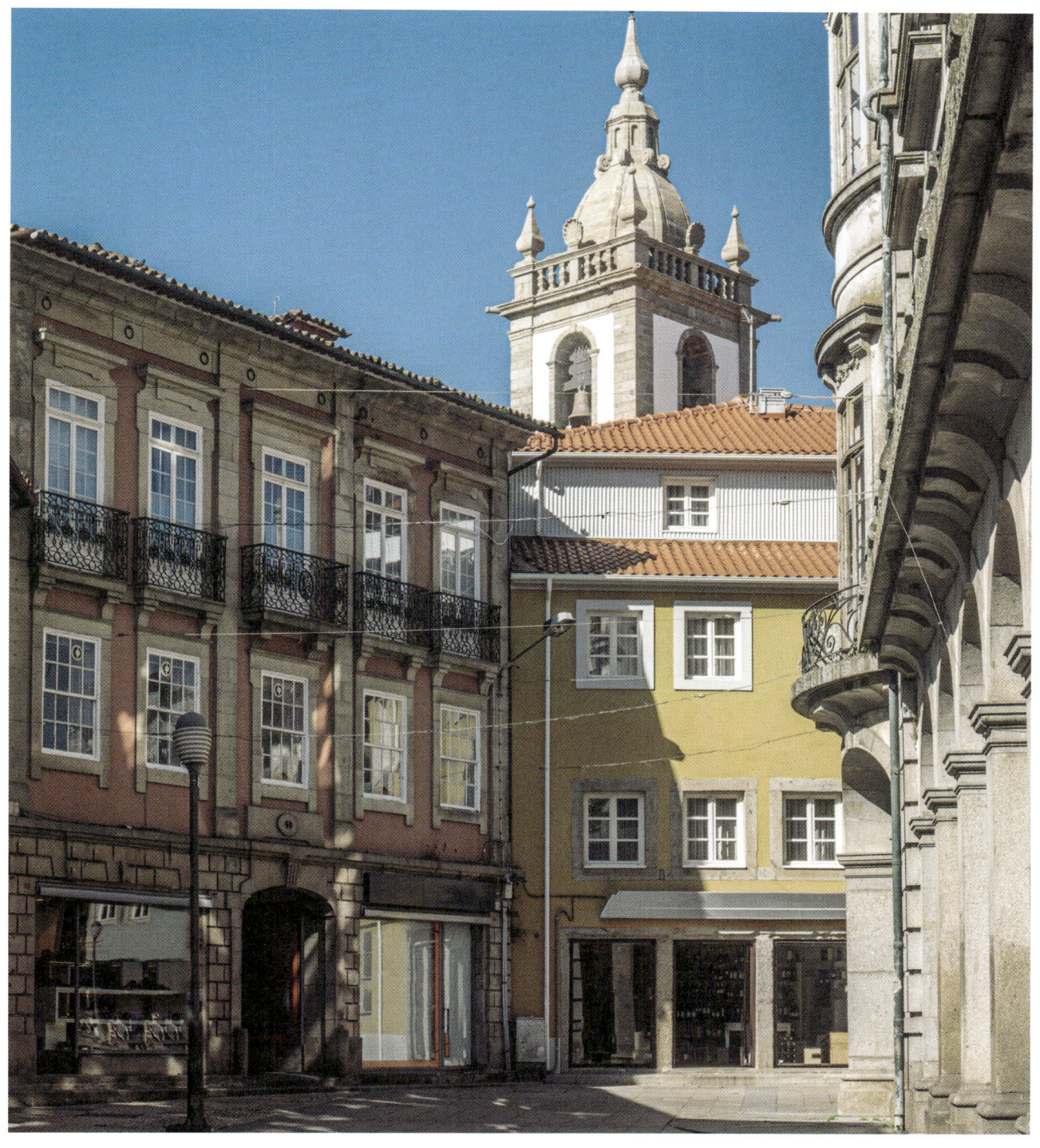

ABOVE: *Here, the church tower of Igreja dos Terceiros de São Francisco rises above the surrounding roofs in Braga. There are more than 30 church buildings in the city.*

LEFT: *The sixteenth-century Arco da Porta Nova marks the entrance to Braga's old town. It was redesigned in the late eighteenth century, again by architect André Soares in his striking style.*

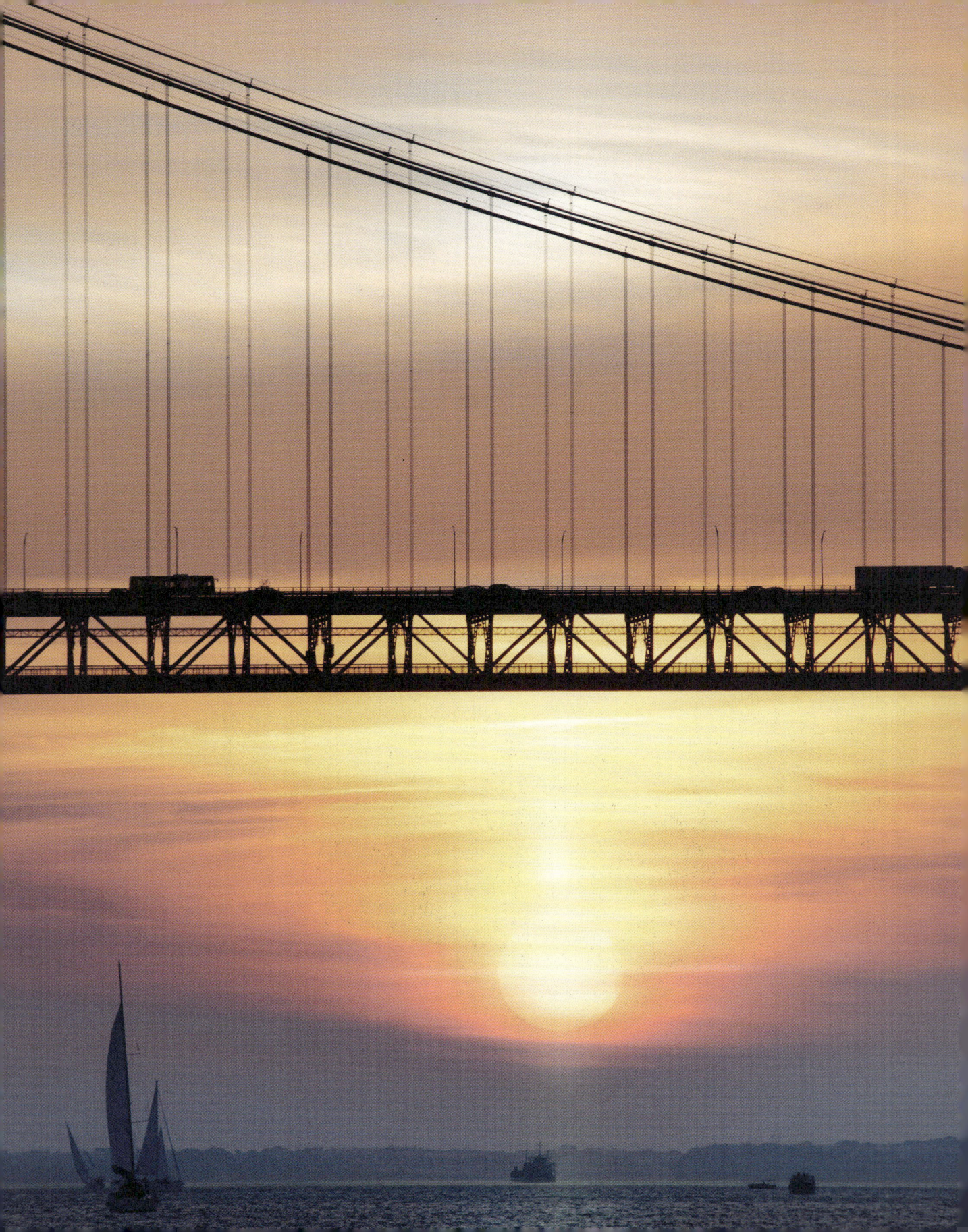

GOLDEN HOUR

WHEN THE EVENING SUN REACHES PORTUGAL'S COAST, A BRIEF INTERVAL OPENS BETWEEN DAY AND NIGHT. LIGHT SOFTENS, COLORS WARM, AND THE LANDSCAPE TAKES ON A MUTED GLOW

This is the *hora dourada*, the golden hour that painters and photographers have long tried to capture on canvas and film: the stretch between late afternoon and dusk when edges soften and color deepens. A certain unreality sets in. The effect is especially strong along Portugal's Atlantic coast, where long sightlines over open water heighten the sense of space and longing. That helps explain why the hills of Lisbon and Porto are dotted with *miradouros*. These vantage points offer clear sightlines across river and city as the light changes. In Lisbon, the Tagus often catches the low sun and turns it into a wide sheet of reflected gold. From the riverbank near Cais de Colunas or from the romantic Miradouro de Santa Luzia above Alfama, the light pools beneath the Ponte 25 de Abril, tracing its red span against the darkening sky. Northern Portugal has its own version of this daily shift. As evening approaches, the steeply stacked rooftops of Porto above the Douro take on subdued reds and ochres. From Vila Nova de Gaia, the cable car to Jardim do Morro provides a clear view across the river to the Ribeira quarter. From this vantage point, the arc of the Dom Luís bridge, the cathedral, and the bishop's palace align in a single frame, while the sky moves poignantly through orange, pink, and purple, like the final seconds of a performance before the curtain falls.

LEFT: *The majestic Ponte 25 de Abril crosses the Tagus south of Lisbon. The nearly 3,200-meter-long suspension bridge defines the river crossing, especially at sunset.*

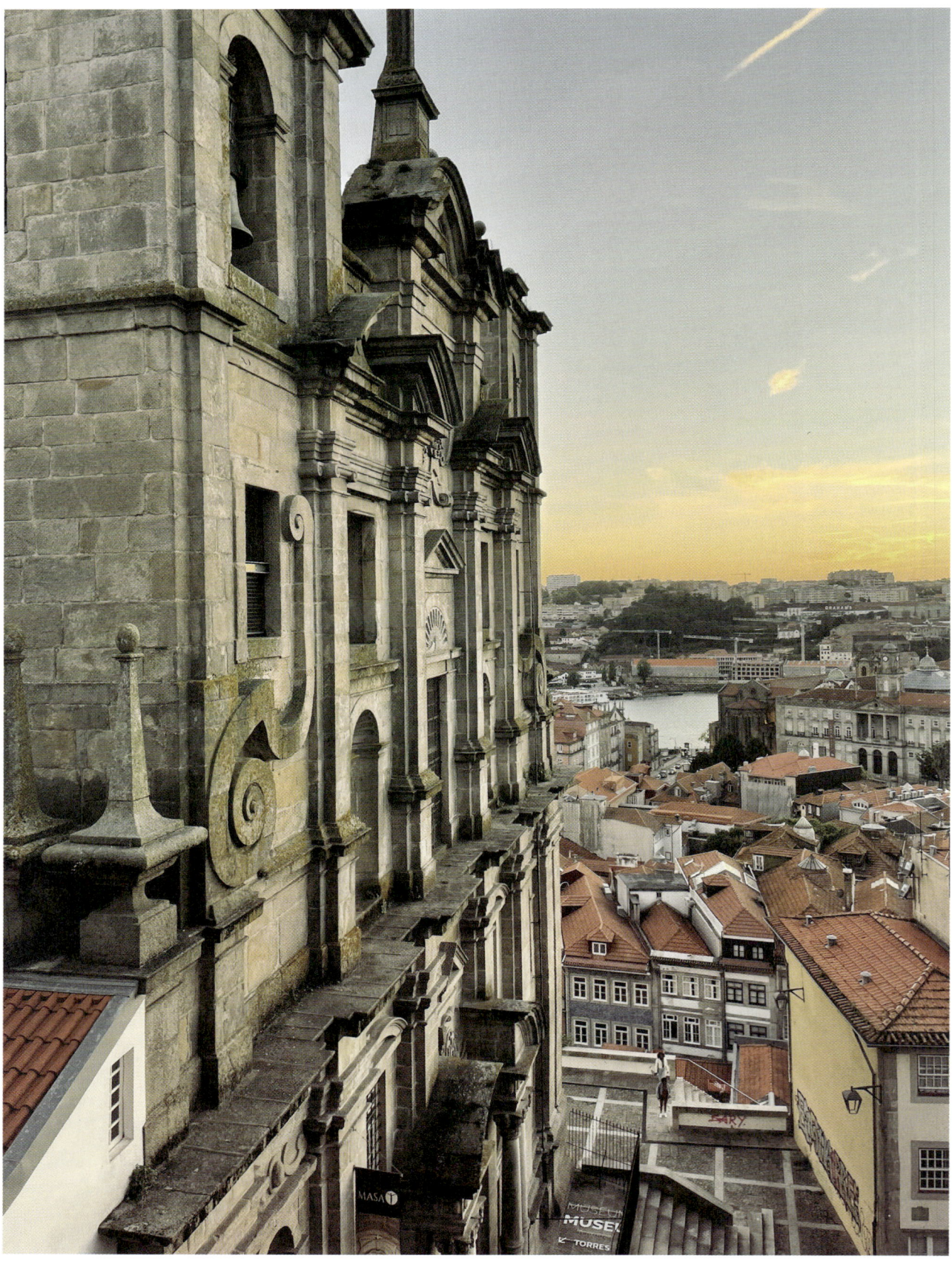

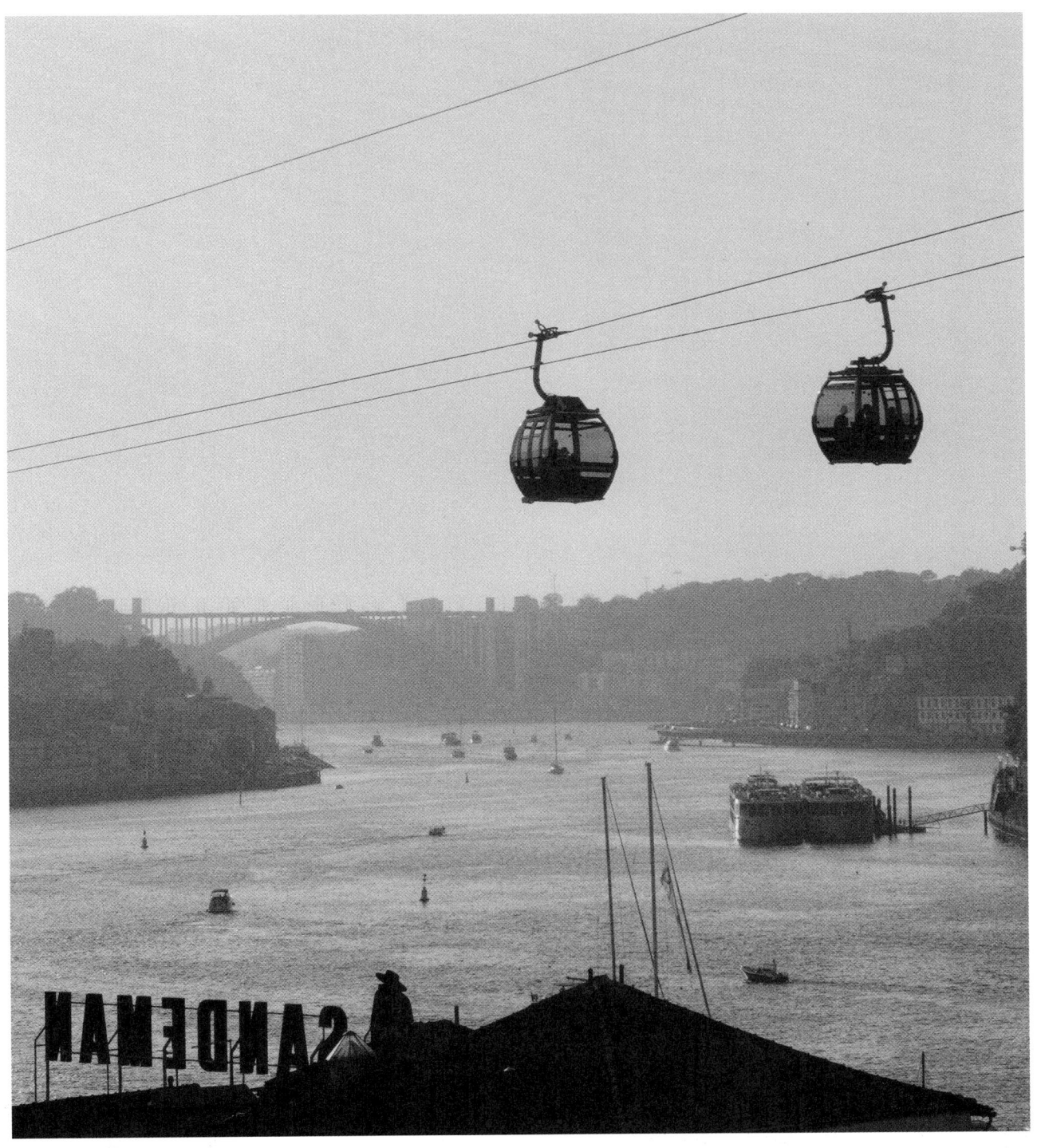

ABOVE AND LEFT: *Sunset views in Porto from a gondola on the Teleférico de Gaia as it moves above the Douro. Evening light settles across the old town, dipping the Mannerist façade of the Igreja dos Grilos in gold.*

FOLLOWING PAGES: *From the Miradouro Jardim do Morro in Vila Nova de Gaia, the late light spreads across the Douro and the city of Porto.*

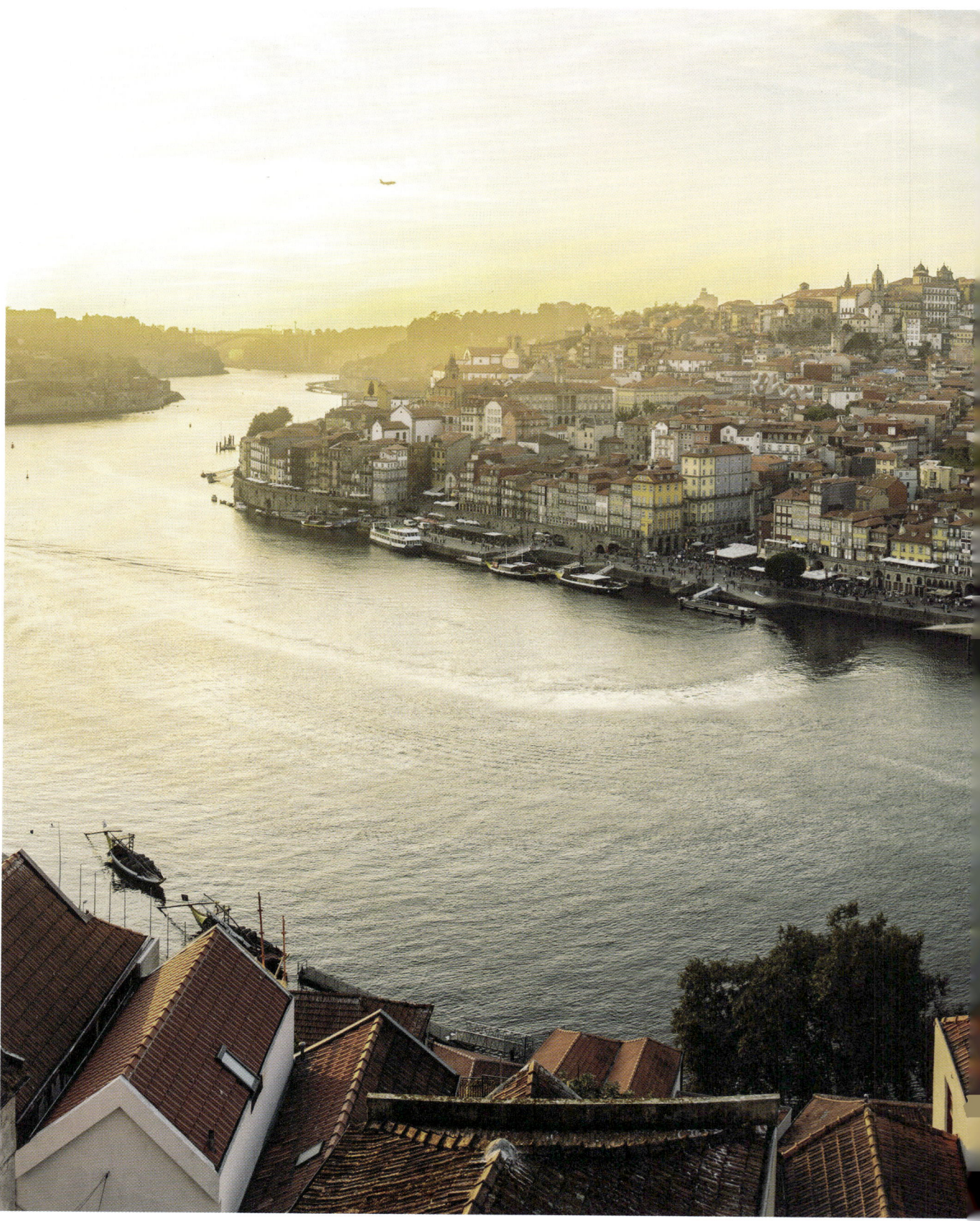

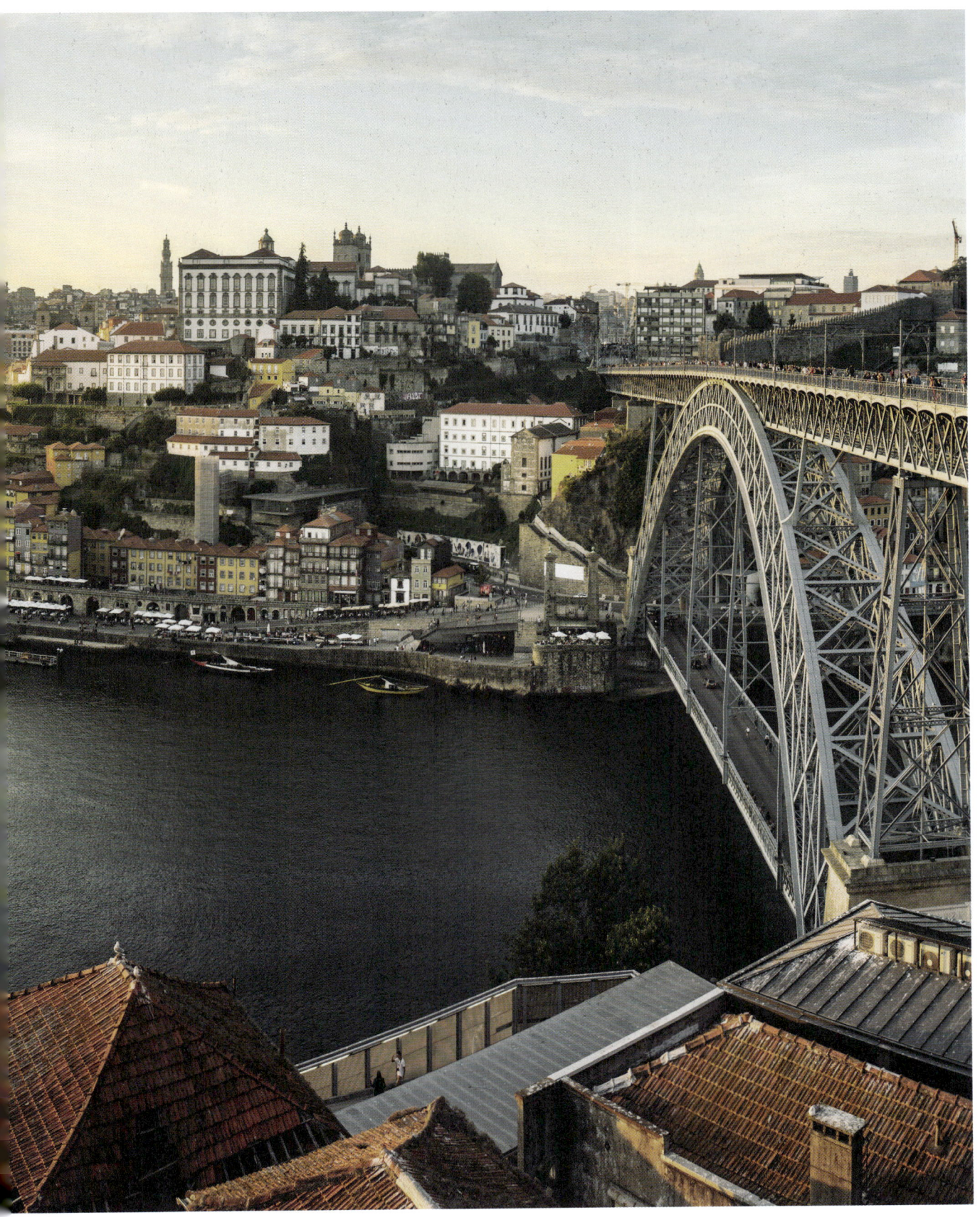

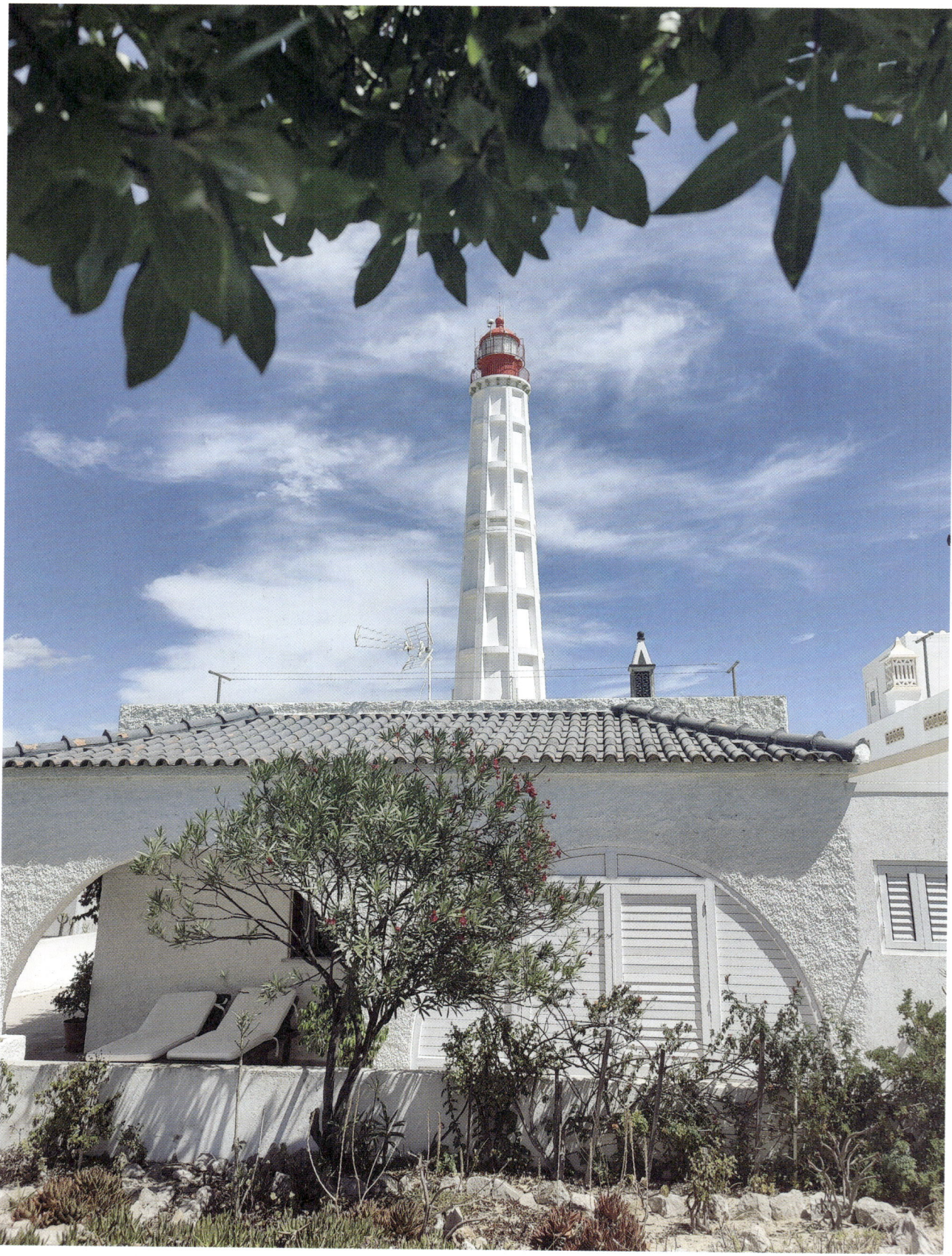

IMAGE CREDITS

OBRIGADO A TODOS!

A book is never created in isolation. Its content and execution depend on the right people, working with passion and dedication. My particular thanks go to Anja Klaffenbach for her inspiring writing, which forms the very heart of this book. I would also like to thank Marcus Taeschner for his steady hand at layout and typesetting. I am equally grateful to all the photographers who share my passion for photography (see previous page). Their evocative images take us all on an inspiring visual journey and awaken a profound affinity with the "Land of Light" that I can only second. Working with the team at teNeues remains a pleasure—*obrigado a todos!*

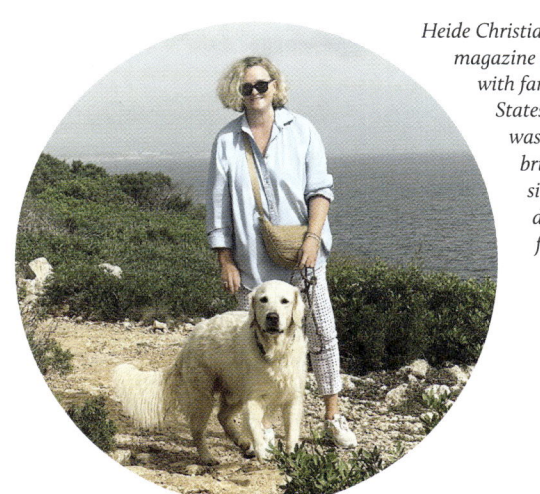

Heide Christiansen began her career as a photo editor at a well-known travel magazine and is now a bestselling author. Born and raised in Canada, with family spread across Europe, Canada, Australia, and the United States, she is an enthusiastic globetrotter. Her passion for Portugal was sparked by her daughter, who returned from her travels there brimming with undiminished enthusiasm. Several friends have since moved to Portugal as well, and through them Heide has developed a special appreciation for the openness and friendliness of the people of Charming Portugal.

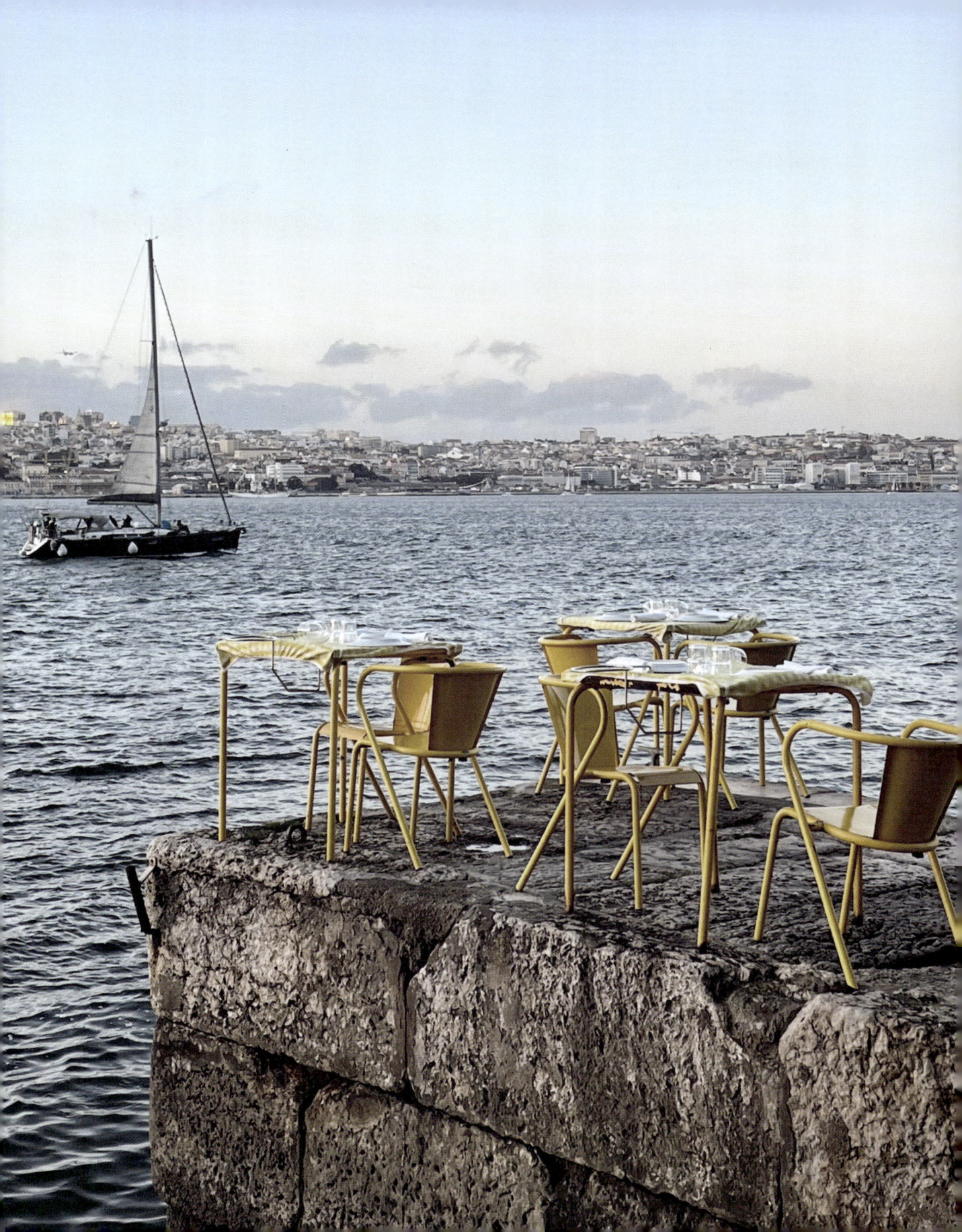

IMPRINT

CHARMING PORTUGAL
This book was conceived, edited,
and designed by teNeues.
Edited by Heide Christiansen

Text/preface by Anja Klaffenbach, www.klarkonzept.de
Translation by John Foulks
Copyediting by Robin Limmeroth
Editorial Management by Stephanie Rebel,
    gestalten Verlag
Proofreading by Benine Mayer, gestalten Verlag
Design by Marcus Taeschner
Layout by Marcus Taeschner
Photo Editorial by Heide Christiansen
Production by Sandra Jansen-Dorn, gestalten Verlag
Picture editing by Jens Grundei
Map graphic by Thomas Vogelmann

Printed in the Czech Republic by Finidr

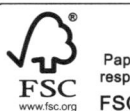

MIX
Paper | Supporting
responsible forestry
FSC® C014138
FSC
www.fsc.org

Published by gestalten, Berlin 2026
ISBN 978-3-96171-763-7
1st printing, 2026

The german edition is available under
ISBN 978-3-96171-764-4

© teNeues, an Imprint of
Die Gestalten Verlag GmbH & Co. KG, Berlin 2026

For more information and to order books, please visit
www.teneues.com and www.gestalten.com

Die Gestalten Verlag GmbH & Co. KG
Mariannenstrasse 9–10
10999 Berlin, Germany
hello@gestalten.com

Krefeld Office
Uerdinger Str. 265/Villa Pattberg
47800 Krefeld, Germany
verlag@teneues.com

teNeues Press Department
press@gestalten.com

Bibliographic information published by the Deutsche
Nationalbibliothek. The Deutsche Nationalbibliothek
lists this publication in the Deutsche
Nationalbibliografie; detailed bibliographic data is
available online at www.dnb.de

https://instagram.com/teneuespublishing

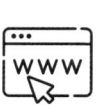

www.teneues.com